CRIMINAL LAW

AND THE CANADIAN CRIMINAL CODE

Second Edition

Richard Barnhorst, LL.B.
Sherrie Barnhorst, LL.B.
Kenneth L. Clarke, LL.B.

McGraw-Hill Ryerson Limited

Toronto Montreal New York Auckland Bogotá
Caracas Lisbon London Madrid Mexico Milan
New Delhi Paris San Juan Singapore Sydney
Tokyo

CRIMINAL LAW AND THE CANADIAN CRIMINAL CODE
Second Edition

4 5 6 7 8 9 10 BG 1 0 9 8 7 6 5

Printed and bound in Canada by Best Gagné Book Manufacturers

Care has been taken to trace ownership of copyright material contained in this text. However, the publishers will gladly take any information that will enable them to rectify any reference or credit in subsequent editions.

Canadian Cataloguing in Publication Data
Barnhorst, Richard, 1947–
    Criminal law and the Canadian criminal code

2nd ed.
Includes index.
ISBN 0-07-551099-5

1. Canada. Criminal code.   2. Criminal law —
Canada. I. Barnhorst, Sherrie, 1948–   .
II. Clarke, Kenneth L., 1946–   .   III. Title.

KE8809.B37 1992   345.71   C91-095499-2
KF9219.B37 1992

Sponsoring Editor: Ann Byford

Copy Editor: Susan Marshall

Designer: Michelle Losier

Preface to Second Edition

This second edition of *Criminal Law and the Canadian Criminal Code*, like the first edition, has been prepared for people who want to understand the principles of criminal law and the offences in the Criminal Code. Police officers, security personnel, probation officers, parole officers, criminologists, law clerks, and any other people involved in the criminal justice system will find this book helpful.

Since the first edition of this book was published in 1977, there have been major changes in the criminal law. Some of the most significant changes have occurred as a result of the enactment of the Canadian Charter of Rights and Freedoms and the application of the Charter to the criminal law by the Supreme Court of Canada. In this edition the Code references are completely updated. As far as possible, the most up-to-date Supreme Court decisions are included.

The format of the second edition is similar to that of the first. Part One introduces criminal law: Chapters One to Six discuss law in general, principles of criminal law, defences, pre-trial procedure, and trial procedure.

Part Two of the book is devoted to a discussion of offences contained in the Criminal Code. The offences are presented in the same order as they appear in the Code. Code sections are often reproduced and elements are defined. Actual case decisions, which appear frequently, help to interpret and apply the Code. It is not possible to cover every Criminal Code offence; however, we have fairly represented the different types of offences and all of the major offences.

There are two appendices. Appendix A deals with drug offences in the Food and Drugs Act and the Narcotic Control Act. Appendix B explains the major provisions of the Young Offenders Act. In addition, there is a glossary that defines terms **boldfaced** in the text.

A new feature of this edition is the margin notes, which provide a quick reference to specific sections of the Criminal Code. Margin notes for *offences* give the section number where the offence is set out, the type of offence, and the penalty. Where the penalty is set out in a section different from that creating the offence, the section number is stated [in brackets]. For summary conviction offences, or hybrid offences treated as summary conviction offences, if no penalty is stated the general penalty of a fine up to $2 000 and/or up to six months' imprisonment applies.

The author would like to sincerely thank the reviewers of the manuscript whose helpful comments and insights helped to ensure the accuracy and quality of the text.

Sherrie Barnhorst

Contents

Chapter **THREE**

Chapter **FOUR**

Chapter **FIVE**

Pre-Trial Criminal Procedure   89

Part Two   Criminal Code Offences

Chapter **SIX**

Offences Against Public Order, Offences Involving Firearms, and the Administration of Law and Justice: Parts II, III, and IV of the Code   125

Chapter **SEVEN**

**Sexual Offences, Public Morals, and Disorderly Conduct: Part V
of the Code** 151

---*Chapter* **EIGHT**

Soliciting and Procuring, Disorderly Houses, Betting, and Lotteries: Part VII of the Code   169

Chapter NINE

Homicide and the Offences of Murder, Manslaughter, and Infanticide: Part VIII of the Code 188

Chapter TEN

Criminal Negligence and Legal Duties: Part VIII of the Code 212

Chapter **ELEVEN**

Chapter **TWELVE**

Chapter **THIRTEEN**

Chapter **FOURTEEN**

Chapter **FIFTEEN**

Abbreviations Used for Case Report Publications

All E.R.	All England Reports (English)
Alta. L.R.	Alberta Law Reports
C.C.C.	Canadian Criminal Cases
Ch.	Chancery (English)
Cox's C.C.	Cox's Criminal Cases (English)
C.R.	Criminal Reports
Cr.App.R.	Criminal Appeal Reports (English)
C.R.N.S.	Criminal Reports New Series
D.L.R.	Dominion Law Reports
E.R.	England Reports
K.B.	King's Bench (English)
M.P.R.	Maritime Provincial Reports
M.V.R.	Motor Vehicle Reports
N.S.R.	Nova Scotia Reports
O.W.N.	Ontario Weekly Notes
P.E.I.S.C.	Prince Edward Island Supreme Court
Q.B.	Queen's Bench (English)
Que. Sess. Ct.	Quebec Sessions Court
R.L.	La Revue Légale (Quebec)
Sask.R.	Saskatchewan Reports
S.C.R.	Supreme Court Reports
Upper Can.Q.B.	Upper Canada Queen's Bench
W.C.B.	Weekly Criminal Bulletin
W.W.R.	Western Weekly Reports

The Criminal Law

ONE

An Introduction to Law

A. THE NATURE OF LAW

Before beginning the subject of this book, the criminal law, we will find it helpful to consider the nature of the law in more general terms. Let us first start with a definition. Law can be defined as that body of rules which regulates the conduct of members of society and is recognized and enforced by the government. There are, of course, many rules that regulate our conduct which are not, by this definition, part of the law. For example, the rules of a private club regarding the duties of club members are not part of the law. Likewise, the moral values which govern a person's conduct are not part of the law; although moral convictions and legal rules often, but not always, overlap. These types of rules are not rules of law for two basic reasons. First, they are not officially recognized by the government as laws applying to all members of society. Second, their violation does not involve a penalty or other legal consequence imposed by the government.

1. Functions of the Law

The definition given above, although suitable for our purposes, does not indicate the wide range of functions served by the law. The law not only tells us what our rights, privileges, and obligations are, but also determines the structure of our government and assigns duties and powers to its various branches. The law even tells us how and by whom laws are to be made. An example of a law-making law is the Constitution Act, 1867 (formerly the British North America Act (BNA Act), 1867). This statute creates our federal system of government, and it divides the authority to make law on various subjects between the federal parliament and provincial legislatures. For example, certain subjects such as property and education are given exclusively to the provinces. This jurisdiction means a federal law on the topic of provincial schooling, for example, would be *ultra vires*, or beyond the scope of the federal government's law-making authority. If a statute is *ultra vires*, it will not be enforceable. Similarly, if a province enacts a law which touches an area given to the federal government, that law is also *ultra vires* and unenforceable.[1]

2. Classes of Law

The two main classes of law are: (1) *public law* and (2) *private law*. Public law consists of the rules which govern the relations among various branches of the government, and between the government and private citizens. The main types of law within the class of public law are constitutional, criminal, and administrative. Private law, or civil law, as it is also known, consists of the rules governing the relations among private persons or groups. Types of private law include contract law, which consists of the rules for making legally enforceable agreements; property law, which includes the rules for owning or passing property; and tort law, which is the law regarding **civil wrongs**.

3. Substantive and Procedural Law

Each class or type of law consists of *substantive rules* and *procedural rules*. Substantive rules of law are the laws which describe our rights and duties. For example, the substantive part of the criminal law defines certain prohibited forms of conduct from which society has a right to be protected. Procedural rules are the laws which tell us how the substantive law can be enforced, that is, how our rights can be protected and our wrongs redressed. Thus, the rules which must be followed when an **arrest** is made are part of the law of **criminal procedure**. Whether an accused has a jury trial is a matter of procedure.

Most of the material in the following chapters is concerned with substantive law. For example, specific criminal offences will be defined and discussed. However, some areas of criminal procedure will also be covered. In the next chapter, such procedural matters as the classification of offences and methods of trial will be examined. Chapter Five discusses other topics of procedure such as the powers of arrest and search.

4. Sources of Canadian Law

a. *Common Law and Civil Law*

There are two major systems of law in the western world today. Most English-speaking countries have what is called a *common law system*. The second type is called the *civil law system*. Notice that the term "civil law"

---

1. Conversely, if a law is within the authority of the government that made it, it is *intra vires*.

has two meanings: It may refer to civil or private law, discussed above, or it may refer to the system of law used by many continental European countries. Except for Quebec provincial law, which operates under the civil law system, Canadian law is part of the common law tradition.

The civil law system is the older of the two. Its beginnings can be traced to the law of the Romans. In the sixth century, the Roman emperor Justinian compiled a code or book of law which contained all of the great Roman laws. This code then became the law in the areas of Europe under Roman control. After the fall of the Roman Empire, many of the people of Europe continued to use *Justinian's Code* or laws derived from it. In the early 19th century, Napoleon had written a similar code which was then adopted by many European countries. The *Napoleonic Code* also greatly influenced the writers of the *Quebec Civil Code*.

From about 55 B.C. to 412, England was occupied by the Roman army and naturally Roman law was used. However, in the fifth century, various Anglo-Saxon tribes invaded the country, forcing the Romans to withdraw their troops. These invasions largely erased the influence of Roman law in England. For many centuries after the departure of the Romans, England was occupied by diverse tribes and groups who had little contact with each other. Each community had its own law based on its traditions and customs. Thus, there was no body of law that could be called English law.

It was not until William, the Duke of Normandy, conquered England in 1066 that a unified England started to take form. One of William's first tasks was to set up a centralized government for the purpose of effectively controlling his new land. Part of the strong central government developed by William and his successors consisted of a royal court system. Under this system, the king's judges would travel through the country holding court in large villages and trading centres. Each judge's route was called a *circuit* and court sittings were known as *assizes*.

These early judges were in the difficult position of not having a set of rules or a code of law to guide them when making decisions. Sometimes Norman law and at other times local law could be used. Often, though, neither was appropriate and the judges had to rely on their common sense and base decisions on what seemed to them principles of justice and fairness. Eventually, the judges began discussing among themselves the cases they had heard and the decisions they had made. Gradually, it became a practice of the judges to follow the decision made in an earlier case if the case being heard and the earlier case had the same or similar facts involved. In other words, rather than rely only on their own judgment, judges would think back to previously decided cases. If they found one that matched, or was very similar to, the case presently being heard, they would make the same decision as that made in the first case. Of course, the facts in one case were frequently not the same or even very similar to the facts in other cases, so the judges could not always find a case to follow. But each time a decision was made in a particular situation, it created a ***precedent***, or example, to be followed in future cases. The principle that was emerging was that like cases should be treated alike. Even today, we accept this principle as a basic rule of justice.

Once accurate written reports of cases became available to judges in about the 16th and 17th centuries, it became much easier for judges to follow precedent. By the 19th century, this practice became a strict and binding rule called ***stare decisis*** which means literally "to stand by." Today, judges in Canada still follow precedent. What this process means, generally speaking, is that lower courts must follow the decisions of higher courts and courts of equal rank should try to follow each other's decisions if at all possible. Thus, by the process of making decisions in case after case, guided by the rule of precedent, these early English judges created a body of law that applied to all the people in England. This law was then common to all, or the ***common law***. Since the common law consists of the decisions of judges in particular cases it is also sometimes called ***case law***.[2] Today, however, Canadian law also includes many statutes which are laws made by our elected governments. So, although Canada is called a "common law country," it has both case law and statute law as well as administrative law (discussed below).

b. Statute Law

Another way to make law is to pass a statute or an Act that contains all the rules on a particular subject. As mentioned previously, the Constitution Act, 1867 divides the authority to make ***statute law***, which is also called legislative law, between the federal parliament and the provincial legislatures. Municipalities, which receive their law-making authority from the province, make a type of legislative law. Municipal laws are called by-laws.

With one exception, in Canada, statute law always has priority over case law. In other words, if there is a conflict between a court decision and a statute, the statute will overrule the court decision. In fact, it is the obligation of judges to apply statute law, where it exists, regardless of what the case law has been on the same topic. This principle is called the supremacy of parliament rule. The exception to this rule is found in cases where the ***Canadian Charter of Rights and Freedoms*** applies. We will discuss the specific nature of this exception later.

Statutes do not always conflict with case law. Sometimes statutes only *codify* the case law. That is, all the principles of law that are contained in a number of cases are put into one statute. Statutes may also clarify an area that has been left unclear by case law. There are also statutes which are concerned with modern topics that have never been dealt with by case

---

2. In one sense, case law is a broader term than common law since, strictly speaking, case law includes the decisions of the English courts of equity. Courts of equity were combined with common law courts in the 19th century so that today we have only one court system. However, equity still exists as a separate body of case law.

law. However, we still have large areas of law in the form of case law which have never been the subject of a statute and are still being developed by the courts. For example, much of the law of evidence which consists of the rules for presenting evidence in court is still in case law form.

An important point is that the judges' law-making function does not end once an area has been put into statute law. Statutes quite frequently need interpreting and this task becomes the responsibility of the courts. The interpretations given to statutes, in turn, become part of the law. Why do statutes need interpreting? First, because statutes usually contain only general rules and it may be questionable how the general rule applies to specific situations. Second, because legislators, like all other people, do not always communicate clearly. Even if a statute seems quite straightforward, it still may be possible to read in more than one meaning. In either situation, the judge becomes the final interpreter who must decide the intent of the legislators when enacting the statute.

For example, the ***defence*** of insanity is set out in statute law. This law states that a person is insane if he or she suffers from a disease of the mind. It has been up to the courts to determine the meaning of the term "disease of the mind."

c. *Administrative Law*

Administrative law is a growing source of law created by the executive branch of government. It consists largely of regulations made by members of federal and provincial cabinets and of the decisions made by administrative boards and tribunals. For example, the decisions of the Workers' Compensation Board in determining the eligibility of an injured worker for compensation form part of administrative case law. Administrative law is not generally concerned with criminal law.

B. THE CANADIAN CHARTER OF RIGHTS AND FREEDOMS

Any discussion of criminal law must include a consideration of the Canadian Charter of Rights and Freedoms. Although this part of the Constitution applies generally to areas of public law, it has special relevance to criminal law.

In 1982, when the Constitution was repatriated, an important addition was made to it, the Charter of Rights and Freedoms. The Charter not only consolidated existing rights but also created new rights and freedoms for Canadians. Although the Canadian Bill of Rights was law, it is not a part of the Constitution. For this reason the courts hesitated to use it to overturn legally enacted legislation. The Charter made it quite clear that the courts were, in certain situations, no longer bound by the principle of supremacy of Parliament.

The Charter of Rights and Freedoms sets out certain individual rights and freedoms that cannot be infringed upon by the government. In other words, since the government acts through statute law, the Charter limits the legislative authority of the government. If a court finds that a statute violates a right or freedom protected by the Charter, the court will rule that the statute is unenforceable. There are two important limitations on our rights and freedoms, however. The first is set out in s.1 of the Charter. Section 1 of the Charter states:

> **1. The Canadian Charter of Rights and Freedoms guarantees the rights and freedoms set out in it subject only to such reasonable limits prescribed by law as can be demonstrably justified in a free and democratic society.**

In other words, a court may find that, although a statute violates the Charter, it is a *justifiable limitation* on our rights. For example, most provinces today have laws which allow the police to randomly stop cars to check for drunk drivers. These laws have been challenged as a violation of our right to be free from arbitrary *detention*. The Supreme Court of Canada has held that these laws do violate our right to be free from arbitrary detention, but that the laws are justified because they are attempting to control the social evil of drunk driving.[3]

A second limitation is set out in s.33. This section allows a legislative body to pass a law which violates certain rights and freedoms if certain procedures are followed. It states:

> **33.(1) Parliament or the legislature of a province may expressly declare in an Act of Parliament or of the legislature, as the case may be, that the Act or a provision of thereof shall operate notwithstanding a provision included in section 2 or sections 7 to 15 of this Charter.**

Section 33 is referred to as the *notwithstanding* or *override clause*. To override the Charter, the statute itself must state that the Charter does not apply. The statute will only be valid for five years; after that time, it must be re-enacted. Also, the override clause can only be used for certain rights. Some rights and freedoms are absolutely protected such as our right to vote.

At the time the Charter became law, many law analysts thought that the override clause would not be used because it would be politically unpopular. This has not been the case. For example, Quebec has used the override clause to enact legislation requiring public signs such as advertisements and posters to be in the French language only. This law was challenged by several store owners who claimed that it violated their freedom of expression guaranteed in s.2(b) of the Charter. The Supreme Court of Canada agreed that the legislation violated s.2(b) because the right to choose one language of expression is part of the freedom of

---

3. *R. v. Hufsky* (1988), 40 C.C.C. (3d) 398 (S.C.C.).

expression. However, the legislation could not be struck down because the Quebec government had included a valid override provision.[4]

a. *Rights and Freedoms in the Charter*

Examples of the rights and freedoms to which all Canadians are entitled are illustrated in the following table:

Table 1-1

EXAMPLES OF RIGHTS AND FREEDOMS IN THE CHARTER

TYPE OF RIGHT/FREEDOM	EXAMPLES
Fundamental freedoms	freedom of conscience, religion, thought, belief, opinion, and expression; freedom of peaceful assembly and association
Democratic right	the right of Canadian citizens to vote or to run for office
Mobility rights	the right of Canadian citizens to enter, remain in, and leave Canada and the right of Canadian citizens and permanent residents to live and work in any province of Canada
Equality rights	the right to be treated equally before and under the law, the right to the equal protection of the law and benefit of the law without discrimination based on race, national or ethnic origin, colour, religion, sex, age, or mental or physical disability

The Charter also protects the two official languages of Canada, French and English.

The Charter has special importance to criminal law. To enforce the law, protect the public, and prosecute offenders, police and others in the criminal justice system are given certain powers and authority to interfere with individual liberty. For example, the power to search and to make arrests are significant infringements of personal freedom. The Charter serves an important function of setting out rules of procedure for exercising these powers and limitations on the authority allowed to law enforcement personnel.

---

4. See *Ford v. Quebec (A.G.)* [1988] 2 S.C.R. 712 and *Devine v. Quebec (A.G.)* [1988] 2 S.C.R. 790.

The most important rights for criminal law are the legal rights set out in s.7–s.14.

Section 7 states:

> **7. Everyone has the right to life, liberty and security of the person and the right not to be deprived thereof except in accordance with the principles of fundamental justice.**

This general statement says that a person cannot be denied life, liberty, or security of the person without the principles of *fundamental justice* being followed. The Supreme Court of Canada has said that the principles of fundamental justice are to be found in the basic tenets of our legal system and that it is up to the courts to develop the limits of these tenets.[5] In other words, the courts will decide on a case-by-case basis whether a tenet of fundamental justice has been violated. For example, the Ontario Court of Appeal has held that the right to remain silent when an offence is being investigated is and always has been a principle of fundamental justice. Therefore, the police violated this right when an accused was told that he would be held until the keys to the car that the police believed he had stolen could be found. In other words, he would be held until he gave the police the keys or told the police where the keys could be found.[6] The Supreme Court of Canada held recently that a provincial law which imposed a minimum seven-day sentence on a person who was driving with a suspended licence — even though he was unaware that his licence had been suspended — violated a principle of fundamental justice. The Court also said that s.8–s.14 are specific situations involving the deprivation of life, liberty, or security of the person.[7]

Sections 8, 9, and 10 concern pre-trial procedure:

> **8. Everyone has the right to be secure against unreasonable search or seizure.**
> **9. Everyone has the right not to be arbitrarily detained or imprisoned.**
> **10. Everyone has the right on arrest or detention**
> **(a) to be informed promptly of the reasons therefor;**
> **(b) to retain and instruct counsel without delay and to be informed of that right; and**
> **(c) to have the validity of the detention determined by way of habeus corpus and to be released if the detention is not lawful.**

Sections 11, 12, 13, and 14 relate to trial procedure:

---

5. Reference re s.94(2) of the Motor Vehicle Act (1985), 23 C.C.C. (3d) 289 (S.C.C.).
6. *R. v. Wooley* (1988), 40 C.C.C. (3d) 531 (Ont.C.A.).
7. *Supra*, note 5.

11. Any person charged with an offence has the right

(a) to be informed without unreasonable delay of the specific offence;

(b) to be tried within a reasonable time;

(c) not to be compelled to be a witness in proceedings against that person in respect of the offence;

(d) to be presumed innocent until proven guilty according to the law in a fair and public hearing by an independent and impartial tribunal;

(e) not to be denied reasonable bail without just cause;

(f) except in the case of an offence under military law tried before a military tribunal, to the benefit of trial by jury where the maximum punishment for the offence is imprisonment for five years or a more severe punishment;

(g) not to be found guilty on account of any act or omission unless at the time of the act or omission, it constituted an offence under Canadian or international law or was criminal according to the general principles of law recognized by the community of nations;

(h) if finally acquitted of the offence, not to be tried for it again and if found guilty and punished for the offence not to be tried or punished for it again; and

(i) if found guilty of the offence, and the punishment for the offence has been varied between the time of commission and time of sentencing, to the benefit of the lesser punishment.

12. Everyone has the right not to be subjected to any cruel and unusual treatment or punishment.

13. A witness who testifies in any proceedings has the right not to have any incriminating evidence so given used to incriminate that witness in any other proceedings, except in a prosecution for perjury or for the giving of contradictory evidence.

14. A party or witness in any proceedings who does not understand or speak the language in which the proceedings are conducted or who is deaf has the right to the assistance of an interpreter.

There have been several important court decisions on the applications of these sections to criminal law. These decisions will be discussed in the following chapters. In particular, s.8, s.9, and s.10 and parts of s.11 will be outlined in Chapter Five which discusses pre-trial procedure. Cases concerning the rights of the accused at trial will be illustrated in Chapter Two.

C. FINDING THE LAW

1. Statute Law

Statutes are published by the official government press. Usually all the statutes (or Acts) passed in one legislative session are contained in one volume. About every ten years, all the statutes are revised and consolidated into one set of volumes. Parliament then repeals the former statutes and enacts as law the newly revised ones. Revisions are necessary mainly to correct any errors in the original statutes and to incorporate into each any subsequent amendments. The last revision of the federal statutes occurred in 1985. So, a law first passed in 1983 can be found in the 1985 revised statutes. Here, each Act is given a separate chapter number and is listed alphabetically. A statute passed in 1986 will be found in the sessional volume for that year. Statutes in the sessional volumes are usually listed in order of enactment. At the back of each sessional volume is a table of public statutes which lists the acts by title or subject matter. These tables are very useful for locating statutes and checking for amendments.

The titles of the volumes are often referred to in abbreviated form. Revised statutes are abbreviated to ''R.S.'' followed by the initial of the province or a ''C'' for Canada. If a sessional volume is referred to, the ''R.'' is dropped. Next the year of enactment is given. Thus, ''R.S.C. 1985'' stands for ''Revised Statutes of Canada enacted in 1985.'' If a particular statute is mentioned, its chapter number is given after the year. Statutes are divided into sections. If a section is referred to, a small ''s'' followed by the section number is written after the chapter number. An example is: Narcotic Control Act R.S.C. 1985, c.N-1 s.24.

2. Case Law

There are many different series of case reports including national, regional, and provincial series. Some of these are official publications, while others are printed by private publishing companies. Only the more important cases are contained in these reports. The cases which would typically be reported would be the decisions in cases that have been appealed, cases which set precedents, and cases involving unclear areas of law. Not everything that has occurred in a case is reported. Usually, only the judge's written decision, which may often include a recital of the facts and the reasons for his or her decision, is reported. If more than one judge has heard the case (an appeal court frequently has more than one judge sitting) and there is a *dissenting opinion*, this will often be included in the report. A dissenting opinion results when the judges who have heard the case fail to reach an unanimous decision. In this situation the decision agreed to by a majority of the judges becomes the official decision of the court. The decision of the minority becomes the dissenting opinion. The court's decision is often referred to as the **holding in the case**. Similarly, a reference may be made to what the judge (or court) "held" in a case.

The most frequently referred to case series in the following pages will be Canadian Criminal Cases, abbreviated C.C.C. and Criminal Reports, abbreviated C.R. A table, "Abbreviations Used for Case Report Publications," at the beginning of the book is a complete list of the names and the accepted abbreviations of other mentioned series.

To locate a case it is important to understand the case citation. The following chart indicates the form used for citing cases and the meaning of each element of the citation.

Figure 1-1

READING A CASE CITATION

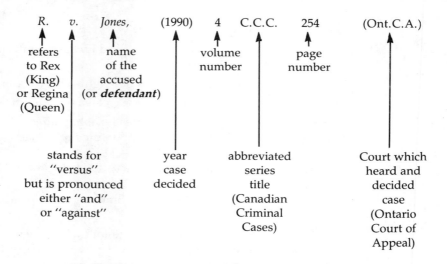

Notice that the first name given in the case is Rex or Regina, which indicates that the state or the Crown is proceeding against the (prosecuting) the accused. If the court's decision is appealed to a higher court, the name of the **appellant** (the party appealing) is given first, followed by the name of the **respondent** (the party responding).

QUESTIONS FOR REVIEW AND DISCUSSION

1 Define the term "law".

2 **a** Why are the rules of a private club not considered law?

  b Can you think of other types of rules that govern our conduct but are not laws?

3 What are some functions served by the law? (Try to think of specific functions not mentioned in the chapter.)

4 **a** What are the two main classes of law?
  b Define each class.

5 **a** What is the difference between substantive law and procedural law?
  b Indicate whether the following are procedural or substantive types of law:
  i the legal definition of murder
  ii the law that states how a search warrant is obtained
  iii the law that requires the appeal of a court decision to be made within a certain time limit

6 **a** Explain the origin of the common law system.
  b Why is this system called the common law system?

7 **a** Explain the operation of the rule of *stare decisis*.
  b What is a precedent?

8 How does a judge make law?

9 Explain how the Charter of Rights and Freedoms affects the principle of supremacy of Parliament.

10 What are the two limitations on our rights and freedoms?

11 Why does the Charter have special relevance to criminal law?

12 How should the following statutes be abbreviated?
  a Young Offenders Act, Revised Statutes of Canada, 1985, Chapter Y-1
  b Criminal Law Amendment Act, 1990, Chapter 13, Statutes of Canada
  c Canada Evidence Act, Revised Statutes of Canada, 1985, Chapter C-5

13 What should the citations be for the following cases?
  a John Smith was prosecuted by the Crown Attorney. The decision of the court was reported in Canadian Criminal Cases, the fifth volume at page 305. The trial was held in 1984 in the province of New Brunswick before a provincial court judge.
  b After being found guilty, Smith appealed the decision of the court to the provincial Court of Appeal. The decision of the appeal court was reported in volume 12 at page 305 of Canadian Criminal Cases. The appeal was heard in 1986.
  c In 1988, Sharon Brown was prosecuted by the Crown in the Court of Queen's Bench in Manitoba. The decision of the court was reported in volume 7 of Criminal Reports at page 46.

TWO

An Introduction to Criminal Law

A. THE NATURE OF THE CRIMINAL LAW

1. A Wrong Against Society

Most crimes have victims; however, crimes are also wrongs committed against society as a whole. In other words, when a crime is committed, not only the victim but also the community suffers. When the crime rate goes up, everyone feels less secure and individuals may actually change their activities if they believe the streets are no longer safe. Therefore, the primary aims of the criminal law are protecting the public and preserving the peace. Ensuring that our community is safe and secure is a duty carried out by the government through the police, court, and correctional systems.

2. The Distinction Between Criminal and Civil Proceedings

As mentioned previously, the civil law governs the interactions of private persons. For example, the law of contract sets out the rules which must be followed before an agreement between private parties will be enforced by the courts.

A breach of a civil rule of law is considered a *civil wrong*. Many civil wrongs are also criminal wrongs. For example, if Yaman is accused of taking Helen's car without Helen's permission, Yaman may have committed both the criminal offence of theft and the civil offence of trespass to goods. This civil wrong is a type of offence called a tort. Very briefly, torts are acts (or omissions) which all people have a duty to refrain from committing against other people. The usual remedy a victim of a tort may seek through a civil proceeding is compensation (e.g., money) for the loss he or she has suffered. So, in the above example, Yaman may be *prosecuted* (proceeded against) in a criminal court and if *convicted* (found guilty), *sentenced* to a suitable punishment. If Yaman is found not guilty, Yaman will be **acquitted** and the criminal charge *dismissed*. If Helen wishes to seek a civil remedy, she must sue (or proceed against) Yaman in a civil court. If Helen is successful against Yaman, Helen will be *awarded* compensation, usually money. If Helen is not successful, *judgment* will be given in favour of Yaman.

In the early days of the English law, there was little distinction drawn between a civil wrong and a criminal wrong. If a person or the person's property were injured, either that person or the person's family would seek revenge. Consequently, blood feuds between families were frequent events, although the community might attempt to encourage the victim to accept compensation in the form of money.

At the same time, the idea of the king's peace was becoming established. The king could put certain people or property under his protection. If anyone injured the persons or property being protected by the king, the wrongdoer would have to pay the king a money fine. Some offences were so serious that a fine would be inadequate. In this case, the offender's "life and limbs" would be at the king's mercy. Gradually, the king extended the area of his peace so that it finally encompassed all the territory and persons under his rule. Since the wrong was an offence against the king, breaches of the peace came to be prosecuted by the king's agents in the name of the king.

Today, most prosecutions are undertaken by **Crown Attorneys** (i.e., **prosecutors**) who are the agents of the federal or provincial **Attorney General**. The Attorney General's office is occupied by a person appointed by the executive branch of the government. This person's role is to act as the government's legal advisor and **counsel**. There are a few situations in which a criminal offence can be prosecuted by a private individual (i.e., private prosecutions). These situations will be mentioned in the discussion of the classification of offences.

Two important differences between civil and criminal wrongs should be emphasized. First, where a possibility of a civil action exists, the community has no interest in whether the victim decides to go to court. However, where a crime has occurred, it is usually the Crown Attorney's decision whether to prosecute, even if the victim would rather not take any steps against the offender. Second, an important aim of the criminal law is to punish convicted offenders (e.g., by fine or imprisonment). However, the civil law generally only permits the victim to be compensated, or repaid, for actual loss.

B. CRIMINAL LAW IN CANADA

1. Jurisdiction

The authority to enact criminal legislation has been assigned to the federal government by the Constitution Act, 1867, although the provinces are authorized by the Act to organize the courts of criminal jurisdiction. The provinces have also been given the power to impose punishment by fine, penalty, or imprisonment for the purposes of enforcing provincial laws. Strictly speaking then, all criminal law is federal. However, provincial offences are similar to crimes, particularly because of the types of punishment possible. In Ontario, for instance, a person may be imprisoned for "two years less a day" for violating a provincial law. Also, the court procedure can be similar and even the same courtrooms may be used. However, crimes are more serious than provincial offences. The offences we think of as crimes, such as assault, theft, and murder, are federal crimes. While provincial offences include traffic violations and liquor offences.

2. Sources of Canadian Criminal Law

The main source of both substantive and procedural criminal law in Canada is the *Criminal Code*. This is a federal statute which was first enacted in 1869. At that time, it attempted to consolidate the English common law crimes applicable to Canada and the colonial laws. A significant addition was made in 1953 by what is now s.9, which states that no person can be convicted of an offence, except for criminal contempt of court, at common law. This section was necessary to clarify the question of whether a person could be convicted of a common law offence that was not in the Code. However, s.8(3) of the Code preserves all common law defences. Thus, for example, the law regarding the use of intoxication as a defence is in case law form.

Although the main focus of this book will be on the Criminal Code, there are many other federal statutes which create criminal offences. Two of these, the Food and Drugs Act and the Narcotic Control Act, are discussed in Appendix A.

C. THE CRIMINAL CODE

1. Structure

The Criminal Code contains twenty-eight parts. The sections within each part are related to each other by subject matter. For example, Part IX consists of offences against the rights of property.

The official Criminal Code can be found in the 1985 Revised Statutes of

Canada, c. C-34. Subsequent sessional volumes must be checked for amendments. Private companies also publish up-to-date editions of the Code each year. One very helpful study aid is an *annotated code*. Codes which are annotated list after each section a brief description of important cases which interpret and apply the section. Annotated codes are useful since the Code, like other statutes, is constantly being interpreted and applied by the courts, and reference to these court decisions is necessary to fully understand the meaning of particular sections.

The Code contains both substantive rules and procedural rules. Substantive rules define offences and set out penalties for offences. Procedural rules include the rules for making arrests, conducting searches, holding trials, and appealing decisions.

2. Classification of Offences

The Code divides offences into three categories: (1) *indictable offences*, (2) offences punishable upon summary conviction, and (3) *hybrid* or *dual procedure offences*. Generally speaking, the difference between the first two is that indictable offences are more serious crimes than *summary conviction offences*. Examples of indictable offences are murder, kidnapping, and robbery. Causing a disturbance in or near a public place and loitering on private property at night are types of summary conviction offences. A hybrid or dual procedure offence may be tried as either an indictable or a summary conviction offence. The decision on how to treat a hybrid offence is made by the Crown Attorney, usually at the time of the trial. The Crown will base its decision on facts such as whether the offence is a first or second occurrence. A second offence is treated more seriously. The existence of mitigating or, on the other hand, aggravating circumstances surrounding the commission of the offence will also influence the prosecutor's decision. Until a decision is made, a hybrid offence is treated like an indictable offence. In other words, a hybrid offence is indictable unless and until the Crown chooses to have the offence tried as a summary conviction offence.

D. TRYING INDICTABLE OFFENCES AND SUMMARY CONVICTION OFFENCES

The specific differences between indictable offences and summary conviction offences are mainly related to procedure and to the types of penalties that can be given. Some of the more important differences between trying indictable offences and summary conviction offences are discussed below. Further comparison will be made in Chapter Five, where powers of arrest and search are discussed.

1. Summary Conviction Offences

Part XXVII of the Code describes the procedure for the trial of offences punishable upon summary conviction. Section 788 provides that to begin a court proceeding (i.e., the trial), an *information* must be laid before a justice of the peace. This means that the *informant* swears, under oath, in an affidavit either that he or she has personal knowledge, or that he or she has **reasonable grounds** for believing that an offence has been committed by a certain person. The information is then signed by the informant and the justice of the peace. If the accused is present, either personally or represented by counsel or agent, the trial can proceed immediately. If the accused is not personally present and not represented by counsel or agent, the justice of the peace can issue a warrant for the arrest of the accused, or a summons which orders the accused to appear in court on a certain date. The accused does not have to appear personally; instead, an agent or lawyer can appear on behalf of the accused.

Although informations are usually laid by police officers, any person may lay an information. A private person can prosecute a summary conviction offence if the Crown does not. However, most offences are prosecuted by a Crown Attorney, although a police officer can be authorized to prosecute cases also.

Section 786 provides that the proceedings must begin (i.e., the information must be laid) no later than six months after the offence is alleged to have occurred. In other words, there is a six-month limitation period on starting the prosecution of a summary conviction offence. In general, there is no limitation period for indictable offences.

Trials of summary conviction offences are held before "summary conviction courts" as defined in s.785. Usually the trials are held before a provincial court judge or justice of the peace. Jury trials are not held in summary conviction proceedings. Similarly preliminary inquiries are never held. A preliminary inquiry is a hearing which takes place before the trial to determine if there is enough evidence to commit the accused to trial. This hearing is only used for certain indictable offences.

After the information has been laid, and with both the accused (or his or her agent or counsel) and the prosecutor present, the accused is arraigned. The procedure used for arraignment is set out in s.801. It provides that the substance of the information must be stated to the accused who is then asked to enter a plea of guilty or not guilty. If the accused pleads guilty, the court will enter a conviction. If the accused pleads not guilty or refuses to plead, the court will enter a not guilty plea and proceed with the trial. This means that the prosecutor will present evidence, through the testimony of witnesses, and the accused may present evidence in defence. Both parties also have an opportunity to cross-examine each other's witnesses.

Once the court has heard the prosecutor, the accused, and the witnesses, it will decide whether to convict the accused or dismiss the information.

Where the accused is convicted, the penalties which may be imposed are limited by s.787. This section provides that unless the law states otherwise, a person who is convicted of a summary conviction offence is liable to a fine of up to $2 000 and/or imprisonment for not more than six months.

2. Indictable Offences

a. *Origins of the Procedure*

Starting in the 12th century, the English method for bringing suspected criminals to justice was by the *presenting of an indictment* by a grand jury. The jury consisted of members of the local community whose duty it was to report all suspected crimes committed by their neighbours to the king or his agent. This report, which would accuse certain persons of specific crimes, was called an indictment. At first the jurors based their report on their own personal knowledge. Gradually, as the jury system evolved, the grand jurors became persons without direct knowledge of the crime, who based their report upon the testimony of witnesses to the offence.

A grand jury system was used in some parts of Canada until recently. The Attorney General, or someone authorized by him or her or the court, would *prefer* (i.e., present) a bill of indictment before a grand jury. The jury would then hear the testimony of witnesses called by the prosecutor. The accused and his or her counsel were not allowed to be present during the hearing. In fact, the proceedings were conducted in complete secrecy. One reason for the secrecy was to protect the reputations of innocent persons falsely accused of crimes.

After hearing the evidence presented by the prosecutor, the jurors would decide whether there was enough evidence to send the accused to trial before a judge and jury. If a majority of the jurors decided that there was enough evidence for a trial, the indictment would be endorsed with the words "true bill". If a majority of the jurors decided that there was insufficient evidence for a trial, the indictment would be endorsed "no bill".

Today, the Attorney General, his or her agent, or someone with his or her consent or the consent of the court (e.g., a private person) prefers the written indictment before the court. This means, in effect, that the Attorney General or his or her agents are performing the functions that had been performed by the grand jury.

b. *Preliminary Inquiries*

One reason for abandoning the use of grand juries is that preliminary inquiries serve a similar function. These hearings take place before the indictment is preferred and just after the accused has been charged with an offence. Depending on the province, preliminary inquiries are usually held before a provincial court judge or justice of the peace. The main purpose of the hearing is to determine if there is enough evidence to commit the accused to trial. During the hearing the prosecutor presents evidence through the testimony of witnesses. The accused has a right to present evidence and to make a statement on his or her own behalf. Each party can also cross-examine each other's witnesses. After considering the evidence, the justice or provincial court judge will decide whether there is enough evidence to commit the accused to trial. Just because an accused has been committed to trial does not mean that the justice or judge has found the accused guilty. If the accused is committed to trial after a preliminary inquiry, this means simply that there is "sufficient evidence" for a trial to be held.

The procedure described above serves a somewhat similar purpose as that once served by the grand jury in that weak cases can be disposed of without the time and expense of a full trial. For the accused, the preliminary hearing has the added advantage of allowing an opportunity for the nature and strength of the Crown's case to be determined.

The relevant Code sections on preliminary hearings are s.535 to s.551.

c. *Methods of Trial*

There are three methods of trial for indictable offences:

1. by a provincial court judge
2. by a judge without a jury
3. by a judge and jury

Some offences in the Code must be tried by a provincial court judge (i.e., a judge appointed by the province — other judges who try criminal cases are appointed by the federal government). Other offences must be tried by a judge and jury. For the majority of offences, however, the accused can elect the method of trial, that is, whether the trial is held before a provincial court judge, judge alone, or judge and jury. The accused may lose the right of election if he or she is charged with an offence that is punishable by more than five years of imprisonment. In this situation, s.568 allows the Attorney General to require the accused to be tried by judge and jury.

Section 553 lists the indictable offences which must be tried before a provincial court judge. These are the less serious indictable offences such as keeping a common gaming house, bookmaking, and betting and hybrid offences such as theft of subject matter that does not exceed $1 000 in value. These offences are tried in the same way as summary conviction offences are tried in that a formal indictment is not necessary and preliminary inquiries are not held.

Section 469 lists the indictable offences which must be tried by the province's *superior court of criminal jurisdiction*. This court is the province's highest ranking trial court with criminal jurisdiction. Section 2 gives the name of the superior criminal court for each province. Generally, it is called the Supreme Court or the Court of Queen's Bench of the province. In Quebec, it is called the Superior Court, in Ontario, the Ontario Court.

Generally, all trials before superior criminal courts are by judge and jury. The one exception is that the accused and the Attorney General may jointly consent to a trial by a superior criminal court without a jury. This exception is set out in s.473.

The offences contained in s.469 are considered the most serious offences; they include: treason, sedition, piracy, and murder.

All other indictable offences in the Code are electable except those, as mentioned above, for which the Attorney General can require a trial before judge and jury. If the accused elects to be tried by judge without a jury, he or she will be tried by a judge as defined for each province in s.552. Until recently, some provinces, like Ontario for example, had a middle level of court called the county or district court which tried these electable offences. However, today all provinces, except Nova Scotia, have only two levels of trial court, the provincial court and the superior court. Generally then, the judges listed in this section are superior or supreme court judges.

Part XIX of the Code, which starts with s.552, describes the procedure to be used where the trial is without a jury and is held before either a judge or provincial court judge.

If the accused elects to be tried by judge and jury, he or she may be tried by a superior court of criminal jurisdiction or a court of criminal jurisdiction. Courts of criminal jurisdiction are defined in s.2. Generally, they are courts of general or quarter sessions of the peace presided over by a superior or county court judge.

Unlike summary conviction offence proceedings, the accused must be personally present (unless the court orders otherwise) for the trial of an indictable offence. Generally speaking, during the trial each party calls its own witnesses who give evidence under oath. Each party also has a right to cross-examine the other party's witnesses. After both the accused and the prosecutor have finished presenting evidence, each one has the right to sum up the evidence and make closing arguments to the jury, if there is one, or to the judge.

If the trial is before a jury, the judge will then sum up the case for the jury. He or she will instruct them on questions of law and may express an opinion regarding credibility of witnesses or the importance of the evidence.

If there is a jury, it will return a verdict of guilty or not guilty. If the trial is before a judge only, the judge will find the accused guilty or not guilty. If the verdict is guilty, the accused will be convicted; if the verdict is not guilty, the accused will be acquitted by the court. If the accused is convicted, the judge will then sentence the accused to a punishment.

The possible penalties for indictable offences are much harsher than those allowed for summary conviction offences. The Code sets out maximum terms of imprisonment for each offence, such as life, 14 years, or 10 years. In a few situations, the Code sets out a minimum punishment that must be imposed if the accused is convicted. Usually, however, the judge can choose a sentence up to the maximum term set out in the Code. So, for example, a first offender would usually be sentenced to a term far less than the maximum allowed. Section 718 allows the court to impose fines in addition to, or instead of, imprisonment if there is no minimum term of imprisonment required. If the offence is punishable by more than five years of imprisonment, the fine cannot be in lieu of but only in addition to a term of imprisonment.

E. THE CHARTER AND THE RIGHTS OF THE ACCUSED AT TRIAL

The rights in the Charter are not all new. Some of our rights such as the *presumption of innocence* have a long history in the development of English common law. The Charter has, however, given the courts new authority to examine legislation and to expand and further define our rights and freedoms. Section 11 of the Charter lists the rights and freedoms that apply to criminal trials. In the following paragraphs, we will look at each of the rights and at some of the more important decisions the courts have made in applying this section.
Section 11 states:

> **11. Any person charged with an offence has the right**
> **(a) to be informed without unreasonable delay of the specific offence; . . .**

The purpose of this paragraph is to ensure that the accused understands the substance of the allegation so that he or she can make a full defence. This right applies not only to criminal but also to quasi-criminal (e.g., provincial) offences, or wherever the accused is subject to penal consequences (a fine or imprisonment).[1]

> **(b) to be tried within a reasonable time; . . .**

This paragraph has recently been considered by the Supreme Court of Canada. In *R. v. Askov*,[2] the accused were charged with several offences, including conspiracy to commit extortion and assault with a weapon. It was alleged that the accused had demanded that the victim pay them a 50% commission for allowing the victim to furnish "exotic dancers" to clubs in Toronto. They were charged in November 1983.
One of the accused was released on a *recognizance* in December, while the others were held until May, at which time they were released also on recognizances. Although the accused made several court appearances, the trial date was put off for various reasons until almost two years after the charges were laid, that is, in September 1985. At that point, the

---

1. *Wigglesworth v. The Queen* (1987), 37 C.C.C. (3d) 385 (S.C.C.).
2. (1990), 59 C.C.C. (3d) 499 (S.C.C.).

defence counsel asked that the proceedings be stayed because the delay breached the accused's rights to a trial within a reasonable time. The Supreme Court of Canada agreed with the defence and ordered that the proceedings be stayed.[3] The court found that the delay was largely due to systemic problems in the particular court district. The courts were overburdened with a backload of cases, and there was, as the trial judge noted, a chronic shortage of courtrooms and judges. As a result, long delays were common in this jurisdiction. The court compared this court district to others in Canada and described it as one of the worst. For example, a comparable court district in Montreal had a median delay of 82 1/2 days compared to this district's median delay of 607 days. The court concluded: "Justice delayed is an affront to the individual, to the community, and to the very administration of justice. The lack of institutional facilities cannot in this case be accepted as a basis for justifying the delay."

The court set some general guidelines for determining whether a delay violates the Charter. It said that six to eight months should be the outside limit in most cases between the time of committal for trial and the actual trial. Factors a court should take into account to decide whether the delay is reasonable include:

- length of the delay: that is, the longer the delay, the more likely it is unreasonable
- explanation for the delay: for example, if a delay is caused by inadequate resources, it will go against the Crown; if a delay is caused by the complexity of a case, it will go against the accused
- waiver: if the accused consents to a delay, the consent must be a fully informed and freely given consent
- prejudice to the accused: presumably, the longer the delay, the greater the prejudice to the accused

The immediate result of this decision has been the staying of proceedings in many cases that were waiting for trial. The decision has also forced the provincial governments to take action to remedy the problems caused by lack of resources.

(c) not to be compelled to be a witness in proceedings against that person in respect of the offence; . . .

---

3. To stay proceedings means to withdraw the information that commences the proceedings. The Crown can stay proceedings under s.579 of the Code. Proceedings that are stayed are then suspended. The Crown has one year from the time that the proceedings were stayed to recommence the proceedings. After that time, the proceedings are deemed to have never commenced, and the courts will not allow the Crown to lay a new information. Courts also have the authority to direct a stay of proceedings to prevent an abuse of process where the Crown is acting oppressively. So, for example, in *Askov*, proceedings were stayed because of the abuse of process caused by the lengthy delay in trying the accused.

This paragraph can be considered along with s.13:

> **13. A witness who testifies in any proceeding has the right not to have any incriminating evidence so given used to incriminate that witness in any other proceedings, except in a prosecution for perjury or for the giving of contradictory evidence.**

These two rights ensure that an accused person has the ***right to remain silent*** and the right not to give self-incriminating evidence. For example, assume Henry is convicted at trial and appeals the conviction. The appeal court would then order a new trial. The Crown cannot use the accused's testimony from the first trial to prove the accused's guilt in the second trial.

Section 11 continues:

> **(d) to be presumed innocent until proven guilty according to the law in a fair and public hearing by an independent and impartial tribunal; . . .**

This right is one of our oldest and most important. It means that the accused does not have to prove that he or she is innocent; instead, the Crown has the burden of proving the accused's guilt. This right is consistent with the right to remain silent. The fact that a person is charged with an offence does not mean the person has committed the offence, but only that the police or the Crown have reasonable grounds for believing that the person committed the offence. The accused is presumed innocent until the Crown proves otherwise in a court of law.

The prosecution's burden of proof is proof ***beyond a reasonable doubt***. If at the end of the trial, the judge or jury has a reasonable doubt as to the guilt of the accused, the accused must be found not guilty. ***Reasonable doubt*** has been explained as follows:

". . . real doubt . . . which an honest juror has after considering all the circumstances of the case and as a result of which [the juror] is unable to say: I am morally certain of his guilt. Moral certainty does not mean absolute certainty."[4]

The doubt must be based on the evidence given at the trial. It is not necessary for the Crown to disprove every possible defence to the charge, but, if the accused does raise a defence which is supported by some evidence, the Crown must disprove the defence beyond a reasonable doubt. When the Crown must prove that a person intentionally committed an act, the Crown can rely on the presumption that a person intended the natural consequences of his or her acts. For example, if Jacqueline fires a gun at Armand, a judge or jury *may*, but not must, presume that she intended to wound him.

---

4. *R. v. Sears* (1947), 90 C.C.C. 159 at 163 (Ont.C.A.).

The burden of proof in a criminal trial is much higher than the burden of proof in a civil trial. In a civil trial, the plaintiff must prove his or her case on a *balance of probabilities*. In other words, he or she must prove that it is more likely than not that his or her claim is true. For example, Anne claims that Boris negligently drove a car and caused damage to Anne's car in an accident. Anne will sue Boris for the cost of repairing the car plus any other expenses incurred because of the accident. Anne must prove that it was more likely than not that Boris drove his car in a negligent manner and caused damage to her car. It is not necessary to prove Boris's negligence beyond a reasonable doubt. However, if Boris were charged with murdering Anne, the prosecution would have to prove beyond a reasonable doubt that Boris caused Anne's death.

Although the burden of proving that the accused committed the offence is on the prosecutor, some Criminal Code offences contain "reverse onus clauses." A *reverse onus clause* shifts part of the burden of proof onto the accused. Similar to a reverse onus clause is a *statutory presumption* where a fact is presumed to exist unless the accused can disprove its existence. Since the enactment of the Charter, many of these clauses and presumptions have been found to be violations of the Charter and unenforceable. For example, in *R. v. Oakes*,[5] the accused was charged under the Narcotic Control Act with possession of narcotics for the purpose of trafficking (i.e., selling). Section 8 of the Act states that once the Crown has proven possession, the burden shifts to the accused to prove on a balance of probabilities that he or she did not possess the drugs for the purpose of trafficking. The Supreme Court of Canada in *Oakes* held that s.8 offended s.11(d) of the Charter because a judge could convict an accused of trafficking even if the judge had a reasonable doubt about whether the drugs were possessed for the purpose of trafficking, an essential element of the offence. In other words, the accused, to avoid conviction, had to disprove on the balance of probabilities the existence of a presumed fact.

Although reverse onus provisions and statutory presumptions offend the *presumption of innocence*, it is possible for these provisions to be upheld as reasonable limitations on a right under s.1 of the Charter. The Supreme Court in *Oakes* laid out the test for deciding if a clause is a justifiable limitation. First, the court must look at whether the objective of the law is sufficiently important to warrant overriding a right. For example, in *Oakes*, the objective of the law was to control trafficking in narcotics. Second, the law in question must be reasonable and justifiable. To decide if the law is reasonable and justifiable, the court should ask three questions.

1. Is the law carefully designed to achieve its objective? That is, is the law rationally, not unfairly or arbitrarily, connected to its objective?

---

5. (1986), 50 C.R. (3d) 1 (S.C.C.).

2. Does the law impair the right as little as possible?
3. Is the effect of the law on the right in proportion to the importance of the objective? In other words, the more serious the impairment of the right, the more important the objective must be.

The court in *Oakes* held that the objective of protecting society from the ills associated with drug trafficking is sufficiently important to override a Charter right. However, s.8 failed the proportionality test because there was no rational connection between possession and the presumed fact of possession for the purpose of trafficking. In other words, it is not rational to presume that because a person possesses a narcotic he or she intends to traffick it.

In *R. v. Whyte*,[6] the Supreme Court upheld a clause which infringes s.11(d). In this case, the accused was charged with having care and control of a car while impaired. For this offence, an accused can be charged even if he or she is not driving. For example, a person who is impaired and is sitting on the driver's side of a car could be charged with this offence. In other words, the police do not have to wait for the accused to drive the vehicle before laying a charge. Section 258(1) of the Code sets out a presumption that a person in the driver's seat of a car is there for the purpose of driving the car. This presumption, in effect, shifts the burden of proof onto the accused to show that his or her purpose for being in the driver's seat was not to set the car in motion. This section states:

> **s.258(1)(a) where it is proved that the accused occupied the seat or position ordinarily occupied by a person who operates a motor vehicle . . ., the accused shall be deemed to have had the care or control of the vehicle . . ., unless the accused establishes that the accused did not occupy the seat . . . for the purpose of setting the vehicle . . . in motion.**

The court allowed this infringement under s.1 because protecting the public from drunk driving is sufficiently important to override a constitutionally protected right. The presumption is a minimal interference since the accused can avoid a conviction by giving a reason for being in the driver's seat. On the other hand, it is impractical to require the Crown to prove an intent to drive.

A situation the court has said is not a reverse onus clause and is allowable is one where a person must produce a certificate or permit to legally carry on a certain activity. For example, s.91 of the Code requires a person to have a permit to possess certain types of firearms. Section 115(1) of the Code states that where there is a question of whether a person has a permit, the onus is on the accused to prove that he or she

---

6. (1988), 64 C.R. (3d) 123 (S.C.C.).

has the permit. In *R. v. Schwartz*,[7] the Supreme Court of Canada held that s.115(1) does not create a reverse onus provision (a minority of the court disagreed and said that it offends s.11(d) of the Charter). The court said that s.115(1) creates a rule of evidence and does not require the accused to prove or disprove an element of the offence. In other words, all the accused must do is present the permit to show that he or she is exempt from the provision under which the charge was laid.

Section 11(d) of the Charter also requires that the accused has a right to a fair and public hearing by an impartial and independent tribunal. This right prevents "secret trials" and ensures fairness. As one court said, "Publicity is the hallmark of justice, and trial in open court is the instrument through which publicity is effectively obtained."[8] However, in some circumstances the public can be excluded. For example, under s.486 of the Code, the judge or justice may exclude the public if he or she is of the opinion that ". . . it is in the interests of public morals, the maintenance of order or the proper administration of justice to exclude all or any members of the public from the courtroom for all or part of the proceedings . . . ."

The Supreme Court of Canada has referred to impartiality as "a state of mind or attitude of the court in relation to . . . issues and parties . . . it connotes an absence of bias actual or perceived".[9] One of the reasons for appointing judges to the bench for life is to ensure their independence and impartiality. A judge can only be removed from the bench for a serious breach of duty. Thus, judges are able to make decisions without the influence of public opinion or of the governments that appointed them.

Section 11 goes on:

> **(e) not to be denied reasonable bail without just cause; . . .**

This right entitles a person who has been arrested to pre-trial release on reasonable bail unless reasonable grounds exist for not releasing the person. This right flows from the presumption of innocence. That is, if a person is presumed innocent until proven guilty, it would be unjustifiable to detain that person until a finding is reached. Pre-trial release will be discussed in more detail in Chapter Five on pre-trial procedure.

> **(f) except in the case of an offence under military law tried before a military tribunal, to the benefit of trial by jury where a maximum punishment for the offence is imprisonment for five years or a more severe punishment; . . .**

---

7. (1988), 45 C.C.C. (3d) 97 (S.C.C.).
8. *F.P. Publications (Western) Ltd. v. R.* (1980), 51 C.C.C. (2d) 110 (Man.C.A.).
9. *Valente v. The Queen*, [1985] 2 S.C.R. 673.

The Supreme Court of Canada has said that s.11(f) confers a benefit on the accused which the accused may choose to waive. However, the waiver must be clear and unequivocal, and the accused must be aware of the consequences of the waiver.[10]

> **(g) not to be found guilty on account of any act or omission unless at the time of the act or omission, it constituted an offence under Canadian or international law or was criminal according to the general principles of law recognized by the community of nations; . . .**

This section sets out the basic right *not* to be convicted of a retroactive offence. In other words, this section prevents the government from creating a new offence and applying it to previous conduct.

> **(h) if finally acquitted of the offence, not to be tried for it again and, if finally found guilty and punished for the offence, not to be tried or punished for it again; . . .**

This paragraph states the protection against double jeopardy — being tried twice for the same offence.

> **(i) if found guilty of the offence and if the punishment for the offence has been varied between the time of commission and sentencing, to the benefit of the lesser punishment.**

This section gives a convicted person the right to the lesser punishment if the penalties have changed between the time the offence was committed and the time of sentencing.

One other Charter right should be mentioned here:

> **12. Everyone has the right not to be subjected to any cruel and unusual treatment or punishment.**

The Supreme Court of Canada has stated in *R. v. Smith*[11] that cruel and unusual punishment is such that it is so excessive as to outrage standards of decency. The guidelines set by the court for determining whether punishment is cruel and unusual are:

- whether the punishment is necessary to accomplish a valid penal objective
- whether the punishment is based on valid sentencing principles
- whether there are valid alternatives to the punishment

---

10. *Turpin and Siddiqui v. The Queen* (1989), 48 C.C.C. (3d) 8 (S.C.C.); *Lee v. The Queen* (1989), 52 C.C.C. (3d) 289 (S.C.C.).
11. (1987), 34 C.C.C. (3d) 97 (S.C.C.).

These guidelines help the court determine whether the punishment is grossly disproportionate in relation to the offence.

In *R. v. Smith*, the Supreme Court held that s.5 of the Narcotic Control Act, which imposes a minimum seven-year term of imprisonment for the offence of importing narcotics, violated s.12 of the Charter.

F. APPEALS

Whether the decision of a court can be appealed, and if so, what procedure is used, depends upon a number of factors. The most important factor is the type of the offence, that is, whether the offence is indictable or is a summary conviction offence. The following is a general discussion of appeal procedure which applies to both types of offences.

In every trial there are two main issues which must be determined: the *facts* of the case and the *law* that applies to those facts. The grounds for appeals are based on *questions of fact*, *questions of law*, or *questions of mixed fact and law*. For example, Roberta is charged with murdering Jean by shooting her. Whether Roberta was the person who aimed and fired the gun at Jean is a question of fact. Once the facts of the case are decided, whether the offence of murder has been committed is a question of law. That is, assuming that Roberta intentionally shot Jean, does this conduct constitute the offence of murder as defined by the Code? When an accused is tried by a judge and jury, the jury's function is to determine the facts of the case while the judge's function is to determine the law that applies to the facts. If the trial is before a judge alone, he or she performs both of these functions (i.e., the judge acts as both the **trier of fact** and the **trier of law**).

Both parties to a proceeding (i.e., the accused and the prosecutor) have a right to appeal in certain situations. Sometimes, the accused must have permission to appeal. The accused may be able to appeal the conviction or the sentence. In other words, the appeal can be based on the decision of the court finding the accused guilty or only the punishment imposed by the Court. So, for example, Owen is convicted of assault under s.266 — the least serious type of assault — and sentenced to six years' imprisonment. Owen can appeal the sentence on a question of law because s.266 of the Code provides that the maximum term of imprisonment for this type of assault is five years.

The prosecutor can appeal a dismissal of the information, the acquittal of the accused, or the sentence ordered by the court.

If the appeal court agrees that the trial court's decision was wrong, it may *allow* the appeal. If the appeal court finds that the trial court's decision was proper, it will *dismiss* the appeal. If the appeal is allowed, the appeal court can do things such as: order a new trial, direct an **acquittal**, enter a verdict of guilty (except where there has been a jury trial), or vary the sentence. An appeal court's decision can sometimes be appealed to a higher court. The final and highest court of appeal in Canada is the Supreme Court of Canada.

G. HIERARCHY OF PERSONS AND COURTS WITH JURISDICTION OVER CRIMINAL MATTERS

One way of picturing the criminal court system is to imagine a pyramid. At the top of the pyramid is the Supreme Court of Canada, which only hears appeals. At the base of the pyramid are the justices of the peace. Lower levels of the pyramid are occupied by trial courts. Upper levels are occupied by appeal courts which only review cases appealed from trial courts. At the middle of the pyramid are those courts in which both trials are held and appeals heard. Generally speaking, as the offence becomes more serious or as an offence is appealed, it moves up the pyramid.

The following is a brief description of some of the main functions of the several levels of judicial authority in criminal matters, starting with the lowest level. This is only a general description since each province is responsible for the administration of criminal law in the province and provincial variations are common.

Table 2-1

MAIN FUNCTIONS OF JUDICIAL AUTHORITY

TITLE	DUTIES
Justice of the Peace	— receives informations — issues summonses and warrants for search and arrest — holds bail and preliminary hearings — in some jurisdictions may try summary offences
Provincial Court Judge	— exercises all the duties of a justice of the peace — can try all but the most serious indictable offences
County or District Court*	— trials of certain indictable offences, either with or without jury are held here — hears appeals of summary offences

*N.B.: Only Nova Scotia still has this level of court.

Supreme or Superior Court	— the province's highest level trial court
	— trials of the most serious indictable offences are held here with or without a jury
	— hears some appeals involving summary conviction offences
Court of Appeal	— the province's highest appeal court, hears appeals from the trial courts and lower level appeal courts
Supreme Court of Canada	— hears appeals from provincial Courts of Appeal

QUESTIONS FOR REVIEW AND DISCUSSION

1 Explain why crimes are wrongs against society.

2 Discuss the differences between civil wrongs and criminal wrongs.

3 Which level of government has the authority to make criminal law in Canada?

4 Name and describe the main source of criminal law in Canada.

5 a Discuss some of the differences between indictable offences and summary conviction offences.
  b What is a hybrid offence?

6 What is the purpose of a preliminary inquiry?

7 What are the three methods of trial for indictable offences?

8 What are the similiarities in the trial of a summary conviction offence and in the trial of an indictable offence?

9 a What did the case of *R. v. Askov* decide?
  b What has been the effect of this decision on the court system?

10 What is the difference between a question of fact and a question of law?

11 a What does the presumption of innocence mean?
  b What other Charter rights are consistent with it?

12 a What are reverse onus clauses?
  b How has the Supreme Court dealt with them?

chapter

THREE

Some General Principles

A. THE ELEMENTS OF A CRIME

In general, every crime has a physical element and a mental element. If either element is missing, then no crime has been committed.

1. The Physical Element of a Crime: *Actus Reus*

The physical element of a crime is usually referred to as the *actus reus*. **Actus reus** is a Latin term which is loosely translated as "guilty act" or "wrongful act". Although the term frequently refers to prohibited acts, it is more accurate to say that this term refers to all the parts of the crime other than the **mens rea** or the state of mind of the accused.

In order to determine what is the *actus reus* of a particular offence, it is necessary to look at the definition of the offence. For example, consider s.265 that defines one way of committing the offence of assault:

> **265.(1) A person commits an assault when**
> **(a) without the consent of another person, he applies force intentionally to that other person, directly or indirectly; . . .**

In this offence, the *actus reus* or physical element consists of (1) applying force to another person (2) without the other person's consent. These are the parts of the crime which do not pertain to what was going on in the mind of the accused. Rather, they pertain to a physical occurrence (applying force) and a circumstance (without consent). The mental element or *mens rea* of the offence consists of the intention to apply force. This is indicated by the word "intentionally". This intention relates to what was going on in the mind of the accused and, therefore, is not part of the *actus reus*.

In general, the *actus reus* of a crime consists of a certain type of *conduct*, a *consequence* of that conduct, and *circumstances* surrounding the conduct. Each of these terms will be discussed separately.

a. *Conduct*

The conduct involved in a crime may be an act, an omission, or a "state of being," depending on the particular crime.

Most crimes require that some *act* be committed. In criminal law, an act is a voluntary movement. For example, when Albert throws a punch at Bruce, Albert is voluntarily moving his arm. Or, when Carol shoots a gun, she is committing an act if she voluntarily pulls the trigger.

An *omission* is the failure to act when there is, under the criminal law, a duty to act. For example, s.215(l)(a) refers to such a duty:

> **215.(1) Every one is under a legal duty**
> **(a) as a parent, foster parent, guardian or head of a family, to provide necessaries of life for a child under the age of sixteen years.**

In brief, a parent has a legal duty to provide food and shelter for his or her children. If a parent omits or fails to perform this duty, without a reasonable excuse, then he or she has committed an offence.

Another example is the duty to assist a police officer when requested to do so:

> **129. Every one who . . .**
> **(b) omits, without reasonable excuse, to assist a public officer or peace officer in the execution of his duty in arresting a person or in preserving the peace, after having reasonable notice that he is required to do so . . .**
> **is guilty of . . . an indictable offence . . . or an offence punishable on summary conviction.**

This section is clearly not prohibiting an act. Rather, it creates a duty, and a person who omits or fails to perform this duty has committed an offence, unless there is a reasonable excuse.

Some offences require neither an act nor an omission. Rather, they simply require a state of being. For example, s.354 prohibits a person from "having in his possession" anything which was obtained by crime:

> **354.(1) Every one commits an offence who has [anything] in his possession . . . knowing that [it] was obtained . . .**
> **(a) [by] the commission in Canada of an offence punishable by indictment, or**
> **(b) [by] an act or omission anywhere that, if it had occurred in Canada, would have constituted an offence punishable by indictment.**

For example, if Bill is wearing a stolen watch, then he has it in his possession. Simply having it is enough. It is not necessary that there be some act or omission for the *actus reus* of this offence.

Another example of a state of being is found in s.201(2)(a):

> **201.(2) Every one who**
> **(a) is found, without lawful excuse, in a common gaming house or common betting house, . . .**
> **is guilty of an offence punishable on summary conviction.**

Again, no act or omission is necessary. Simply being "found in" a common gaming house or common betting house is sufficient.

A state of being is not really conduct; however, it does form part of the *actus reus* of crimes which do not require some act or omission.

(i) Voluntariness

It is a general principle of criminal law that a person's act or omission must be voluntary if he or she is to be held responsible for it. An act was defined above as a voluntary movement. If a movement is involuntary, then under the criminal law, there is no act and, therefore, no criminal responsibility.

An example of an involuntary (or automatic) movement is the beating of a heart. Other examples are the bodily movements of a person undergoing an epileptic seizure, or the actions committed while sleep-walking. The general point is that, if a person has no control over his or her physical actions, then he or she will not be held criminally responsible.

If the conduct which forms part of the *actus reus* of a crime is not voluntary, then the accused can use the defence of automatism. Automatism, along with other defences, is discussed in Chapter Four.

(ii) Innocent agent

A person will not escape criminal responsibility by using the innocent actions of someone else to achieve unlawful purposes. For example, Meloche might try to sell drugs to Brigit by using his 12-year-old son to deliver a package containing the drugs and collect the payment. The son may have no idea that he is delivering drugs and thus would be innocent of any wrongdoing. However, Meloche could be found guilty of trafficking even though he was not involved in the actual sale. Under the criminal law, the acts of Meloche's son are considered to be the acts of Meloche and thus Meloche is held responsible for the *actus reus* of the crime.

b. Consequences

Another part of the *actus reus* or physical element of a crime is a consequence. The consequence involved in a crime is the result of an act or an omission. For example, the consequence or result in homicide is the death of a human being:

> **222.(1) A person commits homicide when, directly or indirectly, by any means, he causes the death of a human being.**

Another example is mischief in which the "consequence" part of the offence is damage to property:

> **430.(1) Every one commits mischief who wilfully**
> **(a) destroys or damages property.**

In both these examples, the Code section does not mention any particular conduct which must cause the consequence to occur. In other words, a person may cause the death of a human being by shooting or stabbing the person, by throwing a bomb in the person's car, or by some other act. Regardless of which act is done, a homicide will have been committed if the act caused a person to die. Similarly, a person commits mischief if he or she causes damage to property such as a house by throwing rocks through the windows, by breaking down the front door, or by some other destructive act.

The point here is that the definitions of most crimes mention a consequence, but they do not mention any particular act or omission. In most situations, this distinction between conduct and consequence is not necessary. For example, it is usually precise enough to say simply that Joan killed Maria or that Joan damaged Maria's property. However, the distinction can be very helpful when trying to understand the concepts of causation, intention, and recklessness, which are discussed below.

c. Circumstances

Conduct (an act or omission) is usually not criminal unless it is committed under certain circumstances which form part of the *actus reus* of a crime. For example, s.280(1) includes many circumstances:

> **280.(1) Every one who, without lawful authority, takes . . . an unmarried person under the age of sixteen years out of the possession of and against the will of the parent or guardian of that person . . . is guilty of an indictable offence.**

The relevant circumstances which must be present for this particular offence to have been committed are: (1) the taker must not have lawful authority (an example of a taker with lawful authority might be a social worker acting under a court order); (2) the taken person must be unmarried; (3) he or she must be under the age of 16; (4) at the time of the taking, he or she must have been in the possession of his or her parent or guardian; and (5) the taking must have been against the will of the parent or guardian of the person. If any one of these circumstances is not present, then the *actus reus* is not complete and, thus, the offence has not been committed.

Another example of relevant circumstances in a crime can be found in s.177, trespassing at night:

> **177. Every one who . . . loiters or prowls at night on the property of another person near a dwelling-house situated on that property is guilty of an offence . . . .**

Here, the circumstances which form part of the *actus reus* are (1) the loitering or prowling must occur at night, (2) it must occur on another person's property, (3) it must occur near a **dwelling-house**, and (4) the house must be situated on that property. All these circumstances must be present for the offence to have been committed. For example, if the loitering or prowling occurs during the day or if there is no dwelling-house on the property, then there is no *actus reus* and thus no offence under s.177 has been committed.

d. *Causation*

When the *actus reus* of a crime includes certain consequences, the crime has been committed only if the conduct of the accused caused the consequences to occur. So, if Frank is charged with murdering Paul, then it must be shown that Frank's conduct caused the death of Paul. In most criminal cases, there is no problem in establishing a causal link between the conduct of the accused and the consequence. For example, Irma punches Noreen, breaking Noreen's nose. It is clear that there is a direct cause-and-effect relationship between Irma's act and Noreen's broken nose.

In some cases, the question of causation is not so clear. In *R. v. Wilmot*,[1] the accused was charged with "causing the death of a human being by means of an unlawful act" (manslaughter). The accused was driving his car on a highway when he collided with a person on a bicycle who was riding in the opposite direction. The collision killed the bicyclist. The accused was intoxicated at the time of the accident. Just before the collision, the accused was driving at a moderate, not excessive, rate of speed. At the moment of impact, the car was standing still or practically so and it was slightly across the centre line on the wrong side of the road. Also, the bicyclist, who had a carton of empty beer bottles on the handle bars, swerved or wavered into the left-hand front corner of the car. The court found the accused not guilty because it was not proven that there was a causal relation between the unlawful act of driving a car while intoxicated and the killing of the bicyclist. The court said that it is not enough to show that while a person was doing an unlawful act another

---

1. (1940), 74 C.C.C. 1 (Alta.C.A.).

person was killed. It must be proven that the act (driving while intoxicated) was a direct cause or at least a contributing cause of the death. Neither the fact that the accused was intoxicated nor the other facts in the case proved that his driving caused or brought about the death of the bicyclist.

In *R. v. Dubois*[2] the problem was whether the accused had indirectly caused the death of a person. The accused, Dubois, started a fight with Miron in a tavern. After the fight was over, Dubois left the tavern to get into his car. A few minutes later, Miron ran out and fired a shot at Dubois. The shot missed Dubois but killed Petit, an innocent passer-by. Miron was convicted of manslaughter. Dubois was then charged with murder. The prosecution argued that Dubois had indirectly caused the death of Petit by assaulting Miron. The court found the accused not guilty because, in law, there was no causal relation between the assault of Dubois on Miron and the death of Petit. The connection between the conduct and the consequence was too remote.

2. The Mental Element of a Crime: *Mens Rea*

You have now learned that the *actus reus* of a crime consists of certain conduct, consequences of that conduct, and surrounding circumstances. In addition, for a crime to occur, the *actus reus* must be accompanied by a certain state of mind, the *mens rea*. Basically, there are three types of *mens rea*:[3] (1) intention, (2) knowledge, and (3) recklessness.

a. *Intention*

In most crimes, it is necessary that the accused person intended to or "meant to" cause a certain wrongful consequence. For example, if Alfred hits Bryce without Bryce's consent, then he will be guilty of assault, but only if he intended or meant to hit Bryce. If Alfred accidentally hits Bryce, then he did not have intention and thus no assault has been committed.

Many Code sections clearly require intention by using such words as "intentionally", "wilfully", or "means to". One example is the offence of obstructing a peace officer in the execution of his duty:

> **129. Every one who**
> **(a) resists or *wilfully* obstructs a public officer or peace officer in the execution of his duty or any person lawfully acting in aid of such an officer, ...**
> **is guilty of an indictable offence . . . or . . . an offence punishable on summary conviction.**

---

2. (1959), 32 C.R. 187 (Que.Q.B.).
3. Intention and knowledge are sometimes referred to as one type of *mens rea*: intention. For the purpose of this chapter, these terms are discussed separately.

In the offence of obstructing a peace officer, a person is guilty only if he or she intends or means to wrongfully obstruct or interfere with the officer.

Even if the Code section does not use a word such as "wilfully", intention usually will still be required. For example, in s.129 above, a person may be charged with resisting a peace officer rather than wilfully obstructing the officer. The section does not indicate that the person must "wilfully" or "intentionally" resist. However, despite the absence of these words, the person will be guilty of the offence only if he intended or meant to resist the peace officer.

(i) Specific intent

Some offences require a special or specific kind of intent. These are called *specific intent offences*. In general, specific intent offences are indicated by the words "with intent" or similar words such as "for the purpose of."[4] For example, consider s.348(1)(a):

> **348.(1) Every one who**
> **(a) breaks and enters a place *with intent to commit an indictable offence* therein . . .**
> **is guilty of an indictable offence . . . .**

In this offence, it must be shown not only that the accused intended to break and enter but also that he or she did it with the specific intent to commit an indictable offence such as theft. If it could be shown that the person broke into a place in order to obtain shelter from a storm, then the offence in s.348(l)(a) has not been committed. On the other hand, it is not necessary to show that the person actually committed an indictable offence. It is enough to show that the person broke and entered with the intent to commit an indictable offence.

Another example of a specific intent offence is robbery. One form of robbery is found in s.343(c):

> **343. Every one commits robbery who . . .**
> **(c) assaults any person *with intent to steal* from him.**

To commit this crime, a person must not only assault someone but also intend to steal from the victim. If it could be shown that Marla assaulted Blake, but it could not be shown that the assault was done for the specific intent to steal, then Marla would be guilty of assault, but not robbery.

Offences, such as assault, which do not require a specific intent are called *general intent offences*. The distinction between a general intent offence and a specific intent offence has been explained by the Supreme Court of Canada in the following way:

---

4. However, this is not always the case. A notable exception is murder (s.229).

In considering the question of mens rea, a distinction is to be drawn between "intention" as applied to acts done to achieve an immediate end on the one hand and acts done with the specific and ulterior motive and intention of furthering or achieving an illegal object on the other hand. Illegal acts of the former kind are done intentionally in the sense that they are not done by accident or through honest mistakes, but acts of the latter kind are the product of preconception and are deliberate steps taken toward an illegal goal. The former acts may be purely physical products of momentary passion, whereas the latter involve the mental process of forming a specific intent. [5]

In other words, in a general intent offence, the acts are done to achieve an immediate consequence or result. For example, assault is committed when Tony throws a punch at Handley in order to hit him and he does hit him without Handley's consent. In a specific intent offence, the acts are done with some additional or further intention in mind. For example, Tony's further intention in hitting Handley might be to steal Handley's money.

The distinction between general intent and specific intent is important for two special reasons:

(1) A greater burden of proof is placed on the prosecution in a specific intent offence. That is, the prosecution must prove not only that the accused intentionally committed the prohibited act, but also that the accused committed the act with a specific intent.

(2) The defence of intoxication (by alcohol or drugs) can be successfully used with a specific intent offence. In most situations, it is not a defence to a charge of committing a general intent offence. The defence of intoxication will be discussed in detail in Chapter Four.

(ii) Intention and motive

Intention is different from motive. Motive refers to some reason for committing the crime. It is not part of the *mens rea* of a crime. A person may commit a crime for a good motive and still be found guilty. For example, a man may want to free his father from the pain of cancer. So he gives his father a poisonous drug which results in the death of his father. Here, the *actus reus* (killing the father) and the *mens rea* (intending to kill his father) of murder were both present and thus a crime has been committed. The motive, to put his father out of his misery, was irrelevant to the issue of criminal responsibility and the son would be guilty of murder.

The important point to remember is that the motive is not part of the actual crime. Therefore, if the *actus reus* and the *mens rea* of a crime were present, then it makes no difference to criminal responsibility whether the accused acted with a good or a bad motive.

However, motive can be relevant in at least two ways. First, it can be

---

5. *R. v. George* (1960), 128 C.C.C. 289 (S.C.C.).

used as evidence to help prove the intention of the accused. For example, if the prosecution can show that Betty would inherit $100,000 when Greta died, then it can be seen that Betty would have a motive or purpose for killing Greta.

A second way in which motive is relevant concerns sentencing. An accused who has been found guilty of a crime may receive a lighter sentence from the judge if he or she acted with a good motive rather than a bad one. For example, Betty might receive a lighter sentence for murdering Greta if the act was done as an act of mercy (e.g., "mercy killing") rather than as an act of greed (e.g., to inherit money).

(iii) Intention and voluntariness

Intention is part of the *mens rea* of a crime and it should be distinguished from the voluntariness of a person's conduct which is part of the *actus reus* of a crime. In general, voluntariness refers to control over bodily movements. Intention refers to the state of mind regarding the consequences or results of those bodily movements. For example, a person may voluntarily shoot a gun but the person may not be intending to kill anyone. The act of shooting is under the person's control and, therefore, is voluntary. But, if the person did not intend human death or serious bodily harm as a consequence of the act, then the person did not have the *mens rea* for the offence of murder.

b. *Knowledge*

In many crimes it is necessary that the accused have knowledge or awareness of certain circumstances. This is sometimes indicated by the word "knowing" or "knowingly" in the definition of the crime. For example, s.131(1) states:

> **131.(1) Subject to subsection (3), every one commits perjury who, with intent to mislead, makes before a person who is authorized by law to permit it to be made before him a false statement under oath . . . knowing that the statement is false.**

If a person gives false evidence at a trial but he or she does not realize that the evidence is false, then the crime of perjury has not been committed. Without knowledge of this circumstance, there is no *mens rea* and thus no offence is committed.

The general rule is that the word "knowingly" in the definition of an offence applies to all the elements of the *actus reus*. Even if "knowing" or "knowingly" is absent from the definition of the offence, knowledge of relevant circumstances will usually be required. For example, in *R. v. McLeod*,[6] the accused was charged with assaulting a police officer, contrary to what is now s.270(1)(a):

---

6. (1954), 111 C.C.C. 106 (B.C.C.A.).

> **270.(1) Every one commits an offence who**
> **(a) assaults a public officer or peace officer engaged in the execution of his duty or a person acting in aid of such an officer.**

The police officer, dressed in plain clothes, tried to stop a fight between two youths. The accused was one of the many bystanders watching the fight. When the officer tried to stop the fight, the accused, not knowing that he was a police officer, pushed the officer and told him to mind his own business. The court held that the accused was not guilty because he lacked the necessary knowledge to commit the offence. Without the knowledge that the person interfering was a police officer, the accused had no *mens rea*.

c. *Recklessness*

Recklessness is a third type of *mens rea* or mental element of a crime. In some offences, it is not necessary that the accused actually intended to commit the offence. Instead, it may be enough for criminal responsibility that the person was reckless about committing the offence.

In general, a person is reckless when he or she is extremely or grossly careless. Court decisions have not been consistent on a more specific definition of recklessness. Some decisions have held that a person is reckless when he or she foresees the possibility of a harmful consequence and then takes the risk that the harm will not result.[7] In other words, the person must be aware of the danger involved. If he or she does not have this **subjective foresight** or **awareness**, then the person is not reckless. For example, Alice wants to practice her target shooting. So, she attaches a target to a tree in a public park. She sees that the tree is in front of a children's play area and that the area is being used by a few children. Alice's first shot misses the target and wounds one of the children. Alice was clearly reckless because she foresaw the possibility of injury even though she had no intention to cause injury. She did not intend the harmful consequence but she foresaw the possibility of it and took the risk.

Under this definition of recklessness, the risk which is taken must be an unjustifiable one. Some risks are justifiable. For example, the doctor who performs heart surgery foresees the possibility of causing the death of the patient, but the doctor is not being reckless by operating. The risk is reasonable or justifiable. On the other hand, in the target shooting example above, it was not reasonable or justifiable for Alice to take the risk.

Other court decisions have said that a person may be reckless even though he or she does not foresee the possibility of a harmful consequence. These decisions have stated that the question is not whether the

---

7. *O'Grady v. Sparling* (1960), 128 C.C.C. 1 (S.C.C.).

accused actually foresaw the consequence. Rather, the question is whether a reasonable person, in the position of the accused, would have foreseen the consequences and whether the conduct of the accused represents a gross departure from the conduct of a reasonable person.[8] This is sometimes called *objective foresight*.

The Supreme Court of Canada appears to have come down in favour of a subjective standard for recklessness. The court in *Sansregret v. The Queen* stated:

> . . . *recklessness, to form part of the criminal* mens rea, *must have an element of the subjective. It is found in the attitude of one who, aware that there is a danger that his conduct could bring about the result prohibited by the criminal law, nevertheless persists, despite the risk.*[9]

Some Code sections clearly require recklessness by using the words "reckless" or "recklessly". An example is one type of the offence of arson:

> **434.(1) Every person who intentionally or recklessly causes damage by fire or explosion to property that is owned, in whole or in part, by that person is guilty of an indictable offence . . . where the fire or explosion seriously threatens the health, safety or property of another person.**

Even if the Code does not include the word "reckless", courts have, for some offences, held that recklessness is a sufficient *mens rea* where the *mens rea* is knowledge of certain circumstances. For example, for the offence of sexual assault, where lack of consent is an element, recklessness regarding whether the victim consented or not to the sexual contact is sufficient for the *mens rea*. In other words, an accused person may be convicted of sexual assault if he or she did not know the victim wasn't consenting but was reckless as to whether the victim consented. Similarly, for the offence of possession of property obtained by the commission of a crime (e.g., possession of stolen property), a person must know that the property has been obtained through the commission of an offence. Recklessness can be a sufficient *mens rea* for this offence.

(i) Wilful blindness

A concept that is closely related to recklessness is *wilful blindness*. The Supreme Court in *Sansregret*[10] defined wilful blindness as follows:

> . . . *wilful blindness arises where a person who has become aware of the need for some inquiry declines to make the inquiry because he does not wish to know the truth. He would prefer to remain ignorant.*

---

8. *R. v. Nelson* (1990), 75 C.R. (3d) 70 (Ont.C.A.).
9. (1985), 18 C.C.C. (3d) 223 (S.C.C.).
10. *Ibid.*

An example of the application of wilful blindness is in *R. v. Blondin*.[11] In this case, the accused was charged with importing narcotics, contrary to s.5 of the Narcotic Control Act. Twenty-three pounds of hashish were found inside a scuba-diving tank which the accused was trying to bring into Canada. The accused admitted that he knew that there was something illegal in the tank but stated he did not know that it contained a narcotic. Knowledge that the substance being imported is a narcotic is an essential ingredient of the offence of importing narcotics. The court held that this requirement was satisfied if it was proven that the accused had been reckless about what the substance was or had wilfully shut his eyes to what it was.

(ii) Recklessness and the offence of criminal negligence
The offence of *criminal negligence* appears to require recklessness for its *mens rea*. It states:

> **219.(1) Every one is criminally negligent who**
> **(a) in doing anything, or**
> **(b) in omitting to do anything that is his duty to do,**
> **shows wanton or *reckless* disregard for the lives or safety of other persons.**

However, courts have not been able to agree on whether the *mens rea* for this offence requires subjective or objective foresight. Recent Supreme Court of Canada decisions have not clarified the issue since the justices themselves have not been able to agree. This issue is discussed in more detail in Chapter Ten, and also with regard to driving offences in Chapter Eleven.

d. Strict Liability

Despite the general rule that *mens rea* is an essential element of an offence, some offences do not require *mens rea*. These are called **strict liability offences**. The Crown needs only to prove the *actus reus* of the offence in order to have the accused convicted, unless the accused can show that he or she acted as a reasonable person in the circumstances or with due diligence. In other words, a person charged with a strict liability offence may be convicted of the offence merely because of his or her conduct, and it is not necessary to consider whether the person was reckless or intended to commit the offence. The only defence is that the accused acted with due diligence under the circumstances.

Strict liability offences are often created by statutes dealing with health, safety, and the general welfare of the public (e.g., the Food and Drugs Act). These offences are contained in provincial legislation and

---

11. (1970), 2 C.C.C. (2d) 118 (B.C.C.A.).

federal statutes other than the Criminal Code. For example, the Ontario Water Resources Act makes the discharging of materials into a lake that might impair the quality of the water an offence. The Supreme Court of Canada in *R. v. Sault Ste. Marie*[12] held that the offence created by the act is one of strict liability. The court stated that pollution offences are "undoubtedly public welfare offences enacted in the interests of public health." An example of a federal offence of strict liability has been treated by the Migratory Birds Convention Act regulations, which provide that no person shall hunt for migratory birds within 400 m of where bait has been deposited. The Migratory Birds Convention Act makes the violation of the act or any regulation passed under the act an offence. In *R. v. Chapin*,[13] the accused was charged with this offence after a conservation officer had found her hunting about 46 m from a pile of grain. Chapin testified that she was unaware of the bait and the officer stated that the bait was difficult to notice. The Supreme Court of Canada held that the offence was of strict liability and that Chapin should be acquitted since she had acted reasonably under the circumstances.

Generally, offences in the Criminal Code are not strict liability offences but require a greater degree of fault.

There is one other possible type of offence, that is, offences of absolute liability. For these offences, the Crown has only to prove the *actus reus* of the offence to gain a conviction. The accused cannot use the defence of due diligence. A person who has no moral blameworthiness at all can be convicted of committing an offence. In general, these offences have been found to violate the Charter. The Supreme Court of Canada has held that a law that allows a person who has done nothing wrong to be convicted of a crime offends the principles of fundamental justice, and, where penal consequences are attached (i.e., a term of imprisonment or probation), the law deprives a person of his or her right to liberty.[14] The Supreme Court of Canada has yet to decide whether an absolute liability offence, the penalty for which is a fine and imprisonment if the fine is not paid, would also offend the Charter.

Courts have not looked favourably on laws which exclude *mens rea* as an element of an offence. They have required that the language of the statute which sets out the offence must be very clear in excluding *mens rea*. If the statute is silent in regard to *mens rea*, then it will usually be interpreted as requiring it. For example, the offence of driving while disqualified has been interpreted as requiring *mens rea*. In other words, the person must know that he or she is disqualified from driving. In *R. v. Prue*,[15] the accused was charged with driving while his licence was suspended. He argued that he had not received notice of the cancellation and, therefore, *mens rea* did not exist. On appeal, the Supreme Court of

12. (1978), 40 C.C.C. (2d) 353 (S.C.C.).
13. [1979] 7 C.R. (3d) 225 (S.C.C.).
14. Reference Section 94(2) of the Motor Vehicle Act (1985), 23 C.C.C. (3d) 289 (S.C.C.).
15. (1979), 46 C.C.C. (2d) 257 (S.C.C.).

Canada held that the driving suspension is a question of fact and ignorance of that fact is a valid defence to the charge.

3. Concurrence of *Mens Rea* and *Actus Reus*

It is a general principle of criminal law that for an offence to occur, both the *mens rea* and the *actus reus* must be present at the same time. In most cases, there are no problems with this principle. For example, in the case of theft, the act of stealing and the intent to steal usually occur at the same time. However, in some cases, it is not so clear. For example, Alphonse picks up a coat in a restaurant thinking that it belongs to him. When he gets home, he realizes that the coat does not belong to him. He also realizes that the coat is a much better and more expensive coat than his own. So, he decides to keep it. Here, the *actus reus*, the taking of the coat, occurred at the restaurant, but the *mens rea*, the intention of depriving the owner, did not occur until later. The question is whether Alphonse should be found not guilty because the *actus reus* and *mens rea* did not occur at the same time. In answering this question, the criminal law relies on the fiction that the act of taking the coat continued until the point at which Alphonse formed the *mens rea* to commit the crime. Thus, Alphonse would be guilty of theft.

In an English case,[16] the accused accidently drove his car onto a police officer's foot. When he learned of the officer's predicament, he refused to move the car. The accused was convicted of assault based on the fiction that the act continued until the intention to assault occurred.

B. PARTIES TO A CRIME

AIDING AND ABETTING s.21

In general, **parties** are certain persons who are involved either before or during the commission of the offence. All persons who are classified as parties are subject to the same penalty regardless of their role in the commission of the crime. Sections 21 and 22 define parties as those who actually commit the crime, or who aid and abet or counsel the commission of a crime.

1. Aiding and Abetting

21.(1) Every one is a party to an offence who
(a) actually *commits* it,
(b) does or omits to do anything for the purpose of *aiding* any person to commit it; or
(c) *abets* any person in committing it.

---

16. *Fagan v. Metropolitan Police Commissioner* (1969) 1 Q.B. 439.

The person who actually commits an offence is a party to the offence. This person is referred to as the ***principal offender*** or simply the principal or the perpetrator. A person who acts through an innocent agent is considered to actually commit the offence himself and, thus, is a principal.

Parts (b) and (c) of s.21 mean, in general, that anyone who helps or encourages another person to commit an offence is a party and is thus responsible for its commission. More specifically, "aid" means to help or give assistance and "abet" means to encourage another to commit a crime.

In order to find a person guilty of ***aiding or abetting***, it is only necessary to show that he or she understood what was taking place and by some act on his or her part encouraged or assisted in the attainment thereof."[17] The encouragement or the assistance given by the person must be intentional. If the conduct of a person has the effect of helping the principal to commit a crime, but the person did not intend to help the principal, then the person did not aid or abet. For example, Ziad lends his tools to Bernice because he thinks Bernice needs them for house repairs. Instead, Bernice uses them to break into a shop. Ziad would not be guilty of aiding or abetting the commission of the offence. Or, Anna, a bank security officer, forgets to lock the door to the bank. This omission helps Betty to rob the bank. Anna would not be guilty of aiding or abetting because she did not intend to help in the commission of the crime.

In general, a person who is merely present at the commission of an offence will not be guilty of aiding and abetting. There must be some active assistance or encouragement. Simply being present and not objecting to the offence is not aiding and abetting. However, a "lookout man" aids and abets. In *R. v. Cunningham*,[18] the accused was stationed at the entrance of a common betting house for the purpose of signalling to the keepers of the house if the police approached. The court held that the accused was assisting in the continued operation of the house by preventing the police from obtaining evidence.

In some cases, the issue of whether there is active assistance or encouragement is more difficult. For example, in *R. v. Kulbacki*,[19] the accused, a 20-year-old man, allowed a 16-year-old girl to drive his car. While he was sitting beside her, she drove the car over 90 m.p.h. and the accused did not do or say anything to stop her. He was charged with aiding and abetting the commission of the offence of dangerous driving. His defence was that he did nothing to encourage the commission of the offence, since he was merely a passive observer, and, therefore, should not be liable for aiding and abetting. The court held that the failure of the accused to stop or prevent the girl from committing the offence, when he was in a position to do so and when he had the authority to do so,

17. *Preston v. R.* (1949), 93 C.C.C. 83 (S.C.C.).
18. (1937), 68 C.C.C. 176 (Ont.C.A.).
19. [1966] 1 C.C.C. 167 (Man.C.A.).

amounted to encouragement and thus, he was aiding and abetting. The court also pointed out that every passenger in an unlawfully driven car is not necessarily aiding and abetting because he or she might not have any authority over the car or any right to control the driver.

An accused may be charged with aiding and abetting in the commission of a particular offence or may simply be charged with the particular offence. In *R. v. Harder*,[20] the accused was charged with rape but his only involvement was assisting the other person to commit the rape. (This offence is now one type of sexual assault.) The Supreme Court of Canada held that the accused was properly convicted of rape and that it was not necessary to spell out in the charge that the accused only assisted in the commission of the offence.

2. Common Intention

COMMON INTENTION s.21(2)

A person is also a party if his or her conduct falls within s.21(2):

> **21.(2) Where two or more persons form an intention in common to carry out an unlawful purpose and to assist each other therein and any one of them, in carrying out the common purpose, commits an offence, each of them who knew or ought to have known that the commission of the offence would be a probable consequence of carrying out the common purpose is a party to that offence.**

To convict someone under this section: (1) there must be a common intention formed by the accused and at least one other person to carry out an unlawful purpose and to help each other in doing so; (2) one of them in carrying out the unlawful purpose must commit an offence different than the unlawful purpose; and (3) the offence must be one which they knew or should have known would probably result from carrying out their common purpose.

The Supreme Court of Canada has recently considered this section, specifically, the third requirement, and the words "ought to have known," along with the issue of the *mens rea* required for murder. In a series of decisions, the court held that the offences of murder and attempted murder require a subjective intent,[21] that is, the accused must actually intend to commit the offence of murder. The Court said:

> *Murder has long been recognized as the worst and most heinous of peacetime crimes. It is, therefore, essential that to satisfy the principles of fundamental justice, the stigma and punishment attaching to a murder*

---

20. (1956), 114 C.C.C. 129 (S.C.C.).
21. *R. v. Martineau* (1990), 58 C.C.C. (3d) 353 (S.C.C.); *R. v. Luxton* (1990), 58 C.C.C. (3d) 449 (S.C.C.); *R. v. Arkell* (1990), 59 C.C.C. (3d) 65 (S.C.C.); *R. v. Logan and Johnson* (1990), 58 C.C.C. (3d) 391.

conviction must be reserved for those who either intend to cause death or who intend to cause bodily harm that they know will likely cause death.

The Court then considered s.21(2). With the words "ought to have known" in s.21(2), it was possible for someone to be convicted of murder who did not have the subjective intent the offence of murder requires. In other words, a person who was not the principal could be convicted of murder with a lesser degree of fault than is required for the principal. This was the situation in one of the cases before the Court, *R. v. Logan and Johnson.*[22] The accused were parties to a robbery of a convenience store. They had entered the store wearing masks and armed with revolvers. One of the other parties shot the clerk, who was severely injured. They were convicted of attempted murder. Logan and Johnson appealed their conviction. Their conviction for attempted murder was based on s.21(2). That is, they had a common intention with the other party to commit an unlawful purpose, the robbery, and that they either knew or ought to have known that the other party might shoot and that a death would result. This application of s.21(2) was clearly unfair, and the Court ruled that the section was unenforceable as it was a violation of fundamental justice under the Charter. More generally, the court also held that in order to convict a person under s.21(2), the accused must have the necessary intent for the actual offence. In other words, if the offence requires subjective intent, then the accused must have that intent. These are very recent decisions. In the future it will be up to the court to consider other situations and offences which will clarify when the objective standard in s.21(2) can be used.

3. Counselling an Offence

COUNSEL-
LING
s.22
[s.464]

    22.(1) Where a person counsels another person to be a party to an offence and that other person is afterwards a party to that offence, the person who counselled is a party to that offence, notwithstanding that the offence was committed in a way different from that which was counselled.

    (2) Every one who counsels another person to be a party to an offence is a party to every offence that the other commits in consequence of the counselling that the person who counselled knew or ought to have known was likely to be committed in consequence of the counselling.

To counsel means to advise or recommend. Counselling also includes procuring (instigating or persuading), soliciting, or inciting.

The general idea in s.22(1) is that a person is a party to an offence if the person advises or gets another person to commit an offence, even if the

---

22. *Ibid.*

crime is committed in a way that is different from what was suggested. Here is an example. Tom suggests to Peter that Peter rob the corner store on Saturday night using a gun Tom provides. Peter robs the store but instead uses a fake gun that he had. Tom has counselled the commission of the offence.

In the case of *R. v. Soloway*,[23] the victim met a woman in a bar and offered to take her home. She invited him in when they reached her home. Inside were several other people including the accused, Soloway. The victim fell asleep on the couch. He woke up when he felt the woman taking his wallet out of his back pocket, and he pretended to be asleep to avoid a fight. There was no money in his wallet and she started to put it back. Soloway then told her to keep the identification papers because they could be sold. Soloway was convicted of theft because of his role in counselling the crime.

Under s.22(2) a person is a party to any other crime that is committed if the person knew or ought to have known that it was likely to be committed as a result of the counselling. Section 22(2) raises the same issue as does s.21(2) concerning objective and subjective foresight. As yet, this section has not been challenged in court.

Counselling is an offence in itself. Therefore, an offence is committed even if the counselled offence is not committed. For the offence of counselling, it does not matter whether the person counselled was persuaded or ever had the intent to commit the crime. If the accused is convicted of the offence of counselling instead of being convicted as a party to the offence, the accused will be punished under s.464:

> **464. Except where otherwise expressly provided by law, the following provisions apply in respect of persons who counsel other persons to commit offences, namely,**
>
> **(a) every one who counsels another person to commit an indictable offence is, if the offence is not committed, guilty of an indictable offence and liable to the same punishment to which a person who attempts to commit that offence is liable; and**
>
> **(b) every one who counsels another person to commit an offence punishable on summary conviction is, if the offence is not committed, guilty of an offence punishable upon summary conviction.**

If the offence counselled is committed , the accused will be punished as a party and can receive the same punishment as if the accused actually committed the offence. For example, if Andrew counsels Megan to commit an offence and Megan commits the offence, then Andrew will be punished as a party to the offence and is liable to receive the same punishment as Megan.

---

23. (1975), 28 C.C.C. (2d) 212 (Alta.C.A.).

4. Accessory After the Fact

Section 23 creates a separate offence of helping someone who has committed an offence. The person who provides such assistance is not a party to the offence but may be convicted of being an *accessory after the fact* (i.e., a helper after the offence has been committed) if the person's actions fall within s.23:

> **23.(1) An accessory after the fact to an offence is one who, knowing that a person has been a party to the offence, receives, comforts or assists that person for the purpose of enabling that person to escape.**
>
> **(2) No married person whose spouse has been a party to an offence is an accessory after the fact to that offence by receiving, comforting or assisting the spouse for the purpose of enabling the spouse to escape.**

There are three main requirements for this offence. First, there must be *knowledge* that the other person has been a party to an offence. In *R. v. Vinette,*[24] the accused did not deny having assisted another person in disposing of a corpse by throwing it to the bottom of a flooded quarry in a weighted trunk. The court decided that this was enough evidence in itself to indicate that the accused knew that the other party had been a party to the crime of homicide. The accused must only know of the party's participation; it is not necessary that he or she be aware of the legal classification of the offence.

Second, the accused must assist the party to the offence escape. A person who does not disclose that an offence has been committed in his or her presence or who does not assist in apprehending the party is not an accessory. In general, assistance is anything that goes beyond a mere omission to aid in the capture of the offender. In *Young v. R.,*[25] the accused told two murderers that their names were known to the police and that the police had the license plate number of their car. The court held that this was assistance because it went beyond a mere omission to aid in their capture and actually helped them escape apprehension.

Third, the assistance must be given with the *intention* of helping the criminal to escape. For example, in *R. v. McVay,*[26] the accused was charged with murder. A witness at the trial had, at the accused's request, disposed of a pair of jeans which the accused was allegedly wearing at the time of the offence. An issue was whether the witness was in fact an accessory since he had helped the accused to escape by disposing of the jeans. The court stated that it was a question for the jury, after weighing the evidence, to decide whether the witness knew that the accused had

---

24. (1974), 19 C.C.C. (2d) 1 (S.C.C.).
25. (1950), 98 C.C.C. 195 (Que.C.A.).
26. (1982), 66 C.C.C. (2d) 512 (Ont.C.A.).

committed a murder at the time he disposed of the jeans. Only if the accused knew of the murder would he then be an accessory after the fact.

Notice that the law recognizes that it would be unfair to make a spouse who assists his or her spouse an accessory after the fact.

WHERE PRINCIPAL OR OTHER PARTY NOT INDICTED OR CONVICTED s.592; s.23.1

If the principal is acquitted of the offence, then the accessory will be acquitted. However, it is possible for an accessory to be convicted if the principal cannot be tried or convicted. Section 592 provides:

> **592. Any one who is charged with being an accessory after the fact to any offence may be indicted, whether or not the principal or any other party to the offence has been indicted or convicted or is or is not amenable to justice.**

Section 23.1 sets out a similar rule for an accused charged with aiding, abetting, counselling, or procuring:

> **23.1 For greater certainty, sections 21 to 23 apply in respect of an accused notwithstanding the fact that the person whom the accused aids or abets, counsels or procures or receives, comforts or assists cannot be convicted of the offence.**

So, for instance, if the principal offender cannot be found or the principal offender cannot be charged because of the offender's youth, the accessory is still liable for the offence. In *R. v. McAvoy*,[27] the accused, a taxi driver, gave an unknown person a ride to a department store. The person entered the store, stole some items, and ran out of the store with two store employees in pursuit. The accused drove off with the thief while the pursuit was still on. The person who actually committed the theft was never found, but the accused was charged with being an accessory. His conviction was upheld by an appeal court.

However, before an accessory can be convicted, the Crown must still prove that the principal committed the offence if the principal has not been previously convicted.[28]

Unless there is a section which sets out a penalty for being an accessory to a specific offence, the penalties for being an accessory are set out in s.463:

> **463.(a) every one who attempts to commit or is an accessory after the fact to the commission of an indictable offence for which, on conviction, an accused is liable to . . . imprisonment for life is guilty of an indictable offence and liable to imprisonment for a term not exceeding fourteen years;**
>
> **(b) every one who attempts to commit or is an**

---

27. (1981), 60 C.C.C. (2d) 95 (Ont.C.A.).
28. For example, see *R. v. Anderson* (1980), 57 C.C.C. (2d) 255 (Alta.C.A.).

accessory after the fact to the commission of an indictable offence for which, on conviction, an accused is liable to imprisonment for fourteen years or less is guilty of an indictable offence and liable to imprisonment for a term that is one-half of the longest term to which a person who is guilty of that offence is liable;

(c) every one who attempts to commit or is an accessory after the fact to the commission of an offence punishable on summary conviction is guilty of an offence punishable upon summary conviction; [i.e., six months' imprisonment and/or a fine of up to $2 000]

(d) every one who attempts to commit or is an accessory after the fact to the commission of an . . . [hybrid offence]

(i) is guilty of an indictable offence and liable to imprisonment for a term not exceeding a term that is one-half the longest term to which a person who is guilty of that offence is liable, or

(ii) is guilty of an offence punishable upon summary conviction.

C. CONSPIRACY

CONSPIRACY s.465

In general, a conspiracy is an agreement (or "common design") by two or more persons to do an unlawful act or to do a lawful act by unlawful means. It is immaterial whether the unlawful act is committed or not. Even though the conspirators may change their minds or may not get the opportunity to perform the unlawful act, they have committed the offence of conspiracy when their agreement is reached. So, if Bibi and Irene plan to kidnap Michelle and they are arrested before they can carry out the kidnapping, both of them would be guilty of conspiracy.

Assume Bibi and Irene made the same agreement as above but Irene only pretended to agree. That is, Irene agreed but had no intention of carrying out the agreement. This was the situation in the case of *R. v. O'Brien*[29] where the accused was charged with conspiracy to commit kidnapping. O'Brien asked Tulley to help him kidnap a woman named Pritchard. He offered to pay him for his help. Tulley agreed and received several payments. When O'Brien started pressuring him to actually carry out the kidnapping, Tulley went to the police and to Pritchard's husband and told them the plan. At O'Brien's trial, Tulley testified that he never intended to carry out the kidnapping but was just going along with O'Brien. On appeal, the Supreme Court of Canada ruled that O'Brien could not be convicted of conspiracy because there was no true agreement between Tulley and O'Brien. For the agreement to exist there must be a common intention to carry out the unlawful plan. In this case Tulley

29. (1954), 110 C.C.C. 1 (S.C.C.).

was only pretending to have the intention to commit the kidnapping. On the other hand, the court in *O'Brien* also said that the offence of conspiracy is committed even if one party later withdraws from the plan since the offence is already complete.

The Supreme Court of Canada has said that a husband and wife cannot be found guilty of conspiring together because in law they are considered to be one legal person. However, if a third party is involved, all three can be convicted.[30]

The main section dealing with conspiracy is s.465:

> **465.(1) Except where otherwise expressly provided by law, the following provisions apply in respect of conspiracy:**
>
> **(a) every one who conspires with any one to commit murder or to cause another person to be murdered, whether in Canada or not, is guilty of an indictable offence and liable to a maximum term of imprisonment for life;**
>
> **(b) every one who conspires with any one to prosecute a person for an alleged offence, knowing that he did not commit that offence, is guilty of an indictable offence and liable**
>
> > **(i) to imprisonment for a term not exceeding ten years, if the alleged offence is one for which, on conviction, the person would be liable to . . . imprisonment for life or for a term not exceeding fourteen years, or**
> >
> > **(ii) to imprisonment for a term not exceeding five years, if the alleged offence is one for which, on conviction, the person would be liable to imprisonment for less than fourteen years; and**
>
> **(c) every one who conspires with any one to commit an indictable offence not provided for in paragraph (a) or (b) is guilty of an indictable offence and liable to the same punishment as that to which an accused who is guilty of that offence would, on conviction, be liable; and**
>
> **(d) every one who conspires with any one to commit an offence punishable on summary conviction is guilty of an offence punishable on summary conviction.**

Sections 465(1)(a) and (b) provide for specific conspiracy offences, that is, conspiracy to commit a murder or to unlawfully prosecute a person.

Section 465(1)(c) makes it an offence to conspire to commit any other indictable offence.

Section 465(1)(d) makes it an offence punishable on summary conviction to conspire to commit a summary conviction offence.

---

30. *Kowbel v. The Queen* (1954), 110 C.C.C. 47 (S.C.C.).

It is also a conspiracy offence to conspire while in Canada to do something outside of Canada if that something is a crime by the laws of the other place. Similarly, it is conspiracy to agree outside of Canada to commit a crime inside of Canada. (See s.465(3) and (4).)

D. ATTEMPTS

ATTEMPTING s.24 A person can commit an offence by merely trying to commit an offence. The offence of attempting a crime is defined in s.24:

> **24.(1) Every one who, having an intent to commit an offence, does or omits to do anything for the purpose of carrying out his intention is guilty of an attempt to commit the offence whether or not it was possible under the circumstances to commit the offence.**

There are three essential elements to an attempt: (1) the intent to commit the offence, (2) some act or omission toward committing the offence, and (3) noncompletion of the offence.

The *intent* required in an attempt is the same as the intent required in the completed offence. For example, in an attempted theft, there must be the intent to steal. In an attempted murder, there must be an attempt to cause a death. For example, if Angela shoots at Ricardo, intending to kill him, but she misses, then Angela has attempted to murder Ricardo.

In addition to intent, there must be some *act* or *omission* done for the purpose of carrying out the intent. The rule is that the act or omission must be more than mere preparation to commit the crime. It must be immediately, not remotely, connected with the commission of the crime. In other words, if a person is only preparing to commit a crime, then no offence is committed. But if the person commits some act or omission which amounts to more than mere preparation, then the person may be guilty of an attempt.

At what point a person's conduct goes beyond preparation and becomes an attempt will depend on the circumstances of the case. However, the conduct must go so far forward to the stage that if there had not been some intervention or interruption, the offence would have been committed. The following are some examples:

In *Henderson v. R*,[31] the accused and two others planned to rob a bank. They obtained the necessary equipment which included guns and ammunition. On their way to commit the robbery, they saw a police car parked in front of the bank. They drove away in another direction and were later apprehended by the police. The Supreme Court of Canada ruled that their conduct amounted to an attempt to commit robbery.

In *R. v. Cline*,[32] the accused disguised himself in large, dark sunglasses

31. (1948), 5 C.R. 112 (S.C.C.).
32. (1956), 115 C.C.C. 18 (Ont.C.A.).

and approached a 12-year-old boy in a dark area of a street and asked him if he would carry his suitcases. The accused had no suitcases with him. The boy refused and ran away. The accused chased the boy, caught up with him and then let him go after telling the boy not to tell anyone of the incident. Evidence at the trial showed that the accused had previously tried to lure boys into alleys by asking them to carry his suitcases. On some occasions, the accused succeeded and committed indecent assaults. The appeal court in this case held that no indecent assault was committed but the accused was guilty of an attempted indecent assault. The court distinquished the acts of preparation from the actual attempt in the following way: the accused chose a time and place where he might obtain a victim; he went to that place at the chosen time; he disguised himself and waited for an opportunity. These were all acts of preparation and he was ready to embark on the course of committing the crime. When he approached the boy and tried to lure him away, the accused was going beyond mere preparation and, thus, these actions amounted to an attempt to commit the offence.

Section 24(1) makes it clear that an accused cannot use as a defence to an attempt charge that it was impossible under the circumstances to commit the offence. In *R. v. Detering*[33] the accused was charged with fraud under what is now s.380.

> **380.(1) Every one who, by deceit, falsehood or other fraud-ulent means, whether or not it is a false pretence within the meaning of this Act, defrauds the public or any person, whether ascertained or not, of any property, money or valu-able security . . . is guilty of an offence . . . .**

Detering operated a car repair business. The Ontario Ministry of Consumer and Commercial Affairs was investigating car repair businesses suspected of cheating the public. Harris, an inspector from the Ministry of Consumer and Commercial Affairs, brought a car to Detering's garage. The transmission had been slightly damaged so that it could be easily repaired. Detering told her that the transmission needed rebuilding. Harris had the work done and paid the bill which stated that the transmission had been rebuilt. When the car was examined, it was found that the transmission had not been rebuilt.

Detering was found not guilty of fraud because Harris was not actually deceived. However, the Supreme Court of Canada held that he could still be found guilty of attempted fraud even though it was impossible for the offence to be committed since the investigator could not be deceived.

The penalties for attempts are contained in s.463 quoted above. The penalties are the same as for being an accessory after the fact.

Section 24(2) states that the issue of whether the act of the accused is an

---

33. (1982), 142 D.L.R. (3d) 87 (S.C.C.).

attempt or mere preparation is a question of law. Thus the judge's function is to decide whether the actions of the accused, as found by the jury, amount to an attempt.

QUESTIONS FOR REVIEW AND DISCUSSION

1 Define *actus reus* and *mens rea*.

2 What constitutes the *actus reus* of a crime?

3 In the cases of *R. v. Wilmot* and *R. v. Dubois*, why were the accused found not guilty?

4 What are the types of *mens rea?*

5 What words are often used in the Code to indicate that intention is required? If these words are not used, is intention required?

6 How have the courts dealt with offences of absolute liability?

7 What is the difference between a general intent offence and a specific intent offence? Give an example of each offence.

8 Why is the difference between general intent offences and specific intent offences important?

9 Explain the difference between intention to commit an offence and the motive for committing an offence. Make up an example illustrating the difference between motive and intention.

10 Explain the difference between a voluntary act and an intentional act.

11 What are the two positions courts have taken on the meaning of recklessness?

12 How are strict liability offences different from other offences?

13 What are the essential elements of aiding and abetting?

14 What does it mean to counsel an offence? When can counselling itself be an offence?

15 What are the essential elements of being an accessory after the fact?

16 What is the difference between conspiracy and aiding and abetting?

17 What are the essential elements of attempting an offence?

18 Marion asked Sarah to take care of her infant boy for a few days. Marion also asked Sarah to give the infant a teaspoonful of "medicine" every night. In fact, the medicine was poison. Sarah did not think that the infant needed medicine so she did not give it to him. She put the medicine on a shelf in her living room. Later, Sarah's five-year-old son gave the infant a large dose of the "medicine" and the infant died. Marion was charged with murder. Should she be convicted? What else, if anything, do you need to know?

19 Eva, Donna, and Claudia are walking through the park when they see their enemy Jim who is walking with a friend. They decide to "have

some fun." So Donna and Claudia hold back Jim's friend while Eva punches and kicks him. Donna and Claudia laugh and yell their support to Eva. Meanwhile Mike, who is walking his dog, stops for a moment to see what is going on. Mike decides not to get involved and walks on. Eva is convicted of assault causing bodily harm. Should Donna or Claudia be convicted of anything? What about Mike? Explain.

20 Murray, Josey (Murray's wife), and Rosa agree to steal some money from Pete's clothing store. They also agree that Pete will not be harmed and that no weapons will be used. Murray enters the store and gets Pete's attention by asking him questions about an article of clothing. Then Josey enters the store and walks toward the cash register while Rosa acts as a lookout near the store entrance. Pete notices Josey reaching into the drawer of the cash register and yells loudly. Rosa panics, pulls a gun, and shoots Pete, severely wounding him. Murray, Josey, and Rosa run from the store and go to Russ's apartment around the corner. Russ agrees to let them use his car and Murray, Josey, and Rosa drive to a hiding place. Pete later dies from the wound he received.

Explain the responsibilities of Murray, Josey, Rosa, and Russ in this case.

FOUR

Defences

COMMON
LAW
DEFENCES IN
FORCE
EXCEPT AS
ALTERED
s.8(3)

A defence is a justification or excuse for conduct which would otherwise be criminal. Defences to criminal charges are contained in the Criminal Code and the common law. Section 8(3) of the Code states that all common law defences apply to criminal charges, except as they are changed by Parliament:

> **8.(3) Every rule and principle of the common law that renders any circumstance a justification or excuse for an act or a defence to a charge continues in force and applies in respect of proceedings for an offence under this Act or any other Act of the Parliament [of Canada] except in so far as they are altered by or are inconsistent with this Act or any other Act of the Parliament [of Canada].**

This section should be read with s.9 which abolishes common law criminal offences. In other words, there are no longer any common law crimes, except for contempt of court, but the defences that developed through the common law are still available unless they are altered by or are inconsistent with an act of Parliament (i.e., legislation).

The general rule is that an accused does not have to prove his or her defence. It is sufficient if merely some evidence is produced which could raise a reasonable doubt in the mind of the jury. For example, Mikhail is charged with murder and his defence is that he was too drunk to form the specific intent to kill his victim. It is not necessary that Mikhail prove his intoxication beyond a reasonable doubt or even on a balance of probabilities. It is enough if Mikhail shows some evidence of his intoxication which could lead a jury to have a reasonable doubt as to whether he had the specific intent to kill his victim. If the jury does have a reasonable doubt, then the prosecution has failed to prove its case and Mikhail should be acquitted.

A. INCAPACITY OF CHILDREN

Section 13 of the Criminal Code states:

INCAPACITY
OF CHILDREN
UNDER
TWELVE
s.13

> **13. No person shall be convicted of an offence in respect of an act or omission on his part while that person was under the age of twelve years.**

The law presumes that children under the age of 12 do not have the mental capacity to understand the nature and consequences of their acts and to distinguish between right and wrong. Without this mental capacity there can be no *mens rea* or "guilty mind" and, thus, no offence.

A child under the age of 12 whose conduct would be a crime for an older person will be dealt with under provincial legislation, usually child welfare or protection laws. Children who are at least 12 and under 18 at the time of the alleged offence are held responsible for their criminal acts. However, they are treated separately and differently from adults. The Young Offenders Act governs the treatment of young people between 12 and 18 who break the law. An overview of this statute is given in Appendix B.

B. INSANITY

The defence of insanity is that the accused did not have the *mens rea* for the offence.

1. The Test of Insanity

The defence of insanity is contained in s.16:

INSANITY
s.16

> **16.(1) No person shall be convicted of an offence in respect of an act or omission on his part while that person was insane.**
>
> **(2) For the purposes of this section, a person is insane when the person is in a state of natural imbecility or has disease of the mind to an extent that renders the person incapable of appreciating the nature and quality of an act or omission or of knowing that an act or omission is wrong.**

Subsection (1) establishes that insanity is a valid defence and subsection (2) lays down the test of insanity. According to this test, a person is insane if the person is in a state of natural imbecility, or has a disease of the mind which makes the person:

• incapable of appreciating the nature and quality of the person's act or
• incapable of knowing that the act is wrong.

In brief, there must be one of the mental incapacities mentioned above and the mental incapacity must be caused by either imbecility or a disease of the mind. If the disease or the imbecility caused the accused *either* to be incapable of appreciating the nature and quality of his or her act *or* to be incapable of knowing that his or her act was wrong, he or she is considered to have been legally insane at the time of the alleged offence.

a. Natural Imbecility

Natural imbecility refers to a state of incomplete mental development. This condition can be caused by a congenital defect or natural decay.

b. Disease of the Mind

Whether a specific condition is a disease of the mind is a question of law for the judge to decide. Courts have considered a number of mental disorders such as schizophrenia, senile dementia, paranoia, melancholia, and certain types of epilepsy as diseases of the mind. Excluded, however, are self-induced states caused by alcohol or drugs and temporary conditions such as hysteria and concussion. Legally, any illness, disorder, or abnormal condition which impairs the mind and its functions may be a disease of the mind. However, whether the accused suffered from a disease of the mind at the time the offence was committed is a question of fact for the jury.

c. Appreciating the Nature and Quality of an Act

Appreciating the nature and quality of the act refers to the physical act and its consequences. The following passage, taken from a Royal Commission Report on the law of insanity in Canadian criminal law, sets out a test for determining whether the accused appreciated the nature and quality of an act:

> . . . *was the accused person at the very time of the offence — not before or after, but at the moment of the offence — by reason of disease of the mind, unable fully to appreciate not only the nature of the act but the natural consequences that would flow from it?*[1]

This test was adopted by the Supreme Court of Canada in *R. v. Cooper*.[2] The accused had killed the victim by choking her to death. The psychiatrist testified that the accused — because of the state of his mind — was incapable of forming the intent to kill and was unaware that his action would result in the taking of a life. However, the accused was capable of

---

1. Quoted and adopted in *R. v. Leech* (1972), 10 C.C.C. (2d) 149 (Alta. S.C.). Reproduced by permission of the Minister of Supplies and Services Canada.
2. (1977), 34 C.C.C. (2d) 18 (S.C.C.).

forming the intent to choke the victim.

The court said, with regard to the meaning of "appreciates":

> *"appreciates" imports [more than] mere knowledge of the physical quality of the act. The requirement . . . is that of perception, an ability to perceive the consequences, impact and results of the physical act. An accused may be aware of the physical character of his actions (i.e. choking) without necessarily having the capacity to appreciate that, in nature and quality, that act will result in the death of a human being.*[3]

Therefore, the court held in this case, there was evidence upon which a jury could find that the accused did not appreciate the nature of his act. The case was sent back for a new trial.

d. *Knowing That an Act Is Wrong*

A person may appreciate the nature and quality of his or her act, but if he or she is not capable of knowing that the act is wrong, he or she still may be found insane.

In a 1990 decision the Supreme Court of Canada held that if a person knows an act is wrong then the person knows the act is morally wrong, not just legally wrong.[4] The facts in *R. v. Laycock*[5] demonstrate the difference between knowing something is morally wrong and knowing something is legally wrong. The accused was charged with murdering his neighbour K. His defence was insanity. There had been many disputes between Laycock and K, involving mainly charges by him that K trespassed on his property. Finally, the accused shot and killed K. Laycock was 66 years old, and had been a soldier in World War I and had tried to serve in World War II but was not accepted. He regarded K as an enemy of democracy and justice and like a Hitler or Mussolini. He believed that when he shot K he was fighting for justice, liberty, and freedom and that he was protecting democracy from a dictator. A psychiatrist testified that the accused was suffering from a disease of the mind, and that, *although the accused knew the act was against the law, he believed it was the right thing to do.* The accused felt that he was morally obligated to undertake the mission of stopping the dictator and that the killing was absolutely justified. The court concluded that this was evidence which could indicate that the accused was incapable of knowing that this act was wrong.

---

3. *Ibid.*, at 147.
4. *Chaulk v. The Queen* (1990), 2 C.R. (4th) 1 (S.C.C.).
5. (1952), 104 C.C.C. 274 (Ont.C.A.).

e. Delusions

Section 16(3) states:

16.(3) A person who has specific delusions, but is in other respects sane, shall not be acquitted on the ground of insanity unless the delusions caused that person to believe in the existence of a state of things that, if it existed, would have justified or excused the act or omission of that person.

If an accused suffers from a specific delusion, he or she may plead not guilty by reason of insanity. A delusion is a belief that is not in touch with reality. The delusion must cause the accused to believe in a situation which, if it were real, would make his or her act legal.

Suppose, for example, that Barney suffered from the specific delusion that he had $1 000 000 in his bank account. In actual fact, Barney had less than $100 deposited. If Barney wrote "bad" cheques as a result of his delusions, he could plead insanity pursuant to s.16(3), on the basis that if he actually had $1 000 000 in his account his cheques would not have been "bad".

2. Presumption of Sanity

Section 16(4) states:

16.(4) Every one shall, until the contrary is proved, be presumed to be and to have been sane.

The effect of this presumption is that, in general, the burden of proving insanity is on the accused. The accused's lawyer does not have to establish the insanity of the accused beyond a reasonable doubt. It is sufficient to prove that it is probable that he or she was insane at the time the offence was committed. This presumption of sanity has been challenged under the Charter of Rights and Freedoms since it violates the right to be presumed innocent. The Supreme Court in a recent decision rejected this argument. In *Chaulk v. The Queen*,[6] the Supreme Court of Canada held that the presumption of sanity does violate the constitutional right to be presumed innocent but that the violation is justified in a free and democratic society. The court stated that the Crown would have an "onerous burden" in having to disprove insanity in every case (i.e., to prove that the accused is sane). In other words, if an accused cannot be presumed sane, in every case, the prosecution would then have to prove beyond a reasonable doubt that the accused was sane, a heavy burden indeed.

---

6. *Supra*, note 4.

3. Disposition on the Finding of Not Guilty by Reason of Insanity and the Charter

DISPOSITION ON FINDING OF INSANITY s.614(2)

Until the Supreme Court of Canada's decision in *R. v. Swain*[7] in 1991, when an accused was found not guilty by reason of insanity, s.614(2) required the trial court to order that the accused be kept in "strict custody . . . until the pleasure of the lieutenant governor of the province is known." In other words, the trial judge had no choice regarding the dispositon of the case. This practice was referred to as *automatic detention*. Even though the accused was found not guilty, he or she was not free to go but was automatically detained for an indefinite period and usually in a facility for the criminally insane.

The facts in *Swain* were that the accused was charged with assaulting his wife and two children. The evidence was that he had swung his children around his head, splashed them with water, and carved an "X" on his wife's chest. He explained that he was ridding them of devils. While on bail, awaiting trial, he received drug therapy for seven weeks as an in-patient. He was then released and lived with his family for 18 months until his trial. The Crown raised the issue of insanity over the accused's objections and he was found not guilty by reason of insanity. The court ordered his detention.

The trial court's decision was appealed to the Ontario Court of Appeal which upheld the decision of the trial court. There was a further appeal to the Supreme Court. A majority of the Supreme Court of Canada justices held that the automatic detention provisions under s.614 violated Swain's Charter rights under s.7 (the right not to be denied liberty unless the principles of fundamental justice are followed) and s.9 (the right not to be arbitrarily detained). The court also found that the violations of s.7 and s.9 were not justifiable limitations under s.1 of the Charter.[8] Therefore, s.614 was unenforceable. There were two basic reasons:

1. There was no requirement that a hearing be held before detention was ordered to determine if the accused was a present danger to the community. Detaining Swain without a hearing was a violation of the rules of fundamental justice.

2. Even if a hearing were required, there were no criteria or standards set out in the law for a judge to apply to decide whether the accused should be detained or released. For example, the judge was not

---

7. (1991), 63 C.C.C. 481 (S.C.C.).
8. Section 1 of the Charter states: "The Canadian Charter of Rights and Freedoms guarantees the rights and freedoms set out in it subject only to such reasonable limits prescribed by law as can be demonstrably justified in a free and democratic society." In other words, even if a law violates a charter right or freedom, it may still be enforceable if the limitation of the right or freedom is justifiable in a free and democratic society. See Chapter One under The Canadian Charter of Rights and Freedoms for further discussion.

directed to consider whether it was likely that the accused would commit a violent crime in the future. The lack of criteria made the detention arbitrary.

The facts in the *Swain* case made the unfairness of the automatic detention procedure especially apparent. It appeared that he had been successfully treated before his trial and was no longer a danger to the community, yet the trial judge had no choice but to order his detention.

The court stated that it would give the federal government a six-month transition period to change the law. During this period, an accused found not guilty by reason of insanity could be confined, but the accused's case would have to be reviewed within 30 to 60 days to determine if the accused was still insane. At the time of this writing the government has not yet enacted a new law to replace s.614.

Sections 617 and 619 set out the review process once the accused has been ordered into custody by the court. After the accused is placed in custody, his or her case is reviewed by a provincial board of review whose members are appointed by the lieutenant-governor. The board makes a recommendation to the lieutenant-governor who then orders the accused to be released or detained. The validity of s.617 and s.619 was not an issue in the *Swain* case. However, the court did indicate that the lieutenant-governor review system might also violate the Charter. It is likely therefore that if and when the court has the opportunity to review this procedure it too will be found unenforceable. Also, it is possible that the federal government will amend s.617 and s.619 along with s.614 to avoid a decision finding the procedure **unconstitutional**.

Another aspect of the defence of insanity which was challenged in *Swain* was a rule developed by judges or a common law rule. This rule stated that the issue of insanity could be raised by the prosecution over the objections of the accused. The trial judge had to give permission for the Crown to do this. Permission would only be given if it could be shown that there was substantial evidence of insanity and that there was convincing evidence that the accused committed the offence. The Crown might raise insanity where, for example, the Crown believed that the accused was a danger to the public and that the likely term of imprisonment the accused would receive if found guilty of the offence would not be sufficient to protect the public.

The Supreme Court held that the common law rule that allows the Crown to raise insanity in certain situations violates the accused's Charter right under s.7. The court stated that it is a rule of fundamental justice that the accused can control his or her defence. Since this rule was a judge-made rule and not a statutory law, the Supreme Court stated that the rule could be reformulated by the court so that it did not offend the Charter. To safeguard the accused's right to control his or her trial the court stated that the rule should be that the Crown can only raise insanity if the accused has already put his or her mental capacity in issue or if the accused had been found otherwise guilty. In this latter situation, the trial would have two parts: the first part in which to determine whether the accused is guilty of the offence and the second to determine if the accused is not guilty because of insanity.

C. AUTOMATISM

If a person's conduct is involuntary, he or she may raise the defence of automatism. Automatism refers to a state in which a person has no conscious control over his or her bodily movements. In other words, his or her behaviour is "automatic". Examples of involuntary, unconscious behaviour occur while a person is sleepwalking or suffering from an epileptic seizure. In other words, a person raising the defence of automatism is saying that he or she did not commit the *actus reus* of the offence.

In general, for automatism to be a defence, the cause of the automatism must be something other than a disease of the mind or intoxication by alcohol or drugs. If an involuntary, unconscious act is caused by a disease of the mind, the defence is insanity, not automatism. Similarly, if the involuntary, unconscious act is caused by intoxication, the defence is, in most cases, intoxication, not automatism.

Automatism caused by a physical injury was a successful defence in *Bleta v. R.*[9] In that case, the accused was charged with murder. Several witnesses testified that they watched a fight between G and the accused which culminated in the accused stabbing G fatally in the neck. Although the stories of the eyewitnesses differed as to the details of the fight, it is clear that blows were exchanged between the two men. The accused was knocked down or fell down striking his head forcibly on the pavement. G started to walk away when the accused, having regained his feet, followed him and pulled out a knife with which he delivered the fatal blow. Two of the onlookers observed that when the accused got up, he staggered and appeared to be dazed, and one police officer also commented on his apparently dazed condition.

The accused contended that the blow to his head deprived him of all voluntary control over his actions. In other words, the accused was saying he was in a state of automatism when he stabbed G.

A psychologist gave evidence which supported the accused's defence. The trial judge summarized the psychologist's evidence as follows:

> *The doctor says that the actions of the accused when he stabbed the deceased were purely automatic and without any volition on the part of the accused. He was, in fact, in the condition of a sleepwalker or an epileptic and since he had been in a fight, he automatically continued it.*[10]

---

9. [1965] 1 C.C.C. 1 (S.C.C.).
10. *Ibid.*

The jury believed that the accused was in a state of automatism when he stabbed G and he was acquitted on the charge of murder.

Automatism may also be used as a defence if an involuntary, unconscious act results from taking a drug without knowing its effect. For example, in *R. v. King*[11] the accused was charged with impaired driving. He had been given an injection of a drug from his dentist. He did not know the drug's effects nor was he made aware of the effects. Shortly after driving away from the dentist's office the drug caused the accused to become unconscious and he ran into a parked car. His act of driving while impaired was considered to be an involuntary act and he was found not guilty. The result would have been different if the accused had known that the drug would produce unconsciousness.

If an accused was aware that he was subject to states of unconsciousness, automatism will not be a successful defence. For example, in *R. v. Shaw*,[12] the accused was suffering from a physical disability which, the court concluded, was probably epilepsy. Although the accused knew that he was subject to attacks which caused unconsciousness, he continued to drive his car. On one occasion, he suffered an attack while driving. He slumped or fell and caused the car to accelerate. The car went off the highway and collided with a tree. Two passengers were killed and three others were injured. Unlike the *King* case, the accused in this case was aware that he could become unconscious while driving and the court held that he could be found criminally responsible for his conduct.

A person who is sleepwalking is considered to be in a state of automatism. For example, in *R. v. Parks*,[13] the accused was charged with murdering his mother-in-law and attempting the murder of his father-in-law. The evidence was that he drove 14 miles (23 km) from his home to his in-laws' home where he attacked his in-laws in their bed. His defence was that he was sleepwalking at the time. He testified that he had been under great stress because he had a gambling addiction and was stealing from his employer to cover gambling debts. The jury accepted the psychiatric evidence that Parks was sleepwalking even though very elaborate complex behaviour was taking place. He was acquitted of both charges.

The possibility of automatism being caused by a severe psychological blow was recognized by the court in *R. v. K.*[14] The accused killed his wife and was charged with manslaughter. The trial judge summarized the testimony of the accused as follows:

11. (1962), 133 C.C.C. 1 (S.C.C.). The court in this case did not specifically mention automatism. However, as noted in *R. v. Hartridge*, [1967] 1 C.C.C. 346 (Sask.C.A.), automatism would be a defence in this situation.
12. (1938), 70 C.C.C. 159 (Ont.C.A.).
13. (1990), 78 C.R. (3d) 1 (Ont.C.A.); appeal to S.C.C. pending.
14. (1970), 3 C.C.C. (2d) 84 (Ont.H.Ct.).

He gave evidence concerning his depression in the months before this tragedy and following the sale of his farm. He described the affection he had for his wife . . . . He described his worry over his own depression and the problem that he was facing, whether he was going to leave with his family to go to Vancouver or not. He also described his actions on the day of the tragedy: the telephone call from Mrs. S. saying repeatedly, "your wife is leaving, your wife is leaving," how he went outside looking for the girls (his daughters), met his wife on the street, returning home, going upstairs and then coming down again, and then seeing his wife and putting his arms around his wife, saying to her, "please don't leave." To the accused, in his evidence, the rest is like a dream. He remembers falling and getting up, his wife being on the floor calling for help.

People who saw the accused after the incident agreed that he appeared to be in shock. His eyes were glazed and he repeatedly answered questions by saying that he did not know what had happened.

A psychiatrist supported the accused's evidence by stating that, in the days before the incident, the accused had become extremely depressed about the problems arising from the sale of his farm and the possibility of his wife leaving him. The psychiatrist felt that a state of automatism was caused by the severe psychological blow of learning that his wife was actually leaving him. This psychological blow produced a state in which "the mind registered little, and from then on the accused did not know what was happening, his mind no longer being in control of his actions."

The judge instructed the members of the jury that if they accepted the above evidence, they should find the accused not guilty. However, if they believed that the state of automatism was caused by a disease of the mind, they should find the accused not guilty by reason of insanity. The jury returned a verdict of not guilty.

On the other hand, the ordinary stresses and disappointments of life are not sufficient to be considered psychological blows to induce automatism. This was the decision of the Ontario Court of Appeal (affirmed on appeal to the Supreme Court) in the case of *R. v. Rabey*.[15] Rabey, a male student, had a crush on a classmate and he learned that she had written a note making fun of him. He took a rock and attacked her. His defence of automatism failed.

Unlike the defence of insanity, if an accused is found not guilty because he or she was in a state of automatism at the time he or she committed the offence, he or she is immediately released from custody.

Automatism is a defence to the charge of committing a strict liability offence. Recall from Chapter Three that a strict liability offence involves an *actus reus* (physical element) but no *mens rea* (mental element). Since the acts of a person in a state of automatism are not voluntary, the *actus reus* is absent.

---

15. (1977), 37 C.C.C. (2d) 461 (Ont.C.A.) affd. 54 C.C.C. (2d) 1 (S.C.C.).

D. INTOXICATION

In general, intoxication by alcohol or drugs is not a defence to a criminal charge. However, it may be a partial defence to a charge of committing a specific intent offence. That is, if it can be shown that the accused was too intoxicated to form the specific intent required, then he or she will not be guilty of the offence. However, the accused may still be found guilty of any *included offence* if it is a general intent offence. An included offence has all its elements contained within another offence; for example, assault may be an included offence of the offence of robbery, as the next case illustrates.

In *R. v. George*[16] the accused was charged with robbery and the included offence of common assault. The accused had violently man-handled an 84-year-old man. The man was badly injured, dumped into a bathtub, and then pulled out when he agreed to give the accused his money. The accused raised the defence of intoxication by alcohol. He was found not guilty of robbery because robbery requires the specific intent to steal and the accused was too drunk to form this specific intent. However, the accused was guilty of the included offence of assault because assault requires only the general intent to apply force to another person. It is possible that a person could be too drunk to know that he or she is applying force to someone else, but in such a case, his or her defence would be insanity or automatism, not intoxication. In this case, insanity was not suggested and the accused clearly admitted that he knew that he was applying force to his victim.

1. Degree of Intoxication Required

The Supreme Court of Canada, in *Perrault v. R.*,[17] considered to what extent an accused must be intoxicated before he or she can successfully use drunkenness as a defence. The court quoted with approval a statement made by a British judge, Lord Denning:

> . . . *If a man is charged with an offence in which a specific intention is essential (as in murder, though not in manslaughter), then evidence of drunkenness, which renders him incapable of forming the intention, is an answer. This degree of drunkenness is reached when the man is rendered so stupid by drink that he does not know what he is doing, . . . as where a drunken man thought his friend (lying in his bed) was a theatrical dummy placed there and stabbed him to death. In this case it would not be murder but it would be manslaughter.*

---

16. (1960), 128 C.C.C. 289 (S.C.C.).
17. [1970] 5 C.C.C. 217 (S.C.C.).

In another case, *R. v. Reece*,[18] the trial judge explained the relationship between drunkenness and criminal responsibility in the following terms:

> *A man may drink, he may drink to excess, he may become quarrelsome, vicious, nasty, belligerent — none of that makes any difference. He is still criminally responsible if he knows what he is doing, if he knows what he is doing even through an alcoholic haze. It is a matter of mind. It may be that he gives way to temptation more readily after drinking and after drinking to excess. That makes no difference to his criminal responsibility, if he knows what he is doing.*

In *R. v. Bucci*[19] the accused was charged with theft of a motor vehicle. His defence was intoxication caused by drugs. The accused had been standing in a small crowd of people beside a car which had been driven into a ditch. The operator of a tow truck asked the accused to put the car in neutral; the accused did so and the tow truck pulled the car out of the ditch. When the car was released from the tow truck, the accused promptly drove it into the ditch again. When it was again pulled out of the ditch, the accused drove the car into the back of the tow truck. The accused then made a manoeuvre with the car which the tow-truck driver assumed was an attempt at parking it nearby. Instead, the accused drove off. The tow-truck operator gave chase and caught up with the accused about a block and a half away when the accused again drove the car into the ditch. The accused ran away but was apprehended by the truck driver.

The accused testified that on the day of his arrest he had taken some valium pills in order to get a "high". Within a two-hour period he had swallowed at least 16 valium pills (10 mg each or 160 mg in total) and drank some whisky. He said he recalled nothing of the events of the next four days except driving a car around a curve, his body going limp, the car going into the ditch, his putting the key in the ignition, and getting into the police car.

Several witnesses testified about his condition. The truck driver said the accused was "tripping all over the place, like tripping over his own two feet." Both police officers who testified said the accused seemed to be under the influence of something — his speech was incoherent, slow and slurred, and his walk was a little unsteady. There was no odour of alcohol. He seemed to understand a direction from one of the officers to get into the police car.

Another witness said the accused was "stoned" during the afternoon of the day on which these events occurred. She said he walked "funny", his eyes were red, and he was not "himself". When they parted, a friend

---

18. (1954), 109 C.C.C. 26 (Ont.C.A.).
19. (1974), 17 C.C.C. (2d) 512 (N.S.).

took or led him up the steps of the bus he was taking and more or less put him on a seat in the bus.

A professor of pharmacology testified that valium was a minor tranquillizer used in the treatment of anxieties. He said the normal daily dosage prescribed was 10 to 30 mg. In his opinion an ingestion of 100 mg would be very high. He stated that he would expect profound effects in a person who had consumed 150 mg of valium over an eight-hour period, including euphoria, depression, a desire for sleep, loss of memory, depression of the normal activity of the central nervous system with resulting loss of inhibitions. He likened its effects to those of alcohol. He said a person might do things while under the influence of valium which he might not otherwise do.

In his reasons for judgment the judge pointed out that a charge of theft (s.322) requires proof of a specific intent — the accused must have the specific intent of depriving the owner of his property, either permanently or temporarily. The judge found that the accused was unable to form this intent because of the drugs he had consumed. He stated:

> *Normally, the prosecutor would have the benefit of the presumption that a man intends the natural and probable consequences of his acts, with the result that when the accused was, for instance, driving the motor vehicle away from the place where it had been driven into the ditch, he was then intending to deprive the owner of the use of his motor vehicle. But such presumptions are easily displaced. The evidence here points very strongly to the fact that the accused's mental processes were deeply affected by the drug he had taken and I have no hesitation in reaching the conclusion that the presumption has been displaced in this case . . . there being no positive proof of the specific intent on the part of the accused to deprive the owner of his motor vehicle, I hold that the prosecution has failed to prove this ingredient of the first charge and I acquit the accused on the charge of theft.*

On the other hand, the fact that a person was drunk when the specific intent offence was committed does not necessarily mean that the defence will succeed. In *R. v. Shea*,[20] the accused already had drank a large amount of alcohol and had taken valium pills when he broke into his son's school. He broke a lock on the principal's office door, forced open a file drawer, and stole a cash box containing $140. He buried the cash box under a pile of brush. He claimed at his trial to have no memory of these events.

He was questioned by the police a few days after the break-in because the police found his fingerprints at the school. He realized what he might have done and searched for the metal box with a metal detector. He found the box and contacted the police. He also arranged to return the box to the principal and pay for the damage caused by the break-in.

---

20. (1981), 24 C.R. (3d) 189 (P.E.I.S.C.).

The judge held that he could not use the defence of intoxication. The fact that he broke into the office, forced open the file-cabinet drawer, stole the box, and then hid it was evidence that he was aware of what he was doing at the time. Shea was convicted of break and enter with intent to commit theft.

2. Intoxication Leading to Insanity or Automatism

The Supreme Court of Canada has recently suggested that severe intoxication which leads to a state like insanity or automatism could allow a defence to a general intent crime.[21]

Courts have recognized "delirium tremens" as a disease of the mind caused by severe intoxication. However, the defence would be insanity, not intoxication.

E. DURESS OR COMPULSION

There are two defences of duress. One is in the Criminal Code and the other is in the common law. The two defences apply in different situations.

The Criminal Code defence states:

COMPULSION BY THREATS s.17

17. A person who commits an offence under compulsion by threats of immediate death or bodily harm from a person who is present when the offence is committed is excused for committing the offence if the person believes that the threats will be carried out and if the person is not a party to a conspiracy or association whereby the person is subject to compulsion, but this section does not apply where the offence that is committed is high treason or treason, murder, piracy, attempted murder, sexual assault, sexual assault with a weapon, threats to a third party or causing bodily harm, aggravated sexual assault, forcible abduction, hostage taking, robbery, assault with a weapon or causing bodily harm, aggravated assault, unlawfully causing bodily harm, arson or an offence under sections 280 to 283 (abduction and detention of young persons).

Clearly, before an accused can rely on the defence of compulsion or duress as outlined in s.17 it must first be established that:

1. the accused committed an offence not listed in s.17;

2. the accused committed the offence because of threats of immediate death or immediate bodily harm;

---

21. *R. v. Bernard* (1988), 45 C.C.C. (3d) 1 (S.C.C.).

3. threats were delivered by a person who was present at the time the accused committed the offence; and

4. the accused was not a member of a group planning to commit the offence.

In *R. v. Carker*,[22] the accused was charged with having unlawfully and wilfully damaged public property. The damaged property consisted of plumbing fixtures in the accused's prison cell. The accused testified that he committed the offence during a disturbance in the course of which a substantial body of prisoners, shouting in unison from their separate cells, threatened the accused, who was not joining in the disturbance. The threats were that, if he did not break the plumbing fixture in his cell, he would be kicked in the head, his arms would be broken, and he would get a knife in the back at the first opportunity.

The court decided that although there was little doubt that the accused committed the offence under the compulsion of threats of death and grievous bodily harm, they were not threats of *"immediate* death" or *"immediate* grievous bodily harm." The court arrived at this decision because it was virtually impossible that immediate death or grievous bodily harm could come to the accused as the persons who were uttering the threats were locked up in separate cells.

The common law defence of duress applies to any offence, but it can only be used by a person who is not the principal actor in a crime. For example, if a person aids and abets a crime because of duress, this defence can be used.

F. NECESSITY

The defence of duress is a specific type of the general defence of necessity. The general defence of necessity is rarely used. The Supreme Court of Canada has said that in situations of emergency, where normal human instincts compel a person to break the law, this defence may be used. The emergency must present a threat to the self or the accused must be acting for altruistic motives.

The case that decided this point was *Perka et al. v. The Queen*.[23] The accused were smuggling drugs from Columbia to Alaska. The drugs were delivered to the accused's ship by plane in international waters off Columbia and were to be dropped in international waters off the coast of Alaska. The ship encountered poor weather conditions and developed mechanical problems. For the safety of the crew, the ship entered a Canadian bay to make repairs, and by doing so became grounded. The next day, the police investigated, found the drugs, and charged the accused with importing drugs into Canada. Their defence was that they

---

22. [1967] 2 C.C.C. 190, 2 C.R.N.S. 16 (S.C.C.).
23. (1984), 14 C.C.C. (3d) 385 (S.C.C.).

never intended to enter Canada but acted out of necessity to save themselves. The Supreme Court of Canada held that the accused could raise this defence, but a jury would have to decide if the facts were as the accused claimed them to be. However, if the facts were as claimed by the accused, compliance with the law was impossible since the situation was such that failure to act would endanger their lives and safety. The court also noted that the accused were not doing anything illegal in Canada until they brought the boat ashore.

G. CONSENT

In limited circumstances an accused may use as a defence the fact that the victim consented to the accused's act. For example, if the accused engaged in a fight with another individual, and as a result of the fight was charged with assault, he or she might be able to argue that the other person consented to the fight. If it can be established that both parties consented to the fight, the accused may be entitled to an acquittal.[24]

Lack of consent is an element of some offences. For example, if Paula had Taufic's consent to take Taufic's car, then Paula would not be guilty of theft. Similarly, if Nick had Evelyn's consent to cut down Evelyn's tree for firewood, then Nick would not be guilty of the offence of wilfully damaging Evelyn's property. Where lack of consent is an element of the offence, it is not actually a defence. That is, the Crown will have to prove beyond a reasonable doubt that there was no consent. It is not up to the accused to raise lack of consent as a defence.

1. Specific Offences for Which Consent Is *Not* a Defence

CONSENT
NOT A
DEFENCE
WHERE
DEATH
INFLICTED
s.14

There are several offences for which consent is specifically not a defence.

For example, the victim's consent to be killed is no defence to a murder charge because s.14 of the Code states:

> **14. No person is entitled to consent to have death inflicted upon him, and such consent does not affect the criminal responsibility of any person by whom death may be inflicted upon the person by whom consent is given.**

There are several offences involving sexual offences against children where consent may not be a defence unless certain circumstances exist. These offences include sexual interference (s.151), invitation to sexual touching (s.152), sexual exploitation (s.153), and the offences of sexual assault (s.271–s.273); see Chapter Seven and Chapter Twelve.

---

24. The Supreme Court of Canada in *R. v. Jobidon* (1991), 66 C.C.C. (3d) 454 (S.C.C.) held that a person cannot consent to a fist fight that causes serious hurt or nontrivial bodily harm. Therefore, consent can only be valid where minor hurt results from a fist fight. This issue is discussed further in Chapter Twelve.

2. Consent by Fraud or Threats of Bodily Harm

When consent is available as a defence, the consent of the victim must be a real or valid consent. If the consent is obtained by fraud, it will not be considered real and therefore it will not constitute a defence. For example, if a doctor tells a patient that the treatment requires the patient to have sexual intercourse with the doctor, the patient's consent would not be valid. Similarly, consent obtained through the threats of bodily harm would not be valid.

H. THE PERMISSIBLE USE OF FORCE: SELF-DEFENCE, THE DEFENCE OF OTHERS, AND THE DEFENCE OF PROPERTY

1. Responsibility for Excessive Force

LIABILITY FOR EXCESSIVE FORCE s.26

In some situations a person is justified in using force. Self-defence, defence of others, and the defence of property are justifications for using force against another person. The general rule is that only as much force as necessary under the circumstances can be used. A person who uses an excessive amount of force will be held criminally and civilly responsible. In other words, the person could be sued in a civil action or charged with a crime. Section 26 of the Code sets out a person's criminal responsibility:

> **26. Every one who is authorized by law to use force is criminally responsible for any excess thereof according to the nature and quality of the act that constitutes the excess.**

So, for example, a person who uses excessive force in protecting himself or herself from an assault could be charged with assault or even murder, depending on the circumstances.

2. Self-Defence

a. *Against an Unprovoked Assault*

SELF-DEFENSE AGAINST UN-PROVOKED ASSAULT s.34

Section 34 of the Code provides that a person may use force in order to protect himself or herself against an unprovoked assault:

> **34.(1) Every one who is unlawfully assaulted without having provoked the assault is justified in repelling force by force if the force he uses is not intended to cause death or grievous bodily harm and is no more than is necessary to enable him to defend himself.**
> **(2) Every one who is unlawfully assaulted and who causes death or grievous bodily harm in repelling the assault is justified if**
> **(a) he causes it under reasonable apprehension of death or**

> grievous bodily harm from the violence with which the assault was originally made or with which the assailant pursues his purposes, and
>> (b) he believes, on reasonable grounds, that he cannot otherwise preserve himself from death or grievous bodily harm.

The offence of assault includes threats and attempts to apply force to another person. Therefore, it is not necessary for the person defending himself or herself to be physically assaulted before acting in self-defence. However, with an exception discussed below, courts have required that the person acting in self-defence be in imminent peril of attack.

PROVO-
CATION
DEFINED
s.36

An accused can rely on s.34 of the Code as a defence only if he or she did not provoke the other person to commit the assault. If he or she provoked the other person to commit the assault, then the accused may be able to rely on s.35, discussed below. For the purposes of s.34 and s.35, provocation includes provocation by blows, words, or gestures (s.36).

Section 34(1) applies to situations where the accused did not intend to cause death or grievous bodily harm. The important points are (1) what the accused intended and (2) whether the force used was no more than necessary and *not* whether death or grievous bodily harm does result.

Section 34(2) applies in situations where the accused did intend to cause bodily harm or death. Under s.34(2) a person who causes grievous bodily harm or kills another in self-defence must meet two requirements:

1. the accused must have been under a reasonable fear of death or serious bodily harm; and

2. the accused must have believed on reasonable grounds that there was no other way to save himself or herself.

Both requirements have objective and subjective elements. The first requirement will only be satisfied if a person in the position of the accused would have been in reasonable fear of death or serious bodily harm. In other words, it is not what a reasonable person looking in from the outside would think but what a reasonable person in the situation of the accused would think. For example, in the case discussed below involving a woman who had been repeatedly battered over a four-year period by her husband, the question was whether a woman in the accused's situation and with her experience would have a reasonable apprehension of death or serious physical harm.

The second requirement demands that the accused's subjective belief that he or she cannot otherwise save himself or herself be based on reasonable grounds. In other words, although the belief must be based on reasonable grounds, it is not necessary to consider whether an ordinary, reasonable person would have held the same belief. Rather, the important question is whether the accused actually believed that there was no other way to save himself or herself and that this belief was based on reasonable grounds.

The recent decision of the Supreme Court of Canada in *R. v. Lavallee*[25] has expanded this defence by accepting evidence of "the battered woman syndrome." In this case, experts testified that the accused felt "trapped, vulnerable, worthless . . ." and unable to leave the relationship despite being repeatedly abused by her husband over a four-year period. On the day of the killing he found her hiding in a closet. He handed her a gun and dared her to shoot him. He said that, if she did not shoot, he would kill her later. When he turned to leave the room, she shot him in the head. The Court held that where the battered woman syndrome applies, the accused does not need to prove imminent peril but only that a well-founded anticipation of peril existed.

b. *Against a Provoked Assault*

SELF-DEFENSE AGAINST PROVOKED ASSAULT s.35

Section 35 of the Code deals with situations in which a person provokes an assault on himself or herself by another person (e.g., by insulting or assaulting the other person or by assaulting him or her):

> **35. Every one who has without justification assaulted another but did not commence the assault with intent to cause death or grievous bodily harm, or has without justification provoked an assault upon himself by another, may justify the use of force subsequent to the assault if**
>
> **(a) he uses the force**
>
> **(i) under reasonable apprehension of death or grievous bodily harm from the violence of the person whom he has assaulted or provoked, and**
>
> **(ii) in the belief, on reasonable grounds, that it is necessary in order to preserve himself from death or grievous bodily harm;**
>
> **(b) he did not, at any time before the necessity of preserving himself from death or grievous bodily harm arose, endeavour to cause death or grievous bodily harm; and**
>
> **(c) he declined further conflict and quitted or retreated from it as far as it was feasible to do so before the necessity of preserving himself from death or grievous bodily harm arose.**

In other words, to justify the use of force under s.35 the accused must satisfy the following criteria:

1. he or she must have assaulted another or in some other way provoked an assault on himself or herself;

---

25. (1990), 55 C.C.C. (3d) 97 (S.C.C.).

2. he or she must at no time have intended to cause death or grievous bodily harm;

3. after being assaulted he or she must have been in reasonable danger of death or bodily harm;

4. he or she must have believed on reasonable grounds that the force used was necessary to prevent his or her death or grievous bodily harm occurring to himself or herself; and

5. before he or she used force he or she must have exhausted all other ways, such as retreat, of avoiding the use of force.

In *R. v. Doiron*[26] the accused, without excuse, assaulted another person (the victim). The victim then broke a beer bottle and attacked the accused. The accused shot the victim with a pistol, and wounded him slightly. The accused argued that he fired his pistol in self-defence using s.35 as his justification. The court held that the accused had reasonable grounds to fear at least that the victim would cause him grievous bodily harm and that firing the pistol was necessary, on reasonable and probable grounds, to stop the accused from injuring him. The court concluded, therefore, that the accused's actions were justified by s.35 and he was acquitted of the charge of discharging a firearm with intent to wound.

c. Preventing Assault and the Defence of Others

Sections 34 and 35 of the Code deal with situations in which an assault actually occurred. Section 37 is concerned with situations in which force is used to prevent an assault from occurring.

USING FORCE TO PREVENT ASSAULT s.37

37.(1) Every one is justified in using force to defend himself or any one under his protection from assault, if he uses no more force than is necessary to prevent the assault or the repetition of it

(2) Nothing in this section shall be deemed to justify the wilful infliction of any hurt or mischief that is excessive, having regard to the nature of the assault that the force used was intended to prevent.

Sections 34, 35, and 37 overlap to some extent; however, s.37 does specifically allow a person to defend anyone under his or her protection from assault. The type of person that may be placed under protection is not defined but presumably it would include members of a person's immediate family and any others with whom the person has a close relationship. In addition, s.27 allows a person to use as much force as is reasonably necessary to prevent the commission of an offence which

---

26. (1972), 18 C.R.N.S. 127 (B.C.C.A.).

would likely cause serious and immediate injury to the person or property of anyone.

In *R. v. Wiggs*[27] the accused was charged with assaulting a boy who, with several other boys, attacked the accused's son. They threw the son to the ground, sat on him, and punched and kicked him. The father rushed to the defence of his son and in stopping the attack struck one of the boys, causing injury to his face. The court found the father not guilty because in defending his son he had used no more force than was necessary in the circumstances.

3. Defence of Property

The defence of property applies to two types of property: real property and personal property. ***Real property*** refers to land and things such as structures, trees, and shrubs attached to the land. ***Personal property*** refers to things which can be moved such as a car, television set, a chair, etc.

Besides the specific sections discussed below, recall s.27 discussed previously. This section provides a general defence to anyone who uses force to prevent the commission of an offence ". . . that would be likely to cause immediate and serious injury to the person or property of anyone; . . . ."

a. *Personal Property*

Sections 38 and 39 of the Code pertain to a person's right to defend personal property which is in his or her possession:

DEFENCE OF PERSONAL PROPERTY s.38

38.(1) Every one who is in peaceable possession of personal property, and every one lawfully assisting him, is justified

(a) in preventing a trespasser from taking it, or

(b) in taking it from a trespasser who has taken it, if he does not strike or cause bodily harm to the trespasser.

(2) Where a person who is in peaceable possession of personal property lays hands upon it, a trespasser who persists in attempting to keep it or take it from him or from any one lawfully assisting him shall be deemed to commit an assault without justification or provocation.

DEFENCE OF PERSONAL PROPERTY WITH CLAIM OF RIGHT s.39

39.(1) Every one who is in peaceable possession of personal property under a claim of right, and every one acting under his authority, is protected from criminal responsibility for defending that possession, even against a person entitled by law to possession of it, if he uses no more force than is necessary.

---

27. [1931] 3 W.W.R. 52 (B.C.C.A.).

Both these sections apply to persons in possession of personal property. This does not necessarily mean that they own the property. For example, Gina may be renting furniture from Janice. Even though Gina does not own the furniture, if she is in peaceable possession of it, then Gina has a right to defend it.

Under s.38(1) force may not be used to prevent a trespasser from taking the personal property. Under s.39(1) force may be used, even against the lawful owner, but only if the person in peaceable possession has possession under a *claim of right.* In other words, the person must honestly believe, on reasonable grounds, that he or she has a right to possess the property. Thus, a possessor under a claim of right is in a much stronger position than a possessor who does not have some basis for claiming that he has a lawful right of possession.

Under s.38(2) a trespasser commits an assault if he or she tries to take personal property from a person in peaceable possession if the possessor puts his hands on the property. In *R. v. Doucette,*[28] C had failed to make his payments on a television set which he was purchasing under a conditional sales agreement. Three bailiffs, acting for the seller of the television, entered C's house to repossess the set. They were not acting under the authority of a court order and C told them to leave. While C was leaning on the television set, the bailiffs grabbed it and began carrying it away. C followed "in a threatening manner" and the bailiff Doucette, believing that C was about to strike him, hit C in the mouth knocking him to the floor. Doucette was charged with assault. In its decision the court found the accused guilty and made the following points:

1. It was illegal for the bailiffs to repossess the television set by the use of force.

2. C was a peaceable possessor of personal property under a claim of right and was protected from criminal responsibility for resisting the taking of the property.

3. The bailiffs were trespassers at least from the point at which C protested against their being in his house.

4. Apart from the actual force applied to C, they could be held responsible for committing an assault under s.38(2) because they persisted in taking the property after C had leaned on it.

b. Real Property

Sections 40 and 41 set out a person's right to defend real property (including a dwelling-house) which is in his or her possession:

---

28. (1960), 33 C.R. 174 (Ont.C.A.).

DEFENSE OF DWELLING-HOUSE FROM BREAK-IN s.40

40. Every one who is in peaceable possession of a dwelling-house, and every one lawfully assisting him or acting under his authority, is justified in using as much force as is necessary to prevent any person from forcibly breaking into or forcibly entering the dwelling-house without lawful authority.

DEFENSE OF DWELLING-HOUSE OR REAL PROPERTY FROM TRESPASSER s.41

41.(1) Every one who is in peaceable possession of a dwelling-house or real property and every one lawfully assisting him or acting under his authority is justified in using force to prevent any person from trespassing on the dwelling-house or real property, or to remove a trespasser therefrom, if he uses no more force than is necessary.

(2) A trespasser who resists an attempt by a person who is in peaceable possession of a dwelling-house or real property, or a person lawfully assisting him or acting under his authority to prevent his entry or to remove him, shall be deemed to commit an assault without justification or provocation.

Section 40 allows a person to use as much force as is necessary to prevent a person from forcibly entering his or her home without lawful authority.

Section 41(1) is broader in that it allows a person to use force to remove trespassers not only from his or her home but from any part of his or her real property. For example, a person could forcibly remove a trespasser from the front lawn. However, the force used must be no more than is necessary.

In *R. v. Ryan*[29] the accused was charged with unlawfully assaulting a police officer. His defence was that the police officer was a trespasser and that he was using reasonable force in the defence of his property against the trespasser. The facts were summarized by the court as follows:

> *A report was received at the police station . . . that a store selling electrical appliances . . . was keeping open to an hour later than that permitted by the city by-law. Accordingly, two women, who were police officers, one in uniform, were sent to investigate. These officers arrived at the store at approximately 6:55 p.m., entered and found there the accused, who was the general manager and in charge of the store, two other employees, and a man, woman, and two children. The accused asked the officers to leave . . . (one officer) refused and insisted she was going to another part of the store to interview the man and the woman. The accused, having asked her to leave then stood in the aisle to prevent her going to interview these people. She endeavoured to force her way past the accused and he put his hands on her arms to stop her.*

---

29. (1956), 116 C.C.C. 239 (B.C.C.A.).

The court found the accused not guilty of assault for two reasons. First, the officers had no right to be in the store. They had no permission by law (e.g., a search warrant). Even though they had an implied permission from the accused to enter like any other member of the public, that permission was revoked when the accused requested them to leave. Second, the accused did not use excessive force in defending his possession of the store.

In *R. v. Montague*[30] the issue was whether the accused had used more force than was necessary in removing a person from his property. Atkinson, a member of the Jehovah's Witnesses, came to the door of the accused's home and asked him if he would be interested in a discussion of the Bible. The accused said he was not interested and told him to leave. Atkinson agreed to leave. At this point in the case, there was a conflict in the evidence. However, the accused admitted that he pushed Atkinson in order to get him to leave. He then followed Atkinson to a point on his property about 20 feet from the house and pushed him down in a snowbank. Atkinson got up and ran to the road with the accused chasing after him. The court concluded that, even if Atkinson was a trespasser, the accused had used more force than was necessary. The court said that Atkinson was actually leaving as requested when the accused proceeded to follow him out. There was nothing to suggest that Atkinson would not have continued leaving if the accused had simply closed the door and stayed in his house. His attack on Atkinson at the snowbank was an assault and was clearly not necessary for the defence of his property.

Under s.41(2) a trespasser who resists an attempt by the possessor of property to remove him from the property is guilty of an assault. However, in order to be guilty, the trespasser must do some overt act of resistance. Passive resistance is not sufficient to justify a conviction. In *R. v. Kellington*,[31] about 25 people came to the offices of the Social Services Department of the city of Vancouver at about 5:00 p.m. They were there to get information about the Department's policy regarding funerals for indigent persons. The Director of the Department discussed the policy with them for about 30 minutes. Then disagreements arose between the Director and the group and he asked them to leave the building. They refused and the police were called to remove them. One member of the group simply remained seated in a chair until arrested. She was charged with assault under s.41(2). The court found her not guilty because she had done no overt act to resist her removal from the property.

I. MISTAKE OF FACT

If a person commits a prohibited act while believing that certain circumstances exist, but which do not actually exist, he may be able to rely on

---

30. (1949), 97 C.C.C. 29 (Ont.Cty.Ct.).
31. (1972), 7 C.C.C. (2d) 564 (B.C.S.C.).

the defence of ***mistake of fact***. A mistake of fact is an error as to some circumstance. For example, if Albert takes Brian's book, believing it to be his own, he is acting under a mistake of fact. A mistake of fact will be a defence to a criminal charge if:

1. the mistake was an honest one, and
2. no offence would have been committed if the circumstances had been as the accused believed them to be.

So, in the example above, Albert would not be guilty of theft if he had an honest belief that the book belonged to him. If the book did belong to him, no offence would have been committed.

Mistake of fact is a defence to most charges under the Code because if a person is acting under a mistaken belief in the facts, the person does not have the *mens rea* or guilty mind required to commit the offence. In the example above, Albert did not have the *mens rea* to commit theft (i.e., the intent to deprive the owner) because he believed that he owned the book.

The Supreme Court of Canada has dealt with the defence of mistake of fact in *Beaver v. R.*[32] The accused was charged with illegal possession of a narcotic drug. He had sold heroin to an undercover RCMP officer. His defence was that he honestly believed that he was selling sugar, not heroin, even though he had told the officer that he was selling a narcotic. The court found the accused not guilty because "[t]he essence of the crime is the possession of the forbidden substance and in a criminal case there is in law no possession without knowledge of the character of the forbidden substance." In short, to be guilty of illegal possession of a narcotic, the accused must know that he has a narcotic. If he has an honest, but mistaken, belief that the substance is sugar, then he does not have the knowledge required for possession. The mistaken belief must be honest, but it is not necessary that it be reasonable. Whether a reasonable person would have believed that the heroin was sugar is merely one factor to be considered by the jury in determining if the accused's mistake was an honest mistake.

LIMITATIONS ON DEFENCE OF MISTAKE OF FACT s.150.1(4)

A mistake of fact will not be a defence if an offence would have been committed if the circumstances would have been as the accused believed them to be. For example, Jane is charged with possession of narcotics. Her defence is that she thought she was in possession of counterfeit money. Mistake of fact in this example would not be a defence because if the facts were as she believed them to be, an offence would still have been committed.[33]

There are several sections in the Code which limit the defence of mistake of fact for sexual offences involving young people. For example, s.150.1 states:

---

32. (1957), 118 C.C.C. 129 (S.C.C.).
33. See *R. v. Kundeus* (1976), 24 C.C.C. (2d) (S.C.C.).

150.1 . . .

(4) It is not a defence to a charge under section 151 or 152, subsection 160(3) or 173(2), or section 271, 272, or 273 that the accused believed that the complainant was fourteen years of age or more at the time the offence is alleged to have been committed unless the accused took all reasonable steps to ascertain the age of the complainant.

(5) It is not a defence to a charge under section 153, 159, 170, 171 or 172 or subsection 212(2) or (4) that the accused believed that the complainant was eighteen years of age or more at the time the offence is alleged to have been committed unless the accused took all reasonable steps to ascertain the age of the complainant.

This section is a recent amendment to the Code. The previous section also took away the defence of mistake of fact without, however, allowing the defence if the accused "took all reasonable steps to ascertain the age of the complainant." In other words, the offence was committed regardless of the nature of the accused's belief about the age of the complainant. There are several provincial Court of Appeal decisions that have held this previous section violates the right to fundamental justice under the Charter. By denying the defence of mistake, this section takes away the fault requirement necessary for criminal offences. The present section basically allows an honest mistake if it is reasonable. It is likely that in the near future the Supreme Court will be required to determine if this section also violates the Charter.

J. MISTAKE OF LAW

IGNORANCE OF THE LAW NO EXCUSE s.19

The general rule "ignorance of the law is no excuse" is contained in s.19:

19. Ignorance of the law by a person who commits an offence is not an excuse for committing that offence.

In other words, everyone is presumed to know the criminal law. A mistake of fact is an error as to some circumstance or fact. A *mistake of law* is an error as to the legal status of the circumstance or fact. For example, in *Beaver v. R.*, discussed above, Beaver was found not guilty of possession of heroin because he honestly believed that the heroin was sugar. This was a mistake of fact. However, if Beaver knew that he had heroin, but honestly believed that it was legal to possess heroin, he would be making a mistake of law and would be guilty.

In some situations, a mistake of civil law may be a defence. A mistake of civil law occurs when a person has an honest belief that he has a legal right under the civil law, but in fact does not have the right. In *R. v.*

Harrison[34] the accused, the operator of a car-towing service, was charged with theft. Haines had parked his car on private property. There were signs on the property stating that unauthorized cars would be towed away at the owner's expense. The owner of the private property asked the accused to remove the car. The accused towed it to a yard surrounded by a high fence and guarded by an attendant and a dog. When Haines arrived at the yard, the attendant told him that he could not have his car unless he paid $12 for the towing and storage. Haines did not get his car back until the next evening when he paid the towing and storage charges.

The offence of theft is committed if a person deprives a property owner of the property "without colour of right." The term *colour of right* refers to an honest mistake of fact or law which leads a person to believe that he or she has a legal right to possess the property. In this case, the accused had no legal right to refuse to release the car, but he honestly believed that he had the legal right to refuse until the money was paid. The court found the accused not guilty because he acted with colour of right. He made a mistake of law and thus acted without the *mens rea* required in the offence of theft. However, the court warned the accused that now that he was aware of his legal position he could not rely on the same mistake of law as a defence to any similar charges in the future.

There is one other situation where mistake of law may be a defence. If a person breaks a regulatory law, that is, a law passed for the health or protection of the public (not a true criminal offence) because an official in charge of enforcing the law which has been broken has mislead the person, the accused may raise the defence of *officially induced error* which is actually a type of mistake of law. For example, in *R. v. Patrick Morningstar*,[35] an official from the Ontario Ministry of Natural Resources had told the people of a native band that they could fish in certain waters. This advice was wrong and one of the band members was charged with unlawfully fishing in a prohibited area. In dismissing the charge, the judge relied on a decision of the Ontario Court of Appeal which stated:

> *In order for the accused to successfully raise this defence, he must show that he relied on the erroneous legal opinion of the official and that his reliance was reasonable. The reasonableness will depend upon several factors including the efforts he made to ascertain the proper law, the complexity or obscurity of the law, the position of the official who gave the advice, and the clarity, definitiveness and reasonableness of the advice given.*

---

34. [1966] 3 C.C.C. 348 (Ont.C.A.).
35. Reported in *The Lawyers Weekly*, November 27, 1987.

K. ENTRAPMENT

In a 1988 decision, *R. v. Mack*,[36] the Supreme Court of Canada held that the defence of entrapment exists as part of the doctrine of abuse of process. The defence of entrapment may be allowed when someone has been "set up" or trapped into committing a crime by the police or police informants. These situations often occur in drug investigations. In *Mack* the accused had been repeatedly asked by a police informer over a six-month period to sell him drugs. The accused refused to sell drugs to the informer until the informer threatened him. At that point he agreed to find him some drugs. The accused testified that, although he had once been involved with drugs, at the time he was approached by the informer he had given up his drug-related lifestyle.

The court held that the police conduct was unacceptable in this case and that the charges against Mack should be stayed. The court set out guidelines for deciding whether police conduct is an abuse of process. First, the police cannot provide opportunities for people to commit crimes unless (1) the police are acting on reasonable suspicions that the people are already engaged in crime or (2) the police are carrying on a bona fide investigation. As one judge said, the police cannot randomly test the virtue of people. Second, even when the police do have reasonable suspicions or are carrying on a bona fide investigation, the police cannot actually induce a person to commit a crime. A more recent decision of the Supreme Court, *R. v. Barnes*,[37] dealt with the issue of what a bona fide investigation is. In this case, a police officer approached the accused in a Vancouver shopping mall and asked him if he had any "weed". At first the accused said no, but the officer continued asking until, finally, the accused agreed to sell the officer a small amount of hash. The trial judge allowed the defence of entrapment because the police had been engaged in "random virtue testing". The British Columbia Court of Appeal overturned the trial court decision. The Supreme Court of Canada upheld the decision of the British Columbia Court of Appeal. The Supreme Court held that the defence did not apply in this case. The accused had been approached in an area known for drug trafficking and the police were conducting a bona fide investigation. It did not matter that the police did not have reasonable grounds to suspect the accused was involved in crime. His physical presence in an area defined with sufficient precision and where it was reasonably suspected that particular criminal activity was occurring was enough to justify the police actions.

---

36. (1988), 44 C.C.C. (3d) 513 (S.C.C.).
37. (1991), 3 C.R. (4th) 1 (S.C.C.).

QUESTIONS FOR REVIEW AND DISCUSSION

1 Define the term "defence to a crime".

2 Does the accused have to "prove" his defence? Explain.

3 What is a common law defence? Give an example.

4 What is the age at which the law presumes children do not have the capacity to commit crimes?

5 What must be established on behalf of the accused if he or she is to be found not guilty by reason of insanity?

6 What is the meaning of "wrong" as the word is used in the defence of insanity?

7 Define the defence of automatism.

8 How is automatism different from insanity?

9 What degree of intoxication must exist before an accused can rely on intoxication as a defence?

10 Could intoxication be used as a defence to common assault, a general intent crime? Explain.

11 Explain the differences between the Code defence of compulsion and the common law defence of duress.

12 When can the defence of necessity be used?

13 What must the Crown prove when lack of consent is an element of an offence?

14 Give examples of when consent is specifically not a defence.

15 **a** What did the court decide in the case of *R. v. Lavallee*?
   b In what way did this case change the law?

16 In general, how much force can be used to defend property?

17 What does mistake of fact mean when it is used as a defence?

18 Can mistake of law be a defence to a crime? Explain.

19 How is mistake of fact different from mistake of law?

20 **a** What is the defence of entrapment?
   b What guidelines must the police follow to avoid this defence being raised?

21 Angela is charged with the theft of one pound of butter from a grocery store. Theft requires the specific intent to deprive another person of his or her property. Angela's defence is that she was too intoxicated to form this specific intent. In making a decision, the judge considers the following points in favour of the accused's defence:
   (1) Angela drank 10 bottles of beer between 12:00 noon and 5:00 p.m. in a beer parlour.
   (2) While waiting for the police to arrive, Angela suddenly went to sleep or lost consciousness in the manager's office.

(3) She did not need the butter since she had an ample supply in her apartment.

(4) She did not remember what happened to the money given to her by her roommate an hour before the incident.

(5) She had no lunch that day.

(6) She had no memory of taking the butter.

(7) She seemed to have taken the butter without caring whether anybody saw her or not.

The judge also considers the following points against the accused:

(1) Angela caused no drunken disturbance either in the beer parlour, store or in the police station.

(2) She had a perfectly lucid conversation with the store manager a few minutes before she took the butter.

(3) Although her breath smelled of alcohol, there was no clinical evidence that the accused was drunk.

(4) She walked perfectly steadily, even on an icy street without rubbers.

(5) Neither the police nor the store manager recognized Angela as being drunk. She appeared normal to them except that her breath smelled of alcohol.

Should Angela be convicted? Explain.

See *R. v. Regehr* (1952), 13 C.R. 53 (Sask.).

22 Henrik owes $500 to Borje, a well-known underworld figure. Borje threatens Henrik by saying: "If you don't pay me by 10:00 p.m. tonight, you'll be dead tomorrow morning". Henrik knows that Borje is serious and will carry out the threat if necessary. So, Henrik breaks into a store, steals $500, and makes the payment to Borje. Henrik is charged with break, enter, and theft. Henrik raises the defence of compulsion. Will his defence be successful? Why?

FIVE

Pre-Trial Criminal Procedure

People working in the criminal justice system have the job of preventing crime and, when crime does occur, the duty to investigate it. They must find, charge, prosecute, and determine the punishment for offenders. Criminal procedure consists of the rules these people must follow in carrying out their duties. The rules of criminal procedure also set out the framework of the criminal justice system. For example, the rules which create the system for trying crimes that was discussed in Chapter Two is part of the law of criminal procedure.

Generally criminal procedure can be separated into three distinct phases: pre-trial procedure, trial procedure, and post-trial procedure. This chapter will consider only the more important aspects of pre-trial procedure including the powers of arrest and search, pre-trial release, and rights of the accused before and after arrest.

A. BRINGING THE ACCUSED BEFORE THE COURT

1. General

When the police have reasonable grounds for believing someone has committed a crime, their next step is to decide how to bring the suspect before a court where the person's guilt or innocence can be determined. The police have three possible choices, not all of which are available in all situations. The police can (1) issue an appearance notice, (2) go before a justice of the peace to ask for a summons to be issued, or (3) make an arrest. Generally speaking, arrests are only made when an appearance notice or summons is inadequate, for example, if there are reasonable grounds for believing the accused will not show up in court.

2. Appearance Notice (Form 9)

An appearance notice is a form given to an accused by the police usually at the scene of the crime. It contains the accused's name, the substance of the charge, and the time and place for the accused to attend court to answer the charge. The accused signs the form (in duplicate) and receives a copy; he or she is then free to go.

ISSUE OF
APPEARANCE
NOTICE
s.496

Section 496 of the Code provides that, where a peace officer does not make an arrest, the officer may issue an appearance notice if the offence is one of the following:

1. an indictable offence mentioned in s.553

2. a hybrid offence

3. an offence punishable on summary conviction

CONTENTS
OF
APPEARANCE
NOTICE
s.501

The contents required for an appearance notice are set out in s.501 of the Code.

3. Summons (Form 6)

The police may go before a justice of the peace and ask that a summons be issued. A summons is a court order commanding the accused to appear in court on a certain day and at a certain time. To obtain a summons, the officer must lay an information before the justice of the peace. If the officer makes out a case against the accused and an arrest warrant is not necessary, a summons will be issued. Section 509 of the Code sets out the requirements for a summons:

> **509.(1) A summons issued under this Part shall**
> **(a) be directed to the accused;**
> **(b) set out briefly the offence in respect of which the accused is charged; and**
> **(c) require the accused to attend court at a time and place to be stated therein and to attend thereafter as required by the court in order to be dealt with according to law.**
> **(2) A summons shall be served by a peace officer who shall deliver it personally to the person to whom it is directed or, if that person cannot be conveniently found, shall leave it for him at his last or usual place of abode with some inmate thereof who appears to be at least sixteen years of age.**

4. Arrests

a. General

An *arrest* can be made by seizing the accused's body. It is sufficient for the arresting person to merely touch the accused and to announce to that person he or she is under arrest.

An arrest can also be made by words alone.[1] The arresting person must use words such that the person being arrested understands his or her freedom is being restricted and that he or she is compelled to follow the instructions of the arresting person.

Whether an arrest had actually been made was the question for the court in *Lebrun v. High-Low Foods Ltd.*[2] At the beginning of a visit to the supermarket, L picked up a carton of cigarettes. He subsequently made a trip to his car and returned. When he "checked out" the cigarettes were not among his purchases. The manager of the supermarket called Constable P, told him that several employees had seen L pick up the cigarettes and that they had neither been returned nor been paid for. The constable came to the store and stopped L's car as it was leaving the parking lot.

The constable told L, "There appears to be a mix-up in your order. The store believes that you have something for which you have not paid." Constable P then asked L to move his car to where the police car was parked. The police officer asked L if he could search the vehicle. L replied, "Go ahead. I'd like to get this cleared up." The constable then proceeded to search the main area of the car, the glove compartment, the trunk, and the back seat.

The police officer was polite and almost apologetic for the inconvenience he was causing. L was co-operative, polite, calm, and not visibly upset. L made no attempt to leave and made no request to be allowed to leave. L did not deny this but said that he felt he had no alternative but to submit to the search; that he unlocked the trunk of his car at the request of Constable P because he felt he would be arrested if he refused to do so.

The court decided that L, notwithstanding that Constable P had neglected to inform him of the fact, had indeed been arrested. L *believed* that he was under total restraint and was compelled to do as directed by Constable P.

b. Use of Force

USE OF
FORCE BY
PERSON
AUTHORIZED
BY LAWS
s.25

A peace officer may, if necessary, use force in making an arrest. This power is granted by s.25. However, no more force than is reasonably necessary to make the arrest is justified. For example, in situations where merely grasping an arm would suffice, an "armlock" would be an unjustifiable use of force. Section 25(3) specifically states that the arresting person cannot use force that is intended or likely to cause death or grievous bodily harm unless the person believes on reasonable grounds that it is necessary to prevent death or grievous bodily harm to himself or herself or anyone under his or her protection. In general, grievous bodily

---

1. *R. v. Whitfield*, [1970] 1 C.C.C. 129 (S.C.C.).
2. (1970), 70 D.L.R. (2d) 718 (B.C.S.C.).

harm refers to serious hurt or pain.[3] The one exception to this rule is in s.25(4) which states that if a person "takes flight" from arrest a police officer is justified " . . . in using as much force as is necessary to prevent the escape by flight, unless the escape can be stopped by reasonable means in a less violent manner."

The Supreme Court of Canada has held in *Priestman v. Colangelo and Smythson*[4] that this section justifies the conduct of the police even if other members of the community are injured as long as the force is exercised in a reasonable and non-negligent manner.

In *Priestman* a police officer used s.25(4) as a justification for his actions. Constables P and A were on patrol duty when they received a message on the radio telephone reporting the theft of a car. Almost immediately they saw a motor vehicle which they believed to be — and which later turned out to be — the stolen vehicle, driven by S. The police car pulled up alongside the stolen car and P ordered S to stop. Both officers were in uniform and S, no doubt, realized that they were police officers. Instead of stopping, he pulled around the corner quickly and drove away at a high rate of speed. The police car followed and on three occasions attempted to pass the stolen car in order to cut it off, but each time S pulled to the south side of the road and cut off the police car. On the third occasion the police car was forced over the south curb on to a boulevard and was compelled to slow down in order to avoid colliding with a hydro pole. Following this third attempt and as the police car went back on the road, P fired a warning shot into the air from his .38 calibre revolver. The stolen car increased its speed and when the police car was one-and-a-half to two car lengths from the stolen car, P aimed at the left rear tire of the stolen car and fired. The bullet hit the bottom of the frame of the rear window, shattered the glass, ricocheted and struck S in the back of the neck, causing him to lose consciousness immediately. The stolen car went over the curb on the south side of the road, grazed a hydro pole, crossed a street, and, coming to a stop, struck the veranda of a house. Before hitting the house, the car ran into and killed two people waiting for a bus.

Constable P took the position that S's escape could not have been prevented by reasonable means in a less violent manner. In other words, P believed he was justified in firing his revolver. The court agreed with P. They found that his actions were justified by s.25(4). He used no more force than was *reasonably necessary* to prevent S's escape.

c. Liability for Excessive Use of Force

If the arrest of the accused was accompanied by more force than was necessary to make the arrest, the arresting person may be sued for

---

3. *R. v. Bottrell* (1981), 60 C.C.C. (2d) 211 (B.C.C.A.).
4. (1959), 19 D.L.R. (2d) 1 (S.C.C.).

LIABILITY FOR EXCESSIVE FORCE s.26

damages based on an assault. In addition, the arresting person can be prosecuted in a criminal court for the offence of assault or one of the more serious criminal offences involving bodily harm. Section 26 of the Code provides:

> **26. Every one who is authorized by law to use force is criminally responsible for any excess thereof according to the nature and quality of the act that constitutes the excess.**

d. Trespass and the Right to Arrest

Whether the arrest is made with or without a warrant, the police have the authority to enter private premises to make an arrest. This issue was recently considered by the Supreme Court in *R. v. Landry*.[5]

The accused was charged with an offence under s.270 of the Code for assaulting a peace officer in the execution of his duty. A public transit inspector observed two youths trying to open car doors in a parking lot at the back of a shopping centre. The inspector called the police. When the police arrived, the inspector gave them a description of the youths and told them that he had seen the youths enter an apartment building. One of the officers approached the building and looked through a basement window where he saw two males who matched the description given by the inspector. The officer then went to the door of the apartment. There was conflicting evidence on whether the door to the apartment was opened by the accused or whether it was already open when the officer arrived. However, it was agreed that the officer stood in the doorway of the apartment and asked the accused if he lived there. The officer then told the two youths they were under arrest. Landry indicated he did not want to go anywhere. The office then entered the room and took physical control of Landry. A fight then broke out which resulted in Landry being charged with assaulting a peace officer in the execution of his duty.

The issue for the court was whether the arrest was legal, that is, whether the officer had the authority to enter a private premises without permission and without a warrant for arrest. If the arrest was not legal, then the charge against Landry could not stand. Landry was acquitted at his trial on the grounds that the officer was not acting in the execution of his duties because he had no power to enter a private premises to make a warrantless arrest. An appeal by the Crown to the Ontario Court of Appeal was dismissed. The Supreme Court of Canada allowed the Crown's appeal and ordered a new trial. The Supreme Court held that the Criminal Code is silent on the spatial limits on arrest without a warrant (i.e., whether an arrest without a warrant is lawful on private premises). Therefore, the court considered the common law on this point. The court held that according to common law the police have the

---

5. (1986), 25 C.C.C. (3d) 1 (S.C.C.).

authority to make a forcible entry into a private premise in order to effect an arrest. Thus, where the police have the authority to make an arrest without a warrant under s.495(1) (discussed below) in proper circumstances, the police may enter a private premises to make an arrest. The policy underlying this law, the court said, is ". . . there should be no place which gives an offender sanctuary from arrest." The circumstances which must exist for entering private premises to make an arrest are:

- The officers must have reasonable and probable grounds for believing that the person is on the premises.
- The officers must give notice of their presence (e.g., by knocking or ringing the doorbell).
- The officers must give notice of their authority (i.e., by identifying themselves).
- The officers must give notice of their purpose.

5. Arrest Without a Warrant

a. *Arrest by Any Person*

ARREST WITHOUT WARRANT BY ANY PERSON s.494

In England, under the common law, every person had a duty to apprehend persons who broke "the King's peace." The persons who had been arrested would then be turned over to the King's agents for trial. Canadian law continues this tradition in the Criminal Code by providing that in certain situations a private person can make an arrest. Section 494 spells out three such situations:

> **494.(1) Any one may arrest without a warrant**
> **(a) a person whom he finds committing an indictable offence; or**
> **(b) a person who, on reasonable grounds, he believes**
> **(i) has committed a criminal offence, and**
> **(ii) is escaping from and freshly pursued by persons who have lawful authority to arrest that person.**
> **(2) Any one who is**
> **(a) the owner or a person in lawful possession of property, or**
> **(b) a person authorized by the owner or by a person in lawful possession of property,**
> **may arrest without a warrant a person whom he finds committing a criminal offence on or in relation to that property.**

The first situation occurs when the arresting person finds the accused in the act of committing an indictable offence. This situation includes hybrid offences since they are treated as indictable until the Crown chooses to have the offence tried as a summary conviction offence. This choice is usually made just before the trial (see Chapter Two).

The second situation described in s.494 occurs when a person believes on reasonable grounds that the accused has *committed a criminal offence* and is escaping from and being *freshly* pursued by persons having lawful authority to arrest him. The term "criminal offence" applies to summary conviction offences as well as to those that are indictable, but not to provincial offences.

To be "freshly pursued" means that the accused must be followed in a manner which is *continuous* and conducted with *reasonable effort,* such that the pursuit and capture of the accused, together with the actual commission of the crime, form a single transaction.

Here is an example of a fresh pursuit. Robert robs a store. He is chased from the store by three customers and the owner and they follow him for several blocks. Robert finally loses them by hiding in an alley. The pursuers search the area for a few minutes but they cannot find Robert. At this point Robert is still being "freshly pursued." After several more minutes of fruitless searching, they decide to go to the police station, and then afterwards, to return to continue the hunt. At this point Robert is no longer being freshly pursued and, therefore, the search is no longer continuous.

A person who has "lawful authority" would include, of course, a peace officer or any person who is granted the power to make an arrest by the Criminal Code. Thus, if, as described above in s.494, a citizen finds an accused committing the offence of robbery (an indictable offence), the citizen has lawful authority to arrest the accused.

The third situation under s.494 in which anyone may make an arrest occurs when the owner of property, or a person such as a tenant who is lawfully in possession of property, *finds an accused committing a criminal offence on or in relation to that property.* Thus, if Arif was renting a house, Arif could arrest Daniel if Arif saw Daniel deliberately break a window in the house.

ARREST FOR BREACH OF PEACE s.30

Section 30 of the Code provides additional power of arrest to the private person. Anyone who sees a breach of the peace is justified in interfering to prevent the continuance or renewal of the breach and may detain any person involved in or about to join in the breach. Thus, if a person is in a bar and a brawl starts, the person may grab and hold back anyone who wants to join in, or who has already joined in, until the police arrive.

OMITTING TO ASSIST OFFICER IN MAKING AN ARREST s.129(b) Hybrid Max: 2 years

The criminal law also imposes a duty on persons to assist in making an arrest when a request is made by the police. Section 129(b) states:

> **129. Every one who . . .**
> **(b) omits without reasonable excuse, to assist a public officer or peace officer in the execution of his duty in arresting a person or in preserving the peace, after having reasonable notice that he is required to do so . . . is guilty of . . . an . . . offence . . . .**

DELIVERY OF ARRESTED PERSON s.494(3)

Section 494(3) states that whenever an arrest is made by a person who is not a peace officer, the person must deliver the arrested person to a peace officer "forthwith". One court has said that "forthwith" does not mean instantly but as soon as is reasonably practicable under the circumstances.[6]

b. Arrest by Peace Officer

Peace officers have the authority of any person to make an arrest and have other authorities as well.

ARREST WITHOUT WARRANT BY PEACE OFFICERS s.495

Section 495 of the Criminal Code defines the situations in which a peace officer may make an arrest without a warrant. Subsection (1) lists the general rules for making an arrest without a warrant. However, these general rules are limited by the exceptions in subs.(2) of s.495. In other words, to decide whether an officer can make an arrest without a warrant, you must first look at the general rules in subs.(1) then check the limitations in subs.(2).

This two-step scheme is a result of the bail reform legislation, passed in the 1970s. The philosophy underlying this legislation is that people should only be held before trial if there is a clear reason for doing so. Until this time it was felt by those responsible for law reform that too many people were being arrested and detained while awaiting trial. Therefore, one purpose of the legislation is to limit the authority of the police to arrest when other methods such as giving an appearance notice or having a summons issued would do just as well. Section 495(1) provides:

> **495.(1) A peace officer may arrest without warrant**
> **(a) a person who has committed an indictable offence or who, on reasonable grounds, he believes has committed or is about to commit an indictable offence;**
> **(b) a person whom he finds committing a criminal offence; or**
> **(c) a person in respect of whom he has reasonable grounds to believe that a warrant of arrest or committal, in any form set out in Part XXVIII in relation thereto, is in force within the territorial jurisdiction in which the person is found.**

PEACE OFFICER DEFINED s.2

The term "peace officer" is defined in s.2 of the Code. It includes a mayor, a warden, a sheriff, a prison guard, certain customs officials, a pilot in command of an aircraft while the aircraft is in flight, certain military personnel and, of course, police officers. Note, a private security officer employed by a department store or business is not a peace officer. This person has only the same power of arrest that any other ordinary person possesses as previously discussed.

---

6. *R. v. Cunningham and Ritchie* (1979), 49 C.C.C. (2d) (Man.Co.Ct.).

Section 495(1) sets out five situations in which a police officer may make an arrest without a warrant.

1. The arresting officer knows the person has committed an indictable offence.

2. The arresting officer believes on ***reasonable grounds*** that the accused has committed an indictable offence. This situation demands that a "reasonable grounds" test be used to determine if an arrest can be made. It is not necessary that an indictable offence has actually been committed. The arresting officer must personally believe that he or she has reasonable grounds to make the arrest (i.e., that an indictable offence has been committed) and it must be objectively established that the reasonable grounds existed.

Generally, reasonable grounds are grounds which would lead any ordinary, prudent, and cautious person to have a strong and honest belief that the person to be arrested has committed the offence. If the accused is later acquitted of the charge, the arrest may still be lawful. The important questions are: (1) whether a reasonable person standing in the shoes of the peace officer would have believed that reasonable grounds existed for making the arrest and (2) whether the officer personally believed that the reasonable grounds existed.

For example, in *Koechlin v. Waugh and Hamilton*[7] the neighbourhood in which the accused was arrested had been subject to a number of break-ins a few nights earlier. The accused and a friend were stopped by the police at approximately 11:00 p.m. The accused was observed to be wearing shoes that matched the shoes worn by the suspect. The accused explained that he was returning home from a show. The police decided to arrest him on the suspicion of having committed the break-in. The court held that these facts did not amount to reasonable and probable grounds for believing the accused committed the break-in.

3. The arresting officer has reasonable grounds to believe an indictable offence is about to be committed. This situation also demands that the police use a reasonable grounds test in determining if an indictable offence is about to be committed. If a police officer has an honest belief based on reasonable grounds that an individual is about to commit an indictable offence, even though that person has not yet made an attempt to commit the offence, then the police officer may make the arrest. Of course, this leads to the odd situation that the person arrested cannot be charged with any offence. Also, the officer cannot hold the person since the arrested person has not committed any offence. However, this power is necessary to prevent the commission of offences that are reasonably foreseeable.[8]

---

7. (1957), 118 C.C.C. 24 (Ont.C.A.).
8. See, for example, Roger E. Salhaney, *Canadian Criminal Procedure*, 5th ed. (Aurora: Canada Law Books, 1989), pp. 46–47.

4. The arresting officer finds the accused committing any criminal offence. The Supreme Court of Canada has held that this situation applies when the officer finds the accused "apparently" committing an offence. This interpretation protects the officer from being sued for false imprisonment if the accused is later found not guilty of the offence.[9] Any criminal offence includes summary conviction offences as well as those that are indictable. It does not include provincial offences. Arrest powers for provincial offences are contained in provincial statutes.

Note, the only power that a police officer has to arrest for a summary conviction offence, without a warrant, is that granted by situation four and by the power that everybody has under s.494 to arrest anyone where there are reasonable grounds to believe that the person has committed a criminal offence and is being freshly pursued by persons with lawful authority to make an arrest.

5. The arresting officer believes on reasonable grounds that the accused is the subject of a warrant, which is in force within the jurisdiction in which the accused is found. This situation considers the circumstance where a police officer has reasonable grounds to believe that there is a warrant in effect for the arrest or commital of the accused. The warrant must be in force in the territorial jurisdiction in which the accused is found at the time of his or her arrest. In other words, if a warrant is in force in only one county or district of a province, it cannot be used to arrest an accused who is found in a different county or district.

c. *Section 495(2) Limitations on Power to Arrest Without a Warrant*

LIMITATIONS ON ARREST WITHOUT WARRANT s.495(2)

A police officer's right to arrest without a warrant is limited by s.495(2) which states that an arrest cannot be made without a warrant for the indictable offences listed in s.553, hybrid offences, or summary conviction offences unless certain circumstances exist. Indictable offences which are contained in s.553 are:

. . .

   (i) **section 201 (keeping a gaming or betting house)**
   (ii) **section 202 (betting, pool-selling, book-making, etc.),**
  (iii) **section 203 (placing bets),**
   (iv) **section 206 (lotteries and games of chance),**
    (v) **section 209 (cheating at play),**
   (vi) **section 210 (keeping a common bawdy-house),**

. . .

---

9. *R. v. Biron* (1975), 23 C.C.C. (2d) 513 (S.C.C.).

**(viii) section 393 (fraud in relation to fares).
and counselling, attempting to commit or being an accessory
after the fact to any of the above offences.**

If a police officer is confronted with one of the three categories of offences described in subs.(2) of s.495, then an arrest without a warrant cannot be made unless the officer considers, on reasonable grounds, that it is in the public interest to make the arrest. "In the public interest" is a general term which means the safety and well-being of the public is to be given priority.

In order to determine whether the public interest would be served by an arrest, the police officer must consider all the circumstances of the offence, including:

(a) the need to establish the identity of the person;

(b) the need to protect and/or keep evidence; or

(c) the need to prevent the continuation or repetition of the offence or the commission of another offence.

The arresting officer must also decide whether there exist any good reasons for believing that the accused, if not arrested, will fail to show up on the court appearance date.

An example of when an arrest could be made for an offence listed in s.495(2) would be if the accused refused to give his or her name to the officer making the charge. In such a situation, an arrest would be in the public interest.

If the peace officer decides that an arrest is not needed, the officer may issue an appearance notice to the accused or obtain a summons. If the officer issues an appearance notice, the officer must also lay an information before a justice of the peace.

d. *Summary of Power of Arrest Without a Warrant*

The following briefly summarizes a police officer's power to arrest without a warrant:

1. The officer must be presented with one of the five situations outlined in s.495(1), or with that part of s.494 that entitles any person to make an arrest.

2. If the officer is presented with such a situation, the officer must then consider whether the offence in question is one which falls within the three categories of s.495(2). If it is not, an arrest can be made.

3. If the offence does fall within one of the three categories, then the officer must decide whether an arrest should be made on the basis of the public interest. If an arrest should not be made, the officer can issue an appearance notice to the accused or go before a justice to have a summons issued.

ARREST FOR BREACH OF PEACE s.31(1)

The Criminal Code provides two additional police powers of arrest without a warrant. Section 31(1) reads:

> **31.(1) Every peace officer who witnesses a breach of the peace and every one who lawfully assists the peace officer is justified in arresting any person whom he finds committing the breach of the peace or who, on reasonable grounds, he believes is about to join in or renew the breach of the peace.**

It has been up to the courts to define "breach of the peace" since this term is not defined in the Code and is not an offence. Generally, courts have said that a ***breach of the peace*** involves the threat of violence, such as when a group of people are loitering and becoming unruly.

The British Columbia Court of Appeal[10] has said that s.31 only applies to breaches of the peace that have actually happened. The court went on to say, however, that under the common law, a police officer can arrest without a warrant where the officer honestly and on reasonable grounds believes that a breach of the peace is about to occur.

Since there is no offence of committing a breach of the peace, the situation is similar to where an officer arrests a person about to commit an offence; that is, the person cannot be charged and or be held. It is possible, though, for the arrested person to be taken before a justice and required to enter a peace bond at common law. This procedure is discussed in more detail in Chapter Twelve under Recognizances to Keep the Peace.

ARREST OF PERSON FOUND IN GAMING HOUSE s.199(2)

The second offence which specifically includes the power to arrest without a warrant is related to the keeping of gaming houses. Section 199(2) allows a police officer to take into custody any person whom he finds in a gaming house.

6. Arrest With a Warrant (Form 7)

An ***arrest warrant*** is a document issued by a justice of the peace or judge which commands the police to arrest a named person.

WARRANT FOR ARREST s.507

A justice of the peace or judge may issue a warrant pursuant to s.507 for the arrest of a person where there are reasonable grounds to believe that the person has committed a criminal offence. The justice or judge must also believe that an arrest is in the public interest before issuing the warrant. The procedure followed is for the person seeking the warrant to go before the justice and "make out a case" against the accused. In other words, the person will provide information for the justice so that the justice can determine whether there are reasonable grounds for believing a warrant is necessary. Note that any person can go before a justice and lay an information.

---

10. *Hayes v. Thompson et al.* (1985), 18 C.C.C. (3d) 254 (B.C.C.A.).

An arrest warrant may also be issued if the accused disobeys an appearance notice or a summons.

Under s.29(1), anyone who executes a warrant has a duty to have the warrant where it is feasible to do so and to produce it for the inspection of the accused if requested.

7. Pre-Trial Release

The general principle of the law is that a person should not be held before trial unless there is a reason for detaining the person. The Code sets out several stages where the reasons for the arrest are reviewed and where the person who has been detained can be released if the reasons no longer exist.

If the accused has been arrested with or without a warrant and the offence for which the accused has been arrested is one of the following:

(a) an indictable offence listed in s.553,

(b) a hybrid offence, or

(c) a summary conviction offence,

RELEASE BY ARRESTING OFFICER s.497

section 497 provides that the peace officer must release the accused as soon as is practicable once the reason for the arrest no longer exists and either obtain a summons or issue an appearance notice. So, for example, where a police officer has arrested an accused in order to confirm the accused's identity, then the accused must be released once the person's identity is confirmed.

RELEASE BY OFFICER IN CHARGE s.498

If the accused is not released, under s.498 the officer in charge of the lock-up must review the arrest. The "officer in charge" is the person responsible for the place where the accused is taken. The officer in charge has the same obligation to release an accused arrested for one of the above offences as the arresting officer. The officer in charge has an additional authority to release an accused if the offence is one punishable by imprisonment for five years or less and if the reason for the arrest no longer exists. If the accused is released, the officer in charge can proceed to have a summons issued, to have the accused give a promise to appear (Form 10), or to have the accused enter a recognizance. A recognizance is an agreement made by the accused that he or she will pay a certain amount of money if he or she fails to appear in court as required (Form 11).

APPEARANCE BEFORE JUSTICE s.503

If the accused is still in custody, the accused must be taken before a justice within 24 hours or as soon as possible (s.503). The justice will then determine whether the accused should be kept in custody, or, whether the accused should be released upon giving an undertaking (Form 12) or entering a recognizance (Form 32) with or without sureties. An undertaking is a promise to appear in court on a certain day. It may contain conditions, for example, that the accused must remain within a certain territorial jurisdiction or notify the police of any change in address or occupation. A *surety* is a person who agrees to be bound by a recognizance on behalf of the accused. In effect, the surety is responsible for ensuring that the accused appears for his or her court date (Form 32).

For most offences, it is up to the Crown to "show cause" why the accused should not be released. For example, it might be proved that the accused has failed to appear for court appearances before. Where a person is charged with certain serious offences such as murder, the hearing must be held before a superior court judge of the province. (The superior court for each province is listed in s.2 of the Code.) In these cases, the onus is on the accused to "show cause" why a release should be ordered. Where the hearing is before a justice, the onus also shifts to the accused in the situations listed in s.515(6). For example, a person who is charged with committing an indictable offence while on pre-trial release for another indictable offence will have the onus of showing cause for why he or she should be released.

8. Civil and Criminal Responsibility of the Arresting Person

NO
CRIMINAL
RESPONSI-
BILITY
WHERE
GOOD FAITH
IN
EXECUTING
WARRANT
s.28

Section 28 of the Criminal Code states that where a person who is authorized to execute an arrest warrant believes, in good faith and on reasonable grounds, that the person arrested is the person named in the warrant, the person is protected from criminal responsibility.

If the arrest is made without a warrant by either a police officer or a private citizen, the arresting individual must have an honest belief based on reasonable grounds that the accused is guilty of the offence for which he or she is arrested. If, in fact, the accused can prove that the arresting person's belief was not based on reasonable grounds then he or she may sue for damages for false imprisonment.

9. Rights Upon Arrest or Detention and the Charter

a. *The Right to Remain Silent*

The Charter has had a significant effect upon the rules regarding arrest and detention. Chapter Two described the right to remain silent as a principle of fundamental justice under s.7 of the Charter during the trial process. This right also applies at the pre-trial stage. Therefore, the accused has the right not to answer police questions. Usually the police inform the accused that he or she does not have to answer questions but it is generally thought that there is no obligation to inform the accused of this right. However, there is one recent decision which held that the police do have this duty.[11] The right to remain silent is based on the presumption of innocence and the right not to incriminate oneself. In *R*.

---

11. *R. v. Campbell* (1989), 7 W.C.B. (2d) 301.

v. Woolley,[12] the police told the accused that he would not be released until they found the keys to the car they believed he had stolen. The Ontario Court of Appeal held that his right to remain silent had been violated because giving the police the keys would in effect be self-incrimination.

Any statement that the accused does make to the police must be voluntary to be admitted at trial. One test for whether a statement is voluntary is whether the statement was obtained without fear of prejudice or hope of advantage held out by a person in authority. For example, if a person is promised a more lenient sentence or threatened with a greater punishment if a statement is not given, the statement would not be voluntary.

An example of the court's application of this rule is the case of *R. v. Zappone*,[13] a decision of the Alberta Court of Appeal. The accused was involved in a traffic accident in which one person was killed. The accused asked the arresting officer if she would be charged with manslaughter. The officer told her that he was charging her with an offence under the provincial Highway Act, that she would receive a ticket, and that the maximum fine was $2 000 under the Act. The accused then gave a statement to the officer which suggested that she had failed to stop for a stop sign. The accused was charged with the provincial offence and also with dangerous driving causing death, an indictable offence under the Code. At her trial she testified that she gave a statement to the officer because the officer had led her to believe that she would be charged with the less serious offence if she co-operated.

The Court of Appeal held that the officer had offered her an inducement of a lesser charge and therefore her statement should not have been admitted. The court ordered her acquittal.

This is not the only test however for whether a statement has been voluntary. The Supreme Court of Canada in *R. v. Horvath*[14] has held that "voluntary" means among other things "of free will." So if, for example, a statement was given under oppressive or coercive circumstances, it may not be considered voluntary. In *Horvath*, the accused, a 17-year-old male had undergone intensive interrogation that left him in a state of "complete emotional disintegration." His final interview by a skilled interrogator put him in a mild hypnotic trance and resulted in him making a confession. In this situation, the statement could not be considered voluntary.

The case of *Moore v. The Queen*[15] illustrates one exception to the right to remain silent. In this case the accused had run a red light on his bicycle. An officer saw him and attempted to give him a ticket. Moore refused to

---

12. (1988), 40 C.C.C. (3d) 531 (Ont.C.A.).
13. (1991), 80 Alta.L.R. (2d) 424.
14. (1980), 44 C.C.C. (2d) 385 (S.C.C.).
15. (1979), 43 C.C.C. (2d) 83 (S.C.C.).

stop or to give his name to the officer. He was finally charged with the offence of obstructing a police officer in the performance of his duties for failing to identify himself. The Supreme Court of Canada held that Moore had obstructed the officer who was performing his duty when asking Moore his name so that the officer could charge Moore with the offence. The decision is limited to situations where the officer actually observes the accused committing an offence and where there is no power to arrest unless and until the officer tries to identify the accused so that the accused can be charged with the offence. The court distinguished this case from another where a person was acting in what the police regarded as a suspicious manner. The accused refused to identify himself, saying that the police would have to arrest him. In this case, the court held that the accused did not need to identify himself. The difference was that the police did not observe the accused committing an offence.

Moore was decided before the Charter came into effect so it is not known how the Supreme Court would deal with this case today. However, a decision of the Saskatchewan Queen's Bench in 1990 followed the *Moore* decision.[16] In this case, the accused was allowing his dogs to run loose which violated a city by-law. He was observed by a police constable. When asked, the accused refused to identify himself, saying that he would get a ticket if he did. The court held that he had obstructed a police officer in the performance of his duties. The court stated that even if requiring people found committing offences to identify themselves violated the Charter it was a reasonable limitation under s.1 of the Charter.[17]

Another exception to the right to remain silent is under provincial laws which require motorists to produce a driver's licence, vehicle registration, and proof of insurance when requested by an officer.

b. *Fingerprinting and Photographing*

A person under arrest for an indictable offence (including a hybrid offence) is required to submit to fingerprinting and photographing. Mandatory fingerprinting has been challenged under the Charter, but the Supreme Court of Canada has held that it is not a violation of the right against self-incrimination.[18] This requirement is dictated by the Identification of Criminals Act. However, if an accused is under arrest for a summary conviction offence, the police have no right to require fingerprinting or photographing. Note, a person may also be given a date

---

16. *R. v. Hudson* (1990) 18 C.R.D. 725.30-01 (Sask.Q.B.).
17. Section 1 allows a law which violates a Charter right or freedom to be enforced if the violation is a reasonable limitation justifiable in a free and democratic society; see Chapter One under The Canadian Charter of Rights and Freedoms.
18. *R. v. Beare; R. v. Higgins*, [1988] 2 S.C.R. 387.

and time to appear for fingerprinting and photographing with an appearance notice, promise to appear, recognizance, or summons (s.502 of the Code).

c. Arbitrary Detention

Section 9 of the Charter provides:

> **9. Everyone has the right not to be arbitrarily detained or imprisoned.**

Some of the most important issues under s.9 have been the meaning of detention and the meaning of arbitrary.

(i) Meaning of detention

An arrest includes a detention but detention has a broader meaning. There are three ways a person can be detained: (1) by using physical restraint, (2) by using psychological means, that is, where a person is made to believe he or she has no choice but to remain even though no threat has been made, and (3) by giving a demand or direction where there will be legal consequences if the person refuses the demand or direction. In *R. v. Therens*,[19] the accused had a car accident. When the police arrived, they asked him to take a breathalyzer test. The police did not inform him of his right to counsel which is required when a person is arrested or detained. The issue for the court was whether Therens had in fact been detained. The Court stated that a person is detained when he or she submits or acquiesces to the deprivation of liberty when the person reasonably believes the choice to do otherwise does not exist. Since refusing to take the test was an offence, Therens did not have a reasonable choice not to take the breathalyzer. Therefore, the court held that he had been detained.

Another type of case in which the meaning of detention has been considered involves people being questioned by customs officials at border crossings. For example, in *R. v. Simmons*[20] the Supreme Court of Canada said that the routine questions asked at border crossings and even baggage checks and a pat or frisk of outer clothing is not a detention. However, it is a detention if a person is given a strip or skin search in a private room or is taken to a hospital for searches of body cavities.

The issue of detention when the police question a person during the investigation of a crime arose in *R. v. Moran*[21] where the accused was eventually charged with the murder of a person he had known. He was called by the police and asked if he would talk to an officer. He was given a choice of meeting the officer at his home or going to the station. The

---

19. (1985), 18 C.C.C. (3d) 481 (S.C.C.).
20. (1988), 45 C.C.C. (3d) 296 (S.C.C.).
21. (1987), 36 C.C.C. (3d) 225 (Ont.C.A.), affd. 44 C.C.C. (3d) 193 (S.C.C.).

accused went to the station. A few days later he was called again and asked to come to the station to give some details to his statement and he complied. He was then questioned in a pressing manner concerning one of his statements. After this questioning he was allowed to leave the station and was not charged until several months later. The issue before the Ontario Court of Appeal was whether he had voluntarily gone to the station or whether he had been detained. The court stated that in deciding whether a person has been detained a court should look at such circumstances as:

(a) the language used by the police and whether the accused had a choice of being questioned at the police station, or at the accused's home, or whether the accused expressed a preference as to where the interview should be held.

(b) how the accused arrived at the station — escorted or by himself or herself

(c) whether the accused was arrested at the end of the interview

(d) the stage of the investigation, that is, whether the police had concluded that a crime had occurred and the accused was a suspect or whether the police were still gathering information

(e) whether the police had reasonable and probable grounds to believe that the accused had committed the offence

(f) the reasonable belief of the accused as to whether he or she was detained

(g) the type of questions put to the accused, that is, whether the questions were an attempt to gather information or whether the accused was confronted with evidence pointing to the accused's guilt

In this case, the court ruled that the accused was not detained.

(ii) Meaning of arbitrary

In *R. v. Hufsky*,[22] the Supreme Court of Canada considered the meaning of arbitrary. The issue in this case was whether random spot checks of motorists by the police are arbitrary detentions. The court applied the test in *Therens*[23] and said that randomly stopping motorists to check for driver's licence, proof of insurance, and impaired driving is a detention. These detentions are arbitrary because the police can stop any motorist without any criteria. However, even though the legislation allowing for random spot checks violates s.9 of the Charter, the court held that the legislation is justified under s.1 as a reasonable limitation in a free and democratic society. The basis on which the court reached this decision is the need for the police to prevent and stop impaired drivers.

---

22. (1988), 40 C.C.C. (3d) 398 (S.C.C.).
23. *Supra*, note 19.

d. Section 10 Rights

Section 10 of the Charter contains two specific rights upon arrest or detention.[24]

> **10. Everyone has the right on arrest or detention**
> **(a) to be informed promptly of the reasons therefor;**

In general, this means that the accused has a right to know what the charges are. Also recall that if a warrant is used under s.29(2)(a), the officer needs to have the warrant if feasible and the accused has a right to examine it.

> **(b) to retain and instruct counsel without delay and to be informed of that right; . . .**

There have been many cases considering the meaning of the right to counsel. Courts have upheld the right to counsel quite strictly. The Supreme Court of Canada has said that this right includes the opportunity to call a lawyer and the right to privacy when the accused talks to a lawyer. Once a person indicates a desire to speak to a lawyer, the police cannot question the person further until the person has had the opportunity to do so.[25] The Supreme Court of Canada[26] in 1990 held that as a part of this right the police must also inform the accused of the existence and availability of legal aid and duty counsel. Duty counsel is a legal aid lawyer who is available to advise accused persons usually before their first court appearances.

There have been three recent Supreme Court cases that have considered both s.10(a) and (b).

In *R. v. Black,*[27] the accused was arrested for attempted murder. She called her lawyer from the police station and had a brief conversation. Two hours later, the police told her that the victim had died and the charge was being upgraded to first-degree murder. She again asked to speak to her lawyer, but attempts to reach him were not successful. At this time she was intoxicated, upset, and physically injured. The police knew that she had limited intelligence and only a Grade 4 education. She asked the police if she would be held over the weekend and was told yes.

---

24. Section 10 also includes the right to "have the validity of the detention determined by way of *habeas corpus* and to be released if the detention is not lawful." The right of *habeas corpus* is one of our oldest rights. It means that a person has a right to a hearing to determine if the detention is legal, and, if it is not, then the person is to be released. Although an important right, it is not used generally at the pre-trial stage, but it tends to be used to test detention issues that come up when a person is already in an institution, being placed in solitary confinement, or is in special handling units. *Habeas corpus* allows a court to examine whether the decision for detention was made fairly and whether the decision maker had the authority to order the detention.
25. See, for example, *R. v. Manninen,* (1987), 34 C.C.C. (3d) 385 (S.C.C.); *R. v. Ross* (1989), 46 C.C.C. (3d) 129 (S.C.C.); *R. v. Dempsey* (1987), 77 N.S.R. (2d) 284.
26. *R. v. Brydges* (1990), 74 C.R. (3d) 129 (S.C.C.).
27. (1989), 50 C.C.C. (3d) 1 (S.C.C.).

At that point a police officer asked her where the knife was, and she told him it was in the kitchen drawer. He then asked her to tell him the whole story and she complied by giving a long statement to the officer.

The court held that she had been denied her right to counsel. The right to counsel can only be exercised meaningfully if the accused is aware of the jeopardy he or she is in. When she first spoke to her lawyer, the charge was attempted murder, a significantly different offence than first-degree murder. In other words, after the charge was changed to murder the police should have waited until she had spoken to her lawyer again before questioning her.

In another decision several months later, the Supreme Court again considered the issue of whether a waiver of the right to counsel was valid. In *R. v. Smith*,[28] the accused was charged with first-degree murder. He had been drinking with some friends when an argument began. He eventually left his friends but returned with a 12-gauge shotgun. He shot the victim at a distance of 96 feet (29 m) in the face and body. The victim fell back and died immediately. Smith called the police the next morning to surrender. When they arrested him, they had him walk out of his sister's house, while three officers trained guns on him, and then had him fall to his knees before they handcuffed him. He was told he was being arrested for the shooting incident and that he had a right to counsel. The police asked if he understood what that meant. He said that he didn't want a lawyer and then made a statement to the police. After making the statement, he was told that the victim had died. In this case, the court held that it was not necessary for the accused to know exactly what the charge was or be aware of all the factual details of the case to validly waive the right to counsel. In this case the accused must have known he was in serious jeopardy when he chose not to call a lawyer. He saw the shotgun blast and the fact that three officers were sent to arrest him indicated the seriousness of the situation. The Crown conceded that the accused's s.10(a) right had been violated but the court held that the violation was not serious since the accused probably knew that the victim had died. The court held that the waiver was valid.

In *R. v. Evans*,[29] the accused who was mentally handicapped was charged with first-degree murder. He was told that he was being arrested for possession of marijuana and that he had a right to a lawyer. The police continued questioning him about the murders even after he said he didn't understand what they were talking about. He was never told that he was a murder suspect. The police then lied to him by saying that his fingerprints had been found at the murder scene. At this point he confessed. The Supreme Court of Canada held that his rights had been seriously violated.

---

28. (1991), 63 C.C.C. (3d) 313 (S.C.C.).
29. (1991), 63 C.C.C. (3d) 289 (S.C.C.).

B. REMEDIES UNDER THE CHARTER

Where a person's rights under the Charter are violated, the person may attempt to have any evidence that was obtained as a result of the violation excluded from his or her trial.

Section 24(2) of the Charter provides that where . . .

> **24.(2) evidence was obtained in a manner that infringed or denied any rights or freedoms guaranteed by this Charter, the evidence shall be excluded if it is established that, having regard to all the circumstances, the admission of it would bring the administration of justice into disrepute.**

In other words, where evidence was obtained in a way that violated a person's rights, and its admission would bring the administration of justice into disrepute, the evidence will be excluded. Section 24 applies to any right that is violated, including violations of rights upon arrest or search.

Section 24 was used successfully by the accused in the cases discussed above. In *Black*,[30] the accused's confession was excluded. However, there was enough other evidence for her conviction to stand. In *Evans*,[31] however, the result of excluding the accused's confession was the over-turning of the conviction. Similarily, in *Therens*,[32] the results of the breathalyzer test were excluded and since there was no other evidence to support the conviction, the accused was found not guilty.

Excluding evidence which results in an apparently guilty person going free is often criticized in the media. For this reason it is worth looking at a case where the court examined closely the grounds for excluding evidence.

In *R. v. Collins*,[33] the Supreme Court of Canada discussed the steps for deciding whether evidence should be excluded when a Charter right has been violated. Not every situation will lead to the exclusion of evidence that has been obtained through a violation of the Charter. Generally, it is up to the accused to establish on a balance of probabilities that a violation has occurred.[34] Then the accused must show on a balance of probabilities that the admission of the evidence would bring the administration of justice into further disrepute. Disrepute may result if admitting the evidence would deny the accused a fair trial or if admitting the evidence would be a judicial condonation of improper police conduct. The court

---

30. *Supra*, note 27.
31. *Supra*, note 29.
32. *Supra*, note 19.
33. (1987), 33 C.C.C. (3d) 1 (S.C.C.).
34. An exception to this statement is where a warrantless search takes place. The Supreme Court of Canada has said that in this situation it is up to the Crown to show that the search was reasonable.

must consider the long-term consequences of regular admission or exclusion of this type of evidence. In other words, by not allowing the use of improperly obtained evidence, the court is discouraging the police from violating the rights of individuals. However, the court must also consider whether disrepute will result from excluding the evidence. The notion of disrepute includes the idea of community views, but not the views of uninformed members of the public or the community as presented in opinion polls. The court noted that:

> *Members of the public generally become conscious of the importance of protecting rights only when they are in some way brought closer to the system either personally or through some experience of friends or family . . . . The Charter is designed to protect the accused from the majority so the enforcement of the Charter must not be left to the majority.*

The court went on to say that the test is whether admission of the evidence would, in the eyes of a reasonable, dispassionate person who is fully aware of the circumstances, bring the administration of justice into disrepute.

In deciding if admission of the evidence would make the trial unfair, the court should look at a number of factors including the right violated and the type of evidence obtained. For example, it would make the trial unfair to use a confession obtained after the police denied a person the right to counsel. On the other hand, using real evidence, for example, a gun or knife that existed anyway, and which was obtained through a Charter violation, may not be unfair.

Another question the court should ask is: Would the evidence have been obtained if the right had not been violated? If the evidence was obtained illegally when it was possible to do otherwise, then a blatant and serious violation has occurred. Also related to the seriousness of the violation is whether the violation was committed deliberately or inadvertently and whether the violation was technical or serious. Also to be considered is whether the violation occurred in circumstances of urgency or necessity.

Finally, the court should consider the seriousness of the charge. For example, it would create more disrepute by excluding evidence that would lead to an acquittal for a serious charge if the violation was trivial.

C. POWERS TO SEARCH

1. General Powers and the Charter

Section 8 of the Charter states:

> **8. Everyone has the right to be secure against unreasonable search or seizure.**

The Supreme Court of Canada has said that the purpose of this section is to prevent unreasonable searches and seizures before they occur.[35] Therefore, generally, a search requires a prior authorization, that is, a **search warrant.** If the police do search without a warrant, the Crown will have the burden of showing that the search was reasonable. The Supreme Court has said that a search is reasonable if:

1. It is authorized by law.
2. The law itself is reasonable.
3. The search is carried out in a reasonable manner.[36]

As a general rule then, the police cannot search a place without first obtaining a search warrant. There are a few exceptions to this rule. Some warrantless searches are authorized by the Criminal Code and under the common law. Others are authorized by such federal acts as the Narcotic Control Act, the Food and Drugs Act, and the Customs Act. The authority to search under the Narcotic Control Act and the Food and Drugs Act is discussed in Appendix A. It should be noted that the authority given to the police under these two statutes to control the illegal use of drugs is somewhat broader than the general authority given under the Criminal Code. In addition, there are search powers granted to police in certain provincial acts.

A reasonable amount of force may be used in making the search. However, if excessive force is used by the searching officers, they may be liable in a civil action for damages or in a criminal action for assault. Sections 25 and 26 protect any person who is legally authorized to conduct a search from criminal or civil liability if the person acted on reasonable grounds.

If the search violates the Charter, the remedies under s.24 of the Charter (discussed above) apply. In other words, evidence obtained from a search that violates the Charter may be excluded if the court finds that its admission would bring the administration of justice into disrepute.

2. With a Warrant (Form 5)

OBTAINING A SEARCH WARRANT s.487

Section 487 authorizes a justice of the peace to issue a search warrant:

> **487.(1) A justice who is satisfied by information upon oath in Form 1 that there are reasonable grounds to believe that there is in a building, receptacle or place**
>
> **(a) anything upon or in respect of which any offence against this Act or any Act of Parliament has been or is suspected to have been committed,**
>
> **(b) anything that there are reasonable grounds to believe**

---

35. *Hunter v. Southam Inc.* (1984), 14 C.C.C. (3d) 97 (S.C.C.).
36. *Collins v. R., supra,* note 33.

> will afford evidence with respect to the commission of an
> offence against this Act or any other Act of Parliament, or
> (c) anything that there are reasonable grounds to believe is
> intended to be used for the purpose of committing any
> offence against the person for which a person may be arrested
> without warrant,
> may at any time issue a warrant . . . authorizing a person
> named therein or a peace officer . . . to search the building,
> receptacle or place for any such thing, and to seize it, and . . .
> bring the thing seized before or make a report in respect
> thereof to, the justice . . . .

The courts have consistently held that a search warrant should not be lightly granted. A search warrant cannot authorize what in reality would amount to a "fishing expedition" for evidence. When the police request that a search warrant be issued, they must convince the justice in writing and under oath that there are reasonable grounds for believing that the conditions set forth in s.487 are satisfied. The evidence that is being sought needs to be described with enough particularity that the seachers can identify the thing to be seized.[37]

The Supreme Court of Canada considered the standard of reasonable grounds in *R. v. Debot*.[38] In this case the police conducted a search of the accused based on information from an informer that the accused would be conducting a drug transaction. This case did not involve a warrant. (Warrants cannot be used to search a person. However, warrantless body searches are allowed under the Food and Drugs Act in some circumstances.) Nonetheless, the court's statement on what constitutes reasonable grounds for conducting a search is relevant here. The court said that in determining whether the standard of reasonableness has been met, the court must consider all the circumstances, including:

- Was the information predicting an offence compelling?
- When information was based on an informer's tip, was the informer credible?
- Was the information corroborated by a police investigation prior to deciding to conduct the search?

In this case, the information about the offence was specific: the time and location was named as well as the parties to the transaction. Also:

- The informer gave the basis for the allegations.
- The police could take into account the accused's past record of drug offences.

---

37. *Purdy v. R.* (1972), 8 C.C.C. (2d) 52 (N.B.C.A.).
38. (1986), 30 C.C.C. (3d) 207, affd. (1989), 52 C.C.C. (3d) 193 (S.C.C.).

- The informer was known to the police as being reliable.
- Police information had confirmed that the accused and the informer had been seen together.
- Police surveillance confirmed the arrival of the accused's vehicle at the location of the transaction.

Therefore, in this case, the police had reasonable grounds to conduct the search. The court noted that if the informer had not been known as reliable or where fewer details of the transaction were given, greater police corroboration that the offence had occurred would be required. In *R. v. Berger*[39] the Saskatchewan Court of Appeal held that a warrant based on information from unnamed confidential sources, where there was no evidence to support the truth of the sources information, no information about how the sources obtained their information, and no independent evidence to support the informer's information, was not a sufficient basis for issuing a warrant.

A "building, place or receptacle" is given a very wide meaning. It includes, for example, boats, cars, backyards, safety deposit boxes in banks, furniture, household plumbing, dwelling-houses, business offices, and summer cottages. However, it does not include a human body. In *Laporte v. Laganiere*,[40] the police sought a warrant to search in the body of the accused for a bullet which was alleged to have been fired from police revolvers. To conduct the search a major operation would have been necessary because the bullet was deeply imbedded in the accused's shoulder. The Quebec court held that, for the purposes of s.487, the body is not a "place or receptacle." Similarly, one court has held that a warrant will not be issued to seize hair samples from an accused.[41] However, under s.256, it is possible to get a warrant to obtain a blood sample in impaired driving cases (see Chapter Eleven on Offences Involving Motor Vehicles).

The place of search must be specified in the warrant. As well, the owner or occupier of the property must be identified, along with the name of the accused. In addition, the warrant must describe the offence for which the evidence is being sought.

According to s.489, with a warrant issued under s.487, police searchers may seize, in addition to the things mentioned in the warrant, anything that on reasonable grounds they believe has been obtained or used in the commission of an offence. The police must have reasonable grounds and cannot seize property on the mere suspicion that the goods have been used or obtained through the commission of an offence. In *R. v. Askov*,[42]

---

39. (1989), 48 C.C.C. (3d) 185 (Sask.C.A.).
40. (1972), 18 C.R.N.S. 357 (Que.Q.B.).
41. *R. v. Legére* (1988), 43 C.C.C. (3d) 502 (N.B.C.A.), but see *contra R. v. Alderton* (1985), 44 C.R. (3d) 254 (Ont.C.A.).
42. (Ont.D.Ct.) Reported in *The Lawyers Weekly*, October 9, 1987.

the police had a warrant to search Askov's home for weapons. While searching the home, they also seized property they suspected was stolen. The property was taken to the police station for investigation to determine if it was indeed stolen. The court stated that the police action was a deliberate and flagrant disregard of his right under the Charter to be free from unreasonable seizure. The police had no reasonable or probable grounds to believe the goods were stolen.

Section 487 provides that a warrant must be executed by day unless it is specifically authorized to be used at night. *Day* is defined in s.2 as ". . . the period between six o'clock in the forenoon and nine o'clock in the afternoon of the same day." *Night* is defined in s.2 as ". . . the period between nine o'clock in the afternoon and six o'clock in the forenoon of the following day."

There are other sections in the Criminal Code that grant the right of search to the police if certain specific offences are involved. For example, s.164 authorizes a police officer to apply for a warrant to seize obscene publications. Section 199 allows a police officer to apply for a search warrant if he suspects, on reasonable grounds, that a gaming house (s.201), book-making place (s.202 and s.203), a lottery (s.206 and s.207) or a common bawdy-house (s.210) exists in any premises.[43]

When executing the warrant, the police have the same duties as discussed above in the *Landry*[44] case when entering private premises to make an arrest. That is, the police must give notice of their presence, notice of their authority, and notice of their purpose. Section 29 which requires the person to have the warrant on his or her person where feasible and to produce it when requested to do so applies to search warrants as well as to arrest warrants.

If entry is refused, the police are entitled to use force. They do not have to announce themselves if, for example, evidence will be destroyed. However, as the Supreme Court of Canada said in *R. v. Genest*,[45] a case which concerned an illegal search:

> *The greater the departure from the standards of behaviour required by the common law and the Charter, the heavier the onus on the police to show why they thought it necessary to use force in the process of an arrest or a search. The evidence to justify such behaviour must be apparent in the record, and must have been available to the police when they chose their course of conduct. The Crown cannot rely on ex post facto justifications.*

---

43. However, an Ontario court has held that s.199(1) is of no force and effect because it violates s.8 of the Charter by not meeting the normal standards for issuing a warrant, that is, that the information be given under oath and that the justice have reasonable grounds for issuing the warrant. See *Re Vella et al. and The Queen* (1984), 14 C.C.C. (3d) 513 (Ont.H.C.J.).
44. *Supra*, note 5.
45. (1989), 45 C.C.C. (3d) 385 at 408 (S.C.C.).

3. Telewarrants

In most situations the police officer must appear before a justice and lay an information to obtain a search warrant. Recent amendments to the Code allow the police, in certain circumstances, to obtain warrants over the telephone. These are called telewarrants. Section 487.1 states:

> **487.1(1) Where a peace officer believes that an indictable offence has been committed and that it would be impracticable to appear personally before a justice [of the peace] . . . the peace officer may submit an information on oath by telephone or other means of telecommunication to a justice . . .**

The justice will then record the information verbatim and must, as soon as is practicable, file it with the court.

The information must include the following:

> **(a) a statement of the circumstances that make it impracticable for the officer to appear personally before a justice**
> **(b) a statement of the indictable offence alleged, the place to be searched, and the items likely to be seized**
> **(c) a statement as to the officer's grounds for believing the items will be found in the place to be searched**

Once the search warrant is issued the officer must file a written report stating when the warrant was executed and what was seized.

Telewarrants must be executed by day unless the justice authorizes execution of it by night.

4. Search Without a Warrant

a. For Certain Offences

The Code allows the police, in certain limited circumstances, to conduct a search without a search warrant. This power is only granted for specific offences. If the offence the police are investigating is not one which authorizes a search without a warrant, then they must first seek a warrant.

Under s.101, a police officer who has reasonable grounds to believe that an offence has been, or is being, committed with respect to any provisions in the Code that deal with prohibited or restricted weapons, firearms or ammunition, may search, without a warrant, a person or a vehicle or any premises other than a dwelling-house. The power to seize incriminating items, or those items suspected of being incriminating, is the same as if the search had been authorized by a warrant under s.484.

Section 339 allows a police officer who has reasonable grounds to suspect that registered timber is being kept without the consent of the owner to enter the place where the timber is, without a search warrant.

Section 462 allows a peace officer to seize counterfeit money or tokens and anything intended to make counterfeit money or tokens.

b. Incident to Lawful Arrest

Apart from the provisions in the Criminal Code (s.101) and other federal acts such as the Customs Act, Narcotic Control Act, and the Food and Drugs Act *the right to search the person exists only as an incident to arrest.* This power is not conferred by the Criminal Code; it comes from the common law, which is preserved in such matters by s.8 of the Code. After the police have arrested an accused, they are entitled to conduct a search of the accused's person and seize anything in his or her possession or immediate surroundings for the purpose of securing evidence, for preventing escape, and for guaranteeing the safety of the accused and the officer.[46]

The Supreme Court of Canada recently considered the authority to search incident to arrest in *Cloutier v. Langlois.*[47] Cloutier had been stopped by the police for making an illegal right-hand turn with his car. A police check showed that he had several unpaid traffic fines. He became highly agitated and verbally abusive. The police then had him put his hands on the car roof and spread his legs and frisked him (lightly patted him down). He sued the officers for assault. The Supreme Court held that reasonable grounds are not necessary for a "frisk" search incident to an arrest. The court said "a frisk search incidental to a lawful arrest reconciles the public's interest in the effective and safe enforcement of the law on one hand, and on the other its interest in ensuring the freedom and dignity of individuals."

The court set out these limits on the common law right to search incident to arrest:

- The police have discretion whether a search is necessary for the effective and safe application of the law.
- The search must be for a valid criminal justice objective (e.g., to check for weapons or prevent escape).
- The search cannot be used to intimidate, ridicule, or pressure the accused to gain admissions.
- The search must not be conducted in an abusive way.

The Supreme Court has also held that before conducting a frisk search the police must inform the accused of the right to counsel. However, the

---

46. *Cloutier v. Langlois* (1990), 53 C.C.C. (3d) 257 (S.C.C.).
47. *Ibid.*

police do not have to wait until the accused calls a lawyer before conducting the search.[48]

In this case, the court held that the search was justified. Although in retrospect the police did not have any real reason to fear physical violence, there was ample evidence at the time that led them to believe the search was necessary for their safety.

Another recent Supreme Court of Canada case reached a different result. In *R. v. Greffe*,[49] the police had information that the accused would be bringing drugs into Canada from Amsterdam. The accused was detained at the airport by customs authorities and his luggage was searched. Nothing was found. He was then taken to a room for a strip search. At this point he had not been told of his right to counsel. He was then turned over to the RCMP who told him that he was being arrested for outstanding traffic warrants, that he had a right to consult counsel, and that he was being taken to a hospital for a rectal search. He was then taken to a hospital for a rectal exam. Two plastic bags containing heroin were recovered from his body.

The court held that there were two serious violations of Charter rights in this case. First, although the Customs Act authorizes this type of search without an arrest if there are reasonable grounds for the search, the accused was not informed of his right to counsel when he was detained for the strip search at the airport. Second, the intrusive body search which took place at the hospital on the basis of an arrest for traffic violations was a violation of his right to be secure against unreasonable search and seizure. In other words, a rectal search on the basis of an arrest for outstanding traffic warrants was not justifiable. Also, even though he was informed of his right to counsel before the rectal search, the notification was "tainted" because he did not know the true reasons for his arrest. The court also found that the police had not acted "in good faith." In other words, the violation of his rights was not unintentional. The court concluded that the evidence of the heroin had to be excluded because of the cumulative effect of the denial of his rights. The court stated:

> *Therefore, and not without great hesitation given the manifest culpability of the appellant, of a crime I consider heinous, I conclude that the integrity of our criminal justice system and the respect owed to our Charter are more important than the conviction of this offender.*

---

48. *Supra*, note 38.
49. (1990), 55 C.C.C. (3d) 161 (S.C.C.).

D. WIRETAPPING AND ELECTRONIC SURVEILLANCE

PRIVATE COMMUNI- CATION DEFINED s.183

A police officer may obtain permission to intercept private communications. Under s.183 the meaning of "intercept" includes listening, recording, or acquiring a communication. A private communication is defined in s.183 as

> **any oral communication or any telecommunication made under circumstances in which it is reasonable for the originator . . . to expect that it will not be intercepted by any person other than the person intended by the originator to receive it.**

The key point is whether it is reasonable to expect the communication to be private. In *Goldman v. The Queen*,[50] the accused had called a police station and made threatening remarks to an officer. The remarks had been recorded. The Supreme Court of Canada held that in this situation it would not be reasonable to expect that the remarks would not be overheard or recorded by another person.

APPLICATION FOR INTER- CEPTING PRIVATE COMMUNI- CATION s.185

Section 185 sets out the requirements for making an application for authorizing the interception of private communications. An application must be made in writing and put before a judge; it must be signed by the Attorney General of the province, the Solicitor General of Canada, or an agent specially designated by the Solicitor General or Attorney General. The application must be accompanied by an affidavit which may be sworn on the information and belief of a peace or public officer stating:

> **185.(1) . . .**
>
> **(c) the facts relied upon to justify the belief that an authorization should be given together with the particulars of the offence,**
>
> **(d) the type of private communication proposed to be intercepted,**
>
> **(e) the names, addresses, and occupations, if known, of all persons, the interception of whose private communications there are reasonable grounds to believe may assist the investigation of the offence, a general description of the nature and location of the investigation of the place, if known, at which private communications are proposed to be intercepted and a general description of the manner of interception proposed to be used,**
>
> **(f) the number of instances, if any on which the application has been made under this section in relation to the offence and a person named in the affidavit pursuant to**

---

50. (1979), 51 C.C.C. (2d) 1 (S.C.C.).

paragraph (e) and on which the application was withdrawn or no authorization was given, the date on which each application was made and the name of the judge to whom each application was made,

(g) the period for which the authorization is requested, and

(h) whether other investigative procedures have been tried and failed or why it appears that they are unlikely to succeed or that the urgency of the matter is such that it would be impractical to carry out the investigation of the offence using other investigative procedures.

Section 186 requires that before authorizing an interception the judge must be satisfied:

186.(1). . .

(a) that it would be in the best interests of the administration of justice to do so, and

(b) that other investigative procedures have been tried and have failed, other investigative procedures are unlikely to succeed or the urgency of the matter is such that it would be impractical to carry out the investigation of the offence using only other investigative procedures.

There are special restrictions on intercepting private communications at the office or residence of a lawyer [s.186(2) and (3)].

If the judge authorizes the interception, the authorization must:

186.(4). . .

(a) state the offence in respect of which private communication may be intercepted;

(b) state the type of private communication that may be intercepted;

(c) state the identity of the persons, if known, whose private communications are to be intercepted, generally describe the place at which private communications may be intercepted, if a general description of that place can be given, and generally describe the manner of the interception that may be used;

(d) contain such terms and conditions as the judge considers advisable in the public interest; and

(e) be valid for the period, not exceeding sixty days, set out therein.

**UNAUTHOR-
IZED
ELECTRONIC
SURVEIL-
LANCE
INDICTABLE
s.184(1)
Max: 5 years**

Unauthorized electronic surveillance is an indictable offence under s.184 of the Code. Section 184(2)(a) allows interception if one of the parties to the conversation consents. Until recently the police used this exception to intercept conversations between police informers and suspects. A 1990 decision of the Supreme Court of Canada has held, however, that the right to be secure against unreasonable searches and seizures applies to interceptions of private communications. Therefore, where the state (i.e., the police) is recording the conversation, s.8 of the Charter requires that the police get judicial authorization for the interception.[51] In other words, a private person can intercept the conversation if the person has the consent of one of the parties. The police, however, must go before a judge to get permission even though one of the parties consents.

QUESTIONS FOR REVIEW AND DISCUSSION

1   Explain the difference between a summons and an appearance notice.

2   When can an appearance notice be used?

3   When can force be used in making an arrest?

4   Explain the authority of private security officers to make arrests.

5   Summarize the situations where a police officer can make an arrest without a warrant.

6   Outline the pre-trial release procedures which must be followed after an arrest has been made.

7   What can happen to a police officer who makes an illegal arrest?

8   Briefly list the rights of a person upon being arrested.

9   How does the *Moore* case affect the right to remain silent?

10   How have the courts defined detention?

11   When is a detention arbitrary?

12   Explain how the Supreme Court of Canada has interpreted the accused's right to retain and consult counsel.

13   What is the usual procedure the police must follow to obtain a search warrant?

14   What can the police seize with a warrant?

15   What is a telewarrant?

16   Under what circumstances can the police search without a warrant?

17   What must a judge be satisfied about before authorizing the interception of a private communication?

---

51. *R. v. Duarte* (1990), 53 C.C.C. (3d) 1 (S.C.C.).

18 The RCMP were investigating a serious assault on three Americans who had been driving to their homes in Michigan. As they approached the International Bridge in Windsor, the Americans were cut off by another vehicle and forced to stop. The Americans were punched and attacked with a knife. The assailants then sped away. The victims identified the car of the assailants as a 1973 or 1975 blue Thunderbird. They picked out a photograph from police files of a man who looked like one of the attackers. However, it turned out that this man was not in Ontario at the time of the assault.

One of the officers, Larkin, reviewed police files looking for owners of Thunderbirds. He found that a man named Storrey had been stopped numerous times driving a 1973 blue Thunderbird. Larkin discovered that Storrey's police photograph closely resembled the photograph identified by the victims. Also, Storrey had a record of violent crime.

Did the police have authority to arrest Storrey? Explain.

See *Storrey v. The Queen* (1990), 53 C.C.C. (3d) 316 (S.C.C.).

19 a If a police officer finds a person committing an indictable offence listed in s.553, what must the officer first consider before he or she can lawfully make an arrest?

b What might the officer do, if he or she doesn't arrest the person, to compel the person's appearance in court?

20 Sam is walking down the street. Behind him he hears a woman shriek, "My purse! He's stolen my purse!" Sam turns around. He sees the woman who has had her purse stolen. She is standing still, staring at her empty hands. He can also see the head and shoulders of a man who appears to be running through the crowd on the sidewalk. A lot of people are staring at him but nobody is chasing him.

a Explain the authority of a private person to make an arrest.

b Should Sam chase the man who is running and arrest him?

21 Constable Dust has been issued a search warrant in accordance with s.487 of the Criminal Code, empowering him to search Gerry's house. When he arrives at the house, he insists that the warrant also entitles him to search Gerry. Is he right?

22 Constable Armstrong arrests Blaine in a department store for theft. He asks Blaine the whereabouts of his car and is informed the car is outside in the parking lot. Constable Armstrong proceeds to the parking lot. He finds Tom and John sitting in the car. He orders them out and then searches them both. Was he legally entitled to search Tom and John?

part
TWO

Criminal Code
Offences

chapter

SIX

Offences Against Public Order, Offences Involving Firearms, and the Administration of Law and Justice

Parts II, III, and IV of the Code

A. OFFENCES AGAINST PUBLIC ORDER: PART II

The offences in this part have to do with harm to the government or the government's authority. Offences in this Part, which are not discussed in this chapter, include committing an act that intimidates Parliament or the legislature (s.51), inciting to mutiny (s.53), and engaging in an unauthorized prize fight (s.83).

1. Treason

There are two types of treason in the Code. High treason under s.46(1) and treason under s.46(2):

HIGH TREASON
s.46(1), (3)(a)
Indictable
Life imprisonment
[s.47(1)]

46.(1) Every one commits high treason who, in Canada,

(a) kills or attempts to kill Her Majesty, or does her any bodily harm tending to death or destruction, maims or wounds her, or imprisons or restrains her;

(b) levies war against Canada or does any act preparatory thereto; or

(c) assists an enemy at war with Canada, or any armed forces against whom Canadian Forces are engaged in hos-

TREASON
s.46(2)
Indictable
Max: life for
offence under
s.46(a), (c), or
(d) or for
offence under
s.46(b) or (e)
while Canada
at war

TREASON
s.46(2)
Max: 14 years
for offence
under s.46(b) or
(e) if Canada
not at war

tilities, whether or not a state of war exists between Canada and the country whose forces they are.

(2) Every one commits treason who, in Canada,

(a) uses force or violence for the purpose of overthrowing the government of Canada or a province;

(b) without lawful authority, communicates or makes available to an agent of a state other than Canada, military or scientific information or any sketch, plan, model, article, note or document of a military or scientific character that he knows or ought to know may be used by that state for a purpose prejudicial to the safety or defence of Canada;

(c) conspires with any person to commit high treason or to do anything mentioned in paragraph (a);

(d) forms an intention to do anything that is high treason or that is mentioned in paragraph (a) and manifests that intention by an overt act; or

(e) conspires with any person to do anything mentioned in paragraph (b) or forms an intention to do anything mentioned in paragraph (b) and manifests that intention by an overt act.

(3) Notwithstanding subsection (1) or (2), a Canadian citizen or a person who owes allegiance to Her Majesty in right of Canada,

(a) commits high treason if, while in or out of Canada, he does anything mentioned in subsection (1); or

(b) commits treason if, while in or out of Canada, he does anything mentioned in subsection (2).

(4) Where it is treason to conspire with any person, the act of conspiring is an overt act of treason.

This is a rarely used section of the Code and one which is largely self-explanatory. Its general purpose is to prohibit acts which threaten the security of Canada.

High treason includes killing or attempting to kill the Queen, levying war against Canada, and assisting an enemy at war with Canada. High treason is a very serious indictable offence which is indicated by the penalty for its commission: a minimum term of life imprisonment.

Treason, an indictable offence, includes using force or violence to overthrow the government and providing to an agent of another country military or scientific information which might threaten the safety of Canada. Treason also includes conspiring with another person to commit high treason or treason and forming the intention to commit high treason or treason and demonstrating that intention by some overt act. The case of *R. v. Bleiler*[1] provides an example of an overt act which demonstrated

---

1. (1917), 28 C.C.C. 9 (Alta.C.A.).

an intention to commit treason. The accused wrote letters advising the German Emperor during World War One to purchase a certain device or invention which would be of assistance to the German army.

If acts of treason or high treason are committed in Canada, any person, whether he or she is a citizen of Canada, may be convicted. If similar acts are committed outside Canada, only Canadian citizens and persons owing allegiance to Canada may be convicted.

There are few cases on treason in Canada. However, one of them is *Lampel v. Berger*.[2] This case involved the meaning of the phrase "assisting an enemy at war with Canada" [s.46(1)(c)]. Berger had agreed to sell to Lampel a piece of property in Sarnia, Ontario in 1917 (during World War One). Berger was a Hungarian citizen who was living in the United States. Hungary was at war with Canada and the United States was a neutral country at the time of the contract. Therefore, Berger was an alien enemy subject living in neutral territory. Before paying for the property, Lampel (a Canadian citizen) learned that Berger regularly sent money to his wife and children in Hungary. Lampel was in doubt as to whether he could lawfully pay the purchase money to Berger because this might be construed as assisting an enemy at war with Canada. So, he started a civil action to have a court determine the matter. The first issue in the case was whether the contract regarding the property was valid. The court said that it was unlawful for a resident of Canada to trade with "the enemy", but for the purposes of contract law Berger was not considered an enemy because he was not residing or carrying on business in an enemy country. Therefore, the contract was valid. The second issue was whether Lampel could pay the purchase money to Berger, knowing that Berger would be sending some of the money to Hungary. The court said that money sent to Hungary would become part of the financial resources of that enemy country and thus would aid the enemy by contributing to its capacity to prolong the war. Lampel knew of Berger's intention to send the money and if he enabled Berger to carry out his intention by paying to him the purchase money, he would be assisting an enemy at war with Canada, contrary to the Criminal Code. The court concluded that it was its duty to intervene by impounding the money and keeping it in court to the credit of Berger until after the war.

SEDITION
s.61
Indictable
Max: 14 years

2. Sedition

In general, the offence of sedition involves advocating the overthrow of the government by the use of force.

The offence of sedition is set out in s.61:

> **61. Every one who**
> **(a) speaks seditious words,**

---

2. (1917), 38 D.L.R. 47 (Ont.S.Ct.).

(b) publishes a seditious libel, or
(c) is a party to a seditious conspiracy,
is guilty of an indictable offence . . . .

Section 61 contains three separate crimes of sedition. For each offence it is necessary that a seditious intention be involved. The term "seditious intention" is defined in s.59(4):

SEDITIOUS INTENTION DEFINED s.59(4)

59.(4) Without limiting the generality of the meaning of the expression "seditious intention," every one shall be presumed to have a seditious intention who
(a) teaches or advocates, or
(b) publishes or circulates any writing that advocates,
the use, without the authority of law, of force as a means of accomplishing a governmental change within Canada.

That is, spoken words or a published libel (e.g., written words) are seditious only if they express a seditious intention. Similarly, a seditious conspiracy is an agreement between two or more persons to carry out a seditious intention.

Like treason, the offence of sedition is rarely committed. It appears that, in general, seditious intention requires an intention to incite violence or to create a public disturbance or disorder against the state. However, a 1951 Supreme Court of Canada decision split on the issue of whether seditious intention always requires an intention to incite violence or public disorder.[3]

The meaning of seditious intention is further clarified by s.60:

EXCEPTION REGARDING SEDITIOUS INTENTION s.60

60. Notwithstanding subsection 59(4), no person shall be deemed to have a seditious intention by reason only that he intends, in good faith,
(a) to show that Her Majesty has been misled or mistaken in her measures;
(b) to point out errors or defects in
    (i) the government or constitution of Canada or a province,
    (ii) the Parliament of Canada or the legislature of a province, or
    (iii) the administration of justice in Canada;
(c) to procure, by lawful means, the alteration of any matter of government in Canada; or
(d) to point out, for the purpose of removal, matters that produce or tend to produce feelings of hostility and ill-will between different classes of persons in Canada.

---

3. *Boucher v. R.* (1951), 99 C.C.C. 1 (S.C.C.).

This provision recognizes that free criticism is a basic element of modern democratic government. The purpose of s.60 is to protect the widest range of public discussion and controversy, so long as it is done in good faith and for the purposes mentioned. However, this section does not protect a person from criminal liability if, in addition to having good faith, the person intends to incite violence or public disorder.

3. Unlawful Assemblies and Riots

UNLAWFUL ASSEMBLY s.63 Summary conviction [s.66]

a. *Unlawful Assemblies*

It is a summary conviction offence for a group of three or more who have assembled for a common purpose to conduct themselves in such a way that their neighbours have reasonable fears that the peace will be disturbed.

Section 63(1) defines the term "unlawful assembly":

> **63.(1) An unlawful assembly is an assembly of three or more persons who, with intent to carry out any common purpose, assemble in such a manner or so conduct themselves when they are assembled as to cause persons in the neighbourhood of the assembly to fear, on reasonable grounds, that they**
> **(a) will disturb the peace tumultuously; or**
> **(b) will by that assembly needlessly and without reasonable cause provoke other persons to disturb the peace tumultuously. . . .**
>
> **(3) Persons are not unlawfully assembled by reason only that they are assembled to protect the dwelling-house of any one of them against persons who are threatening to break and enter it for the purpose of committing an indictable offence therein.**

The elements of an unlawful assembly are: (1) an assembly of three or more persons (2) who have the intent to carry out a common purpose and (3) whose conduct (or manner of assembling) causes the persons in the neighbourhood to fear that there will be a tumultuous disturbance of the peace. The disturbance of the peace can be caused by the members of the assembly or by others who are needlessly or without reasonable cause provoked to disturb the peace.

An assembly that starts out lawfully can become unlawful if the conduct of the group creates fear of a disturbance [s.63(2)]. Similarly, there may be an unlawful assembly even though the common purpose of the persons involved is lawful. The important point is the manner in which the purpose is, or is likely to be, carried out. If the manner causes persons in the neighbourhood to fear that there will be a disturbance, an offence is committed regardless of the lawfulness of the common purpose. Of course, the fear must be based on reasonable grounds. For example in *R. v. Kalyn*,[4] the accused set up a stereo system in front of Kalyn's cottage and organized a party. The party got out of control and eventually there was a confrontation with the police. The court held that the common intention was to have a party, which was not unlawful. Therefore, the assembly was at first lawful, but became unlawful when the crowd turned unruly and violent. The court also held that the conduct of a few members of the assembly could make the assembly unlawful and that all the members would be liable for the offence.

b. Riots

A riot occurs when the unlawful assembly actually begins to disturb the peace. Section 64 states:

**RIOT
s.64
Indictable
Max: 2 years
[s.65]**

> **64. A riot is an unlawful assembly that has begun to disturb the peace tumultuously.**

The term "tumultuous" is not defined in the Code but in *R. v. Lockhart*[5] the Nova Scotia Court of Appeal said that "the word must connote in a general sense some element of violence or force which may be exhibited by menaces or threats." In this case a person named Keddy was arrested for disturbing the peace. A short while later a group of 20 or 30 people arrived at the police station demanding his release. One person in the crowd threatened to break Keddy out if he wasn't released. Another person offered to fight the police. The court held that in this case a riot had taken place when the threats were made. The threats, swearing, and yelling created an atmosphere of violence that was "tumultuous".

**READING
PROCLAMA-
TION
DURING RIOT
s.67**

Taking part in a riot is an indictable offence under s.65.

Under s.67, where a riot of at least 12 persons is taking place, a justice, mayor, or sheriff, or the lawful deputy of a mayor or sheriff can go to the place and after commanding silence read the following proclamation:

> *Her Majesty the Queen charges and commands all persons being assembled immediately to disperse and peaceably to depart to their habitations or to their lawful business on the pain of being guilty of an offence for which, on conviction, they may be sentenced to imprisonment for life . . . .*

**OFFENCES
RELATED TO
PROCLAMA-
TION
s.68
Indictable
Max: life
imprisonment**

It is an indictable offence under s.68 to oppose, hinder, or assault anyone making or beginning to make a proclamation. It is also an offence under this section not to disperse within 30 minutes after the proclamation has been made or within 30 minutes of when the proclamation would have been made if the person trying to make it had not been opposed, hindered, or assaulted.

---

4. (1980), 52 C.C.C. (2d) 378 (Sask.C.A.).
5. (1976), 15 N.S.R. (2d) 512 (N.S.C.A.).

4. Explosive Substances

DUTY OF CARE RE EXPLOSIVE SUBSTANCES s.79

Section 79 of the Code states that every one who has explosives in his or her possession is under a duty to use reasonable care to prevent harm to property or persons:

> **79. Every one who has an explosive substance in his possession or under his care or control is under a legal duty to use reasonable care to prevent bodily harm or death to persons or damage to property by that explosive substance.**

EXPLOSIVE SUBSTANCES DEFINED s.2

Section 2 defines "explosive substance", as including a bomb, grenade, dynamite, or any other similar incendiary substance or device. The term also includes anything intended to be used to make an explosive substance and anything used or intended to be used to cause an explosion with an explosive substance.

BREACH OF DUTY s.80 Indictable Max: 14 years' imprisonment for causing or likely to cause bodily harm or property damage, life imprisonment for causing or likely to cause death

Section 80 makes it an indictable offence to fail, without lawful excuse, to perform the duty regarding explosives. If an explosion resulted from the breach of the duty and a person was killed, or was likely to have been killed, the punishment is life imprisonment. If the explosion caused or was likely to have caused bodily harm or property damage, the punishment is imprisonment for 14 years. In other words, it is not necessary that death, harm, or damage actually take place, only that death, harm, or damage was likely. On the other hand, if a person fails to perform the duty, but no explosion takes place, then no offence under this section has occurred.

USING EXPLOSIVES s.81 Indictable Max: life imprisonment for s.81(a) or (b), 14 years for s.81(c) or (d)

Under s.81 it is an indictable offence (a) to do anything with the intent to cause an explosion that is likely to cause serious bodily harm, death, or serious property damage; (b) to cause an explosion with the intent to do bodily harm; (c) to throw or place an explosive anywhere with the intent to damage property without lawful excuse; and (d) to make or possess an explosive with the intent to endanger life or cause serious property damage. These and other offences in s.81 require proof of the specific intents mentioned, unlike s.80 offences which simply require proof of a failure to exercise reasonable care.

POSSESSION WITHOUT LAWFUL EXCUSE s.82 Indictable Max: 5 years

A separate offence of making, having in possession, or having care and control of an explosive without lawful excuse is contained in s.82. The section puts the onus on the accused to show a "lawful excuse" for making or having possession of the explosive. This section is open to challenge under the Charter because it sets up a reverse onus clause. (See Chapter Two for a discussion of these clauses.)

B. FIREARMS AND OFFENSIVE WEAPONS: PART III

Part III of the Code outlines offences involving the use, possession, and distribution of weapons. In brief, it forbids the possession of certain weapons and requires certificates or permits for purchasing and possessing other weapons.

1. Firearms

a. Definition

Firearm is defined under s.84 as "any barrelled weapon from which any shot, bullet, or other missile can be discharged and that is capable of causing serious bodily injury or death to a person, and includes any frame or receiver of such a barrelled weapon and anything that can be adapted for use as a firearm."

However, s.84 specifically states that certain types of weapons are not considered firearms in certain situations. These include antique firearms that are not restricted weapons and are not intended to be discharged, devices used for such purposes as distress signals or firing blanks, or devices used for slaughtering or tranquillizing animals.

In *R. v. Covin and Covin*,[6] the Supreme Court of Canada interpreted the last part of this definition, "anything that can be adapted for use as a firearm." The court noted that most pieces of wood, pipe, and metal could, given time and expertise, be adapted for use as a firearm. The court held that the exact meaning of this phrase depends on the offence for which the firearm is being used. In this case the accused were charged with robbery and with using a firearm while committing an indictable offence. Their conviction for robbery was not appealed. However, the conviction for the second offence was appealed on the grounds that the weapon they used was not a "firearm". The gun that they used in the robbery was a damaged airgun with several missing pieces, some of which were necessary for the gun's operation.

To determine whether the airgun was a firearm the court examined the purpose of the offence, stating that it is necessary to protect the victim of an offence (e.g., robbery) from serious injury or death by discouraging the use of firearms during the commission of the offence. The court explained:

> *Therefore, whatever is used at the scene of the crime must be in my view be proven by the Crown as capable, either at the outset or through adaptation or assembly, of being loaded, fired and thereby having the potential of causing serious bodily harm during the commission of the offence, or during the flight after the commission of the main offence . . . .*

In this case, an experienced person would have taken 10 to 15 minutes to replace the missing parts. The court allowed the appeal. It concluded

---

6. (1983), 8 C.C.C. (3d) 240 (S.C.C.).

that there were not the necessary "ingredients" or "ability" to make the gun operable and therefore it was not a firearm.

b. Controlling the Use of Firearms

Section 106 of the Code states a person must obtain a firearms acquisition certificate before buying a gun. A certificate will not be issued to anyone:

REQUIRE-MENTS FOR A FIREARM ACQUISITION CERTIFICATE s.106

- under 16 years of age,
- who has a record of conviction for a violent crime,
- who is on probation and under an order not to possess firearms,
- who has a history of a mental disorder involving violence in the last five years, or
- who has a history of violent behaviour in the last five years.

It is possible for a person under 16 to obtain a certificate under s.110 if the applicant hunts or traps as a way of life.

An additional requirement of s.106 is that the applicant has completed a course and passed a test on the safe handling of guns. This requirement was made part of the Code in 1978; however, s.106(3) states that this paragraph shall come into effect in each province upon proclamation. At this time, it is not yet in effect in any province, partly because of disputes over who will pay for the training of applicants.

USE OF FIREARM DURING COMMISSION OF OFFENCE s.85 Indictable Max: 14 years Min: 1 year for first offence; 3 years for second or subsequent offence

c. Firearm Offences

Section 85 makes it an indictable offence to use a firearm during the commission of an indictable offence or during flight after the commission of an indictable offence. The person must be convicted of an indictable offence before he or she can be convicted of this offence.

Section 86(1) makes pointing a firearm at another person, without lawful excuse and whether or not the firearm is loaded, a hybrid offence.

Under s.86(2), anyone, without lawful excuse, who carries, handles, ships, or stores a firearm or ammunition in a careless manner or without reasonable precautions for the safety of other persons has committed a hybrid offence.

POINTING A FIREARM s.86(1) Hybrid Max: 5 years

Two provincial courts of appeal have held that this latter offence violates the Charter.[7] Both decisions held that s.86(2) creates a strict liability offence since a person could be convicted for acting carelessly or for not taking reasonable precautions. Imposing criminal liability for the violation of a civil standard of liability could not be justified under s.1 of the Charter in this situation.

---

7. *R. v. Durham* (1991), 66 C.C.C. (3d) 66 (Ont.Ct.[Gen.Div.]); *R. v. Finlay* (1991), 64 C.C.C. (3d) 557 (Sask.C.A.).

2. Weapons

a. Definition

CARELESS
USE OF A
FIREARM
s.86(2)
Hybrid
Max: 2 years for
first offence;
5 years for
second or
subsequent
offence

The term "weapon" is defined in s.2. It includes firearms and (1) anything used or intended to be used to cause death or injury to persons, whether it was designed to cause death or injury, and (2) anything used or intended to be used for the purpose of threatening or intimidating any person.

Two provincial courts of appeal have held that it is the subjective intent of the user that determines whether a thing is a weapon and not the objective intent of the manufacturer.[8] For example, a rifle is a weapon. A beer bottle is not a weapon but a container for beer. However, the bottle could be a weapon if a person used it or intended to use it to assault another person. In other words, almost any object could be a weapon, depending on the intention of the possessor.

b. Prohibited Weapons

PROHIBITED
WEAPON
DEFINED
s.84

"Prohibited weapon" is defined in s.84 as:

> **(a) any device or contrivance designed or intended to muffle or stop the sound or report of a firearm,**
>
> **(b) any knife that has a blade that opens automatically by gravity or centrifugal force or by hand pressure applied to a button, spring or other device in or attached to the handle of the knife,**
>
> **(c) a weapon of any kind, not being a restricted weapon . . . that is capable of firing bullets in rapid succession during one pressure of the trigger,**
>
> **(d) any firearm adapted from a rifle or shotgun, whether by sawing, cutting or other alteration or modification, that, so adapted, has a barrel that is less than 457 mm in length or that is less than 660 mm in overall length, or**
>
> **(e) a weapon of any kind, not being an antique firearm or a firearm of a kind commonly used in Canada for hunting or sporting purposes, that is declared by order of the Governor in Council to be a prohibited weapon.**

The New Brunswick Court of Appeal considered the meaning of para.(b), "[a] knife [with] a blade that opens . . . by gravity or centrifugal force." The court stated that a knife can fall within this definition even

---

8. *R. v. Murray* (1991), 65 C.C.C. (3d) 507 (Ont.C.A.); *R. v. Roberts* (1990), 60 C.C.C. (3d) 509 (N.S.C.A.).

though it was not designed to open as such if, because of wear or alteration, it can be opened through gravity or centrifugal force.[9]

c. Restricted Weapons

The term "restricted weapon" is also defined in s.84:

RESTRICTED WEAPON DEFINED s.84

84.(a) any firearm, not being a prohibited weapon, designed, altered or intended to be aimed and fired by the action of one hand,
   (b) any firearm that
      (i) is not a prohibited weapon, has a barrel that is less than 470 mm in length and is capable of discharging centre-fire ammunition in a semi-automatic manner, or
      (ii) is designed or adapted to be fired when reduced to a length of less than 660 mm by folding, telescoping or otherwise, or
   (c) any firearm that is designed, altered or intended to fire bullets in rapid succession during one pressure of the trigger and that on January 1, 1978, was registered as a restricted weapon and formed part of a gun collection in Canada of a genuine gun collector, or
   (d) a weapon of any kind, not being a prohibited weapon or a shotgun or rifle of a kind that, in the opinion of the Governor in Council, is reasonable for use in Canada for hunting or sporting purposes, that is declared by order of the Governor in Council to be a restricted weapon.

d. Restricted Weapons Certificates

A person who is at least 18 may apply for a permit to have a restricted weapon under s.109 of the Code. The weapon must be examined by a firearms registrar and must have a serial number on it for identification, unless it is an antique firearm, in which case it must be described for purposes of identification.

PERMIT FOR RESTRICTED WEAPON s.109

To obtain a certificate, the restricted weapon must be required by the applicant:

• to protect life,

• for use in connection with his or her lawful profession or occupation,

• for use in target practice, under the auspices of a shooting club approved for the purposes of this section by the Attorney General of the province,

---

9. *R. v. Richard and Walker* (1981), 63 C.C.C. (2d) 333.

- for the use in target practice in accordance with conditions proposed to be attached to the permit to be issued in respect of the restricted weapon;

or the restricted weapon must be:

- part of a gun collection of a genuine gun collector, or
- deemed to be a relic.

The certificate will include the address of the applicant's home or business where the weapon may be kept.

PERMIT TO
TRANSPORT
RESTRICTED
WEAPON
s.110

e. *Permit to Transport a Restricted Weapon*

A permit is also necessary to transport a restricted weapon from one place to another (s.110). It is also necessary to obtain a permit to convey a restricted weapon to a firearms registrar when applying for a registration certificate. The same requirements to possess a restricted weapon apply to obtain a permit to transport a restricted weapon.

POSSESSION
OF WEAPON
OR
IMITATION
s.87
Indictable
Max: 10 years

f. *Offences Involving Weapons*

Under s.87, it is an indictable offence to possess a weapon or an imitation of a weapon for a purpose dangerous to the public peace or for the purpose of committing an offence. For a conviction under this section, the prosecution must prove (1) possession and (2) intention.

The fact that a person was carrying a weapon for a defensive purpose does not necessarily mean that the weapon is not possessed for a purpose dangerous to the public. In *R. v. Nelson*,[10] the accused feared being attacked by two men, the Bougie brothers, with whom he had had some previous trouble. Before going to a club where he expected that they would be, he armed himself with a double bladed homemade knife having an 18-inch (45-cm) blade. After drinking some beer at the club, the accused got into a fight with one of the Bougies and the two of them were required to leave the club. Outside the club, the accused was confronted by the Bougie brothers and he began swinging his knife at them, injuring both of them. The accused was convicted of carrying a weapon for a purpose dangerous to the public peace. The court noted that even though the weapon was intended for defence purposes, it was necessary to consider other factors such as the nature of the weapon, how it was acquired, the manner of its use, the time, the place, and relevant statements or actions of the accused. The court concluded:

---

10. (1972), 8 C.C.C. (2d) 29 (Ont.C.A.).

In this instance the character of the weapon and the reasons for its acquisition as well as the clear intention of the [accused] to make use of what was, under the circumstances, a clearly illegal method of defence make it clear that the weapon was being carried for a purpose dangerous to the public peace.

In *R. v. Proverbs*,[11] the court also considered the meaning of the phrase "having possession for a purpose dangerous to the public peace." It stated that the purpose must be determined at the instant of time that precedes the weapon's use. In this case the police had a search warrant to search Proverbs' apartment. When they arrived at the apartment, they knocked on the door and announced they were the police. There was no response, but they believed that someone was inside. Eventually, they had the caretaker open the door and they found the accused crouched over a loaded shotgun. He claimed that he had only heard the knocking and thought someone was breaking in and that he did not know the officers were police. He was convicted of an offence under s.87. On appeal the court stated:

If the jury were satisfied that prior to the entry of the police into his premises, Proverbs did not have the weapon for a purpose dangerous to the public peace, and he only loaded it, on the sudden. . . unaware that it was the police seeking entry, because he was in fear of harm to himself and only intended to use it if necessary to defend himself . . . then the Crown would not have proved [the elements of the offence]. . . .

The court ordered a new trial.

WHILE ATTENDING PUBLIC MEETING s.88 Summary conviction

Under s.88 it is a summary conviction offence to, without lawful excuse, have possession of a weapon while attending or on the way to attending a public meeting.

CARRYING CONCEALED WEAPON s.89 Hybrid Max: 5 years

Section 89 makes carrying a concealed weapon without a permit a hybrid offence.

Under s.90, possession of a prohibited weapon is a hybrid offence.

POSSESSION OF PROHIB- ITED WEAPON s.90 Hybrid Max: 5 years

An interesting recent decision of the Ontario Court of Appeal[12] found the accused not guilty of possession of a prohibited weapon. The weapon, nunchaku sticks, was found in his apartment during a search by the police. The pair of sticks consisted of a hard inner core of plastic covered by soft foam padding and held together by a light chain. The accused testified that the sticks were a "training simile" that he used for martial arts training. The court held that by the subjective intent test of the definition of weapon in s.2 of the Code the sticks were not a weapon

---

11. (1983), 9 C.C.C. (3d) 249 (Ont.C.A.).
12. *Supra*, note 8.

since the accused did not use or intend to use them to cause death or injury. The court stated that Parliament cannot declare an object to be a prohibited weapon unless it is first a weapon as defined in s.2. Therefore, the accused was acquitted. The court also noted that recent proposals to amend the Code dealing with weapons offences would change the definition of weapon to include "anything designed to be used" for causing death or injury, which would have covered the situation in this case.

POSSESSION OF UNREG- ISTERED RESTRICTED WEAPON s.91(1) Hybrid Max: 5 years

Under s.91, possession of a restricted weapon is a hybrid offence unless the person in possession has a permit.

There are several other offences outlined in s.93 to s.117 that concern the sale, delivery, or acquisition of firearms and other weapons.

C. BRIBERY, OBSTRUCTING A POLICE OFFICER, PERJURY, AND OBSTRUCTING JUSTICE: PART IV

1. Bribery

In general, bribery is the accepting or offering of an undue reward or "payoff" in order to influence a public official's behaviour in office. There are several Code sections involving bribery. These sections mention various types of *rewards*, *public officials*, and *behaviours*.

An example of a Code section involving bribery is s.119:

BRIBERY OF JUDICIAL OFFICERS s.119 Indictable Max: 14 years

119.(1) Every one who
(a) being the holder of a judicial office, or being a member of Parliament or of the legislature of a province, corruptly
  (i) accepts or obtains,
  (ii) agrees to accept, or
  (iii) attempts to obtain,
any money, valuable consideration, office, place or employment for himself or another person in respect of anything done or omitted or to be done or omitted by him in his official capacity, or
(b) gives or offers corruptly to a person mentioned in paragraph (a) any money, valuable consideration, office, place or employment in respect of anything done or omitted or to be done or omitted by him in his official capacity for himself or another person,
is guilty of an indictable offence . . . .

In this bribery offence, it is clear that the public official could be a judge, a member of Parliament, or a member of a provincial legislature.

The reward could be money, a job, or practically anything of value. The behaviour involved could be any act or omission by the official in carrying out his or her public duties.

Section 119(2) protects judges from spurious charges by requiring the consent of the Attorney General of Canada before proceedings can be instituted.

Bribery involves two parties: the public official and any other person. Offences may be committed by one or both of them. Paragraph (a) refers to three separate offences which may be committed by the public official: (i) actually accepting a bribe; (ii) simply agreeing to accept a bribe; and (iii) soliciting or trying to obtain a bribe. Paragraph (b) refers to two offences which may be committed by the other person: (i) actually giving a bribe to the official and (ii) simply offering a bribe to the official.

If a person offers a bribe to an official, it is no defence that the official refused it. In other words, the offence is complete when the offer is made.

It is also necessary that the offering, giving, or accepting be done "corruptly". The word "corruptly" means with the intention to accomplish the purpose forbidden by the Code.[13] So, under s.119, it must be shown that the offering, accepting, etc. was done with the intention of having the official do or omit to do some act in his or her official capacity.

In *R. v. Bruneau*,[14] the accused was charged with agreeing to accept $10 000 for the use of his influence in his official capacity as a member of Parliament. Bruneau had agreed to accept the money from B, one of his constituents, to use his influence to have the federal government buy B's property as the site for a post office. The usual practice, which was followed in this case, was that after a number of possible sites were examined by federal officials, the local member of Parliament was consulted for his recommendation. B's property was purchased and Bruneau accepted $10 000 from B. Bruneau's lawyer argued that Bruneau had not been acting "in his official capacity" because that phrase refers to the power of a member of Parliament to take part in legislation and matters directly related to it in the House of Commons. The court rejected this argument and found Bruneau guilty. The court felt that since the accused had been consulted because of his membership in Parliament, any action taken by him would be "in his official capacity."

BRIBERY OF OFFICERS
s.120
Indictable
Max: 14 years

2. Other Bribery Offences

Section 120(a) makes it an offence for a justice, police commissioner, peace officer, public officer, or officer of juvenile court, or other person employed in the administration of criminal law to accept, obtain, agree to accept, or attempt to obtain a bribe with intent:

---

13. *R. v. Gross* (1946), 86 C.C.C. 68 (Ont.C.A.).
14. [1964] 1 C.C.C. 97 (Ont.C.A.).

120.(a)(iv) to interfere with the administration of justice,

(v) to procure or facilitate the commission of an offence, or

(vi) to protect from detection or punishment a person who has committed or who intends to commit an offence, or

(b) gives or offers, corruptly, to a person mentioned [above] . . . any money valuable consideration, office, place or employment with intent that the person should do anything mentioned in . . . (a)(iv), (v) or (vi).

Section 120(b) prohibits the offering of a bribe to any of the officials listed in s.120(a) with any of the intents set out in s.120(a).

A person cannot be convicted under s.120 of offering a bribe to a peace officer with intent to interfere with the administration of justice unless he or she knew that the person to whom the offer was made was a police officer.[15]

The meaning of "administration of justice" was discussed in *R. v. Kalick*.[16] In this case, the accused gave a bribe of $1 000 to a police officer in order to persuade him not to charge him with an offence which he had committed. Kalick argued that there could be no intent to interfere with the administration of justice until after some proceeding, such as the formal charging of the accused, had taken place. The Supreme Court of Canada decided that "administration of justice" must be given a wider meaning which "includes the taking of necessary steps to have a person who has committed an offence brought before the proper tribunal and punished for his offence. It is a very wide term covering the detection, prosecution and punishment of offenders." Because of this broad definition, Kalick was convicted. The court also held that this section applies to provincial offences as well as federal crimes. It was immaterial whether the officer actually intended to lay a charge.

FRAUDS ON THE GOVERNMENT s.121 Indictable Max: 5 years

Section 121 makes it an offence to bribe government officials. "Official" is broadly defined in s.118 as "a person who (a) holds an office or (b) is appointed to discharge a public duty."

MUNICIPAL CORRUPTION s.123 Indictable Max: 5 years

Section 123 makes it an offence to bribe a "municipal official" which refers to a member of a municipal council or a person who holds an office under a municipal government. The term includes persons such as the chief building inspector for a city.[17]

---

15. *R. v. Smith* (1921), 38 C.C.C. 21 (Ont.C.A.).
16. (1920), 35 C.C.C. 159 (S.C.C.).
17. *R. v. Belzberg* (1962), 131 C.C.C. 281 (S.C.C.).

3. Obstructing a Peace Officer

RESISTING,
OBSTRUCT-
ING, OR
FAILING TO
ASSIST A
PUBLIC OR
PEACE
OFFICER
s.129
Hybrid
Max: 2 years

129. Every one who

(a) resists or wilfully obstructs a public officer or peace officer in the execution of his duty or any person lawfully acting in aid of such an officer,

(b) omits, without reasonable excuse, to assist a public officer or peace officer in the execution of his duty in arresting a person or in preserving the peace, after having reasonable notice that he is required to do so, or

(c) resists or wilfully obstructs any person in the lawful execution of a process against lands or goods or in making a lawful distress or seizure,

is guilty of

(d) an indictable offence . . ., or

(e) an offence punishable on summary conviction.

The essential elements of a charge under s.129(a) are that (1) the accused obstructed, (2) the obstruction was wilful, (3) the person obstructed was a public officer or peace officer, and (4) the officer was in the lawful execution of his or her duty.

a. Obstruction

The ordinary meaning of the term "obstruct" is to hinder, block, or stop up.[18]

The obstruction may involve physical force such as assaulting a police officer. For example, in *Bain v. R.*[19] the accused resisted being lawfully arrested by kicking and breaking the leg of one of the officers.

The obstruction may occur without the use of physical force. In *R. v. Matheson*,[20] the accused refused to permit officers to make a lawful search of his house. The accused used no physical force or threats, did not shut a door in the officers' faces, or block an entrance with his body. He simply said that he did not want the officers in his house and that he refused to allow them to search. The court held that the accused had obstructed the officers in the execution of their duty. Also, the court said that physical acts of obstruction are not necessary. All that is necessary is for the accused to do an act which leads the officer to think that there would be violence if the officer proceeded. The accused in this case had obstructed by preventing the officer from proceeding to search the house, unless the officer chose to do so by force.

---

18. *R. v. Matheson* (1913), 21 C.C.C. 312 (N.B.C.A.).
19. (1955), 11 C.C.C. 281 (Man.C.A.).
20. *Supra*, note 18.

In *R. v. Johnson*[21] the driver of a car was stopped for speeding. He gave the officer a false name and was given a ticket under that name. The Saskatchewan Court of Appeal held that the accused's intent was to mislead the officer and therefore obstruct the officer in the execution of his duty. The court referred to *R. v. Moore* discussed in Chapter Five.[22] In that case the Supreme Court of Canada said that the accused had obstructed an officer in the execution of his duty by not providing his name where the officer had no authority to make an arrest except for the purpose of establishing the person's identity. On the other hand, the Alberta Court of Appeal held that the accused was not guilty of obstruction where she refused to give her name when the officer had no evidence that the accused had committed an offence.[23]

In *R. v. B.*[24] the police were looking for a runaway youth. They spoke to the accused who gave them false information about her whereabouts. He was convicted of obstruction.

b. Wilfully

The term "wilfully" as used in this section means deliberately or intentionally. It refers to a deliberate purpose to accomplish something forbidden, a determination to carry out one's own will in defiance of the law.[25]

c. Peace Officer or Public Officer

In general, "peace officer" and "public officer" refer to persons who have the duty of enforcing the law.

The term "peace officer" is defined in s.2 and was discussed in Chapter Five. In most situations, it refers to a police officer.

The term "public officer" is also defined in s.2:

> "public officer" includes
> (a) an officer of customs or excise,
> (b) an officer of the Canadian Forces,
> (c) an officer of the Royal Canadian Mounted Police, and
> (d) any officer while he is engaged in enforcing the laws of Canada relating to revenue, customs, excise, trade or navigation.

d. Execution of Duty

The requirement that the officer must be in the lawful execution of his or her duty when obstructed means that the officer must be carrying out

---

21. (1985), 41 Sask. R. 205 (Q.B.).
22. See note 13, Chapter Five.
23. *R. v. Guthrie* (1982), 69 C.C.C. (2d) 216 (Alta.C.A.).
24. (1985), 41 Alta.L.R. (2d) 341 (Prov.Ct.Youth Div.).
25. *R. v. Griffin* (1935), 63 C.C.C. 286 (N.B.C.A.).

some duty or obligation imposed by law. If the officer is not carrying out such a duty, then there is no offence under s.129.

Following are some cases which involve the question of whether the officer who was obstructed was in the execution of his or her duty: In *R. v. Westlie*[26] two plain-clothed police officers were working in the skid row area of Vancouver. The accused knew that they were police officers and he starting shouting "undercover pigs, undercover fuzz, watch out for the pigs." Many people in the area were attracted by the shouting. One of the officers told the accused that he was on duty in the area and warned him to stop. The accused then began stopping people on the street pointing at the two police officers and referring to them as "undercover pigs" and "undercover fuzz." The accused was charged with wilfully obstructing a peace officer in the execution of his duty. There were three main issues in the case: (1) at the time of the incident was the police officer in the execution of his duty? (2) was there obstruction of the police officer? and (3) was the obstruction wilful? The court held that (1) the officer was in the execution of his general duty as a police officer to take all steps necessary to ensure that the public peace would be kept, to prevent and detect crime, to bring offenders to justice and to protect property from criminal damage. (2) The accused did all he could to identify the officers to the public and thus completely frustrate the officers in the execution of their duty. This amounted to obstruction. (3) There was no question that the conduct of the accused was intentional and deliberate. But, if he had a lawful excuse for his conduct, then he would not be guilty of the offence. However, the court felt that it was clear that the accused was trying to warn law-violators in the area that the two men were police officers and to stop breaking the law until the officers had left the area. Therefore, the accused was convicted.

In *R. v. Potvin*,[27] the accused was charged with resisting a peace officer contrary to s.129(a). The accused and a friend had gone to a park in Montreal. He had placed his kayak on a lake in the park when a police officer told him that boating was not permitted on the lake and warned him that he would be arrested if he did go boating. The accused went for a boat ride and was arrested. He resisted the arrest and two police officers had to push him into a patrol car. The Crown argued that the accused had violated a city by-law which prohibited, among other things, throwing anything in city lakes and playing unauthorized games. The Crown also argued that the arrest was lawful. The court disagreed, saying that the accused had the right to resist the arrest because he had not violated the by-law and, even if he had, it was not an offence which allowed an arrest

---

26. (1971), 2 C.C.C. (2d) 315 (B.C.C.A.).
27. (1973), 15 C.C.C. (2d) 85 (Que.C.A.).

without a warrant. The police officers were acting without authority and thus were not in the execution of their duty. Therefore, the accused had a lawful excuse for resisting the arrest and he was not guilty under s.129(a). Similarly in *R. v. Houle*,[28] a police officer attempted to give the accused a ticket for an offence that no longer existed. The regulation creating the offence had been repealed two days earlier, unknown to the officer. The accused's conviction for obstruction was overturned on appeal because the officer was not in the execution of his duty.

Knowlton v. R.[29] involved the following facts. In 1971, Premier Kosygin of the U.S.S.R. was to visit Edmonton as a part of his official visit to Canada. He was going to make a short stop at the Chateau Lacombe Hotel. A few days before the visit Kosygin had been assaulted in Ottawa by a man who had grabbed the Premier and tried to drag him to the ground. To prevent another such incident, 26 police officers cordoned off an area in front of the entrance of the hotel. The accused wanted to get in the cordoned-off area to take pictures. A police officer told him that he could not enter the area and warned him that if he did, he would be arrested. The accused ignored the warning. He began to go into the restricted area, pushing his way through two constables. He was arrested and charged with wilfully obstructing a peace officer in the execution of his duty. The incident took place at about the time Kosygin was scheduled to arrive. The Supreme Court of Canada said that the police had interfered with Knowlton's right to move freely in a public street. Such an interference could only be justified if the police were carrying out some duty imposed on them by law. The court held that the police were acting in the execution of their general duty to preserve peace, order, and public safety. They had a duty to prevent another criminal assault on Kosygin and the accused had obstructed them in carrying out that duty.

Section 129(b) makes failing to help a peace officer or public officer in arresting a person or in keeping the peace an offence, unless there is a reasonable excuse for not helping. In *R. v. Foster*[30] a police officer observed a car being driven in a dangerous manner. He signalled to the driver to stop, but once the driver stopped and got out of the car, he started to run away. The officer caught up with him in a place where several people were camping. While the officer was struggling with the driver, the officer asked Foster, who was watching, to help him get the man back to his police car. When Foster simply told the man to go with the officer, the officer again requested his help. Foster said, "No way," and walked away. It turned out that the driver was Foster's son. The

---

28. (1985), 24 C.C.C. (3d) 57 (Alta.C.A.).
29. (1973), 10 C.C.C. (2d) 377 (S.C.C.).
30. (1981), 65 C.C.C. (2d) 388 (Alta.Q.B.).

court held that the fact the driver was Foster's son was no excuse for failing to help the police officer.

Section 129(c) prohibits interfering with a person who has the legal authority to seize or hold land or goods. For example, a sheriff's bailiff may be acting under a court order to take possession of a house. If the person living in the house refuses to allow the bailiff to take possession, then he or she would be violating section 129(c).

**PERJURY
s.131
Indictable
Max: life
imprisonment
if perjury
procures
conviction of
another for
offence
punishable by
death;
14 years
otherwise
s.132**

4. Perjury

In brief, the offence of perjury is knowingly making a false statement under oath. Section 131 states:

> **131.(1) Subject to subsection (3), every one commits perjury who, with intent to mislead, makes before a person who is authorized by law to permit it to be made before him, a false statement under oath or solemn affirmation, by affidavit, solemn declaration or deposition or orally, knowing that the statement is false.**
>
> **(2) Subsection (1) applies whether or not a statement referred to in that subsection is made in a judicial proceeding.**
>
> **(3) Subsection (1) does not apply to a statement referred to in that subsection that is made by a person who is not specially permitted, authorized or required by law to make that statement.**

The offence of perjury can take place at a judicial proceeding which is defined in s.118 as including proceedings before a court, the House of Commons, the Senate, or any other body or person authorized to make an inquiry and to take evidence under oath.

In order for a witness to be convicted of perjury, it must be proved beyond a reasonable doubt that (1) evidence given by the witness was false; (2) the witness knew when giving the evidence that it was false, and (3) it was given with the intent to mislead. These requirements were considered by the Supreme Court of Canada in *Calder v. R.*[31] The accused was a witness in a divorce case. He made a false statement at the divorce trial regarding the length of time a woman had been living in a trailer on his business premises. At the perjury trial, he claimed that his evidence had been an honest statement of what he could remember. The court held that he was not guilty of perjury because, even though he had made

---

31. (1960), 129 C.C.C. 220 (S.C.C.).

a false statement, there was no proof that he knew the evidence was false or that he intended to mislead the court. In short, an honest error made by a witness does not amount to perjury.

In *R. v. Regnier*,[32] the Ontario Court of Appeal held that for perjury, it is not necessary that a false statement mislead the court. It is enough if the witness knows that his statement is false and he intends to mislead.

In *R. v. Hayford*,[33] the Saskatchewan Court of Appeal held that if a witness makes a statement which is true in one sense and false in another, the Crown must prove that the statement was false in the sense that the witness used it. The accused had been a witness at a preliminary hearing on a charge of assault. He stated at the hearing that he had not agreed to sell to R certain furniture. A month before he had said to a police officer that he had made an agreement with R to sell the furniture. It was decided at the assault trial that the agreement was void (i.e., it had no legal effect). At the perjury trial the court said that there was an agreement in the sense that the accused and R had gone through the form of an agreement. But, there was no agreement in the sense that it was not legally binding. The Crown failed to prove in which sense the accused had stated that there was no agreement. Thus, the accused could not be convicted of perjury.

5. Obstructing Justice

a. *Professional Bondspersons*

139.(1) Every one who wilfully attempts in any manner to obstruct, pervert or defeat the course of justice in a judicial proceeding,

(a) by indemnifying or agreeing to indemnify a surety, in any way either in whole or in part, or

(b) where he is a surety, by accepting or agreeing to accept a fee or any form of indemnity whether in whole or in part from or in respect of a person who is released or is to be released from custody,

is guilty of . . . an . . . offence.

This subsection outlaws the business of providing bond money. For example, assume Jean-Luc acts as a surety for Ovide by posting bond or giving money to the court to release Ovide from custody on the understanding that Ovide will appear for trial. The idea behind allowing Jean-Luc to post bond for Ovide is that Jean-Luc will have a real interest in seeing that Ovide appears for trial. If Ovide appears, then Jean-Luc gets the money back. If Ovide does not appear, then Jean-Luc does not get the

32. (1955), 112 C.C.C. 79 (Ont.C.A.).
33. (1921), 35 C.C.C. 293 (Sask.C.A.).

money back. Under s.139(l), it is an offence for Jean-Luc and Ovide to attempt to defeat the course of justice by making an agreement that when released from custody, Ovide would pay back ("indemnify") Jean-Luc the amount of the bond or the amount of the bond plus a fee. Under such an agreement, Jean-Luc would have no interest in seeing that Ovide appeared for trial because Jean-Luc would get the money back regardless of whether or not Ovide appeared.

OBSTRUCT-ING JUSTICE
s.139(2)
Indictable
Max: 10 years

b. *Obstructing the Course of Justice*

139. . . .

(2) Every one who wilfully attempts in any manner other than a manner described in subsection (1) to obstruct, pervert or defeat the course of justice is guilty of an indictable offence . . . .

The phrase "course of justice" has been given a broad meaning and is not limited to proceedings which follow the laying of a charge. In *R. v. Morin*[34] the Quebec Court of Appeal held that "course of justice" should be given the same meaning as "administration of justice," which has been interpreted by the Supreme Court of Canada as a very wide term covering the detection, prosecution, and punishment of offenders.[35] In *Morin*, the accused was charged with attempting to obstruct the course of justice by offering a bribe to a peace officer. While being driven to the police station, he offered money to the officers in the hope of avoiding arrest. He was convicted of attempting to obstruct the course of justice. It would seem that Morin could have been charged either with attempting to obstruct justice or with offering a bribe to a peace officer, contrary to s.120.

In *R. v. Zeck*,[36] the accused was observed by a police officer destroying parking tickets that had been placed on cars by the officer. The Ontario Court of Appeal held that he was properly convicted of obstructing the course of justice. The offence applies to wilful attempts to obstruct the enforcement by the police of a municipal parking by-law.

In *R. v. Balaram*,[37] the accused sent a threatening letter to a judge and made two threatening phone calls. The accused was unhappy about a sentence he had received from the judge. He was convicted of obstruction for making the threats even though there was little chance that he could follow them through.

---

34. (1968), 5 C.R.N.S. 297 (Que.C.A.).
35. *R. v. Kalick*, see note 16.
36. (1980), 53 C.C.C. (2d) 551 (Ont.C.A.).
37. Reported in *The Lawyers Weekly*, February 22, 1991.

If something is said or done which obstructs justice, but the person did not have the *mens rea* to obstruct justice, then no offence is committed. In *R. v. Savinkoff*,[38] the accused was charged with attempting to obstruct justice by trying to induce two men to give false evidence at their trial. The Crown failed to prove that the accused knew that the evidence was false. Without this guilty knowledge, the accused had no *mens rea* and was acquitted of the charge.

c. Bribes and Threats

The use of bribes and threats is mentioned in s.139(3) as a specific way of obstructing the course of justice in a judicial proceeding:

BRIBES AND THREATS IN OBSTRUCT- ING THE COURSE OF JUSTICE s.139(3) Hybrid Max: 2 years

139.(3) Without restricting the generality of subsection (2), every one shall be deemed wilfully to attempt to obstruct, pervert or defeat the course of justice who in a judicial proceeding, existing or proposed,

(a) dissuades or attempts to dissuade a person by threats, bribes or other corrupt means from giving evidence;

(b) influences or attempts to influence by threats, bribes or other corrupt means, a person in his conduct as a juror; or

(c) accepts or obtains, agrees to accept or attempts to obtain a bribe or other corrupt consideration to abstain from giving evidence, or to do or to refrain from doing anything as a juror.

In short, it is obstruction of justice to use bribes or threats to try to corrupt witnesses and jurors. It is also obstruction of justice for a witness or juror to accept a bribe. Note that the section refers to judicial proceedings that are already in progress and those that are not yet in progress but are proposed.

Under para.(a), it is no defence that the accused believed that the evidence to be given by a witness was false. In *R. v. Silverman*,[39] the accused offered a bribe to a witness to persuade him not to give certain evidence at a trial. His purpose was to get the witness to tell what the accused believed to be a true version of the facts. The court found him guilty because the offence was complete when he made the offer of a bribe not to give evidence. It made no difference that the accused honestly believed that the witness was going to give an untrue version of the facts.

---

38. (1962), 39 C.R. 306 (B.C.C.A.).
39. (1908), 14 C.C.C. 79 (Ont.C.A.).

QUESTIONS FOR REVIEW AND DISCUSSION

1 Explain the difference between treason and sedition.

2 **a** What are the essential elements of an unlawful assembly?
b How is a riot different from an unlawful assembly?

3 **a** What would be a lawful excuse for being in possession of an explosive substance?
b Would this lawful excuse protect the possessor from criminal liability for an injury caused by the explosion of the explosive substance? Explain.

4 **a** What is a "weapon"?
b Give two examples.
c What is the main effect of classifying a weapon as restricted rather than as prohibited?

5 **a** What is a firearms acquisition certificate?
b Who can obtain one?

6 **a** What was the issue in the case of *R. v. Covin and Covin*?
b What did the court decide in the case?

7 **a** What is the offence of bribery?
b Give an example of bribery.

8 How have the courts defined the term "administration of justice" in the offence of bribery?

9 **a** When is an officer not acting in the execution of duty?
b Give an example of a police officer not acting in the execution of duty.

10 What are the essential elements of the offence of perjury?

11 Why doesn't the law allow the business of providing bond money?

12 Mrs. Cassidy called the police to report damage to her car. The police came to her house to talk to her about the incident. Mrs. C suggested that her son David might know something about the damage. When the officer started questioning D, he became upset and ordered them out of the house. He then ran and got a gun, and the police left the house. D was charged with possession of a weapon for a purpose dangerous to the public.

a What should David be charged with?
b What must the Crown prove to obtain a conviction?
c Should he be convicted? Explain.

See *R. v. Cassidy* (1989), 50 C.C.C. (3d) 193 (S.C.C.).

13 The police received a report that a woman had been stabbed. When they went to the house where the stabbing was reported to have occurred, they were met at the door by C, the victim's husband. C told the police to leave but they insisted on entering the house. A

struggle took place between the police and C. The police had no grounds to believe that C was involved in the stabbing.

Should C be convicted of obstructing the police in the execution of their duty? Explain.

See *R. v. Custer* (1984), 12 C.C.C. (3d) 372 (Sask.C.A.).

14 Rousseau was a lawyer representing clients who were charged with theft. It was alleged that R offered to pay a certain amount of money to the investigating police officer if the charges were withdrawn. What can R be charged with and what must be proved to convict R?

See *Rousseau v. The Queen* (1985), 21 C.C.C. (3d) 1 (S.C.C.).

SEVEN

Sexual Offences, Public Morals, and Disorderly Conduct

Part V of the Code

A. SEXUAL OFFENCES

At one time this part of the Code contained the offence of rape and various offences involving intercourse with female minors. In 1985, the law was amended and most of these offences were repealed. "Rape" is now defined as a type of assault and is contained in Part VII of the Code which deals with offences against the person. Part V now primarily concerns sexual offences against children.

There are several offences involving sexual activity with children.

SEXUAL
INTER-
FERENCE
s.151
Hybrid
Max: 10 years

1. Sexual Interference

151. Every person who, for a sexual purpose, touches, directly or indirectly, with a part of the body or with an object, any part of the body of a person under the age of fourteen years is guilty of an indictable offence . . . or is guilty of an offence punishable upon summary conviction.

INVITATION
TO SEXUAL
TOUCHING
s.152
Hybrid
Max: 10 years

2. Invitation to Sexual Touching

152. Every person who, for a sexual purpose, invites, counsels, or incites a person under the age of fourteen years to touch, directly or indirectly, with a part of the body or with an object, the body of any person, . . . under the age of

fourteen years is guilty of an indictable offence and liable to a term of imprisonment not exceeding ten years or is guilty of an offence punishable on summary conviction.

SEXUAL
EXPLOITA-
TION
s.153
Hybrid
Max: 5 years

3. Sexual Exploitation

153.(1) Every person who is in a position of trust or authority towards a young person or is a person with whom the young person is in a relationship of dependency and who

(a) for a sexual purpose, touches directly or indirectly, with a part of the body or with an object any part of the body of a young person, or

(b) for a sexual purpose invites, counsels or incites a young person to touch directly or indirectly, with a part of the body or with an object, the body of any person including the body of the person who so invites, counsels or incites and the body of the young person

is guilty of an indictable offence . . . or is guilty of an offence punishable on summary conviction.

(2) In this section "young person" means a person fourteen years of age or more but under the age of eighteen years.

Notice that s.153(2) combines elements of the offences of sexual interference and exploitation where the complainant is at least 14 but under 18 years old and the accused is in a position of trust or authority.

There are few reported cases involving these offences. However, in one of them, *R. v. Palmer*,[1] a male teacher was convicted of sexual exploitation under s.153 of the Code. The teacher had become involved in a sexual relationship with a 16-year-old female student. He arranged secret meetings with the student which involved the complicity of other students. The fact that the student agreed to the relationship was not a defence. The court said: "Can the accused's acts be excused because of the cooperation of the victims in this case? I think not. A teacher stands in the place of a parent or the step-parent. Could a parent or step-parent say 'My child cooperated in the sexual activity?' I don't think so."

4. Incest

155.(1) Every one commits incest who, knowing that another person is by blood relationship his or her parent, child, brother, sister, grandparent or grandchild as the case

---

1. Reported in *The Lawyers Weekly*, February 6, 1990.

may be, has sexual intercourse with that person.

(2) Every one who commits incest is guilty of an indictable offence

. . .

(3) No accused shall be determined by a court guilty of an offence under this section if the accused was under restraint, duress, or fear of the person with whom the accused had the sexual intercourse at the time the sexual intercourse occurred.

(4) In this section "brother" and "sister" respectively, include half-brother and half-sister.

Sexual intercourse is defined in s.4(5):

4. . . .

(5) For the purposes of this Act, sexual intercourse is complete on penetration to even the slightest degree, notwithstanding that seed is not emitted.

ANAL INTER-COURSE
s.159
Hybrid
Max: 10 years

5. Anal Intercourse

159.(1) Every person who engages in an act of anal intercourse is guilty of an indictable offence . . . or an offence punishable on summary conviction.

(2) Subsection (1) does not apply to any act engaged in, in private, between
(a) a husband and wife
(b) any two persons, each of whom is eighteen years of age or more,
both of whom consent to the act.

(3) For the purpose of subsection (2),
(a) an act shall be deemed not to have been engaged in in private if it is engaged in in a public place or if more than two persons take part or are present; and
(b) a person shall be deemed not to consent to an act
(i) if the consent is extorted by force, threats or fear of bodily harm or is obtained by false and fraudulent misrepresentations respecting the nature and quality of the act, or
(ii) if the court is satisfied beyond a reasonable doubt that the person could not have consented to the act by reason of mental disability.

Public place is defined in s.150 as including "any place to which the public has access as of right or by invitation, express or implied." For example, private cubicles in public washrooms have been held not to be private places.[2]

BESTIALITY
s.160
Hybrid
Max: 10 years

6. Bestiality

160.(1) Every person who commits bestiality is guilty of an indictable offence . . . or is guilty of an offence punishable on summary conviction.

(2) Every person who compels another to commit bestiality is guilty of an indictable offence . . . or is guilty of an offence punishable on summary conviction.

(3) Notwithstanding subsection (1), every person who commits bestiality in the presence of a person who is under the age of fourteen years, or who incites a person under the age of fourteen years to commit bestiality is guilty of an indictable offence . . . or is guilty of an offence punishable on summary conviction.

The term "bestiality" is not defined in the Code but it generally refers to a human being having sexual intercourse in any way with an animal or bird.

INDECENT ACTS
s.173(2)
Summary conviction

7. Exposing

173.(2) Every person who, in any place, for a sexual purpose, exposes his or her genital organs to a person who is under the age of fourteen years is guilty of an offence punishable on summary conviction.

8. Consent as a Defence

The general rule is that consent is not a defence to these offences. Section 150.1(1) states:

150.1(1) Where an accused is charged with an offence under section 151 or 152 or subsection 153(1), 160(3) or 173(2) . . . it is not a defence that the complainant consented to the activity that forms the subject-matter of the charge.

CONSENT AS DEFENCE
s.150.1(2)

Section 150.1(2) provides exceptions to the general rule, where consent can be a defence if certain circumstances exist:

2. See, for example, *R. v. LeBeau* (1988), 41 C.C.C. (3d) 163 (Ont.C.A.). Note this case is being appealed to the Supreme Court of Canada on the question of whether the use of lookouts and other precautions in a public washroom can make a place not public.

> **150.1** . . . where an accused is charged with an offence under section 151 or 152 or subsection 173(2) or section 271 in respect of a complainant who is twelve years of age or more but under the age of fourteen years, . . .
>
> **(2)** . . . it is not a defence that the complainant consented to the activity that forms the subject matter of the charge, unless the accused
>
> **(a)** is twelve years of age or more but under the age of sixteen years;
>
> **(b)** is less than two years older than the complainant; and
>
> **(c)** is neither in a position of trust or authority towards the complainant nor is a person with whom the complainant is in a relationship of dependency.

In addition, s.150.1(3) provides that:

> **(3) No person aged twelve or thirteen years shall be tried for an offence under section 151 or 152 or subsection 173(2) unless the person is in a position of trust or authority towards the complainant or is a person with whom the complainant is in a relationship of dependency.**

These exceptions mean that no offence has taken place where the victim and accused are in more or less equal positions.

The Code does not define the term "position of trust or authority." Presumably this refers to persons like parents, teachers, babysitters, or employers.

Neither does the Code define the term "sexual purpose", but see the discussion of the meaning of sexual assault in Chapter Twelve.

The rule in s.150.1(1) that does not allow consent as a defence may be challenged under the Charter as violating a principle of fundamental justice under s.7.

B. CORRUPTION OF MORALS

MAKING,
DISTRIBUT-
ING OBSCENE
MATERIALS
s.163
Hybrid
Max: 2 years
[s.169]

1. Pornography

The Criminal Code creates certain offences concerning obscene (i.e., pornographic) materials. These are hybrid offences which are set out as follows:

> **163.(1) Every one commits an offence who**
> **(a) makes, prints, publishes, distributes, circulates or has in his possession for the purpose of publication, distribution or circulation any obscene written matter, picture, model, phonograph record or other thing whatever.**
> . . .

> **(2) Every one commits an offence who knowingly, without lawful justification or excuse,**
> **(a) sells, exposes to public view or has in his possession for such a purpose any obscene written matter, picture, model, phonograph record or other thing whatsoever . . . .**

Subsection (1)(a) is directed toward *publishers* and *distributors* of obscene material, although the Supreme Court of Canada has said that this subsection includes private individuals who make obscene material even if the material is not meant for publication.[3] Courts have held that a person who shows an obscene film in a private home is not "circulating" but a person in the business of renting videos is circulating or distributing.[4]

Subsection (2)(a) is directed toward *sellers* of obscene material (e.g., an operator of a bookstore) and those who expose obscene material (e.g., a manager of an art gallery).

An important difference between subs.(1) and subs.(2) is that under subs.(2) the Crown must prove that the accused acted knowingly, that is, that the accused had knowledge of the nature of the material. Under subs.(1), the Crown does not have to prove knowledge. In fact, subs.(6) states that:

IGNORANCE NOT A DEFENCE
s.163(6)

> **(6) Where an accused is charged with an offence under subsection (1), the fact that the accused was ignorant of the nature of the matter . . . is not a defence to the charge.**

In *R. v. Metro News*,[5] the Ontario Court of Appeal held that subs.(6) violated the Charter by creating an absolute liability offence (i.e., one which has no *mens rea*). (See Chapter Three for a discussion of absolute and strict liability offences.) The court held that it was open to the accused to raise a reasonable doubt that he had acted under an honest and reasonable belief in a state of facts that, if this state existed, would have made his act innocent. This defence is the defence of mistake of fact. (See Chapter Four for a discussion of this defence.) However, the court went on to say, it is not a defence for the accused to say that he honestly believed the material was not obscene. In other words, the offence is made out when the Crown proves that the accused distributed matter that was obscene. The accused may, however, show that he or she acted under a reasonable and honest mistake, for example, if the accused could show that he believed the books being distributed were, for example, encyclopedias.

---

3. *Hawkshaw v. The Queen* (1986), 26 C.C.C. (3d) 129 (S.C.C.).
4. *R. v. Rioux* [1970] 3 C.C.C. 149 (S.C.C.); *R. v. Red Hot Video* (1985), 18 C.C.C. (3d) 1 (B.C.C.A.).
5. (1986), 29 C.C.C. (3d) 35 (Ont.C.A.). The leave to appeal to the S.C.C. was refused.

The requirement of "knowingly" under subs.(2) was considered in *R. v. Britnell*.[6] The accused was the operator of a bookstore who was charged with selling obscene books. The court pointed out that the prosecution must prove that the accused "knowingly" sold obscene books. The court said that "knowingly" meant (1) that the books were sold with knowledge and (2) that he knew of their obscene character. Neither of these requirements were satisfied in the case. The accused carried a stock of nearly 250,000 books in his store. The ordering of the few copies of obscene books was done by a clerk, not the accused. There was no evidence that the accused was aware of the presence of the books in his store or that he had knowledge of their obscene character. Also, there was no evidence that he was present when any of the obscene books were sold. Thus, he was found not guilty.

In *R. v. Cameron*,[7] it was held that "knowingly" does not require that the accused should have the legal knowledge of whether the material is obscene. It is enough if he has knowledge of the subject matter and sells the material or exposes it to public view. In this case, the accused was the manager of an art gallery. She was charged with exposing to public view seven obscene drawings in her gallery. The court held that she must have had the necessary knowledge of the subject matter because: (1) she collected the drawings through other galleries and from the artists themselves; and (2) she arranged for the display of the drawings in her gallery. It was not necessary that she knew that the drawings met the legal definition of obscenity. It was *only* necessary that she was aware of the subject matter or what was depicted in the drawings.

a. *The Meaning of Obscenity*

OBSCENITY DEFINED s.163(8)

A major issue in prohibiting pornography has been the definition of the term "obscenity". The present law was enacted in 1959. Since that time societal values and views have changed. In the past several years there have been many attempts by the government to amend the law of obscenity to make it reflect more modern views. However, each of these attempts has failed.[8] The problem lies in the conflict between allowing free expression and the desire to limit pornography. Although Parliament has been unable to find a definition that is acceptable to the community, the courts have played a significant role in developing the definition of obscenity. The basic definition of obscenity is in s.163(8):

> **163.(8) For the purposes of this Act, any publication a dominant characteristic of which is the undue exploitation of**

---

6. (1912), 20 C.C.C. 85 (Ont.C.A.).
7. [1966] 4 C.C.C. 273, 49 C.R. 49 (Ont.C.A.), aff'd. (1967) 2 C.C.C. 195, 1 C.R.N.S. 227 (S.C.C.).
8. The most recent attempt at new legislation was Bill C-54 which died on the order paper in November 1987.

> **sex, or of sex and any one or more of the following subjects, namely crime, horror, cruelty and violence, shall be deemed to be obscene.**

This definition is not limited to written publications but has been applied to films, videos, and sexual devices and articles.[9]

"Dominant characteristic" seems to refer to a main or distinctive feature or peculiarity of the material. But can there be more than one dominant characteristic? And, how is it decided that a characteristic, such as undue exploitation of sex, is dominant? In *Brodie v. R.*,[10] four judges (not a majority) of the Supreme Court of Canada suggested answers to these questions. First, material (in this case, a book) may have more than one dominant characteristic. Second, in searching for a dominant characteristic, it is necessary to read the whole book, not merely isolated passages and isolated words. Third, it is relevant to consider the purpose of the author and the literary or artistic merit of the book. On the other hand, the Ontario Court of Appeal has said that magazines are to be judged somewhat differently from books.[11] An obscene article cannot be saved by surrounding it with "profound articles on foreign policy." In other words, an allegedly obscene magazine article will be looked at separately from the rest of the publication.

b. What Is "Undue Exploitation of Sex"?

The four judges in the *Brodie* case, mentioned above, suggested that this phrase means that some exploitation of a sexual theme is permitted. In determining whether there is "undue" (excessive) exploitation, the judges said that it depends on (1) the author's purpose, (2) the artistic or literary merit of the work, and (3) whether the material violates the community standards of decency.

Whether the material violates the community standard of decency has become the most important test in deciding whether material is obscene. The meaning of "community standards of decency" was discussed in *Dominion News and Gifts v. R.*[12] In that case, the Supreme Court of Canada was asked to decide whether certain issues of "Dude" magazine and "Escapade" magazine had a dominant characteristic of undue or excessive exploitation of sex. The court relied on the judgment of one of the lower court judges,[13] who said:

> *Those [community] standards are not set by those of lowest taste. Nor are they set exclusively by those of rigid, austere, conservative or puritan taste*

---

9. *Supra*, note 3.
10. (1962), 132 C.C.C. 161, 37 C.R. 120 (S.C.C.).
11. *R. v. Penthouse Int. Ltd.* (1979), 46 C.C.C. (2d) 111 (Ont.C.A.), leave to appeal to the S.C.C. refused, (1979) 46 C.C.C. (2d) 111n (S.C.C.).
12. [1964] 3 C.C.C. 1, 42 C.R. 209 (S.C.C.).
13. [1963] 2 C.C.C. 103, 40 C.R. 109 (Man.C.A.).

and habit of mind. Something approaching a general average of community thinking and feeling has to be discovered.

The judge also noted that the community standards must be Canadian and they must be contemporary (i.e., in keeping with the attitudes of the times):

Times change, and ideas change with them. Compared with the Victorian era, this is a liberal age in which we live. One manifestation of it is the relative freedom with which the whole question of sex is discussed. In books, magazines, movies, television and sometimes even in parlour conversation, various aspects of sex are made the subject of comment, with a candour that in an earlier day would have been regarded as indecent and intolerable. We cannot and should not ignore these present-day attitudes when we face the question of whether "Dude" and "Escapade" are obscene according to our criminal law.

In a more recent case, *Towne Cinema Theatres Ltd. v. R.,*[14] the Supreme Court of Canada stated that, in determining community standards, the test is not what the average Canadian would want to see but is what the average Canadian would tolerate others seeing.

The fact that a film has been approved for public viewing by a provincial censor board can be evidence of community standards of decency. However, this approval does not necessarily mean that a court will not find the film obscene. In fact, courts have held that it is not necessary for the Crown to present any evidence on what community standards are. The judge may determine what community standards are by drawing on his or her own experience. However, the judge cannot impose personal views but must objectively determine the community's views.

c. *Application of the Definition of Obscenity [s.163(8)]*

In *Brodie v. R.*[15] the Supreme Court of Canada held that *Lady Chatterly's Lover* was not obscene. The book included very detailed and explicit descriptions of the sexual relations between a man and a woman. The court said that sex could be described as a dominant characteristic of the book; however, the book, as a whole, did not unduly or excessively exploit sex.

In *R. v. Red Hot Video*[16] the court considered whether three videos were obscene. In judging that they were, the court said:

They constitute a threat to society because they have a tendency to create indifference to violence insofar as women are concerned. They tend to

---

14. (1985), 18 C.C.C. (3d) 193 (S.C.C.).
15. *Supra*, note 10.
16. (1985), 18 C.C.C. (3d) 1 (B.C.C.A.).

dehumanize and degrade both men and women in an excessive and revolting way. They exalt the concept that in some perverted way domination of women by men is accepted in our society.

Similarly in *R. v. Wagner*,[17] the Alberta Court of Queen's Bench stated that material is pornographic if it is sexually explicit with violence or sexually explicit and dehumanizing or degrading.

DEFENCE OF
PUBLIC
GOOD
s.163(3)

d. Defence of the Public Good

A defence to charges under s.163 is the defence of the public good:

> **163.(3) No person shall be convicted of an offence under this section if he establishes that the public good was served by the acts that are alleged to constitute the offence and that the acts alleged did not extend beyond what served the public good.**

There are two parts to this defence which must be proved by the accused: (1) that the public good was served and (2) that the acts (e.g., publishing or selling of obscene books) did not go beyond what served the public good. Material that otherwise would be obscene will not be considered obscene if this defence is established.

Something serves the public good if it is necessary or advantageous to objects of general interest, such as religion, science, literature, art or other objects of general interest.[18] In *Delorme v. R.*,[19] the accused who ran a bookstore was charged with selling an obscene book. The book was about a woman who was subjected to many cruel and violent sexual acts. Experts testified that the book had value as a psychological study and would be useful to students of literature or psychology. One expert testified that the book was difficult to read and not within everyone's grasp. The court held that although the book may have been of benefit to certain students, since it was available in a public bookstore, it could not be said that the public good was being served. Therefore, his defence failed and he was convicted.

e. Obscenity and the Charter

At this time there are conflicting court decisions on how the obscenity provisions are affected by the Charter. For example, one court has held that the obscenity offence violates the protection of freedom of expression under the Charter but that the violation is a reasonable limit under

---

17. (1985), 26 C.C.C. (3d) 242 (Alta.Q.B.), aff'd. on other grounds, 26 C.C.C. (3d) 242 (Alta.C.A.), leave to appeal refused, 26 C.C.C. (3d) 242 (S.C.C.).
18. *R. v. American News Co. Ltd.* (1957), 118 C.C.C. 152 (Ont.C.A.).
19. (1973), 21 C.R.N.S. 305 (Que.C.A.).

s.1.[20] The British Columbia Court of Appeal held that the application of community standards is not so overly vague or broad as to violate s.7 of the Charter.[21]

On the other hand, the Manitoba Court of Appeal has held that "hard-core" pornography is not protected by our freedom of expression under the Charter because it does not convey meaning.[22] The court stated that intellectual meaning rather than sensual arousal is what the Charter is meant to protect. This case as well as others are being appealed to the Supreme Court of Canada which will give the final statement on the effect of the Charter on the offence.

IMMORAL
THEATRICAL
PERFORM-
ANCE
s.167
Hybrid
Max: 2 years
[s.169]

2. Immoral, Indecent, or Obscene Theatrical Performance

> 167.(1) Every one commits an offence who, being the lessee, manager, agent or person in charge of a theatre, presents or gives or allows to be presented or given therein an immoral, indecent or obscene performance, entertainment or representation.
>
> (2) Every one commits an offence who takes part or appears as an actor, performer, or assistant in any capacity, in an immoral, indecent or obscene performance, entertainment or representation in a theatre.

Subsection (1) is directed against the person in charge of the theatre in which the immoral, indecent, or obscene performance takes place. Subsection (2) is directed at those who participate in the performance.

a. *Indecent Performance*

"Indecent" is not defined in the Code and the courts have not developed a clear test. However, in general, something is indecent if it offends community standards of decency or good taste.

b. *Immoral Performance*

Immoral is another term not defined in the Code. In general, it refers to not conforming with accepted patterns of conduct.

The meaning of immoral was clarified somewhat by the Supreme Court of Canada in *Johnson v. R.*[23] In that case, the issue was "whether the performance of a dance in a theatre before a public audience, which would have been unexceptional if performed when fully or partly clad, becomes 'immoral' on the sole ground that it is performed 'in the nude'."

---

20. See note 17.
21. *Supra*, note 16.
22. *R. v. Butler* (1990), 60 C.C.C. (3d) 219 (Man.C.A.). This decision is being appealed to the Supreme Court of Canada.
23. (1973), 23 C.R.N.S. 273 (S.C.C.).

The accused woman appeared on stage in a cabaret in front of about 17 people. She danced five dances. Three dances were "topless" and one was completely in the nude. At the time of the nude dance, she was alone on the stage. She did nothing offensive by way of words or gestures while she danced. The court held that the performance was not immoral. There was nothing immoral about displaying a naked human body and there was no evidence that the dance was "immoral" in any other way. The court noted that the section makes it an offence to be unclothed in a public place. But the simple fact that Parliament makes it an offence does not mean that it is a breach of moral standards. The result was that the dancer was not guilty of engaging in an immoral performance.

In *R. v. MacLean and MacLean (No.2)*,[24] the Ontario Court of Appeal held that the test for whether a performance is immoral is the community standard for tolerance. The judge must consider all of the surrounding circumstances including the performer's purpose.

c. Obscene Performance

The definition of obscenity in s.163(8) applies to this offence. In *Hawkshaw v. The Queen*,[25] the Supreme Court of Canada held that s.163(8) sets out the sole test for obscenity for all offences in the Code even if they are not based on a publication.

C. DISORDERLY CONDUCT

INDECENT ACTS s.173(1) Summary conviction

1. Indecent Acts

173. Every one who wilfully does an indecent act
(a) in a public place in the presence of one or more persons,
or
(b) in any place, with intent thereby to insult or offend any person, is guilty of an offence punishable on summary conviction.

The essential elements of this offence are as follows.

a. Indecency

As mentioned earlier, indecency is not defined in the Code. Generally, it refers to a violation of community standards of decency or good taste. A common example of an indecent act is the exposure of the "private parts" of a person (i.e., indecent exposure). But, simply being nude in public,

---

24. (1982), 1 C.C.C. (3d) 412 (Ont.C.A.), leave to appeal to Supreme Court of Canada was refused.
25. *Supra*, note 3.

such as lying nude on a public beach, is not an indecent act, although the person could be charged under s.174 (see below).

b. Wilfully

The term "wilfully" has the same meaning that it has in most other sections of the Code: to do an act purposely and with a criminal intention.

c. Place of the Act

The act may occur in a public place (any place to which the public may go) but it must be in the presence of one or more persons [s.173(a)]. In *R. v. Hastings*,[26] the court held that urinating on a public street at night, with no exposure to any person other than a police officer, is not an offence.

If an indecent act is done with the specific intent to insult or offend any person, it makes no difference where the act occurs [s.173(b)]. In other words, the indecent act may occur in any place, public or private, but it must be shown that the accused did the act in order to insult or offend someone.

**NUDITY
s.174
Summary
conviction**

2. Nudity

174.(1) Every one who, without lawful excuse,
(a) is nude in a public place, or
(b) is nude and exposed to public view while on private property, whether or not the property is his own,
is guilty of an offence punishable on summary conviction.
(2) For the purposes of this section, a person is nude who is so clad as to offend against public decency or order.

No act is required to commit this offence. Simply being nude is enough. Under ss.(2) nudity does not mean completely naked. The Supreme Court of Canada in *R. v. Verette*[27] held that complete nudity in a public place does not require that the Crown prove that the nudity offended public decency. Proof that public decency was offended is only required under ss.(2) where the person need not be completely nude. So, in *R. v. Giambalvo*,[28] the Ontario Court of Appeal held that a dancer who was only partly clad commits an offence under this section only if he or she has offended public decency or order. The test for this offence is the standard of community tolerance of the circumstances under which the dance was performed.

Section 174(3) states that the consent of the Attorney General is required to commence proceedings under this section.

---

26. (1947), 4 D.L.R. 748 (N.B.C.A.).
27. (1978), 40 C.C.C. (2d) 273 (S.C.C.).
28. (1982), 70 C.C.C. (2d) 324 (Ont.C.A.).

CAUSING
DISTURB-
ANCE
s.175(1)(a)
Summary
conviction

3. Causing a Disturbance

175. Every one who
(a) not being in a dwelling-house, causes a disturbance in or near a public place,
(i) by fighting, screaming, shouting, swearing, singing or using insulting or obscene language,
(ii) by being drunk, or
(iii) by impeding or molesting other persons, . . . is guilty of an offence punishable on summary conviction.

The essential elements of this offence are: (1) that the accused was not in a dwelling-house; (2) that he or she caused a disturbance; (3) that the disturbance occurred in a public place or near a public place; and (4) that the disturbance was caused by the accused's fighting, screaming, etc., or by his or her being drunk or by his or her impeding or molesting other persons.

a. Dwelling-House

Dwelling-house is defined in s.2 as:

. . . the whole or any part of a building or structure that is kept or occupied as a permanent or temporary residence and includes
(a) a building within the curtilage of a dwelling-house that is connected to it by a doorway or by a covered and enclosed passageway, and
(b) a unit that is designed to be mobile and to be used as a permanent or temporary residence and that is being used as such a residence.

In *R. v. Jones*,[29] an issue was whether the administrative office of a university was a dwelling-house. Students of Simon Fraser University conducted a "sit-in" at the university. They occupied the administrative office and prevented officials and administrators from entering the office. They were charged with causing a disturbance by impeding other persons [s.175(a)(iii)]. The lawyer for the students argued that the sit-in occurred in a dwelling-house within the meaning of the definition in s.2 and, therefore, no offence was committed. First, the lawyer argued that for legal purposes such as being sued, the "residence" of a university is its administrative office. The court agreed that for certain legal purposes, the administrative office is the residence of the university but is not for the purpose of s.175. Second, the lawyer argued that because the stu-

---

29. (1970), 1 C.C.C. (2d) 232 (B.C.C.A.).

dents brought and used sleeping bags and food they used the premises as their temporary residence within the meaning of the definition in s.2. The court disagreed again by deciding that trespassers cannot by wrongfully occupying university property convert it into their residence and thereby make it a dwelling-house.

In *R. v. Campbell*[30] the accused was charged with causing a disturbance in a public place by using insulting or obscene language. He was in the hallway near to the television room of a hospital when the incident occurred. The trial court dismissed the charge on the grounds that the television room and hallway were dwelling-houses. An appeal court disagreed and held that, although the rooms of the patients were probably dwelling-houses, a television room and hallway where the public could come and go were not dwelling-houses.

b. Disturbance

The meaning of "disturbance" was discussed in *R. v. C.D.*[31] The accused was charged with causing a disturbance by using insulting language [s.175(a)(i)]. While standing in a public street, the accused shouted at Mr. and Mrs. Smith to "get your f— car out of this f— parking lot or I'll hit your f— car." Then, the accused got in his car and drove it into the rear of the Smith car. The impact threw the Smith's child to the floor of the car. Mrs. Smith and the child both began to cry. There was no person other than the Smiths present when the shouting occurred. The court felt that the language used by the accused was insulting and that it occurred in a public place. But, there was no disturbance. Each of the three judges of the New Brunswick Court of Appeal gave his own interpretation of the meaning of disturbance. One judge said:

> While it is difficult, if not impossible, to define with any degree of precision what is meant by a "disturbance" as used in s.171(a)(i) [now s.175(a)(1)], it is obvious it involves activities constituting a distraction to persons in or near public places who are pursuing their ordinary peaceable pursuits and includes a breach of the peace, a tumult, an uproar, a commotion and any other disorder. Where the acts specified in the section produce only annoyance or emotional upset not accompanied by activities in the nature of a disorder, there is not, in my opinion, a disturbance of the kind contemplated by the section.

A second judge said that for there to be a disturbance, it is not necessary that there be a riot but there must be "something more than mere interruption of tranquillity or peace of some person's mind." He concluded that no act caused by the insulting language was done which could be considered a disturbance.

---

30. (1980), 22 C.R. (3d) 219 (Alta.Q.B.).
31. (1973), 13 C.C.C. (2d) 206 (N.B.C.A.).

The third judge said that disturbance referred to a "disorder or agitation" of the public or interference "with the ordinary and customary use by the public of the public place."

In short, all three judges agreed that although the language was insulting and emotionally upsetting to the Smith family, it did not cause a disturbance. In other words, more is required for a disturbance than for the victim to have been emotionally upset. Therefore, the accused was found not guilty. On the other hand, he probably could have been convicted of intimidation, mischief, or assault.

A contrary result was reached in *R. v. Swinimer*,[32] where all of the judges hearing the appeal agreed that a disturbance occurs when any of the acts listed in the section take place, if such acts could disturb another person.

4. Trespassing at Night

> **177. Every one who, without lawful excuse, the proof of which lies upon him, loiters or prowls at night upon the property of another person near a dwelling-house situated on that property is guilty of an offence punishable on summary conviction.**

This section is sometimes referred to as the "Peeping Tom" section. For the offence to be committed, (1) a person must "loiter or prowl"; (2) the loitering or prowling must occur at "night"; (3) it must be on another person's property; (4) it must be near a dwelling-house on that property. If the person has some lawful excuse for his or her actions, then it is up to him or her to prove it.

a. Night

The term "night" is defined in s.2 as the period between 9:00 p.m. and 6:00 a.m. If the loitering or prowling occurs before 9:00 p.m. or after 6:00 a.m., even if it is dark outside, the offence is not committed.

b. Loiters or Prowls

The meaning of "loiters" was considered in *R. v. Andsten and Petrie*.[33] The accused in the case were private detectives who had been hired by a man to investigate the conduct of his estranged wife. They kept the wife's house under surveillance from about 11:30 p.m. to about 2:30 a.m. by lingering on the property, hanging around the house, listening at the windows and finally demanding admission to speak to a man who they believed to be in the house. The court held that the meaning of "loiters" as used in s.177 is "hanging around" and that the detectives were

---

32. (1978), 40 C.C.C. (2d) 432 (N.B.C.A.).
33. (1960), 33 C.R. 213 (B.C.C.A.).

loitering near the wife's house. The detectives argued that they had a lawful excuse for their actions. They said that they were on the wife's property for the lawful purpose of investigating her conduct. The court agreed that this was a lawful purpose; however, this purpose did not justify or excuse the civil wrong of trespass which they committed by their invasion of the wife's property. Therefore, the detectives were found guilty.

In one of the few reported case on the meaning of "prowls," the court decided that the term was meant to cover behaviour which is more overt than mere loitering. It refers to hunting in a stealthy manner for an opportunity to carry out an unlawful purpose. The court explained that a person who walks quickly through another person's property would not be loitering. But, if it could be proven that he or she was looking for a chance to break into the house or steal something, then he or she would be prowling.[34]

SPREADING FALSE NEWS s.181 Indictable Max: 2 years

5. Spreading False News

181. Every one who wilfully publishes a statement, tale or news that he knows is false and that causes or is likely to cause injury or mischief to a public interest is guilty of an indictable offence.

There are few reported cases of this offence. However, one recent case achieved significant coverage in the media and is useful for showing the court's application of this section in light of the Charter. The case was *R. v. Zundel*.[35] The accused had been charged with this offence for publishing anti-Semitic material which among other things stated that the Holocaust never occurred. The Ontario Court of Appeal held that this offence does not violate the Charter's right to freedom of expression. The court stated that the essence of the offence is the wilful publication of false facts that are known to be false by the person who publishes them and that the publication has caused or is likely to cause injury or mischief to the public interest. This conduct does not fall within the protection of the Charter. Spreading falsehoods knowingly is the antithesis of seeking truth through the free exchange of ideas which is the purpose of protecting the freedom of expression. Furthermore, the Court stated, the public has an interest in preserving racial and religious harmony. In the second appeal of this case, the Court of Appeal said that this offence only applies to the spreading of false statements of fact and not of opinion. Also, the accused must know that the facts are false. Recklessness as to the truth or falsity of the statements is not sufficient for the offence to have been committed.[36]

---

34. *R. v. McLean* (1970), 1 C.C.C. (2d) 277 (Alta.Mag.Ct.). See also *R. v. Willis* (1987), 37 C.C.C. (3d) 184 (B.C.Co.Ct.)
35. (1987), 31 C.C.C. (3d) 97, (Ont.C.A.), leave to appeal to S.C.C. refused.
36. *R. v. Zundel* (1990), 53 C.C.C. (3d) 161 (Ont.C.A.).

QUESTIONS FOR REVIEW AND DISCUSSION

1 List the offences concerning sexual activity and children. Indicate the age at which the victim must be for the offence to occur.

2 Give an example of a person in a position of authority or trust under s.153.

3 a In general, when is consent not a defence to offences involving sexual conduct and children?
b What are the exceptions to situations when consent is not a defence?
c Why do you think these exceptions exist?

4 a What has become the most important test for determining whether material is obscene?
b Explain the nature of the test.

5 What is the test for deciding whether a theatrical performance is immoral, indecent, or obscene?

6 What are the ways in which the offence of nudity can be committed?

7 What are the elements of the offence of causing a disturbance?

8 What are the elements of the offence of trespassing at night?

9 What is involved in the offence of spreading false news?

10 The accused operated a store that sold sex articles and devices. The items were on display inside the store. Outside the store was a sign that stated "For Adults Only." The accused was charged with possession for the purpose of sale of obscene articles.
a What definition of obscenity is used for this offence?
b What questions should the court ask to decide if the articles are obscene?
c Should it matter that the store is restricted to adults?

See *Germain v. The Queen* (1985), 21 C.C.C. (3d) 289 (S.C.C.).

EIGHT

Soliciting and Procuring, Disorderly Houses, Betting, and Lotteries

Part VII of the Code

A. SOLICITING AND PROCURING

It is not an offence to sell sex for money. The Code controls prostitution in three other ways. First, to solicit in public is an offence. Second, to engage in pimping, that is, procuring a person to be a prostitute, is also an offence. Third, there are several offences related to keeping a common bawdy-house (or house of prostitution). Common bawdy-houses are discussed below under Disorderly Houses.

Section 197 clarifies the question, which previously had been the subject of conflicting case decisions, of whether a man can be a prostitute, by stating: "prostitute means a person of either sex who engages in prostitution."

It should also be remembered that the use of the pronoun "he" in these offences, as well as in all parts of the Code, include male and female persons according to the Interpretation Act, R.S.C. 1985, c.I-21.

1. Procuring

Section 212 sets out the offences involving procuring prostitution. These include:

PROCURING
s.212(1)
Indictable
Max: 10 years

212.(1) Every one who
(a) procures, attempts to procure or solicits a person to have illicit sexual intercourse with another person, whether in or out of Canada,

(b) inveigles or entices a person who is not a prostitute or a person of known immoral character to a common bawdy-house . . . for the purpose of . . . prostitution,

(c) knowingly conceals a person in a common bawdy-house . . .

(d) procures or attempts to procure a person to become whether in or out of Canada, a prostitute,

. . .

(g) procures a person to enter or leave Canada for the purpose of prostitution,

. . .

(h) for the purpose of gain, exercises control, direction or influence over the movements of a person in such a manner as to show that he is aiding, abetting or compelling that person to engage in or carry on prostitution with any person, or generally

(i) applies or administers to a person or causes that person to take any drug, intoxicating liquor, matter or thing with intent to stupefy or overpower that person in order thereby to enable any person to have illicit sexual intercourse with that person,

(j) lives wholly or in part on the avails of prostitution of another person.

LIVING ON THE AVAILS OF JUVENILE PROSTITUTE s.212(2) Indictable Max: 14 years

These offences are indictable and the maximum penalty is a ten-year prison term. However, if the accused is charged with living on the avails of a prostitute who is under 18, the penalty is a maximum term of imprisonment of 14 years.

There is an additional offence in this section concerning prostitutes under 18:

OBTAINING SERVICES OF JUVENILE PROSTI-TUTION s.212(4) Indictable Max: 5 years

212.(4) Every person who, in any place, obtains or attempts to obtain for consideration (i.e. money or something else of value) the sexual services of a person who is under the age of eighteen years is guilty of an indictable offence and liable to imprisonment for a term not exceeding five years.

The Supreme Court of Canada said in *Deutsch v. The Queen*[1] that the term "illicit sexual intercourse" in para.(a) refers to sexual intercourse that is not authorized or sanctioned by lawful marriage. In this case the accused, while interviewing a prospective employee, told her that if she took the job she might be required to have sexual intercourse with clients. She was also told that she could make a lot of money doing this. The Supreme Court of Canada held in this case that the offence of attempting

---

1. (1986), 27 C.C.C. (3d) 385 (S.C.C.).

to procure a woman to have illicit sexual relations was made out where the Crown could prove that the employer intended to induce or persuade the woman to seek employment that would require her to have intercourse with clients. In this case, holding out a large financial reward for having intercourse with clients was an inducement.

In *R. v. Celebrity Enterprises Ltd.*, the British Columbia Court of Appeal considered the meaning of "living on the avails of prostitution [ss.(j)]". The court held that the Crown must prove that the accused received some of the proceeds of the prostitute's earnings or that those proceeds somehow supported the accused's living. In this case, the accused were operators of a nightclub that was frequented by prostitutes. Their convictions for living on the avails of prostitution were overturned because indirect benefits such as admission fees to the club could not be considered "avails of prostitution".[2]

A decision of the Ontario Court of Appeal has held that a charge of "living on avails" requires the Crown to prove that the accused "was living parasitically on the earnings of the prostitute for his or her own advantage." So, where the accused and the prostitute are in a legitimate and normal living arrangement as spouses or room-mates, and are sharing living expenses, the accused cannot be said to be "living on the avails." The relationship must have a parasitic aspect for the offence to be made out. Otherwise, any person who lives with a prostitute would be likely to incur criminal responsibility.[3]

2. Soliciting

Section 213 sets out the offences concerning the public solicitation of sex:

**SOLICITING
IN PUBLIC
s.213(1)
Summary
conviction**

    213. (1) Every person who in a public place or in any place open to public view

    (a) stops or attempts to stop any motor vehicle,

    (b) impedes the free flow of pedestrian or vehicular traffic or ingress to or egress from premises adjacent to that place, or

    (c) stops or attempts to stop any person or in any manner communicates or attempts to communicate with any person for the purpose of engaging in prostitution or of obtaining the sexual services of a prostitute is guilty of an offence punishable on summary conviction.

Notice that this section makes it an offence for both the prostitute or the person seeking the services of a prostitute to communicate in public. In other words, either the prostitute or the "client" can be charged. This section of the Code has been the subject of several challenges under the

---

2. (1978), 41 C.C.C. (2d) 540 (B.C.C.A.).
3. *R. v. Grilo* (1991), 64 C.C.C. (3d) 53 (Ont. C.A.).

Charter as a violation of freedom of expression and under s.7 which guarantees the right not to be denied life, liberty, or security of the person except in accordance with the principles of fundamental justice. The Supreme Court of Canada recently considered together three cases which were being appealed on this issue.[4] All of the judges held that s.213(1)(c) [formerly s.195.1(1)(c)] violates the guarantee of freedom of expression. However, four of the judges, a majority, went on to find that this section is a reasonable limitation "prescribed by law as can be demonstrably justified in a free and democratic society under s.1." The aim of the law, the court held, was to prevent the nuisance caused by the public purchase of sex. The court considered the street congestion, noise, and oral harassment of non-participants in urban environments to be part of the social nuisance caused by this conduct. A majority of the judges also agreed that the offence does not violate s.7 of the Charter. A minority disagreed and stated that, where communication is a protected right (freedom of expression) and prostitution itself is legal, the possibility of imprisonment for this offence is too drastic a response. It is a principle of fundamental justice that the penalty must be in proportion to the offence.

B. DISORDERLY HOUSES

"Disorderly house" is a general term which refers to a common bawdy-house, a common gaming house, or a common betting house. It is an offence to "keep" a disorderly house, to be "found in" a disorderly house, or to "knowingly permit" a place to be used as a disorderly house. A keeper is defined in s.197:

KEEPER OF
DISORDERLY
HOUSE
DEFINED
s.197(1)

197. "Keeper" includes a person who:
(a) is an owner or occupier of a place,
(b) assists or acts on behalf of an owner or occupier of a place,
(c) appears to be, or to assist or act on behalf of an owner or occupier of a place,
(d) has the care or management of a place, or
(e) uses a place permanently or temporarily, with or without the consent of the owner or occupier thereof.

The Supreme Court of Canada has held that simply falling within the definition above is not enough to be convicted of "keeping" a disorderly house. There must be something more than simply being the owner or manager of a place which someone else uses as a disorderly house. In

---

4. Ref. re Criminal Code sections 193 and 195.1(1)(c). (1990), 56 C.C.C. (3d) 65 (S.C.C.); *R. v. Skinner* (1990), 56 C.C.C. (3d) 1 (S.C.C.); *R. v. Stagnitta* (1990), 56 C.C.C. (3d) 17 (S.C.C.).

general, a person must participate in the wrongful use of the disorderly house to be a keeper.[5]

If a person is "found in" a disorderly house, then it is up to that person to show some evidence that there was a lawful excuse for being there. For example, a furnace repairperson would have a lawful excuse if he or she were present in the house to repair the furnace.

If the owner or someone else having care or control of a place is charged with "knowingly permitting" the place to be used as a disorderly house, the person will be found guilty only if he or she had knowledge of how the place was being used. For example, a landlord may not know that one of his or her apartments is being used for illegal betting.

Each of the types of disorderly houses will be discussed separately.

1. Common Bawdy-House

A common bawdy-house is defined in s.197(1):

COMMON BAWDY-HOUSE DEFINED s.197(1)

> **197.(1) . . . "common bawdy-house" means a place that is**
> **(a) kept or occupied, or**
> **(b) resorted to by one or more persons for the purpose of prostitution or the practice of acts of indecency.**

Offences regarding bawdy-houses are stated in s.210:

KEEPING A COMMON BAWDY-HOUSE s.210(1) Indictable Max: 2 years

BEING FOUND IN OR OWNING A COMMON BAWDY-HOUSE s.210(2) Summary conviction

> **210.(1) Everyone who keeps a common bawdy-house is guilty of an indictable offence . . .**
> **(2) Everyone who**
> **(a) is an inmate of a common bawdy-house,**
> **(b) is found, without lawful excuse, in a common bawdy-house, or**
> **(c) as owner, landlord, lessor, tenant, occupier, agent or otherwise having charge or control of any place, knowingly permits the place or any part thereof to be let or used for the purposes of a common bawdy-house,**
> **is guilty of an offence punishable on summary conviction.**

The accused must have some degree of control over the care and management of the premises to be convicted of keeping a common bawdy-house. In *R. v. Corbeil*,[6] the accused was charged with keeping a common bawdy-house. She was a masseuse at a masseuse parlour that offered masturbation to its clients. The masseuse kept half the fee and turned the other half over to the owners of the parlour; the masseuse also

---

5. *R. v. Kerin* (1963), 1 C.C.C. 233, 39 C.R. 390 (S.C.C.).
6. *R. v. Corbeil* (1991), 64 C.C.C. (3d) 272 (S.C.C.).

kept a record of the clients. The Supreme Court of Canada held that although she occupied a space and used it, she did not exercise the requisite care and control required for the offence.

One isolated act of prostitution is not enough to make a place a bawdy-house. There must be frequent resort to, or habitual use of, the place for purposes of prostitution or indecent acts. In *Paterson v. R.*[7] two women went with three plain-clothed police officers to a suburban home for the purpose of prostitution. After their arrival, the two women went to another part of the house and later returned wearing nothing but their underwear. At this point, the officers disclosed their identity and charged them with keeping a common bawdy-house. The Supreme Court of Canada held that to be convicted of "keeping", it is necessary that there be a frequent or habitual use of the premises for the purposes of prostitution. The court found the women not guilty because there was no evidence that the home had been used for prostitution on any other occasion.

A similar decision was reached in *R. v. Evans, Lee and Woodhouse*,[8] which involved a house being used for a stag party. Three women had sexual intercourse with a number of men at the party and were paid for their services. The house had never been used before for prostitution. The issue was whether the large number of acts of intercourse which occurred in one evening were enough to convict the women and two male occupants of keeping a common bawdy-house. The court held that they were not guilty because the use of the house on one evening did not amount to frequent or habitual use of the premises for prostitution.

The Ontario Court of Appeal in *R. v. Pierce*[9] has held that any defined space, even a parking lot, can be a bawdy-house if acts of prostitution take place there. However, the prostitutes in this case, although present in a parking lot on a number of occasions, exercised no control over the lot and had no interest in the lot as owners, tenants, or licensees. Therefore, they did not have the required care and control of the lot to be "keepers" for the offence.

It is also necessary that for a place to be a bawdy-house, the acts of prostitution or indecency must be physically performed there. In *R. v. Equigaray*,[10] a prostitute received telephone calls at her apartment from customers but she always met them on the street. Then, she and the customers would go to a hotel. The prostitute was charged with keeping her residence as a common bawdy-house. She was found not guilty because the acts of prostitution did not take place there.

The meaning of "acts of indecency" was considered in *R. v. Laliberte*.[11] The court defined an indecent act as one that offends the general

---

7. (1968), 2 C.C.C. 247 (S.C.C.).
8. (1973), 11 C.C.C. (2d) 130 (Ont.C.A.).
9. (1982), 66 C.C.C. (2d) 388 (Ont.C.A.).
10. (1971), 15 C.R.N.S. 58 (Que.C.A.).
11. (1973), 12 C.C.C. (2d) 109 (Que.C.A.).

standards that decency permits. In this case, masturbation performed by a masseuse on the customers of a massage parlour was considered an act of indecency. Thus, the massage parlour was a common bawdy-house.

"Prostitution" is not defined in the Code but it has been given a wide meaning by the courts. In *R. v. Lantay*,[12] the Ontario Court of Appeal held that prostitution is not limited to sexual intercourse. It includes a woman offering herself for money as a participant in physical acts of indecency for the sexual gratification of men. This case also involved masturbation performed on customers of a massage parlour. The court held that the operator of the massage parlour was guilty of keeping a common bawdy-house because it was being resorted to for the purpose of prostitution.

Other cases have decided that proof of monetary payment for the acts of prostitution is not necessary for the purpose of deciding if a place is a common bawdy-house. In *R. v. Turkiewich*,[13] a hotel registration clerk was charged with knowingly permitting the hotel premises to be used for the purposes of a common bawdy-house. The clerk argued that because there was no evidence that money had been paid to any woman, prostitution could not be proven. The court disagreed and said that prostitution must be interpreted to include illicit or promiscuous sexual relations whether or not these relations took place for payment where it is proved that the accused knowingly allowed a place to be used for illicit sex.

The Supreme Court of Canada has held that the offences of keeping, being found in, or being an inmate of a common bawdy-house are not violations of freedom of expression or liberty.[14]

2. Common Gaming House and Common Betting House

a. *Offences*

The offences involving a common gaming house are set out in s.201:

KEEPING GAMING OR BETTING HOUSE s.201(1) Indictable Max: 2 years

BEING FOUND IN OR OWNING A GAMING OR BETTING HOUSE s.201(2) Summary conviction

> **201.(1) Everyone who keeps a common gaming house or common betting house is guilty of an indictable offence and liable to imprisonment . . . two years.**
> **(2) Everyone who**
> **(a) is found, without lawful excuse, in a common gaming house or common betting house, or,**
> **(b) as owner, landlord, lessor, tenant, occupier or agent, knowingly permits a place to be let or used for the purposes of a common gaming house or common betting house,**
> **is guilty of an offence punishable on summary conviction.**

---

12. [1965] 3 C.C.C. 170 (Ont.C.A.).
13. (1962), 113 C.C.C. 301, 38 C.R. 220 (Man.C.A.).
14. *Supra*, note 4.

b. Common Gaming House

"Common gaming house" is defined in s.197(1):

> 197.(1) Common gaming house means a place that is
>
> (a) kept for gain to which persons resort for the purpose of playing games, or
>
> (b) kept or used for the purpose of playing games
>
> (i) in which a bank is kept by one or more but not all of the players,
>
> (ii) in which all or any portion of the bets on or proceeds from a game is paid, directly or indirectly, to the keeper of the place,
>
> (iii) in which, directly or indirectly, a fee is charged to or paid by the players for the privilege of playing or participating in a game or using gaming equipment, or
>
> (iv) in which the chances of winning are not equally favourable to all persons who play the game, including the person, if any, who conducts the game.

(i) The meaning of gaming and games

Notice that under s.197(1)(a) the definition of common gaming house does not refer to the players making bets or wagering. The Supreme Court of Canada in *Di Pietro v. The Queen*[15] has held that even though the definition of common gaming house under s.197(1)(a) does not appear to require that the patrons are involved in wagering, wagering under the common law is part of the meaning of gaming. The court quoted a 1903 English decision which stated: "To amount to gaming the game played must involve the element of wagering — that is to say, each of the players must have a chance of losing as well as of winning." The Supreme Court concluded:

> *The prosecution must prove, as an element of the offence of gaming, that the participants had the chance of winning and losing money or money's worth. This possible outcome must be a result, direct or indirect, of wagering or hazarding a stake prior to or during the game.*

In this case, the "loser" bought drinks for the "winners" and no money exchanged hands. This practice was not a game under this section, but just a convenient way to take turns for paying for the drinks.

In addition to the common law meaning of gaming, the Code in s.197(1)(b) defines "game" as "a game of chance or mixed chance and skill." A game of chance is one in which luck entirely determines the winner. The Supreme Court of Canada has held that the term "mixed

---

15. *Di Pietro v. The Queen* (1986), 25 C.C.C. (3d) 100 (S.C.C.).

chance and skill" does not imply any particular proportions of skill and chance. For example, the court decided that the card game of bridge is a game of mixed chance and skill.[16] In *R. v. Lebansky*,[17] target shooting at a miniature shooting range was considered to be a game of skill and not of chance. Although some element of chance was involved, it was too small to justify classifying the game as one of mixed chance and skill. In *R . v. McGee*,[18] the game of bingo was held to be a game of chance.

(ii) Kept for gain

Under para. (a) of the definition of common gaming house, it is necessary that the place is "kept for gain" (or profit). In *R. v. James*,[19] the accused was the manager of a cigar shop. In the rear of the shop was a room in which poker games were played. Out of the stakes which were bet during the games a small amount of money was set aside to cover the cigars and refreshments consumed by the players. The court decided that the increased profits of the business derived from the sale of cigars and refreshments were a "gain" and the accused was guilty of keeping a common gaming house. A similar case, *R. v. Forder*,[20] involved the players in a poker game paying a small sum each half hour to the accused for a new pack of cards. The accused made a large profit in this way and the court held that he was guilty of keeping a common gaming house. It seems that these two cases would also fit within para.(b)(ii) of the definition of common gaming house because a portion of the bets was paid to the keeper of the place in each of the cases.

(iii) Kept, used, or resorted to

Under both para.(a) and para.(b), a place must be used more than once to be a common gaming house. The Supreme Court of Canada in *Rockert v. The Queen*[21] held that the words "kept" and "resort" refer to frequent or habitual use and the word "used" in para.(b) means more than one use. Section 197(4) allows for a place which is used once to be a common gaming house "if the keeper or any other person acting on behalf of or in concert with the keeper has used another place on another occasion in the manner described in that paragraph." In other words, this section prevents people from creating "moving" gaming houses.

(iv) Bank

A place is also a gaming house if it is kept or used for the purpose of playing games in which a "bank" is kept by one or more but not all of the players. In *R. v. Rubenstein*,[22] the accused was charged with keeping a

---

16. *Ross v. The Queen*, [1969] 1 C.C.C. 1 (S.C.C.).
17. (1941), 75 C.C.C. 348 (Man.C.A.).
18. (1942), 77 C.C.C. 302 (Man.C.A.).
19. (1903), 7 C.C.C. 196 (Ont.C.A.).
20. (1930), 54 C.C.C. 388 (Ont.C.A.).
21. (1978), 38 C.C.C. (2d) 438 (S.C.C.).
22. (1960), 32 C.R. 20 (Ont.C.A.).

common gaming house in that he was a banker in a game of blackjack played on a picnic table in a public park. The court defined "bank" as the sum of money which the dealer or banker has as a fund from which to draw the stakes and pay his or her losses, or the pile of money which the player who plays against all the other players has before him or her. The accused claimed that, at the time the police interfered, he was only taking his turn as banker and so could not be charged with keeping a common gaming house. However, during the time that the police watched, the deal went completely around three times and the bank did not change hands. The court found that the accused was running a bank which was "kept by one or more but not all of the players." The court also stated that if the bank had been passed around, the offence would not have been committed.

(v) Place

In *Rubenstein*, the accused also argued that he should not be convicted because the "place" where the game was played was a picnic table in a public park. The court held that he should be convicted because the table fell within the definition of "place" in s.197(1). It was not necessary that it be a room or building because the definition includes places which are not "covered or enclosed" and which are used by persons who do not have "an exclusive right of use." The accused also fell within the definition of "keeper" because he was a person using the place "temporarily with or without the consent of the owner or occupier."

(vi) Genuine social club

An exception to the definition of common gaming house is found in s.197(2):

> **197.(2) A place is not a common gaming house within the meaning of paragraph (a) or subparagraph (b)(ii) or (iii) of the definition "common gaming house" in subsection (1) while it is occupied and used by an incorporated genuine social club or branch thereof, if**
>
> **(a) the whole or any portion of the bets on or proceeds from games played therein is not directly or indirectly paid to the keeper thereof, and,**
>
> **(b) no fee is charged to persons for the right or privilege of participating in the games played therein other than under the authority of and in accordance with the terms of a licence issued by the Attorney General of the province in which the place is situated or by such other person or authority in the province as may be specified by the Attorney General thereof.**

In general, a social club is a group of people who get together for a social purpose (e.g., playing games), not for the purpose of making a profit. In *R. v. MacDonald et al.*,[23] a secretary-manager of the Royal Canadian Legion was charged with keeping a common gaming house. The defence was that the Legion was a genuine[24] social club and fell within the exception in s.197(2). Members of the public wishing to play bingo were admitted upon payment of a 50-cent admission fee. In order to participate in prize money, an additional 50 cents was paid. The Legion kept only the admission fees and the other money was returned as prizes to the winning players. The Supreme Court of Canada decided that admission of the public, for a fee, was not occupation and use by a genuine social club. The court went on to say: "It is unnecessary to go into the objects (or purposes) of the Canadian Legion . . . . The use of these premises on such a widespread scale contradicts any possible inference of the use as a *bona fide* [genuine] social club."

There does not seem to be one single test for determining whether a place is being used by a genuine social club. In the *MacDonald* case above, the admission of the general public for a fee on a widespread scale was an important factor in the court's decision that it was not being used by a genuine social club. In *R. v. Tatti*,[25] the Ontario Court of Appeal referred to a genuine social club as a club which is owned and controlled by all members equally. In that case, the accused was the manager of a recreation club which was used for playing card games, ping-pong, and billiards. The court held that the exception for social clubs did not apply in the case because the club was owned and controlled completely by the accused. Other courts have taken into account whether the social objects or purposes of the club are really being carried out and whether non-members are allowed to play the games. However, in *Re Mow Chong Social Club*,[26] the Ontario Court of Appeal decided that the mere fact that a non-member was able to enter the club and that only some of the purposes of the club were being carried out did not necessarily mean that a club was not a genuine social club.

Even if a place is being used by a genuine social club, it may still be considered a common gaming house if there is a payment to the keeper from bets on or proceeds from the games, or the keeper charges unauthorized fees to the players of the games [see s.197(2)(a) and (b)]. In *R. v. Karavasilis*,[27] members of a soccer club leased a building from the accused where they played rummy. The accused sold the soccer club members refreshments during their games. Even though they were a legitimate social club, the fact that the accused earned a profit from selling refreshments made the place a common gaming house.

---

23. (1966), 47 C.R. 37 (S.C.C.).
24. Until recently, amendments to s.197(2), the Code, and court decisions applying to s.197(2) used the Latin term for genuine, "bona fide". For clarity, the term "genuine" will be used even if the court used the term "bona fide".
25. [1965] 4 C.C.C. 268, 47 C.R. 59 (Ont.C.A.).
26. (1964), 47 C.R. 295 (Ont.C.A.).
27. (1980), 54 C.C.C. (2d) 530 (Ont.C.A.).

c. *Common Betting House*

Section 197(1) contains the following definitions:

> **197.(1) "Common betting house" means a place that is opened, kept or used for the purpose of:**
>
> **(a) enabling, encouraging or assisting persons who resort thereto to bet between themselves or with the keeper, or**
>
> **(b) enabling any person to receive, record, register, transmit or pay bets or to announce the results of betting.**
>
> **"Bet" means a bet that is placed on any contingency or event that is to take place in or out of Canada, and . . . includes a bet that is placed on any contingency relating to a horse-race, fight, match or sporting event that is to take place in or out of Canada.**

The recording of one bet is not enough in itself to make a place a common betting house. In *R. v. Weidman*,[28] the accused was the operator of a small store which sold newspapers, magazines, and cigarettes. There was proof that one or two bets had been made at the store. The British Columbia Court of Appeal held that there must be proof that the place is opened, kept, or used for the purpose of betting. This could be proved by one bet if there were other surrounding circumstances which showed that the place was kept for that purpose. In this case, these other circumstances did not exist and the accused was found not guilty of keeping a common betting house.

In *R. v. Woodward and Willcocks*,[29] a newspaper office was held to be a common betting house and the editor and business manager of the paper were convicted of "keeping". The newspaper operated a guessing contest in which the contestants paid a fee and tried to guess the results of football games. Prizes were awarded to the top three contestants. The prize money was taken from the fees paid by the contestants. This type of contest falls within the definition of "bet" because the contestants were betting among themselves "on a contingency relating to a sporting event."

d. *Presumptions*

Section 198 creates certain presumptions in regard to disorderly houses. All of these presumptions may be subject to challenges under the Charter, as a violation of the presumption of innocence. (See Chapter Two for a discussion of reverse onus clauses and presumptions.)

---

28. (1954), 108 C.C.C. 89, 18 C.R. 164 (B.C.C.A.).
29. (1922), 38 C.C.C. 154 (Man.C.A.).

(i) Obstruction

PRESUMP-
TIONS
REGARDING
DISORDERLY
HOUSES
s.198

198.(1) In proceedings under this Part

(a) evidence that a peace officer who was authorized to enter a place was wilfully prevented from entering or was wilfully obstructed or delayed in entering is, in the absence of any evidence to the contrary, proof that the place is a disorderly house; . . . .

For example, in *Ewaschuk v. R.*,[30] a police officer came to the door of a house with a search warrant. A woman opened the door slightly and, realizing that it was a police officer, slammed and locked the door. By this action, she was wilfully obstructing and delaying the officer, who was authorized to enter the house. Because there was no evidence to show that the place was not a disorderly house, the woman's action was enough for the court to decide that it was such a house.

(ii) Gaming equipment

198.(1) . . .

(b) Evidence that a place was found to be equipped with gaming equipment or any device for concealing, removing or destroying gaming equipment is, in the absence of any evidence to the contrary, proof that the place is a common gaming house or a common betting house, as the case may be;

(c) evidence that gaming equipment was found in a place entered under a warrant issued pursuant to this Part, or on or about the person of anyone found therein, is, in the absence of any evidence to the contrary, proof that the place is a common gaming house and that the persons found therein were playing games, whether or not any person acting under the warrant observed any person playing games therein.

For example, in *R. v. Achilles*,[31] there was evidence that a place was set up with forty-eight chairs and eight card tables and other tables on which were cards, score sheets, and pencils. The court said that these items were gaming equipment and were there for the purpose of playing a game of chance or mixed chance and skill. This was enough evidence for the court to presume that the place was a common gaming house. The accused did not testify and no evidence was given on their behalf. In other words, the presumption was not rebutted and, thus, evidence of

---

30. (1955), 111 C.C.C. 377 (Man.C.A.).
31. (1972), 6 C.C.C. (2d) 274 (Ont.C.A.).

the gaming equipment was considered proof that the place was a common gaming house.

(iii) Evidence of conviction

198.(1)(d) evidence that a person was convicted of keeping a disorderly house is, for the purpose of proceedings against anyone who is alleged to have been an inmate or to have been found in that house at the time the person committed the offence of which he was convicted, in the absence of any evidence to the contrary, proof that the house was, at that time, a disorderly house.

For example, Harry is convicted of keeping a common betting house. Jim was found in Harry's place during the time Harry was keeping it as a betting house. Jim is later charged with the offence of being "found in" a common betting house. At Jim's trial, Harry's conviction will be proof that the place was a common betting house unless there is some evidence at the trial to show that it was not.

(iv) Slot machines

198.(2) For the purpose of proceedings under this Part, a place that is found to be equipped with a slot machine shall be conclusively presumed to be a common gaming house.

In general, a slot machine refers to a machine which provides goods or amusement and which involves some element of chance. However, pinball machines are not considered slot machines if the only prize that can be won is one or more free games. The Ontario Court of Appeal has held that the presumption in this subsection violates the presumption of innocence.[32]

e. *Other Betting Offences*

BETTING, POOL-SELLING, BOOK-MAKING, ETC. s.202 Indictable Max: 2 years Min: 14 days for second offence, or 3 months for subsequent offences

Section 202 creates several betting offences which do not require the existence of a common gaming house or common betting house. These include: (a) knowingly allowing a place to be used for recording or registering bets or selling a pool; (b) making or keeping a gambling or betting machine; (c) being the custodian of a wager; (d) recording or registering bets; (e) engaging in bookmaking or in the business of betting; (f) printing or providing bookmaking information; (g) importing bookmaking information; (h) advertising an offer to bet on a contest; (i) wilfully and knowingly sending betting or bookmaking information; (j) aiding or assisting in committing any of these offences. These offences

---

32. *R. v. Shisler* (1990), 53 C.C.C. (3d) 531 (Ont.C.A.).

are directed at prohibiting the business of betting rather than prohibiting the keeping of a gaming or a betting house.

f. Off-Track Betting Shops

Under s.203, off-track betting shops are made illegal:

PLACING BETS ON BEHALF OF OTHERS
s.203
Indictable
Max: 2 years
Min: 14 days for second, 3 months for subsequent offences

203. Every one who

(a) places or offers or agrees to place a bet on behalf of another person for a consideration paid or to be paid by or on behalf of that other person,

(b) engages in the business or practice of placing or agreeing to place bets on behalf of other persons, whether for a consideration or otherwise, or,

(c) holds himself out or allows himself to be held out as engaging in the business or practice of placing or agreeing to place bets on behalf of other persons, whether for a consideration or otherwise, is guilty of an indictable offence and liable,

(d) for a first offence, to imprisonment for not more than two years,

(e) for a second offence, to imprisonment for not more than two years and not less than fourteen days, and

(f) for each subsequent offence, to imprisonment for not more than two years and not less than three months.

The offences in s.203 are basically similar to the offence of engaging in the business of betting. The main difference is that s.203 specifically prohibits off-track betting shops. These shops receive money from customers and, for a fee, wager the money for them at the racetrack.

EXCEPTIONS ALLOWING BETTING
s.204

Section 204 creates certain exceptions which allow for betting in certain situations. For example, it states s.201 and s.202 do not apply to:

(a) any person or association by reason of his or their becoming the custodian . . . of any money . . . to be paid to

    (i) the winner of a lawful race, sport game or exercise,

    (ii) the owner of a horse engaged in a lawful race, or

    (iii) the winner of any bets between not more than ten individuals;

(b) a private bet between individuals not engaged in any way in the business of betting;

This section also sets out the rules for allowing betting at approved race courses.

C. LOTTERIES AND OTHER SCHEMES

1. Lotteries

OFFENCES IN RELATION TO LOTTERIES AND GAMES OF CHANCE s.206(1) Indictable Max: 2 years

A lottery is a scheme for giving a prize by some method of chance, such as drawing numbered tickets from a container. In s.206, a lottery is referred to as a game or any proposal, scheme, or plan for advancing, lending, giving, selling, or in any way disposing of any property by lots, cards, tickets, or any mode of chance whatever. Section 206(1) covers several offences involving lotteries, including: (a) advertising or publishing a lottery; (b) selling or otherwise disposing of lottery tickets; (c) knowingly sending articles which are intended for use in a lottery; and (d) conducting or managing a lottery.

EXCEPTIONS PERMITTING LOTTERIES s.207

For a lottery to exist, it is essential that the prize ("property") be disposed of by some method of chance. If any skill is involved, then there is no lottery. Because of this rule, many contests include a "skill-testing question" which must be answered before the prize is awarded. However, some lotteries are permitted. In general, s.207(1) provides that a lottery scheme may be conducted and managed by the government of a province. Also, if licensed by the provincial government, lotteries may be conducted and managed by: (a) a charitable or religious organization, (b) an agricultural fair or exhibition, and (c) any person at a public place of amusement.

2. Other Schemes

OTHER PROHIBITED SCHEMES s.206(1)(e)–(j) Indictable Max: 2 years

Section 206(1)(e) covers other schemes and games which are not lotteries because they do not involve giving a prize by some method of chance. In brief, it prohibits the conduct or management of any scheme by which a person upon paying an amount of money becomes entitled to receive something of greater monetary value because of the contributions of others to the scheme. In *Dream Home Contests Ltd. v. R.*,[33] the accused were charged with operating such a scheme. They built a house called a "Dream Home" which was put on display to the public. Contestants had to buy a one-dollar ticket and had to estimate the total retail value of the Dream Home. The contestant who most closely estimated the total retail value of the home would win the home. In other words, the winning contestant became entitled to a home which was of much greater value than the amount paid ($1). Giving away such a valuable prize was only made possible by the fact that so many other contestants "contributed to the scheme" (i.e., bought tickets). Therefore, the requirements of the offence were present and the accused were found guilty. The accused were also charged with advertising a lottery, contrary to s.206(1)(a). However, the accused were not guilty of this offence because the contest

---

33. (1960), 33 C.R. 47 (S.C.C.).

was not a lottery since it did not involve giving a prize by some method of chance. In other words, estimating the value of the house was considered to involve skill.

Section 206(1)(e) also covers pyramid selling schemes which operate like chain letters. In *R. v. Cote*,[34] the accused was an officer of the company known as Dare To Be Great of Canada Ltd. The company's operation involved selling a course to persons at a cost of $1 500. The company claimed that the objective of the course was to strengthen the personality of the subscriber (or "member"), to improve the member's self-confidence, and to make the member more successful in work. The subscriber also received a suitcase containing a tape recorder, cassettes, and other materials which had a total value of $100. After completing the course, the subscriber became a sales agent (or "motivator") and received a commission of $900 for every sale of the course to a new subscriber. Each of these new subscribers also had to pay $1 500 for the course. In turn, these new subscribers became sales agents after completing the course. The court held that this scheme fell within s.206(1)(e) because it was a means by which a person, upon paying $1 500, became entitled to receive a larger sum of money by recruiting new members who were the source of the larger sum.

The remaining paragraphs of s.206(1) are reasonably clear:

> **206.(1) Every one is guilty of an indictable offence and is liable to imprisonment for two years who . . .**
>
> **(f) disposes of any goods, wares or merchandise by any game of chance or any game of mixed chance and skill in which the contestant or competitor pays money or other valuable consideration;**
>
> **(g) induces any person to stake or hazard any money or other valuable property or thing on the result of any dice game, three-card monte, punch board, coin table or on the operation of a wheel of fortune;**
>
> **(h) for valuable consideration carries on or plays or offers to carry on or to play, or employs any person to carry on or play in a public place or a place to which the public have access, the game of three-card monte;**
>
> **(i) receives bets of any kind on the outcome of a game of three-card monte; or**
>
> **(j) being the owner of a place, permits any person to play the game of three-card monte therein.**

Three-card monte is a card game in which a person tries to guess the location of one playing card among a total of three. Section 206(2)

---

34. (1973), 11 C.C.C. (2d) 443 (Que.C.A.).

provides that three-card monte includes any other game that is similar to it whether or not cards are used or notwithstanding the number of cards or things used.

QUESTIONS FOR REVIEW AND DISCUSSION

1 Explain the ways the Criminal Code controls prostitution.

2 Name the three types of disorderly houses.

3 Name three offences which can be committed in relation to a disorderly house.

4 Explain the meaning of "prostitution" and "acts of indecency" in the definition of a common bawdy-house.

5 What is a common gaming house?

6 What is the meaning of "game"?

7 What is a genuine social club?

8 What is a common betting house?

9 Give two examples of legal betting.

10 What are the essential elements of a lottery?

11 As part of a scheme for making money, Youssef rents three houses and hires several prostitutes. The Red House is rented from Avril and is to be used for "group sex orgies" among customers and prostitutes. Avril agrees to let Youssef use the house for this purpose. The Pink House is rented from Winona and is to be used for "private sex". The plan is for each room in the house to be used by one prostitute and one customer. Winona has no knowledge that the place is to be used for this purpose. The Purple House is rented from Jackson and is to be used as a meeting place for prostitutes and "cautious" customers. After meeting at the house, the plan is for Youssef to take the customer and the prostitute in Jackson's car to a secluded location for the purpose of having sexual intercourse in the back seat. Youssef and Jackson agree to split the proceeds from this operation.

The Purple House and the Pink House operate for several weeks before the opening of the Red House and prove to be very profitable. On the opening night of the Red House, all three houses are raided by the police and Youssef, a customer, and a prostitute are arrested in Jackson's car. The following charges result: (1) Youssef is charged with keeping four common bawdy-houses: the three houses and the car; (2) Avril, Winona, and Jackson are charged with permitting their places to be used as common bawdy-houses; (3) the prostitutes and customers are charged with being found in a common bawdy-house. On which charges should there be convictions? Why?

12 Eugene operates a shooting range and charges a $2 admission fee. The most accurate shooter on any day wins a free admission. Is Eugene guilty of keeping a common gaming house? Why?

13 Christine is charged with keeping a common gaming house. The only evidence presented at the trial is that a slot machine was found in Christine's basement. Should Christine be convicted? Why?

14 Christine, Mehta, Enni, and Sharon enjoy betting on horse races. Because Enni lives near the track, he places bets for himself, Christine, Mehta, and Sharon each week during the racing season. Is Enni guilty of an offence? Why? Does it matter that Enni received no fee for placing the bets? Why?

NINE

Homicide and the Offences of Murder, Manslaughter, and Infanticide

Part VIII of the Code

A. HOMICIDE

Homicide is defined in s.222 of the Code as follows:

HOMICIDE DEFINED s.222

> **222.(1) A person commits homicide when, directly or indirectly, by any means, he causes the death of a human being.**
> **(2) Homicide is culpable or not culpable.**
> **(3) Homicide that is not culpable is not an offence.**
> **(4) Culpable homicide is murder or manslaughter, or infanticide.**

1. Causation

In most situations, where the act is proved, it is not difficult to determine whether the act caused the death. Caitlin shoots a gun at Millie; Millie dies from the gunshot wound. It is clear that Caitlin's act caused Millie's death. However, there are situations where it is not clear if the act caused the death. For example, an intervening act, such as improper medical treatment, may contribute to the death, or there may be other factors such as the condition of the victim which contributed to the death. The general rule developed by the courts is that the accused takes his or her victim as he or she is. In other words, the accused takes his or her victim with whatever weaknesses or special conditions the victim has. So, if the victim of assault dies because of a weak heart, the accused will still be responsible for causing the death.

An example of a case in which the victim had a special condition that contributed to his death is *R. v. Smithers*,[1] decided by the Supreme Court of Canada. The accused and the victim, Cobby, had been on opposing hockey teams. The game was rough and both were ejected from the game. The accused made repeated threats that he was going "to get" the victim. The victim was apprehensive about the threats and did not want to fight. He waited about 45 minutes before leaving the game, accompanied by his teammates and coach. The accused was waiting and tried to punch him in the head. The victim's teammates grabbed the accused and tried to hold him back, but he was able to kick the victim in the abdomen. The victim died about five minutes later. The medical evidence was that the victim's death had been caused by asphyxia resulting from aspiration of foreign material into his lungs (i.e., breathing in his own vomit) and that the vomiting was probably caused by the kick. Death from this cause was extremely rare in the case of a healthy teenager like the victim. It may have resulted from a malfunction of the epiglottis, which is a flap of skin preventing food from entering the air passage. The Supreme Court held that in this case there was sufficient evidence for a jury to decide that the kick was the cause of death. The accused could be found guilty even though the death was not anticipated and ordinarily would not have resulted.

There are several sections of the Code which deal with other specific issues of causation.

a. *Section 223*

Since homicide is the causing of the death of a *human being* it is important to know when, in the eyes of the criminal law, a human being comes into existence.

Section 223 states:

WHEN A CHILD BECOMES A HUMAN BEING s.223(1)

> **223.(1) A child becomes a human being within the meaning of this Act when it has completely proceeded, in a living state, from the body of its mother whether or not**
> **(a) it has breathed,**
> **(b) it has an independent circulation, or**
> **(c) the navel string is severed.**

CAUSING DEATH BY INJURY GIVEN BEFORE OR DURING BIRTH s.223(2)

Thus, according to the criminal law, a fetus (i.e., an unborn child) is not a human being. The section then goes on to state:

> **223.(2) A person commits homicide when he causes injury to a child before or during its birth as a result of which the child dies after becoming a human being.**

---

1. (1978), 34 C.C.C. (2d) 427 (S.C.C.).

In other words, under this section homicide is committed if an injury causes a fetus to die after being born. If the fetus dies before being born because of the injury, then the death is not homicide. In *R. v. Prince*,[2] the accused attacked a woman who was obviously pregnant. The child was born prematurely and died 19 minutes after birth because of the injuries suffered by the mother. The court held that the accused was responsible for the child's death.

DEATH THAT
MIGHT HAVE
BEEN PRE-
VENTED
s.224

b. Section 224

> 224. Where a person, by an act or omission, does anything that results in the death of a human being, he causes the death of that human being notwithstanding that death from that cause might have been prevented by resorting to proper means.

This section would apply to the following type of situation: Whitney inflicts a minor wound on Foster. Foster fails to get proper medical treatment for the injury, and the wound becomes infected, causing Foster's death. Whitney has caused the death of Foster even though the death could have been prevented if the wound had been given proper treatment.

c. Section 225

This section deals with a situation similar to s.224.

DEATH
CAUSED BY
TREATMENT
s.225

> 225. Where a person causes to a human being a bodily injury that is of itself of a dangerous nature and from which death results, he causes the death of that human being notwithstanding that the immediate cause of death is proper or improper treatment that is applied in good faith.

A case which involved s.225 is *R. v. Emkeit and 12 Others*.[3] Emkeit and the other 12 men were members of a motorcycle gang. During a fight with a rival gang, one of its members was hit on the side of the head with a chain by Emkeit. He died while being driven to the hospital. The victim's injuries consisted of several serious head lacerations. Doctors testified that the causes of death were pulmonary edema caused by the head injuries, and tracheobronchial aspiration which in effect meant that the victim had drowned in his own vomit. This had resulted from the injured man being laid on his back without his tongue being depressed while he was being taken to the hospital by his friends.

Emkeit argued that the jury could have found him not guilty if the jury

---

2. (1988), 44 C.C.C. (3d) 510 (Man.C.A.).
3. (1971), 3 C.C.C. (2d) 309 (Alta.C.A.).

found that the victim's life could have been saved if proper treatment had been given. The court held, however, that the jury did not need to consider this argument. In giving his reasons for rejecting Emkeit's appeal, the judge adopted the following example taken from an English case as an analogous situation to which s.225 would apply:

> . . . *A man is stabbed in the back, his lung is pierced and haemorrhage results; two hours later he dies of haemorrhage from that wound; in the interval there is no time for a careful examination and the treatment given turns out in the light of subsequent knowledge to have been inappropriate and, indeed, harmful. In those circumstances no reasonable jury or court could, properly directed, in our view come to any other conclusion than that the death resulted from the original wound.*

The case from which the example was taken was *R. v. Smith*.[4] The facts were that during a fight at a military barracks, the accused stabbed the deceased in the back and arm. Unknown to anyone, the deceased's lung had been pierced and the wound was hemorrhaging. A fellow member of the company tried to carry him to the medical station. On the way he tripped twice and dropped the injured man on the ground. At the medical station, no one appreciated the seriousness of his injuries and the treatment he was given turned out to have been wrong and probably harmful. The man died about one hour after arriving at the station. If he had been given proper treatment his chances of recovery were as high as 75 percent. The court held that if at the time of death the original wound is still an *operating* and *substantial* cause then the death can be properly said to be the result of the wound, even though some other cause of death is also operating.

In sum, the *Emkeit* and *Smith* cases demonstrate that a person will not be able to escape criminal responsibility where he or she causes a serious injury but where the death is actually caused by improper treatment. The key point is whether the original wound is the operating and substantial cause of death. A case in which the wound was not considered the cause of death is *R. v. Jordan*.[5] The accused had stabbed the victim in the abdomen. Evidence showed the victim had been given an antibiotic to which he had an allergic reaction of severe diarrhea. When the reaction was discovered, the drug was discontinued. However, the next day another doctor gave the victim the same drug. The victim was also given abnormally large quantities of liquid intravenously, and he eventually died from pneumonia caused by the excessive amount of liquid. The stab wound that the victim had suffered, although serious (it had pierced his intestine), had mainly healed by the time the victim died. In this case the accused's conviction was overturned. The cause of death was too far

---

4. (1959), 2 All E.R. 193.
5. (1956), 40 Cr.App.Rep. 152 (C.A.).

removed from the original stabbing; the death was really caused by the grossly improper treatment of the doctors.

Notice also that the treatment must be given in "good faith". Presumably, if Jack was seriously injured and taken to a doctor who decides to kill him by giving him the wrong medication, then Tom, the person who caused the original injury, would escape responsibility for the death.[6]

d. Section 226

INJURY THAT
ACCEL-
ERATES
DEATH
s.226

> **226. Where a person causes to a human being a bodily injury that results in death, he causes the death of that human being notwithstanding that the effect of the bodily injury is only to accelerate his death from a disease or disorder arising from some other cause.**

The effect of this section is that even though a person causes injury to another, and the injury itself has not caused the death, the person has still committed homicide if the injury has accelerated the death from other causes. A case which relied on s.226 is *R. v. Nicholson*.[7] In this case, the accused and the deceased argued one evening at a school house meeting. The accused struck the deceased twice. At that point they were pushed outside the building. The deceased's body was found some hours later. Medical evidence indicated that the deceased was a man in poor physical condition, whose heart was abnormally small, and who suffered from Bright's disease. He had also been indulging freely in alcoholic beverages. The doctor who testified at the trial said that the blows struck by the accused were one cause of death, others being the man's bad health and drinking. A jury found the accused guilty of manslaughter since the blows contributed to the causing of the death.

e. Section 227

DEATH
WITHIN ONE
YEAR AND
ONE DAY
s.227

> **227. No person commits culpable homicide or the offence of causing the death of a human being by criminal negligence . . . unless the death occurs within one year and one day from the time of the occurrence of the last event by means of which the person caused or contributed to the cause of death.**

The rule in this section originated during medieval times when it was very difficult, if not impossible, to accurately identify as the cause of death an event that occurred over a year ago. In modern times there has been some criticism of this rule. The criticism points out that medical

---

6. For example, see *R. v. MarKuss* (1864), 176 E.R. 598. Whether the original assailant would be liable would depend on the court finding that the original injury actually contributed to the death.

7. (1926), 47 C.C.C. 113 (N.S.C.A.).

science has advanced to a stage where, first, it is not difficult to trace a cause of death to an event which happened long ago and, second, because medical science is so advanced, persons who would have previously died immediately now may linger for months before finally dying.[8]

2. Culpable and Non-Culpable Homicide

Whenever a person causes the death of another person, he or she commits homicide. There are, however, two types of homicide, *culpable* and *non-culpable*. Only **culpable homicide** is a criminal offence.

a. *Non-Culpable Homicide*

Non-culpable homicide can be divided into two types, *justifiable* and *excusable*. Homicide is justifiable if it is authorized or ordered by the law. Examples of justifiable homicide are: a soldier killing an enemy during wartime, the execution of a person sentenced to death, or a police officer shooting a person in the course of duty. In these situations, the law may either require the killing as when a death penalty is imposed or it may permit a killing as when a police officer finds it necessary to kill someone. (Note: Canadian law no longer allows the death penalty.)

A homicide may be excusable where caused in self-defence, in defence of others under the person's protection, or in defence of property. These excuses are generally discussed in Chapter Four, Defences. Recall that to rely on an excuse such as self-defence the force used must be no more than that necessary to repel the attack.

Homicide may also be excusable where it is caused accidentally. So, for example, where a person is doing a lawful act and unintentionally and without negligence kills another person, the death is considered accidental and no criminal liability will be attached. However, as will be discussed more fully later, if a person is doing an unlawful act and accidentally causes a death, the homicide will be culpable.

b. *Culpable Homicide*

Culpable homicide consists of three offences: murder, manslaughter, and infanticide. Murder is the most serious type of culpable homicide. Generally speaking, the difference between murder and manslaughter is that murder requires a specific intent (e.g., to cause a person's death), while manslaughter requires a general intent which is usually argued when the accused has recklessly caused a death. So, for example, Alfred is angry at his child Billy and beats the child severely. Billy dies from the beating. If it is clear that Alfred did not specifically intend to cause Billy's death but only had the general intention to do the act of beating, and was

---

8. 1961 *Criminal Law Review*, 348.

reckless about the consequences of the beating, he will probably be charged with manslaughter and not with murder. In contrast to murder and manslaughter, infanticide is a rarely used offence which only applies to certain situations involving newborn children.

Before deciding whether a death involves murder, manslaughter, or infanticide, it is first necessary to decide whether the homicide is culpable or non-culpable.

Section 222(5) lists the methods by which culpable homicide can be committed:

CULPABLE HOMICIDE DEFINED s.222(5)

222.(5) A person commits culpable homicide when he causes the death of a human being,
(a) by means of an unlawful act,
(b) by criminal negligence,
(c) by causing that human being, by threats or fear of violence or by deception, to do anything that causes his death, or
(d) by wilfully frightening that human being, in the case of a child or a sick person.

(i) By an unlawful act

There are many types of unlawful acts ranging from crimes which involve the risk of serious personal injury to municipal or provincial offences which are enacted for the purpose of regulating some activity (e.g., parking by-laws) and have no role in protecting people or property. When considering whether an act is "unlawful" for the purposes of s.222, the courts do not treat all unlawful acts the same. If the unlawful act is criminal, and death results, the accused will have committed a culpable homicide if any reasonable person would have realized that the unlawful act would have subjected another person to some risk of harm, however trivial.[9] For example, in *R. v. Jakerbowych*,[10] the accused was charged with manslaughter for shooting his friend. He had pulled the trigger of the gun to check that it was unloaded and then pointed it at his friend. The gun discharged, killing him. The evidence showed that the gun was faulty and that there was no way the accused could have been aware of the defect. Even though pointing a firearm at another is an offence, the court found him not guilty because a reasonable person in his position would not have realized the risk.

In *R. v. Cole*,[11] the Ontario Court of Appeal considered the situation where the unlawful act which causes death is not criminal. The accused had met the deceased at a bar where they were both drinking. The deceased asked the accused for drugs. The accused gave the deceased

---

9. *R. v. Baron* (1984), 39 C.R. (3d) 379 (Ont.H.Ct.).
10. (1968), 66 W.W.R. 755 (Alta.T.D.).
11. (1981), 64 C.C.C. (2d) 119 (Ont.C.A.).

some prescription pills and later helped her take some of them. The woman died later that evening from a drug overdose and the accused was charged with manslaughter. The Ontario Court of Appeal stated that, where the unlawful act is not criminal, the act must have been committed intentionally, and objectively have been likely to cause harm or injury to another person. In this case, however, the court found that the accused had not committed an unlawful act. The drugs he had given the deceased were listed under the Food and Drugs Act and, although it was an offence to sell such drugs unless authorized, it was not an offence to give the drugs to a person.

(ii) Criminal negligence

Culpable homicide may also occur where a person's death has been caused by criminal negligence. The offences of criminal negligence are discussed in Chapter Ten. The definition of criminal negligence, which is set out in s.219, applies to criminal negligence under s.222(5)(b). The offence of causing death by criminal negligence has the same elements as culpable homicide by criminal negligence (the offence charged would be manslaughter). In other words, a person could be charged either with causing death by criminal negligence or with manslaughter.

(iii) Threats or fear of violence

Another way of committing culpable homicide is by causing a person to do something, through threats, fear of violence or deception, which causes his or her death. An example of a case where the court said that there were facts from which a jury could find that the deceased acted through fear of violence is *R. v. Graves*.[12] In this case, the accused, along with others, and while intoxicated, trespassed on the victim's front lawn. The accused and his friends were using grossly offensive language and refused to leave when asked. The victim, his wife, and others who had been sitting on the front porch eventually went into the house. After a time, the victim loaded his gun, went to the front of the house and asked the accused and his friends to leave. Instead of leaving, they rushed upon the victim. The victim used the gun as a club to ward off the attackers. The gun went off, killing the victim. The court held that the accused was properly charged with manslaughter.

(iv) Frightening a child or sick person

It is also culpable homicide to cause a person's death, where the person is a child or sick person, by wilfully frightening him or her. This provision is set out in s.228:

CAUSING
DEATH BY
INFLUENCE
ON THE
MIND
s.228

> **228. No person commits culpable homicide where he causes the death of a human being:**
> **(a) by any influence on the mind alone, or**

---

12. (1913), 21 C.C.C. 44 (S.C.C.).

(b) by any disorder or disease resulting from influence on the mind alone,

but this section does not apply where a person causes the death of a child or sick person by wilfully frightening him.

An example of a case where the court found that the death was caused by influence on the mind is *R. v. Howard*.[13] In this case, the accused and victim were travelling on a streetcar. The accused was trying to get off and the victim was in his way. The men began to argue and blows were exchanged. A few moments later, the victim became unconscious and then died. The medical evidence showed that the deceased had been an elderly man in poor physical condition. His arteries were weak and death was caused by a brain hemorrhage. The court found that the blows had not caused the hemorrhage but that death was a result of the anger and excitement which caused the artery to burst. In this situation, death was actually caused by influence on the mind. The charges against the accused were dismissed, since the victim, though elderly, was not "a sick person".

B. OFFENCES OF CULPABLE HOMICIDE

Once it is established that the homicide is culpable, the next step is determining whether the homicide is murder, manslaughter, or infanticide.

1. Murder

Culpable homicide is murder where certain additional factors, other than the culpable causing of death, are present. Under the common law, murder was defined as unlawful killing with "malice aforethought"; in other words, where the person intended to cause someone's death. Until recently, the offence of murder covered not only those situations where the death had been specifically intended but also where the death was not intended but certain surrounding circumstances existed. However, since the enactment of the Charter, the Supreme Court of Canada has made drastic changes to the offence of murder which are discussed below.

Sections 229 and 230 set out the situations in which culpable homicide is murder.

MURDER
DEFINED
s.229

a. *Section 229*

229. Culpable homicide is murder

(a) where the person who causes the death of a human being

---

13. (1913), 5 W.W.R. 838 (Man.).

(i) means to cause his death, or

(ii) means to cause him bodily harm that he knows is likely to cause his death, and is reckless whether death ensues or not;

(b) where a person, meaning to cause death to a human being or meaning to cause him bodily harm that he knows is likely to cause his death, and being reckless whether death ensues or not, by accident or mistake causes death to another human being, notwithstanding that he does not mean to cause death or bodily harm to that human being; or

(c) where a person, for an unlawful object, does anything that he knows or ought to know is likely to cause death, and thereby causes death to a human being, notwithstanding that he desires to effect his object without causing death or bodily harm to any human being.

(i) Section 229(a)

Murder under s.229(a)(i) is the simplest form of the offence. All that must be shown is that the accused by a voluntary act caused a person's death and that the accused intended to cause that person's death. Since it may be impossible to produce evidence that shows a person actually had the mental intention to cause another person's death (unless, of course, there is a confession), courts have long taken the position that it may be presumed that a person intends the natural consequences of his or her acts. As one judge stated: "If a man is aware that certain consequences will probably follow the act which the person contemplates doing and yet deliberately proceeds to do that act, the person must be taken to have intended those consequences to follow even though he may have hoped they would not."[14] For example, Hania wants to kill Carl. Hania puts a bomb in Carl's car. Hania knows that Lao always travels with Carl and although Hania does not want Lao to die, she knows that Lao probably will die from the explosion. If Carl and Lao die, Hania can be charged with murder for both their deaths.

Murder under s.229(a)(ii) differs from that under s.229(a)(i) in that the specific intent necessary is to cause bodily harm that the accused knows is likely to cause death, rather than a specific intent to cause death. Before a person can be convicted of murder under s.229(a)(ii), it must be shown that the accused *intentionally* inflicted bodily harm that the accused *knew* was likely to cause death and that the accused was *reckless* as to whether death would result. All of these elements must be present, that is, the intent, knowledge, and recklessness. Thus, a homicide will not fall within this section if the accused did not actually know that the death was a likely result of the bodily harm or if the accused caused the bodily harm recklessly rather than intentionally. Likewise, the homicide does

---

14. *R. v. Krafchenko* (1914), 22 C.C.C. 277 (Man.K.B.).

not fall within this section unless the accused was reckless as to whether or not death would ensue. This means that the accused, who knew death was likely, without justification or without caring, did the act which caused the death. For example, Kim commits an apparently minor assault on Tanya without meaning to cause serious injury and without realizing that it was likely to cause death. However, unknown to Kim, Tanya has a weak heart. The assault causes Tanya to suffer a stroke from which she dies. Kim would probably not be convicted of murder. Although Kim did intend to cause bodily harm, she did not know the injury was likely to cause death and, therefore, s.229(a)(ii) would not apply.

(ii) Section 229(b)

This subsection merely provides that where a person's conduct would fall under s.229(a) but, by accident or mistake, the wrong person dies, the person has still committed murder, even though he or she had no intent to harm the person who died. In *R. v. Droste*,[15] the accused planned to murder his wife by staging a car accident. Instead, his wife was only injured while his two children who were in the back seat died. The court held that he was properly convicted of murdering his children. His intent to kill his wife was "transferred" to the victims of his act.

(iii) Section 229(c)

This subsection makes homicide murder where a person for an *unlawful object* does something which he or she *knows* or *ought to know* is dangerous to life and which causes the death of a human being. It is essential that the accused acted for an unlawful object. In other words, the act which caused the death must have been done to further or to achieve an unlawful purpose. For example, if Rebecca shoots a gun at Owen for the purpose of robbing him and Owen dies, Rebecca can be charged with murder since she fired the gun for the unlawful object of robbing Owen. The Supreme Court of Canada has said that the unlawful object in this section must be a serious crime, that is, an indictable offence requiring *mens rea*. The case in which the Court made this statement was *R. v. Vasil*.[16] The accused had been living with the mother of the two victims. Vasil and the mother were at a party where they had an argument. Vasil left the party, went back to their house, and took the babysitter home. He then returned to the house and spread lighter fluid on various things in the house and set the house on fire. He testified that his purpose in setting the fire was to damage the mother's things. The two children asleep in the house died. The unlawful object in this case was the wilful destruction of property. The dangerous act (the act which the accused should have known may cause death) was setting the fire.

---

15. (1979), 49 C.C.C. (2d) 52 (Ont.C.A.).
16. (1981), 58 C.C.C. (2d) 97 (S.C.C.).

The words "ought to know" mean that an objective test may be used to determine whether the accused is responsible for the death. Unlike s.229(a)(11) which uses a subjective test (i.e., did the accused actually know the harm was likely to cause death?), this section asks, would a reasonable person have known that the thing being done was dangerous to life? One court stated the test this way: "If the accused had the capacity to form the intent necessary for the unlawful object and had knowledge of the relevant facts which made his conduct such as to be likely to cause death, he is guilty of murder if a reasonable man should have anticipated that such conduct was likely to cause death."[17]

There have been many critics of the presence of an **objective mens rea** for an offence as serious as murder. A Justice of the Supreme Court of Canada has indicated that this section violates the Charter. However, in the case in which this comment was made (*R. v. Vaillancourt*, discussed below), it was not necessary to rule on this section to make a decision in the case.[18] So, strictly speaking, the section has not been struck down yet. However, if a case involving this section does come before the court, it is likely to be found unconstitutional. The issue of the type of *mens rea*, that is, subjective or objective, required for murder is discussed more fully in the next section.

**CONSTRUC-
TIVE
MURDER
s.230**

b. *Constructive Murder Under S.230*

Under this section culpable homicide is murder where a person causes a someone else's death whether or not the person knew death was likely and whether or not he or she intended to cause death. The section only applies where the death is caused while one of the offences listed in the section is being attempted or committed. The offences listed in s.230 include such serious crimes as assaulting a peace officer, sexual assault, kidnapping, robbery, and breaking and entering.

The effect of s.230 is that a person can be found guilty of murder even though the death may have been caused accidently. The principle is that a person who attempts or commits one of these serious offences should be held responsible for murder if a death results even though the death was unintended. Murder under s.230 is referred to as constructive murder because subjective intent to cause the death is not required. Three of the paragraphs, (a), (c), and (d), have recently been struck down by the Supreme Court of Canada. It is likely that the remaining section will also be challenged and struck down when the appropriate case arises.

The first paragraph to be challenged was s.230(d). This paragraph has been repealed and no longer appears in the Code:

**230. Culpable homicide is murder where a person causes
the death of a human being [while committing or attempting**

---

17. *R. v. Tennant and Naccarato* (1975), 23 C.C.C. (2d) 80 (Ont.C.A.).
18. See note 20.

listed offences] . . . whether or not the person means to cause death to any human being and whether or not he knows that death is likely to be caused to any human being, if . . .
(d) he uses a weapon or has it upon his person
(i) during or at the time he commits or attempts to commit the offence, or
(ii) during or at the time of his flight after committing or attempting to commit the offence,
and death ensues as a consequence.

Section 230(d) provided the widest circumstances in which culpable homicide could be murder. Under (d) a person who accidently caused a death could be convicted of murder if the other elements of the offence were present. In other words, murder under s.230(d) was an absolute liability offence with regard to causing the death.

Despite criticism by many legal scholars, including members of the federal law reform commission, saying that it is wrong to convict some-one of murder who neither intended to cause death nor intended to cause bodily harm the person knew was likely to cause death, the Supreme Court of Canada, in a 1951 decision, upheld the validity of s.230(d).[19]

However, with the enactment of the Charter, the court was given the opportunity to reexamine this law. The court heard two cases, both involving unintentional killings. In *R. v. Vaillancourt*[20] the accused was charged with murder after his accomplice in a robbery shot and killed a bystander. Vaillancourt was charged with murder because he was a party to the offence [s.21(2)]. Vaillancourt testified that he and the accomplice planned to use knives for the robbery. When the accomplice showed up with a gun, Vaillancourt asked him to take out the bullets before the robbery. In fact three bullets were found in his glove at the scene of the crime. In *R. v. Laviolette*[21] the accused took part in a break and enter. The owner of the house was beaten to death by one of Laviolette's accomplices.

The Supreme Court of Canada held in both these cases that s.230(d) violated the Charter's guarantees of fundamental justice and the pre-sumption of innocence. The court found the violation of fundamental justice on two grounds. First, the court held that for serious offences the *mens rea* required for the offence must reflect the nature of the particular crime. For example, theft requires proof of a mental element of dishon-esty. Murder is distinguished from manslaughter by the type of *mens rea* required — intention rather than recklessness. But murder under s.230(d) does not require any type of intention; therefore, this section cannot be upheld. Second, the court stated that the *mens rea* required for an offence must reflect the stigma and penalty attached to the crime.

---

19. *R. v. Rowe* (1951), 100 C.C.C. 97 (S.C.C.).
20. (1987), 39 C.C.C. (3d) 118 (S.C.C.).
21. (1987), 39 C.C.C. (3d) 238 (S.C.C.).

Convicting a person of the serious crime of murder, the penalty for which is life imprisonment, when the person did not subjectively or objectively intend to cause the death offends the Charter.

The court stated that the presumption of innocence requires that all of the elements of the offence need to be proved against an accused. Murder, the court said, requires at least objective foreseeability. Under s.230(d), a person can be convicted of murder with no *mens rea* proved; therefore, the presumption of innocence is violated.

The court also considered whether s.230(d) could be saved by the reasonable limit test under s.1 of the Charter and held that it could not.

Since murder under s.230(d) was basically an absolute liability offence with regard to causing death, the court did not need to decide whether objective foreseeability would be sufficient for the offence of murder. The court considered this issue a few years later when s.230(a) was challenged:

> **230. Culpable homicide is murder where a person causes the death of a human being [while attempting or committing listed offences] . . . whether or not the person means to cause death to any human being and whether or not he knows that death is likely if . . .**
>   **(a) he means to cause bodily harm for the purpose of**
>   **(i) facilitating the commission of the offence, or**
>   **(ii) facilitating his flight after committing or attempting**
> **to commit the offence, and death ensues from bodily harm.**

The court issued concurrent judgments in five cases.[22] In brief, the court held that the offence of murder requires subjective foreseeability. The decisions repeated the statement in *Vaillancourt* that it is a principle of fundamental justice that the punishment for an offence must be in proportion to the seriousness of the offence. Murder is the most serious peacetime crime. Therefore, it must be reserved for those who either intend to cause death or cause bodily harm that they know is likely to cause death. The court's decision only concerned s.230(a). A year later the court was asked to consider s.230(c) under which murder is committed if, during the commission of one of the offences listed in s.230, the accused:

> **(c) . . . wilfully stops, by any means the breath of a human being for a purpose mentioned in paragraph (a), and the death ensues therefrom.**

In *R. v. Sit*,[23] the accused was charged with murder under this section

---

22. *R. v. Martineau* (1990), 58 C.C.C. (3d) 353 (S.C.C.); *R. v. Luxton* (1990), 58 C.C.C. (3d) 449 (S.C.C.); *R. v. Rodney* (1990), 58 C.C.C. (3d) 408 (S.C.C.); *R. v. Arkell* (1990), 59 C.C.C. (3d) 65 (S.C.C.); *R. v. Logan and Johnson* (1990) 58 C.C.C. (3d) 391 (S.C.C.).
23. (1991), 66 C.C.C. (3d) 449 (S.C.C.).

for causing the death of a victim during an attempted kidnapping. Again the court held that murder requires subjective foreseeability and struck the section down.

The only remaining paragraph is (b) which makes the causing of an unintentional death during the attempt or commission of one of the offences in s.230 murder where a person

> **(b) administers a stupefying or overpowering thing for a purpose mentioned in paragraph (a), and the death ensues therefrom . . . .**

This will likely be challenged and struck down when an appropriate case arises.

c. Classification of Murder for Sentencing

FIRST AND SECOND DEGREE MURDER DEFINED s.231

In 1976 legislation was enacted by Parliament to abolish capital punishment (the death penalty). Before this legislation was brought into effect murder was punishable either by death or by life imprisonment. Generally, the only murder cases punishable by death were those in which a police officer, prison guard, or other similar person was killed while in the course of duty.

Murder is now classified under s.231 as either first degree or second degree murder. First degree murder is planned and deliberate. Murder is also first degree even if not planned and deliberate where the victim is a police officer, prison guard, person working in a prison, or is another similar person acting in the course of duty. It is also first degree murder to cause a person's death, whether or not planned and deliberate, while committing or attempting to commit the following offences: s.76(l) (hijacking aircraft), s.271 (sexual assault), s.272 (sexual assault with a weapon), s.273 (aggravated sexual assault), s.279 (kidnapping and forcible confinement), and s.279.1 (hostage taking). All murder that is not first degree is second degree.

(i) The meaning of "planned and deliberate"

Section 231 does not create a substantive offence; its purpose is to determine the punishment for a person who has committed murder. Therefore, before considering whether the death was planned and deliberate, the Crown must prove beyond a reasonable doubt that the accused is guilty of murder as defined under s.229 and s.230.[24] Once the murder is proved, the Crown must then prove that the murder was both planned and deliberate. The terms "planned" and "deliberate" mean different things. It would be possible for a murder to be planned but not deliber-

---

24. *R. v. Mitchell* (1965), 43 C.R. 391 (S.C.C.); *R. v. Droste, supra,* note 15.

ate. For example, a man might make plans over a period of days to kill his wife but at the moment of the actual killing be acting impulsively and not deliberately. "Planned" refers to a calculated scheme or design that has been carefully thought out. The term "deliberate" as used in the Code means more than intentional and is closer in meaning to "considered, not impulsive."[25] One judge stated, ". . . deliberation proceeds from the will enlightened by an intelligence which has had time to reflect upon the nature and the quality of the incriminating act."[26] In considering whether a murder has been planned and deliberate, the jury must be concerned with the accused's "mental processes". It should consider the accused's actions, conduct, statements, and capacity to plan and deliberate.[27]

(ii) Punishment for first and second degree murder

PENALTY FOR MURDER
Indictable
Min: life imprisonment
s.235

There are special sections of the Code that deal with the penalties for murder. Under s.235 both first and second degree murder are punishable by mandatory life imprisonment. The difference between the two offences with regard to punishment concerns eligibility for *parole* under s.742. In general, a person convicted of first degree murder cannot be paroled until he or she has served 25 years of the sentence. Where a person has been convicted of second degree murder, he or she may be eligible for parole after serving at least 10 years but no more than 25 years. The number of years to be served before parole eligibility is set usually by the trial judge. However, if the person convicted of second degree murder has a previous conviction for murder, the period to be served before he or she is eligible for parole is 25 years.

PAROLE REQUIRE-MENTS
s.742

APPLICATION FOR REVIEW
s.745

Under s.745 a person who has been convicted of first or second degree murder and has served at least 15 years of the sentence can apply for a review of his or her case for the purpose of reducing the years to be served before he or she will be eligible for parole. The application is considered by a judge and jury. They will look at such factors as the character of the applicant, the conduct of the applicant while serving the sentence, the nature of the offence, and any other factors the judge believes are relevant. After hearing the evidence, the jury may order that:

- A lesser number of years of imprisonment without eligibility for parole be served.
- The person's ineligibility for parole be terminated.

If the jury does not order a change in eligibility for parole, the jury must set another time when an application for reduction can be made.

If the jury makes an order which reduces the period for parole eligibility, the applicant must still apply to the federal *Parole Board* for parole. It is possible that a person could successfully have the period of eligibility

---

25. *More v. R.*, [1963] 3 C.C.C. 289 (S.C.C.).
26. *Pilon v. R.* (1966), 2 C.C.C. 53, 46 C.R. 272 (Que.C.A.).
27. *R. v. Mitchell, supra*, note 24.

reduced for parole but still be turned down by the parole board. A person who is given a life sentence and then released on parole is not totally free because he or she will remain on parole for the rest of his or her life. A person on parole is allowed to live in the community only as long as the conditions of the parole are followed. For example, a parolee may need to report address or job changes to a parole officer or live within a certain area.

2. Manslaughter

While the common law defined murder as unlawful killing with malice aforethought, manslaughter was defined as unlawful killing without malice aforethought. Today manslaughter is still defined in relation to murder:

MAN-
SLAUGHTER
s.234
Indictable
Max: life
imprisonment
[s.236]

> **234. Culpable homicide that is not murder or infanticide is manslaughter.**

The effect of this section is that once a homicide is found to be culpable, the next step is determining whether it is murder or infanticide; if the culpable homicide is neither, then the offence is manslaughter. For example, where a person has been charged with murder and if the Crown fails to prove beyond a reasonable doubt all the elements of the offence of murder, the jury may find the accused guilty of the less serious offence of manslaughter. Similarly, if an accused appeals his or her conviction for murder, the appeal court may substitute a verdict of guilty of manslaughter.

a. By an Unlawful Act or Criminal Negligence

Manslaughter most often arises where the death is caused by means of an unlawful act or by criminal negligence.[28] Where the death is a result of an unlawful act, such as assault, it is not necessary to prove that the accused intended to cause the harm. In fact, many cases of manslaughter involve accidental deaths which occur as a result of an unlawful act. For example, in *R. v. Chisholm*,[29] a boy, aged 14, without justification or excuse, rushed at his young playmate, who then fell backwards. The fall dislocated the spinal column at the base of the boy's skull causing his death. Chisholm's defence was that the homicide was accidental. The court, however, found him guilty of manslaughter. In its judgment it stated:

---

28. As explained above, the offence of manslaughter by criminal negligence overlaps the offence of causing death by criminal negligence and either can be charged in a situation. The offence of causing death by criminal negligence is discussed in detail in Chapter Ten.

29. (1908), 14 C.C.C. 15 (N.S.Cty.Ct.).

Homicide by misadventure [i.e., accident], . . . only occurs where an accused is doing a lawful act and accidentally kills another person. In the case before me the blow by the accused was an unlawful act which rendered him amenable for any consequences resulting from it. It is no defence to a charge of manslaughter that the unfortunate fatality was not anticipated by the accused and would not ordinarily result from such a blow.

It is possible that a person could be convicted of manslaughter based on either an unlawful act or criminal negligence. In *R. v. Mack,*[30] three men, including the deceased and the accused, were sitting in a mobile home. Each of the men had taken heroin that evening. While still feeling the effects of the drug the accused found a gun in the bedroom and took it to the kitchen table to examine it. Although he claimed that he did not remember pointing the gun at any person, at some point in the evening he fired three shots striking the deceased twice and the other man once. The court held that a jury could find the accused guilty of manslaughter if its members believed beyond a reasonable doubt either that the accused committed the unlawful act of pointing the gun at the deceased or that the accused was criminally negligent in the manner in which he handled the gun.

b. Murder Reduced to Manslaughter

MURDER REDUCED TO MAN-SLAUGHTER s.232

A person also may be convicted of manslaughter where he has been charged with murder in two situations: (1) where the accused successfully raises the defence of intoxication; (2) where the accused successfully raises the defence of provocation.

(i) Intoxication
The defence of intoxication was discussed in detail in Chapter Four. Since murder requires specific intent, an accused can raise the defence of intoxication to reduce the charge to manslaughter. In other words, where the Crown proves that the accused unlawfully caused a death but cannot prove that the accused had the specific intent for the offence of murder because of intoxication, the accused can be convicted of manslaughter.

THE DEFENCE OF PROVOCA-TION s.232

(ii) Provocation
The defence of provocation can only be used for the offence of murder. If provocation is proved, the accused will be found guilty of the less serious offence of manslaughter.

Section 232 of the Criminal Code provides:

> **232.(1) Culpable homicide that otherwise would be murder may be reduced to manslaughter if the person who com-**

---

30. (1975), 29 C.R.N.S. 270 (Alta.C.A.).

mitted it did so in the heat of passion caused by sudden provocation.

(2) A wrongful act or insult that is of such a nature as to be sufficient to deprive an ordinary person of the power of self-control is provocation for the purposes of this section if the accused acted upon it on the sudden and before there was time for his passion to cool.

(3) For the purposes of this section the questions

(a) whether a particular wrongful act or insult amounted to provocation, and

(b) whether the accused was deprived of the power of self-control by the provocation that he alleges he received, are questions of fact, but no one shall be deemed to have given provocation to another by doing anything that he had a legal right to do, or by doing anything that the accused incited him to do in order to provide the accused with an excuse for causing death or bodily harm to any human being.

"Provocation" as defined in s.232 consists of the following elements:

1. a wrongful act or insult,
2. sufficient to deprive an ordinary person of the power of self-control,
3. the offender acts upon it on the sudden, and
4. before there has been time for his or her passion to cool.

These elements are the basis for two tests for determining whether provocation exists. The accused must satisfy both tests before a defence of provocation will be successful.

"Wrongful Act or Insult"

The first test is to determine whether the wrongful act or insult was of a nature sufficient to deprive an ordinary person of self-control. This is an objective test. The test is not whether the wrongful act or insult deprived the accused of self-control but whether the act would be sufficient to deprive any ordinary person of the power of self-control. For example, a common or casual verbal insult, or act, will not be considered provocation.

An "ordinary" person has a normal temperament and level of self-control. If there are particular characteristics such as age, sex, or race, of the accused that are relevant to the provocation, they should be ascribed to the ordinary person. For example, if the provocation consists of a racial slur, the jury can think of an ordinary person with that racial background when deciding whether the slur would provoke an ordinary person. On the other hand, as part of this test, the jury cannot consider that the cultural background of the accused makes certain acts more provocative.

For example, in *R. v. Ly*,[31] the accused was a Vietnamese man who was charged with murdering his wife who he believed had been unfaithful. The British Columbia Court of Appeal held that the trial judge did not make an error in not instructing the jury that within the accused's culture, marital infidelity is considered a serious act that causes a man to lose honour.

"Upon the Sudden"
If the accused meets the first test for provocation, it is still necessary that he or she satisfy the second. This is a subjective test.

The second test is to determine whether the accused acted upon the sudden, before his or her passion had time to cool. In other words, the accused must have reacted almost instantaneously after the perceived insult. So, for example, in a case where the accused had been insulted but had waited four or five minutes before shooting the victim, the defence of provocation was not available.[32]

3. Infanticide and Offences Concerning Childbirth

a. Infanticide

INFANTICIDE
s.233
Indictable
Max: 5 years
[s.239]

    233. A female person commits infanticide when by a wilful act or omission she causes the death of her newly-born child, if at the time of the act or omission she is not fully recovered from the effects of giving birth to the child and by reason thereof or of the effect of lactation consequent on the birth of the child her mind is then disturbed.

    239. Every female person who commits infanticide is guilty of an indictable offence and liable to imprisonment for a term not exceeding five years.

NEWLY-BORN
CHILD
DEFINED
s.2

Section 2 of the Code defines "newly-born child" as a person under the age of one year.

As mentioned previously, this offence is rarely used. It was first introduced into the law of Canada in 1948. It is based on the reasoning that a woman may be mentally disturbed from the effects of giving birth or of lactation and thus be less responsible for her actions. In this situation the law mitigates the severity of punishment for what would otherwise be murder or manslaughter.

---

31. (1987), 33 C.C.C. (3d) 31 (B.C.C.A.).
32. *Olbey v. The Queen* (1979), 50 C.C.C. (2d) 257 (S.C.C.).

In *R. v. Marchello*,[33] the judge listed the elements of the offence which the Crown would have to prove:

(a) the accused must be a woman;

(b) she must have caused the death of a child;

(c) the child must have been "newly born";

(d) the child must have been the child of the accused;

(e) the death must have been caused by a wilful act or omission of the accused;

(f) at the time the wilful act or omission the accused must not have fully recovered from the effect of giving birth to the child; and

(g) by reason of giving birth to the child the balance of her mind was disturbed.

Since the *Marchello* case, s.663 has been added to the Code. It states as follows:

LACK OF PROOF THAT WOMAN NOT RECOVERED FROM CHILDBIRTH s.663

663. Where a female person is charged with infanticide and the evidence establishes that she caused the death of her child but does not establish that, at the time of the act or omission by which she caused the death of the child,

(a) she was not fully recovered from the effects of giving birth to the child or from the effect of lactation consequent on the birth of the child, and

(b) the balance of her mind was, at that time, disturbed by reason of the effect of giving birth to the child or of the effect of lactation consequent on the birth of the child,

she may be convicted unless the evidence establishes that the act or omission was not wilful.

The purpose of s.663 is to avoid the problems which arise where the Crown is able to prove all the elements of the offence except those concerning the woman's mental state or where the accused raises as her defence that she was fully recovered or that her mind was not disturbed. The result would be that she would be entitled to be acquitted of infanticide and could not be charged later with murder or manslaughter since an accused cannot be tried twice for the same homicide.

b. Neglect and Concealing

NEGLECT TO OBTAIN ASSISTANCE IN CHILD-BIRTH s.242 Indictable Max: 5 years

Two offences somewhat related to infanticide are neglect to obtain assistance in childbirth and concealing the body of a child. They are set out in the Code as follows:

242. A female person who, being pregnant and about to be delivered, with intent that the child shall not live or with

33. (1951), 100 C.C.C. 137, 12 C.R. 7 (Ont.H.Ct.).

intent to conceal the birth of the child, fails to make provision for reasonable assistance in respect of her delivery is, if the child is permanently injured as a result thereof or dies immediately before, during or in a short time after birth, as a result thereof, guilty of an indictable offence and is liable to imprisonment for five years.

CONCEALING BODY OF CHILD s.243 Indictable Max: 2 years

243. Every one who in any manner disposes of the dead body of a child, with intent to conceal the fact that its mother has been delivered of it, whether the child died before, during or after birth, is guilty of an indictable offence and is liable to imprisonment for a term not exceeding two years.

Neither of these offences is used very often today. They seem to be left over from a time when there was greater stigma attached to bearing an illegitimate child.

c. Causing Death in the Act of Birth

Section 238 covers certain situations where the child dies before becoming a human being:

KILLING UNBORN CHILD IN ACT OF BIRTH s.238 Indictable Max: life imprisonment

238.(1) Every one who causes the death, in the act of birth, of any child that has not become a human being, in such a manner that, if the child were a human being, he would be guilty of murder, is guilty of an indictable offence and is liable to imprisonment for life.

(2) This section does not apply to a person who, by means that, in good faith, he considers necessary to preserve the life of the mother of a child, causes the death of that child.

Under s.238 it is essential that the death of the child occur while in the act of birth, and in such a way that it would be murder if the child had been a human being (as defined in the Code). This means that the causing of the death must fall within either s.229 or s.230. The exception provided in s.238(2) is to allow for situations where it is necessary to cause the death of the unborn child to save the mother.

QUESTIONS FOR REVIEW AND DISCUSSION

1 If a person assaults another person and the assaulted person bleeds to death because he suffers from hemophilia, has the person who inflicted the injury caused the death? Explain.

2 How does the Code define "human being"?

3 Is it homicide to cause the death of a child before it becomes a human

being? What if the injury is caused before the child becomes a human being but the child does not die until after it becomes a human being?

4 Barb shoots and wounds Mike. Mike's religion forbids him to have blood transfusions. Mike dies from the wound although he would probably have survived if he would have allowed a transfusion. Has Barb caused Mike's death? Which Code section is relevant?

5 What questions would a judge ask himself or herself to decide if a particular act was the cause of a homicide when there was an intervening act that contributed to the death?

6 What is the difference between culpable and non-culpable homicide?

7 When may a homicide be justified? excused? Make up some examples of justifiable and excusable homicide.

8 List the ways by which culpable homicide can be committed.

9 What questions would a judge ask to decide if an act is unlawful for the purpose of s.222(5)(a)?

10 Would the following acts be unlawful under s.222(5)(a)? Do you need any other information to make a decision?
a Failure of a person to file his or her income tax return at year-end (by the deadline)
b Failure of a person to provide the necessaries of life for his or her children
c Failure of a person to have his or her pet dog vaccinated for rabies
d Driving through a stop sign

11 Why does the Code state that a person has not committed culpable homicide where the death has been caused by influence on the mind alone unless the deceased is a child or sick person? Do you agree with the law on this point? Why does the law make an exception in the case of children and sick persons?

12 Distinguish the offences of murder under s.229:
a Which subsection deals with "transferred intent" and what does this phrase mean?
b Which subsection sets out the simplest form of murder?
c Which subsection uses an "objective test" and what does this mean?
d What may happen to the subsection that allows objective intent?

13 Discuss the basic elements of murder under s.230. What has the Supreme Court of Canada done with s.230?

14 What are the differences between first and second degree murder?

15 How have courts interpreted the words "planned and deliberate" as used in the Code?

16 How did the common law distinguish manslaughter from murder? How is manslaughter defined today?

17 How does manslaughter most often arise?

18 Under what circumstances may a charge of murder be reduced to manslaughter?

19 Why may infanticide be a difficult offence to prove?

20 Brown had been drinking in a tavern for most of the evening with Smith. At closing time he agreed to drive Smith home. However, he first drove to an empty field for the ostensible purpose of drinking some beer. While there, Brown savagely beat Smith, inflicting many minor injuries and several facial wounds, not mortal in themselves. Smith was abandoned in the field, where he died after some extended but uncertain time. The doctor who performed the autopsy stated that in his opinion the deceased died from loss of blood through the facial wounds, but that the injuries would not have caused death if they had received attention. He said that he did not think death was caused by pneumonia resulting from exposure to the cold night air, but he could not exclude that possibility.

a Has Brown caused Smith's death? Does it make any difference whether the death was a result of loss of blood or of pneumonia?

b Does the fact that Brown had been drinking all evening give him any special defence? Explain.

   See *R. v. Popoff* (1959), 125 C.C.C. 116 (B.C.C.A.).

21 John Silvers had lost his job and was deeply in debt. He decided that the only answer to his problems was to commit suicide. He purchased a gun and went home to shoot himself. Just as he put the gun to his head, his wife walked into the room and, realizing what John was attempting, grabbed his arm to push the gun away from his head. The gun fired and Mrs. Silvers was fatally shot in the heart. With what offence, if any, should John be charged? What will the Crown have to prove?

   See *R. v. Hopwood* (1913), 8 Cr.App.R. 143 and *Wexter v. R.* (1939), 72 C.C.C. 1 (S.C.C.).

22 Jane Snow, aged 14, was walking home from school one day when a car pulled up beside her. A man, Sam Luther, rolled down the window and asked Jane for directions to a certain street. When she stopped to answer him Luther pointed a gun at her and told her to get into the car. Jane, very frightened, obeyed him. Luther drove to a highway and started heading out of town. As the car approached an intersection and slowed down to make a turn, Jane opened the door and jumped out. She hit her head on a rock and died almost instantly. Has Luther caused Jane's death? If yes, with what offence can he be charged? Explain.

   See *R. v. Valade* (1915), 26 C.C.C. 233 (Que.C.A.).

TEN

Criminal Negligence and Legal Duties

Part VIII of the Code

A. CRIMINAL NEGLIGENCE

CRIMINAL
NEGLIGENCE
AND DUTY
DEFINED
s.219

219.(1) Every one is criminally negligent who
(a) in doing anything, or
(b) in omitting to do anything that it is his duty to do,
shows wanton or reckless disregard for the lives or safety of other persons.
(2) For the purpose of this section, "duty" means a duty imposed by law.

Section 219 of the Code defines criminal negligence. Notice that it does not refer to a specific type of conduct. Any act that shows wanton or reckless disregard for the lives or safety of other persons may be a criminally negligent act. Similarly, any omission, or failure to act, where there is a legal duty to act, may be criminally negligent if the omission shows wanton or reckless disregard for the lives and safety of others.

"Duty" is defined as a duty imposed by law. Duties include not only those specified in the Code or other statutes but also those imposed by the common law. For example, under the common law, a person carrying a dangerous weapon, such as a rifle, is under a duty to take proper precautions.[1] An example of a duty imposed by the Code is contained in s.79. This section provides that a person who possesses explosive sub-

---

1. *R. v. Coyne* (1958), 124 C.C.C. 176 (N.B.C.A.).

stances is under a duty to use reasonable care to prevent bodily harm or death to persons, or damage to property. Similarly, under s.263(1), a person who makes an opening in ice, which is open to or frequented by the public, is under a duty to guard the opening in a manner adequate to prevent accidents. The duties imposed by the Code such as the duty of a parent to provide the "necessaries of life" for his or her child are discussed later in this chapter.

For a breach of a duty to be criminally negligent, the omission must show reckless and wanton disregard for the lives and safety of others. So, for example, in the case of *R. v. Baker*,[2] the Supreme Court of Canada found the accused not guilty of criminal negligence even though he had breached a very strict duty imposed for the protection of workers. In this case, the accused was operating hoisting machinery in a mine shaft. An unusually loud noise attracted his attention for a moment, causing him to fail to stop the descent of a cage or "skip". The cage struck and killed a worker. Although the accused had breached a duty required by *The Mining Regulations* by not stopping the descending cage, the court held that the almost involuntary act of the accused in directing his attention to the loud noise was not an act of criminal negligence. That is, his failure to act did not show reckless and wanton disregard for the lives and safety of others.

1. Criminal Negligence Distinguished From Civil Negligence

It is important to distinguish criminal negligence from *civil negligence.* Generally speaking, the civil law imposes on all persons a duty to act in a manner that does not cause harm to other persons or to their property. If a person breaches a duty to take care and causes harm to a person, he or she may be found negligent by a civil court and ordered to make compensation to the injured person. A person is civilly negligent when he or she fails to meet the standards of a *reasonable person*. For example: Chrystal is driving home from work one night. It is raining hard and the road is slippery. A pedestrian suddenly appears in front of Chrystal's car and is hit. The pedestrian may sue Chrystal for compensation for any injuries. The question for the court will be whether Chrystal, given the weather and road conditions, was driving in the manner of a reasonable person. In other words, the court is not concerned with what Chrystal's intent was or whether Chrystal actually saw the pedestrian but only with what a reasonable person would have seen or thought. The court is applying an objective test to Chrystal's conduct. If the court determines that Chrystal's conduct has not met the standard of a reasonable person,

---

2. (1929), 51 C.C.C. 352 (S.C.C.).

she will be found civilly negligent and will be ordered to make compensation to the pedestrian.

To be found criminally negligent there must be a greater degree of misconduct than that required for civil negligence. All human beings occasionally fail to meet the standard of the reasonable person. When a failure results in a loss to another person, usually the wrongdoer will not be punished but merely required to compensate the victim for his or her loss. However, when conduct becomes reckless and wanton, the failure is so great that the wrongdoer becomes guilty not only of civil negligence but also of a criminal offence and is then liable to punishment.

The key difference then between criminal negligence and civil negligence is that criminal negligence requires reckless or wanton conduct (i.e., conduct which shows a reckless or wanton disregard for the lives and safety of others), while civil negligence requires only a failure to meet the standard of conduct of the reasonable person. In other words criminal negligence is a great departure from the standard of the reasonable person while civil negligence is any departure.

2. Determining the *Mens Rea* of the Offence

"Reckless and wanton" refers to the type of *mens rea* required for criminal negligence. Surprisingly, courts have not been able to agree on the type of *mens rea* required for this offence. The debate is over whether a subjective standard or an objective standard should be used to judge a person's conduct. A subjective standard asks, "Did the accused know or turn a blind eye to whether the conduct was reckless and wanton?" An objective standard asks, "Would a reasonable person know that the conduct was reckless and wanton?" Under the objective approach, the difference between criminal negligence and civil negligence becomes one of degree. Criminal negligence is a gross or a "marked and significant" departure from the standard of the reasonable person, given the circumstances of the case and the accused's understanding of those facts.

The subjective approach is similar to the objective approach but requires one additional element before conduct can be said to be criminally negligent. The additional element is that the person accused of criminal negligence must have either (1) actually foreseen that his or her conduct would probably cause harm or (2) turned a blind eye to the situation and then chosen, without justification, to run the risk. This approach requires a *subjective* awareness on the part of the accused of the danger involved. In other words, it is not enough that a reasonable person would have realized the dangerous nature of the conduct; the accused must have actually realized or "adverted to" the danger. Thus, this approach says that the law does not punish those persons who are ***inadvertently negligent***, that is, those who did not think about the risk they were taking, but only those who were aware of the risk — ***advertently negligent***. In 1960, the decision of the Supreme Court of Canada in

O'Grady v. Sparling[3] stated that the test for criminal negligence is subjective, that is, it must be proved that the accused adverted to the risk. In spite of the principle of *stare decisis*, lower courts have had difficulty in following this decision. Most court decisions after the *O'Grady* case used a test of gross negligence for a finding of criminal negligence. The position taken by the courts can probably best be understood by considering the kinds of situations often encountered in cases of criminal negligence. Automobile and hunting accidents make up a large portion of these cases. The courts were, perhaps, recognizing the fact that the misuse of guns and cars can result in great suffering and that society expects persons who cause damage through the careless, even though thoughtless, use of these instruments to be punished. For example, the person who has had one drink too many and ends up driving on the wrong side of the road, and causing a major accident, may not have "adverted to" or thought about the dangerous nature of his conduct. However, courts have found it difficult not to condemn such actions through the use of criminal penalties.

The Supreme Court of Canada has recently had the opportunity to again review the *mens rea* required for criminal negligence. Unfortunately, the court was unable to agree on a test for criminal negligence. In *R. v. Tutton*,[4] the accused were Carol and Arthur Tutton, parents of a child who had died. The parents belonged to a religious group that believed in faith healing. Their child was diagnosed as having diabetes. The mother received medical instruction on how to treat the child's condition. However, both parents believed that the child would be cured through faith. At one point the parents stopped administering the insulin the child needed. The child became ill and they were warned by a doctor of the importance of continuing to give the much-needed insulin injections to their son. They again stopped giving him the insulin, and he died three days later. The parents were charged with causing the boy's death by criminal negligence for failing in their duty to provide necessary medical treatment. The evidence was that they were loving and responsible parents. Their defence was that they honestly believed that their son would be cured by divine intervention.

The Ontario Court of Appeal stated that a subjective test must be used to determine whether the Tuttons had been reckless and wanton. The case was appealed to the Supreme Court and heard by six justices. There were three written opinions in the case. Two justices stated that an objective standard should be used. One justice agreed that an objective standard should be used but added that, when applying an objective norm, "a generous allowance" must be made for factors that are particular to the accused, such as youth, mental development, and education.

---

3. (1960), 128 C.C.C. 1 (S.C.C.).
4. (1989), 69 C.R. (3d) 289 (S.C.C.).

The other three justices stated that a subjective test should be used. They reaffirmed the test set out in the *O'Grady* case.

The decision of the two justices who were in favour of the objective test stated:

> *Our concept of criminal culpability relies primarily upon a consideration of the mental state which accompanies or initiates the wrongful act and the attribution of criminal liability without proof of such blameworthy mental state raises serious concerns. Nonetheless, negligence has become accepted as a factor which may lead to criminal liability and strong arguments can be made in its favour. Section 202 [now 219] affords an example of its adoption. . . . Negligence connotes the opposite of thought-directed action. In other words, its existence precludes the element of positive intent to achieve a given result . . . What is punished . . . is not a state of mind but the consequences of mindless action. This is apparent . . . from the words of the section which make criminal conduct which shows wanton and reckless disregard . . . .*

The decision continued to say that, in applying this standard to the facts of this case, it would be up to the jury to decide whether the belief of the Tuttons was reasonable and honest. The jury would have to consider the whole background of the case including "the experience of the Tuttons with the child's illness, that they had seen the effect of the withdrawal of insulin on one occasion, that they had been informed of the necessity of the insulin, and that Mrs. Tutton had received some formal instruction in providing care for the child." As well, the jury would have to consider whether the belief in a miraculous cure, although honest, was reasonable. All six justices agreed that the case would have to be re-tried because the trial judge's instructions to the jury were wrong.

A decision which was released at the same time as *Tutton* was *R. v. Waite*[5] in which the same judges took the same positions. In *Waite*, the accused was found not guilty at trial of four counts of causing death by criminal negligence and one count of causing bodily harm by criminal negligence. In this case, the accused, after drinking several cans of beer, got into his car with two friends and followed a hayride made up of several tractors pulling wagons. The accused passed the hayride, turned his car around, and drove back toward the wagons. There was evidence that he said to his companions, "Let's see how close we can get" or "Let's play chicken." He then drove down the left side of the road, without the headlights of his car on. When he was within 150 feet (45 m) of the wagons, he swerved to the right to go around the wagons and struck five people who were running along that side of the wagons. Four died and

---

5. (1989), 69 C.R. (3d) 323 (S.C.C.).

one was injured. The trial judge instructed the jury to use a subjective standard to decide whether he was guilty of criminal negligence, that is: Did the accused deliberately assume the risk of his conduct? The accused was found not guilty of criminal negligence but guilty of dangerous driving. The case was appealed to the Ontario Court of Appeal which disagreed with the trial judge's directions on criminal negligence. The court held that an objective standard should be used to decide criminal negligence and that the *mens rea* can be objectively determined from the accused's conduct. The Court of Appeal ordered a new trial. The Supreme Court agreed with the Court of Appeal's decision that a new trial was necessary because of errors in the judge's direction to the jury, but took the same inconclusive positions on whether an objective or subjective standard should be used.

There are usually a total of nine Supreme Court justices who hear appeals. At the time when these cases were heard, two were ill and one had resigned. Therefore, it remains to be seen what will happen if another case of criminal negligence comes before the full court. A decision of the Ontario Court of Appeal, which followed these decisions, stated that, until the Supreme Court of Canada rules otherwise, the law in Ontario requires that criminal negligence be decided by an objective standard, which is a marked departure from the standard of a reasonable person.[6] Presumably, other provinces will also continue to apply the standard which each of their courts of appeal have set.

3. The Offences of Criminal Negligence

CAUSING DEATH BY CRIMINAL NEGLIGENCE s.220 Indictable Max: life imprisonment

220. Every one who by criminal negligence causes death to another person is guilty of an indictable offence and is liable to imprisonment for life.

221. Every one who by criminal negligence causes bodily harm to another person is guilty of an indictable offence and is liable to imprisonment for . . . ten years.

CAUSING BODILY HARM BY CRIMINAL NEGLIGENCE s.221 Indictable Max: 10 years

In addition to the offences set out in s.220 and s.221, the Code also provides in s.222(5)(b) that culpable homicide (i.e., homicide that is a criminal offence) can be caused by criminal negligence. In brief, any person who recklessly causes death or bodily harm has committed the offence of criminal negligence. Although many cases of criminal negligence involve the use of cars, any act can give rise to a charge of criminal negligence. The following are a few examples:

1. *R. v. Petzoldt*[7]: The accused was an unemployed animal trainer and

6. *R. v. Nelson* (1990), 75 C.R. (3d) 70 (Ont.C.A.).
7. (1973), 11 C.C.C. (2d) 320 (Ont.Cty.Ct.).

performer. He owned two chimpanzees which he kept in the basement of his house. While he was walking the female chimp, which was five feet (one and one-half metres) tall and weighed 200 lbs. (90 kg), on a busy street, the chimp reached out and grabbed an eight-year-old girl. The girl was bitten on her head and shoulder by the chimp. There had been several previous instances that demonstrated the aggressive and dangerous character of the animal. The animal trainer was found guilty of criminal negligence causing bodily harm. The judge said that in knowing the dangerous nature of the animal and in taking it for a walk on a main street, the accused showed wanton and reckless disregard for the safety of others.

2. *R. v. Barek*[8]: The accused, a farmer's son, was walking home after a day of hunting. Although his gun had been unloaded, he reloaded it when he smelled the odour of a skunk. When he reached the road, he met some school children. One boy, who was walking about three or four feet (one metre) in front of the accused, without warning, turned around and faced the accused. The gun went off, killing the boy. At the accused's trial, it was shown that the gun was in terrible condition. The hammers were so loose that the slightest jar would cause the gun to fire if the hammers were cocked. Furthermore, the accused was carrying the gun at its point of balance or about six inches (15 cm) in front of the hammers. The judge decided, based on the facts, that the gun was cocked. The accused was convicted of criminal negligence causing death.

3. *R. v. Rogers*[9]: This case involved criminal negligence caused by breach of a duty imposed by s.216. This section states that where a person undertakes to provide medical or surgical treatment, he is under a duty to have and use reasonable knowledge, skill, and care in doing so. Rogers was an unlicensed physician. At the time of the events leading to the charge, he was registered as a naturopathic physician. The practice of naturopathy is defined as the art of healing by natural methods or therapeutics. Rogers prescribed a low-calorie, low-protein diet for a young child who was suffering from a skin disease. After following the diet from April 22 to June 11, the child's condition became so severe that he was hospitalized. The day after he entered the hospital, he died. The testimony of medical doctors at Rogers' trial indicated that the child died from gross malnutrition. The court of appeal upheld Rogers' conviction for criminal negligence causing death.

4. *R. v. Gagnon*[10]: The accused with three others was riding in a car travelling at about 60 to 70 m.p.h. (96 to 112 km/h). After the four drank a number of bottles of beer, the accused threw the empty bottles out onto the roadside. One bottle smashed against a rock and its fragments hit and seriously injured a woman sitting nearby. The court considered that the

8. (1947), 90 C.C.C. 189 (Ont.C.A.).
9. [1968] 4 C.C.C. 278 (B.C.C.A.).
10. (1956), 115 C.C.C. 82 (Que.Ct.S.P.).

road was one heavily travelled at that time of year and that it was well known that many travellers stop by the wayside to go for walks or to sit and rest. The accused, the court found, had thrown the bottles at random with no concern for the consequences of his act. The accused was found guilty of criminal negligence causing bodily harm.

B. DUTIES TENDING TO PRESERVATION OF LIFE

The following sections impose certain duties. Unlike most criminal offences which require active misconduct, these sections make it possible for a person to be guilty of a crime by *not* doing something. As discussed previously, a breach of one of these duties may be the basis for a charge of criminal negligence if the failure to act shows wanton and reckless disregard for the lives and safety of others.

DUTY OF PERSONS TO PROVIDE NECESSARIES s.215 Hybrid Max: 2 years

1. Duty of Persons to Provide Necessaries

215.(1) Every one is under a legal duty

(a) as a parent, foster parent, guardian or head of a family, to provide necessaries of life for a child under the age of sixteen years.

(b) as a married person, to provide necessaries of life to his spouse; and

(c) to provide necessaries of life to a person under his charge if that person

(i) is unable, by reason of detention, age, illness, insanity or other cause, to withdraw himself from that charge, and

(ii) is unable to provide himself with necessaries of life.

(2) Every one commits an offence who, being under a legal duty within the meaning of subsection (1), fails without excuse, the proof of which lies upon him, to perform that duty, if

(a) with respect to a duty imposed by paragraph (1)(a) or (b),

(i) the person to whom the duty is owed is in destitute or necessitous circumstances, or

(ii) the failure to perform the duty endangers the life of the person to whom the duty is owed, or causes or is likely to cause the health of that person to be endangered permanently; or

(b) with respect to a duty imposed by paragraph (1)(c), the failure to perform the duty endangers the life of the person to whom the duty is owed or causes or is likely to cause the health of that person to be injured permanently.

(3) Every one who commits an offence under subsection (2) is guilty of

(a) an indictable offence and is liable to imprisonment for two years; or

(b) an offence punishable on summary conviction.

This section places upon parents, spouses, and persons in charge of other persons, the duty to provide the necessaries of life for their children, spouses, or charges. It should be noticed that for an offence to have been committed, it is not enough that there has been a failure to provide without lawful excuse. If the person to whom the duty is owed falls under para.(1)(a) or (b), the person must, because of the failure to provide, either be in destitute or necessitous circumstances, or the person's health or life must be endangered. So, for example, a wife who fails to support her husband cannot be convicted of this offence if her husband has sufficient means of his own. If, however, the person to whom the duty is owed falls under para.(1)(c), the offence is only committed if his or her health or life is endangered.

Child is defined in s.214:

CHILD DEFINED s.214

214. In this Part. . .

"child" includes an adopted child and an illegitimate child;

. . .

"guardian" includes a person who has in law or in fact the custody or control of a child.

Since s.214 defines "child" as including an illegitimate or adopted child, parents of these children are included in s.215. Section 215(4)(b) further provides that evidence that a person has in any way recognized a child as being his or her child, is, in the absence of any evidence to the contrary, proof that the child is the person's child. So, for example, if a man supports a child who is not biologically his, this would be evidence that he has recognized the child as his own. Unless evidence is presented which provides another explanation for his actions, the child will be presumed to be his.

The definition of "guardian" is very broad. It would cover a situation where, for example, a parent has left the child in the care of a person who has then, *in fact*, the custody and control of the child.

Until 1975, only husbands had a duty to support their wives. In that year the (Status of Women) Amendment Act was passed. This act amended certain sections of several statutes, including the Criminal Code, so that men and women could be treated more equally by the law. Because of this act, the duty to provide necessaries is now placed on both spouses.

Where a person has another person under his or her charge, the duty to provide is only imposed if the person under charge is unable, for a reason listed in s.215(l)(c)(i), to withdraw from the charge and if the person under charge is unable to provide for himself or herself. An English example of a case where the court found the accused had failed to provide for a person under his charge is *R. v. Instan*.[11] In this case, the accused was living with her elderly aunt. The aunt became ill with gangrene and was confined to bed. Only the accused was aware of the aunt's condition. The accused did not give or attempt to obtain any medical assistance for her aunt. She also neglected to provide food for her, although the accused accepted food which was brought to the house by tradespeople. Although the aunt died from the gangrene, the court found that the aunt's death was substantially accelerated by neglect, want of food, and of nursing and medical attention. The accused was found guilty of manslaughter.

a. Necessaries of Life

Necessaries in this section of the Code are those things necessary for the preservation of life. Ordinarily, this includes food, shelter, clothing, and medical treatment. However, this is probably not a complete list, especially since what is considered a necessary will depend on the particular circumstances of the case.[12]

b. Lawful Excuses

The failure to provide necessaries must be without "lawful excuse". The Code has not clearly defined what may be considered a lawful excuse. However, courts have stated that inability to provide because of lack of money where, for example, the parents are unable to find employment, is a lawful excuse.[13] Also, the person must be aware that the necessaries are required before he or she can be found guilty of the offence.[14] If the spouse or child has adequate means of his or her own, an accused would also have a lawful excuse since the spouse or child would not be in destitute or necessitous circumstances.

c. Destitute and Necessitous Circumstances

The fact that a spouse or child is on welfare or receiving charity from friends or relatives does not mean that this person is not in destitute or necessitous circumstances. As one judge aptly pointed out, families receive relief because they are in destitute or necessitous circumstances.

---

11. (1893), 17 Cox's C.C. 602.
12. For example, see *R. v. Sidney* (1912), 20 C.C.C. 376 (Sask.C.A.).
13. For example, see *R. v. Bunting* (1926), 45 C.C.C. 135 (Ont.C.A.).
14. *R. v. Steele* (1952), 102 C.C.C. 273 (Ont.C.A.).

They do not cease to be in such circumstances because they have received relief to keep them from famishing or suffering.[15]

Furthermore, s.215(4)(d) states that the fact that a spouse or child is receiving or has received necessaries from a person who is not under a legal duty to provide them cannot be used as a defence by an accused. So, for example: A wife has been deserted by her husband. She is forced to live with her parents because she has no means of her own. Even if the parents support her at a very high standard of living, the husband cannot defend himself on the grounds that she is not destitute or in necessitous circumstances.

d. *Danger to Life or Health*

The offence may be committed where the failure to provide necessaries endangers the life of the person to whom the duty is owed, or causes, or is likely to cause, the health of that person to be permanently endangered. Whether a person's life has been endangered or whether his or her health has been permanently endangered depends on the particular facts of each case. It has been said that the words have no special technical meaning.[16]

2. Duties of Persons Undertaking Dangerous Acts

a. *Where Medical or Surgical Treatment Is Administered*

DUTY OF
PERSONS
ADMINISTER-
ING MEDICAL
TREATMENT
s.216

216. Every one who undertakes to administer surgical or medical treatment to another person or to do any other lawful acts that may endanger the life of another person is, except in cases of necessity, under a legal duty to have and to use reasonable knowledge, skill and care in doing so.

This section does not create an offence but merely defines the duty of persons who administer medical or surgical treatment. Section 216 would most often be used in conjunction with the offence of criminal negligence. This means if a person breaches a duty under s.216, he or she has not committed an offence unless the breach of the duty is criminally negligent. Notice there is an exception "in cases of necessity" where no duty is imposed. Presumably this would apply in an emergency situation to protect a person who attempted to give aid but failed to have or use reasonable knowledge, skill, or care.

---

15. *R. v. Wilson* (1933), 60 C.C.C. 309 (Alta.C.A.).
16. *R. v. Bowman* (1893), 3 C.C.C. 410 (N.S.C.A.).

b. Where Omission Is Dangerous to Life

DUTY WHERE DANGEROUS ACT UNDERTAKEN s.217

217. Every one who undertakes to do an act is under a legal duty to do it if an omission to do the act is or may be dangerous to life.

This section provides that where a person begins to do an act, he or she is under a legal duty to complete it if the omission of the act is or may be dangerous to life. So, for example: Sylvia sees Laurel drowning. Sylvia is under no legal obligation to save Laurel. But if Sylvia throws Laurel a rope and before Laurel can grab it, pulls it back in, Sylvia has breached a legal duty to act. Sylvia undertook to act and Laurel's life has been endangered by the omission. Like s.216, this section does not create an offence but could be used as the grounds for a charge of criminal negligence.

3. Child Abandonment

ABANDONING CHILD s.218 Indictable Max: 2 years

218. Every one who unlawfully abandons or exposes a child who is under the age of ten years, so that its life is or is likely to be endangered or its health is or is likely to be permanently injured, is guilty of an indictable offence and is liable to imprisonment for . . . two years.

"ABANDON," "EXPOSE" DEFINED s.214

214. In this Part
"abandon" or "expose" includes
(a) a wilful omission to take charge of a child by a person who is under a legal duty to do so, and
(b) dealing with a child in a manner that is likely to leave that child exposed to risk without protection; . . . .

This section makes it an indictable offence to abandon a child under the age of ten. Notice that the offence can be committed by either a failure to act (i.e., a "wilful omission") or by positive misconduct (i.e., dealing with the child in a manner that exposes the child to risk). "Abandon" has also been defined by the courts as "leaving children to their fate."[17]

An example of a case of child abandonment is *R. v. Motuz and Motuz*.[18] In this case, the parents left their two children aged four and five, alone and locked in a farmhouse while they went out drinking. The farmhouse was three-quarters of a mile (1206 m) from the nearest neighbour. After the parents had been gone for three hours, the house caught fire, burned

17. *Re Drummond Infants Adoption* (1968), 66 W.W.R. 435 (B.C.S.C.).
18. [1965] 2 C.C.C. 162 (Man.C.A.).

down, killing both children. In finding the parents guilty, the judge described the parents' conduct as a total abandonment of parental responsibility.

QUESTIONS FOR REVIEW AND DISCUSSION

1 What are the main differences between civil negligence and criminal negligence?

2 Discuss the two main approaches used by the courts to determine if a person's conduct has been reckless (i.e., criminally negligent). Which approach do you prefer? Why? Which approach have most courts seemed to use?

3 List the offences of criminal negligence.

4 Give some examples of conduct that would be criminally negligent.

5 What essential elements must be present before an omission to act can be criminally negligent?

6 List the following:
  a The persons who are under a duty to provide necessaries
  b The persons to whom the duty is owed
  c The circumstances under which a breach of duty is an offence

7 What are "necessaries of life"?

8 Under what circumstances may a person who is under a duty to provide necessaries of life have a lawful excuse for not providing them?

9 Why does the law in "cases of necessity" where medical or surgical treatment is administered not impose a duty to have and use reasonable knowledge, skill, and care?

10 Does the law always impose a duty to act if the failure to act will endanger a person's life? If not, under what circumstances does a person have a duty to act?

11 LeMay and Sullivan were midwives who helped women who wished to have their babies at home. They had no formal medical training. They attended at the birth of a child of J.V. at her request. The child was partially born but LeMay and Sullivan were unable to complete the delivery. The woman was taken to the hospital by ambulance where the delivery was completed using "a basic delivery technique." However, the child was dead. LeMay and Sullivan were charged with criminal negligence causing death. What do you think were the issues in this case? How would you resolve them? (Note: You may need to refer to some of the sections covered in Chapter Nine).
  See *R. v. Sullivan* (1991), 63 C.C.C. (3d) 97 (S.C.C.).

12 Mr. and Mrs. Simon and their seven children lived in a two-room house on a farm in Saskatchewan. For the past two months, Mrs.

Simon's 20-year-old brother, Rodney, had been living with them. Because of the limited space, Mrs. Simon did not want her brother staying in the house. She had complained about this to Mr. Simon on several occasions. One night after Mr. Simon and Rodney had returned from work, Mr. and Mrs. Simon argued about whether Rodney should continue living with them. Mrs. Simon finally said there wasn't room for everyone and that she was leaving. She then put on a jacket and hat. She had, however, nothing on her feet except house slippers and stockings and was otherwise thinly clad. Before she left, she told her 10-year-old son, Jimmy, to put on his coat and to come with her. A few minutes after Mrs. Simon and Jimmy left, Rodney asked Mr. Simon if they should go after them. The temperature that night was -40°F. Mr Simon said no, that they had probably gone to a neighbour's house for the night. The neighbour lived one and a half miles to the south. The next day, Rodney went to the neighbours to see if Mrs. Simon and Jimmy were there. On the way, he found their bodies frozen stiff. Apparently they had taken a wrong turn and lost their way.

With what offence or offences, if any, could Mr. Simon or Rodney be charged? What would the Crown have to show? What other information would be relevant?

See *R. v. Sidney* (1912), 20 C.C.C. 376 (Sask.C.A.).

chapter

ELEVEN

Offences Involving Motor Vehicles

Part VIII of the Code

A. INTRODUCTION

We don't usually think of drivers of cars as potential criminals. Yet the careless use of cars by people in our society has become a great cause of death and injury. It has become necessary to use the criminal law to prevent and control the dangerous use of the motor vehicle.

The Criminal Code contains a number of offences that involve the operation of a motor vehicle. Some of these offences are similar to provincial highway traffic offences. For example, the Criminal Code contains an offence for failing to stop at the scene of an accident. Most of the provincial highway traffic statutes also have an offence of failing to remain at the scene of an accident. The provinces create traffic offences under their authority to regulate the use of the roads and highways. For example, to control the flow of traffic, the provinces set speed limits and make rules regarding turns. However, where conduct creates a risk of injury or death, the federal government uses its authority to make criminal law concerning the use of motor vehicles. Therefore, regardless of how similar a provincial offence and federal offence may seem, it is important to remember that the Code offence is more serious and is a crime.

In the following discussion, reference will usually be made to motor vehicles since the bulk of the cases concern cars. However, operators of "vessels" (i.e., boats), aircraft, and railway equipment can also be charged with these offences.

MOTOR VEHICLE DEFINED s.2 "Motor vehicle" is defined in s.2 of the Code as a "vehicle that is drawn, propelled or driven by any means other than by muscular power." The definition of motor vehicle includes, in addition to cars, farm tractors, snowmobiles, and motorcycles.

B. CRIMINAL NEGLIGENCE AND MOTOR VEHICLE OFFENCES

Until 1985, the Code contained the offence of criminal negligence in the operation of a motor vehicle. This offence frequently overlapped with the offences of criminal negligence causing death or bodily harm. In 1985, driving offences were reorganized: penalties were increased and new offences were created. Also, the offence of criminal negligence in the operation of a motor vehicle was repealed. So, today, when a person causes death or injury by driving in a criminally negligent way that person can be charged with the general offence of criminal negligence causing death or causing injury.

The same test for judging whether driving is criminally negligent arises as in any other case of criminal negligence. Recall from Chapter Ten that the Supreme Court of Canada has been unable to agree on whether the test should be objective or subjective for determining reckless and wanton conduct. The court, after the inconclusive decisions in *Tutton* and *Waite* (discussed in Chapter Ten), again considered the question of the test for criminal negligence in a case involving a motor vehicle.

In *R. v. Anderson*,[1] the accused was driving his parents' car in the early evening when he went through a traffic light and struck another vehicle broadside. A passenger in the other car died. There was no other evidence of improper driving except that the accused was given a breathalyzer test by the police who determined that he was legally impaired by alcohol. The police officer who gave the accused the test stated that the accused did not appear to be grossly impaired and that, in fact, the accused "showed very little impairment at all." The trial judge found the accused not guilty of criminal negligence on the basis that his driving was not a "blatant disregard for the lives and safety of others."

The issue put before the Supreme Court of Canada was whether the trial judge had erred in not considering the intent of the accused when he began driving or the consequences of his driving. The Supreme Court of Canada did not need to answer this question and the underlying question of whether an objective or subjective approach should be used. The court held that with either approach the Crown must first establish that the accused's conduct was a marked departure from the standard of the reasonable person. If the objective approach is used, then the accused may be found guilty. If a subjective approach is used, the Crown must move to a second stage and establish that the accused was aware of the risk. In Anderson, the trial judge found as a matter of fact that the accused's conduct was *not* a marked departure from the standard of the reasonable person. The Supreme Court of Canada stated that it did not have the authority to interfere with the trial judge's finding of fact and affirmed the decision of the trial judge. However, the court did suggest

---

1. (1990) 75 C.R. (3d) 50 (S.C.C.).

that the greater the risk created by the conduct, the less difference there is between the subjective approach and objective approach. The court stated: "The greater the risk created, the easier it is to conclude that a reasonably prudent person would have foreseen the consequences. Equally, it is easier to conclude that the accused must have foreseen the consequences." In other words, a person is presumed to have intended the natural consequences of his or her conduct. This presumption is necessary because it is difficult to prove what a person's mental state was at the time of the offence. The court seems to have suggested that, in situations where the risk is great, this presumption will operate so that the question of which test is used is irrelevant.

In *R. v. Nelson*[2] a case that was heard after *Tutton* and *Waite*, the Ontario Court of Appeal had to deal with the uncertainty of the law in this area. The accused had been drinking alcohol from a bottle while driving erratically through traffic. He eventually struck a vehicle going in the opposite direction, and severely damaged the vehicle. The passengers in this vehicle were seriously injured. The Ontario Court of Appeal held that, until the Supreme Court of Canada rules otherwise, the test for criminal negligence in Ontario is objective. In this case, the questions were: was the driver's conduct a marked departure from the standard of a reasonable driver in the circumstances and did the driver either recognize the risk to the lives and safety of others or give no thought to this risk? The court dismissed the accused's appeal.

C. DANGEROUS DRIVING

A less serious offence than criminal negligence is dangerous driving. Dangerous driving does not require reckless and wanton behaviour. A court will look at whether the driver's behaviour endangered the lives and safety of others and whether the behaviour departed from the standard of the reasonable person. It is not necessary that actual danger to the public be proved but only that the driving was dangerous to anyone who might reasonably have been expected to be in the vicinity at the time the driving took place.[3]

Section 249 defines the offence:

DANGEROUS OPERATION OF MOTOR VEHICLES, VESSELS AND AIRCRAFT
s.249(1), (2)
Hybrid
Max: 5 years

249.(1) Every one commits an offence who operates

(a) a motor vehicle on a street, road, highway or other public place in a manner that is dangerous to the public, having regard to all the circumstances, including the nature, condition and use of that place and the amount of traffic that at the time is or might reasonably be expected to be on that place; . . .

---

2. (1990), 75 C.R. (3d) 70 (Ont.C.A.).
3. *R. v. Mueller* (1975), 29 C.C.C. (2d) 243 (Ont.C.A.).

(2) Every one who commits an offence under subsection (1)

(a) is guilty of an indictable offence and liable to imprisonment for a term not exceeding five years; or

(b) is guilty of an offence punishable on summary conviction.

(3) Every one who commits an offence under subsection (1) and thereby causes bodily harm to any person is guilty of an indictable offence and liable to imprisonment for a term not exceeding ten years.

(4) Every one who commits an offence under subsection (1) and thereby causes the death of any other person is guilty of an indictable offence and liable for a term of imprisonment not exceeding fourteen years.

DANGEROUS OPERATION OF MOTOR VEHICLES, VESSELS, AND AIRCRAFT CAUSING BODILY HARM
s.249(3)
Indictable
Max: 10 Years

CAUSING DEATH
s.249(4)
Indictable
Max: 14 Years

A "public place" under s.249 generally means any place to which the public has a degree of access. A privately owned driveway used for customer parking was held to be a "public place" in *R. v. English*.[4] Other cases have described shopping centre parking lots, churchyards, and school grounds as public places.[5] The public may include *passengers* in the car which is being driven dangerously.[6] Note that, for a conviction under s.249, an injury, or death, is not necessary although the penalties are greater if death or injury does result.

In practice, courts tend to use an objective standard for the offence of dangerous driving, although the offence has been the subject of the same debate as criminal negligence regarding objective and subjective standards. The objective approach was used in an Ontario case, *R. v. Beaudoin*[7] which has been cited with approval by other courts. In *Beaudoin* the court said that to support a conviction of dangerous driving the prosecution must prove beyond a reasonable doubt:

1. that the lives or safety of others were endangered by the accused's driving; and

2. that such jeopardizing resulted from the driver's departure from the standard of care that a prudent driver would have exercised having regard to what actually were or might reasonably have been expected to be the condition, nature, or use of the place where he was driving (including the amount of traffic thereon).

The Supreme Court of Canada considered the offence of dangerous

---

4. [1970] 1 C.C.C. 358 (Ont.C.A.).
5. For example, see *R. v. Gaudreault* (1978), 44 C.C.C. (2d) 235 (Ont.C.A.) and *R. v. Mailloux* [1970] 1 C.C.C. 338 (Que.C.A.).
6. *R. v. MacPhee* (1977), 38 C.C.C. (2d) 49 (N.S.C.A.).
7. (1973), 12 C.C.C. (2d) 81 (Ont.C.A.).

driving in *R. v. Peda*.[8] The accused was driving his taxi-cab easterly on an expressway exit lane. The prosecutor contended that the accused was driving dangerously when he drove his car from the exit lane, across the raised strip dividing the exit lane from the road running parallel to the expressway and then across the two eastbound lanes of this road and over the median, striking a car being driven westerly. There was no evidence of the speed at which the accused was driving. The accused stated that he was driving down the exit lane when the driver of the car in front of him suddenly braked and he remembered nothing after from that point until after the accident. The trial judge in his address to the jury said:

> *So, briefly, dangerous driving is driving a car on a street, road, or highway, or other place in a manner that is dangerous to the public, . . ., there is really no ambiguity in that language, it is a matter which you will have to decide: was the manner in which the accused drove the car, under the circumstances which have been related to you, was it dangerous to the public having regard to all the circumstances.*

The jury concluded that the accused's driving was dangerous to the public and found him guilty as charged. The Supreme Court of Canada held that the judge's directions to the jury which merely paraphrased the words of the Code defining the offence were sufficient. The court continued to say that the essence of the offence of dangerous driving is the manner or character of the accused's driving. It is not necessary that the jury finds a given state of mind to convict. It is the task of the jury to determine, from evidence of the observable conduct of the vehicle driven and the attendant circumstances, the actual behaviour of the driver. However, the court stopped short of endorsing an objective standard. In exceptional circumstances, where there is some evidence that the accused was unaware of the risk, the court said this evidence should be considered by the jury. It would then be open to the jury to return a not guilty verdict if the jury found that the accused had not adverted to the risk. In other words, the court seemed to say that in most situations, the subjective mental state can be implied from the dangerous act itself.

Peda was decided in 1969. Since that time the Supreme Court of Canada has given its split decisions in *Tutton* and *Waite* on the standard to be used for criminal negligence. Since dangerous driving is a less serious offence, it seems unlikely that a greater degree of fault, that is, subjective intent, will be required. Therefore, the *mens rea* required for this offence will remain unclear until the Supreme Court makes a more definitive statement.

---

8. (1969), 4 C.C.C. 245; [1969] 4 C.C.C. 245 (S.C.C.).

D. FAILING TO STOP AT THE SCENE OF AN ACCIDENT

Section 252 provides that:

FAILURE TO STOP AT SCENE OF ACCIDENT s.252 Hybrid Max: 2 years

252. Everyone who has the care, charge or control of a vehicle, vessel or aircraft that is involved in an accident with
(a) another person,
(b) a vehicle, vessel or aircraft, or
(c) in the case of a vehicle, cattle in the charge of a person, and with intent to escape civil or criminal liability fails to stop his vehicle, vessel or, where possible, his aircraft, give his name and address and, where any person has been injured, or appears to require assistance, offer assistance, is guilty of an indictable offence and is liable to imprisonment for . . . two years or . . . an offence punishable on summary conviction.

The elements of the offence are:

1. Having the care, charge or control of a vehicle;
2. Involvement in an accident with a person, another vehicle, or cattle; and
3. Failure to stop and to give assistance or name and address with the intent to escape civil or criminal liability.

1. Care, Charge, or Control

To commit this offence a person must have care, charge, or control of the vehicle. Ordinarily this person is the driver. In *R. v. Slessor*,[9] one of the judges hearing the case on appeal stated that it would be possible for a passenger to have care, charge, or control where, for example, the car is being driven by a chauffeur or employee of the passenger. On the other hand, where a person allows another person to drive his or her car, in a social or business situation, it will usually be the driver who has the care, charge, or control of the vehicle.

2. Involved in an Accident

As a general rule, an "accident" occurs the instant two vehicles, a vehicle and a person, or a vehicle and an "object" come into contact. It is immaterial whether or not damage actually occurs as a result of the contact. In certain circumstances, involvement in an accident does not require the accused's car to have actually collided with another car, person, or object. If the accused, for instance, caused an accident, or helped to cause it, and witnessed the accident occurring, then he or she

---

9. [1970] 2 C.C.C. 247 (Ont.C.A.).

would be "involved" in the accident. For example, if a person changed lanes abruptly and caused a car travelling behind to brake suddenly, go out of control, hit the curb, and roll off the highway, the person would have been involved in the accident. However, if the person could prove that he or she did not see the accident and was unaware that it had occurred even though he or she caused it, the person would not be involved in an accident.

3. Failure to Render Assistance

This failure does not refer to applying first aid. Rendering assistance means taking the necessary steps to ensure that medical assistance or first-aid help reaches the scene of the accident as quickly as possible.

4. Failure to Stop With Intent to Escape Criminal or Civil Liability

Courts have held that the intent required for this element of the offence is to escape liability arising from the accident and not from another cause. For example, if a person fails to stop to avoid liability for unpaid parking tickets, the intent for the offence has not been proved.[10]

The offence contains a reverse onus clause concerning this element of the offence. Section 252(2) states:

PRESUMP-
TION
REGARDING
INTENT
s.252(2)

> **252.(2) In proceedings under subsection (1), evidence that an accused failed to stop his vehicle, vessel or, where possible his aircraft, as the case may be, offer assistance where any person has been injured or appears to require assistance and give his name and address is, in the absence of any evidence to the contrary, proof of an intent to escape civil and criminal liability.**

In other words, an accused is required to give an explanation for not stopping once it has been demonstrated he or she was involved in an accident. This section was applied in *R. v. Gosselin.*[11] The accused was the driver of a car which hit two pedestrians who were walking on the shoulder of the road. He drove a brief distance past the accident and then stopped his car and walked back. There was conflicting evidence regarding whether he offered any assistance. Another car had stopped and some of its occupants had already gone to a farmhouse for help by the time he arrived at the scene. He then went back to his car and drove 2.1 km to a restaurant where he called the police to report the accident. The police told him that an ambulance and police car were already on the

---

10. *R. v. Hofer* (1982), 2 C.C.C. (3d) 236 (Sask.Q.B.).
11. (1988), 45 C.C.C. (3d) 568 (Ont.C.A.).

scene. He did not give his name to the police or state that he was the driver. He called the police back 22 minutes later and gave his name and stated that he was the driver of the vehicle. The police told him to remain at the restaurant until they arrived, which he did. His statement to the police was that he left the accident to get help. At trial he was found guilty of failing to remain. The trial judge relied on s.252(2) to convict him. On appeal, the Ontario Court of Appeal held that the trial judge made an error in applying this section and sent the case back for a new trial. In this case there was "evidence to the contrary" that he did not leave the scene to escape liability. If the judge did not either reject this evidence or disbelieve it, then the presumption in this section cannot be applied and the Crown must prove beyond a reasonable doubt that the accused left the scene to escape liability. The trial judge, although he doubted the accused's evidence, did not reject it. In fact, the Court of Appeal stated that the two phone calls to the police and the fact that he stayed at the restaurant were evidence to the contrary that would be difficult to reject. Once it is established that the Crown cannot rely on s.252(2), the judge must then consider all the evidence to determine whether the Crown has proved beyond a reasonable doubt that the accused left the scene of the accident with the intent to escape liability. The trial judge did not do so in this case.

This type of reverse onus clause is open to challenge under the Charter for offending the presumption of innocence. The Court of Appeal in *Gosselin* considered this issue as well. It concluded that although the clause does offend the presumption of innocence, it is a justifiable limitation under s.1 of the Charter. The court used the test set out by the Supreme Court of Canada and asked these questions:

1. Is the objective of the challenged law sufficiently important to override the protected right or freedom?
2. Is the law carefully and rationally designed to achieve its objective?
3. Does the law impair the right or freedom as little as possible?
4. Are the effects of the law on the right proportional to the attainment of the objective?

The Court of Appeal held that the objective of the law, that is, the curbing of injuries to persons and damage to property, is sufficiently important to override the Charter right and that the duties imposed by the section are reasonable and not out of proportion to the objective of the law. The Court of Appeal in Nova Scotia has also held that this section is a justifiable infringement of the Charter.[12]

---

12. *R. v. T.* (S.D.) (1985), 18 C.C.C. (3d) 125 (N.S.C.A.).

E. IMPAIRED DRIVING AND HAVING OVER 80 mg OF ALCOHOL IN 100 mL OF BLOOD

1. The Offences

There are two offences which may involve drinking and driving. One offence is operating a vehicle while impaired. A person can be impaired by drugs or alcohol. The other offence (discussed below) is driving with more than 80 mg of alcohol in 100 mL of blood.

OPERATING WHILE IMPAIRED; 80 mg ALCOHOL IN 100 mL BLOOD s.253

Section 253 sets out these offences:

> **253. Every one commits an offence who operates a motor vehicle or vessel or operates or assists in the operation of an aircraft or of railway equipment or has the care or control of a motor vehicle, vessel, aircraft or railway equipment, whether it is in motion or not,**
>
> **(a) while the person's ability to operate the vehicle, vessel, aircraft or railway equipment is impaired by alcohol or a drug; or**
>
> **(b) having consumed alcohol in such a quantity that the concentration in the person's blood exceeds eighty milligrams of alcohol in one hundred millilitres of blood.**

Whether a motor vehicle can move under its own power at the time of the offence is not material. It is the type or nature of the vehicle and not its actual state of operability that is the determining factor. In *Saunders v. R.*,[13] even though the motor vehicle in question was wedged into a ditch so that it could not move under its own power (it was eventually moved by a tow truck) the accused, who was in the car and impaired at the time, was found guilty of impaired driving.

Offences under s.253 do not require that the vehicle be on a highway or road or other "public place". For example, in *R. v. Murray*,[14] a Prince Edward Island case, the accused was convicted of impaired driving while the car was in the private driveway beside his house.

There are two ways these offences can be committed: a person can be actually operating, that is, driving, a vehicle, or a person can have care or control of the vehicle whether or not the vehicle is in motion. In other words, a person can have care or control of a vehicle even if the person is not driving the vehicle. For example, if a police officer sees an obviously impaired person enter the driver's side of a car and put the key in the ignition, the police officer can charge the person with having care or control even if the person is stopped before the vehicle is set in motion.

---

13. [1967] 3 C.C.C. 278 (S.C.C.).
14. (1973), 11 C.C.C. (2d) 296 (P.E.I.S.C.).

2. Having Care or Control

If a person is found in the driver's seat, s.258(1)(a) creates the following *rebuttable presumption*:

PRESUMP-
TION WHERE
FOUND IN
DRIVER'S
SEAT
s.258(1)(a)

(a) Where it is proved that the accused occupied the seat ordinarily occupied by the driver of a motor vehicle, he shall be deemed to have had the care or control of the vehicle unless he establishes that he did not enter or mount the vehicle for the purpose of setting it in motion.

In other words, this presumption means that, if a person is in the driver's seat of a car, it will be presumed that the person had the care or control of the vehicle unless the person can show that he or she did not intend to put the vehicle in motion. Until the case of *R. v. Ford*, discussed below, some courts had held that this presumption meant that if an accused who was found in the driver's seat could show that he or she did not intend to set the car in motion, a conviction could not be made. For example in *R. v. Mcphee*,[15] the accused, a taxi driver, realized that he was impaired. He attempted to call his superviser to request that someone take his taxi off the road. The line was busy so he went to his cab and turned on the ignition to use the car radio to call the dispatcher who could relay the message to his supervisor. Before anyone arrived, he was found by the police asleep in the car. He was acquitted of having care and control while impaired because he did not enter the vehicle for the purpose of setting it in motion.

This interpretation of the presumption was changed by the decision of the Supreme Court of Canada in *Ford*.[16] The accused had been attending a party on a cold winter night. During the evening he started the car to warm the engine so the car would start when he was ready to go home. He did not intend to drive home, however, and had arranged for someone else to drive since he knew he was impaired. The police found him behind the wheel with the motor running. The Supreme Court affirmed the decision of the Court of Appeal which held that intent to drive the vehicle is not necessary for the offence. The court stated: "Care or control may be exercised where the accused performs some acts or series of acts involving the use of the car, its fittings or equipment . . . whereby the car may be unintentionally set in motion creating the danger that the section is designed to prevent." Thus, the presumption cannot be used as a defence. If the accused rebuts the presumption by showing that he or she did not enter the vehicle for the purpose of putting it in motion, it is still open to the Crown to prove that the accused had care or control by showing that the accused performed an act or series of acts that might have put the vehicle in motion.

---

15. (1976), 25 C.C.C. (2d) 412 (Ont.C.A.).
16. (1982), 65 C.C.C. (2d) 392 (S.C.C.).

3. The Charter and S.258

The presumption under s.258, like other reverse onus clauses, has been challenged under the Charter as a violation of the presumption of innocence. The Supreme Court of Canada has held that even though the presumption violates the right to be presumed innocent, the provision is a justifiable limitation under s.1 of the Charter. The Court stated that the objective of protecting the public from drunk drivers is "sufficiently important to warrant overriding a constitutionally protected right."[17]

4. The Meaning of Impaired

In general an accused is impaired under s.253 if having been so affected by the consumption of alcohol, or drugs, the accused is no longer in complete control of the motor vehicle. The proof of impairment can come from a number of sources: for example, actual driving behaviour, a breathalyzer test, or appearance and behaviour (i.e., slurred speech, smell of alcohol on the breath, etc.) of the accused when he or she is examined by the police.

In *R. v. McKenzie*[18] the court made the following statement about proof of impairment:

> *There appears to be no single test or observation of impairment of control of faculties, standing alone, which is sufficiently conclusive. There should be consideration of a combination of several tests and observations such as general conduct, smell of the breath, character of the speech, manner of walking, turning sharply, sitting down and rising, picking up objects, reaction of the pupils of the eyes, character of the breathing.*

In *R. v. Graat*,[19] the Supreme Court of Canada affirmed a decision of the Ontario Court of Appeal which held that non-expert opinion evidence is admissible regarding the impairment of a person. Medical expertise is not necessary to identify whether a person is impaired since most people can express an opinion on impairment from their own experience.

As mentioned, impairment can be from alcohol or drugs. One court has said that the term "drug" should include any substance that if consumed will bring about impairment.[20] Another court has held that it is not necessary to prove whether the impairment is from alcohol or drugs.[21]

---

17. *R. v. Whyte* (1988), 42 C.C.C. (3d) 123 (S.C.C.).
18. (1955), 111 C.C.C. 317 (Alta.S.C.).
19. (1982), 31 C.R. (3d) 289 (S.C.C.).
20. *R. v. Marionchuk* (1978), 4 C.R. (3d) 178 (Sask.C.A.).
21. *R. v. MacAuley* (1975), 25 C.C.C. (2d) 1 (N.B.C.A.).

5. The Question of Voluntariness

The Supreme Court of Canada has held that there is a rebuttable presumption that a person who is impaired by alcohol or drugs voluntarily became impaired.[22] The question of voluntariness often comes up when the accused claims that he or she was unaware of the effects of the drug or alcohol. For example, a person may claim that he or she became unwittingly impaired because of taking a presciption drug. In general, if the person can establish that he or she was not aware, and should not have reasonably been aware, that the medication would cause impairment, the person will avoid conviction for impairment. On the other hand, a mistaken belief as to how much one can drink before becoming impaired or overestimating the time it would take for medication to take effect is not a defence.[23]

Whether or not an accused's impairment was voluntary was discussed in *McLeod v. A.G. Sask.*[24] The accused was charged with impaired driving. He testified that he had two drinks of whisky and then, intending to take two "222" pills, he mistakenly took two pills prescribed for his diabetes. A doctor testified that the diabetes medication could cause symptoms of impairment, and that the accused would be unaware of such symptoms. The court held that through no act of his own will, the accused became incapable of appreciating that he was, or might become impaired. In such circumstances, the accused could not be convicted of impaired driving.

In *R. v. Saxon*[25] the accused after taking two tranquillizers at approximately 3:00 p.m. drove to a local beer parlour and consumed four beers between 4:00 p.m. and 5:00 p.m. At 5:00 p.m. he left, entered his car, drove it, and was involved in an accident. The accused, at his trial, testified that a year before the trial he consulted a doctor who prescribed some tranquillizers for him, and told him not to drink alcohol for a period of six weeks. He took the tranquillizers for about three days. The accused stated that the pills made him very drowsy and that because of their effect he was unable to work and therefore he stopped taking them. However, some months later, on the day of the accident, the accused stated that he was feeling nervous so he decided to start taking the tranquillizers again. He took a single pill at 8:00 a.m., and another at 11:00 a.m., and at 3:00 p.m. he took two more. He was supposed to have only one pill every six hours. The accused then went to the beer parlour and the last thing he said he remembered before the accident was pushing the door open to leave. The accused was charged with impaired driving.

The accused's doctor gave the following evidence about the effect of the tranquillizers and the alcohol:

22. *R. v. King* (1962), 38 C.R. 52 (S.C.C.).
23. *R. v. Penner* (1974), 16 C.C.C. (2d) 334 (Man.C.A.), *R. v. Murray* (1985), 22 C.C.C. (3d) 502 (Ont.C.A.).
24. (1972), 6 C.C.C. (2d) 81 (Sask.D.C.).
25. (1975), 22 C.C.C. (2d) 370 (Alta.C.A.).

Q. **A person who has had four tranquillizers, two of them at the same time in the day, what would be the effect of one bottle of beer on such a person? Would he begin to feel upset after the first bottle of beer?**

A. I think he would begin to notice it, yes.

Q. **He would begin to notice and the second beer would make the condition worse?**

A. Likely, yes.

Q. **Four would make it very bad?**

A. By four I think he would notice it absolutely.

The accused argued that his impairment was not voluntarily induced in that he had taken tranquillizers prescribed by his doctor, and that he did not know, and had not been told by his doctor, what their effect would be when the tranquillizers were combined with alcohol. The court did not accept the accused's defence and found him guilty of impaired driving. The court stated that if an accused knew, or had any reasonable grounds for believing, that the consumption of drugs and alcohol might cause him to be impaired, then if he consumes these substances and becomes impaired, he has voluntarily become impaired. The accused in this case should have known from his own prior use of the drugs that they would impair his judgment and make him drowsy and less alert. Yet, after taking four pills over seven hours, instead of the prescribed one pill every six, he proceeded to a beer parlour and consumed alcohol. He should have known the beer would increase the impairment caused by the tranquillizers alone. Furthermore, the accused's doctor testified that two beers, let alone the four he had actually consumed, when taken in conjunction with the tranquillizers, should have alerted him to the fact that he was impaired.

6. Having More Than 80 mg of Alcohol in 100 mL of Blood

The development of machines capable of measuring the amount of alcohol in a person's blood has greatly simplified the task of controlling impaired driving. The offence of driving with more than 80 mg of alcohol in 100 mL of blood does not require any proof of bad driving or any other evidence of impairment.

There are two types of tests used today. The first test uses a screening device and it is usually administered on the spot when the driver is stopped. This method is sometimes called roadside testing. If a person "fails" this test, the person will be asked to take a breathalyzer test at the police station. It is the results of the second test which are used to determine the exact amount of alcohol in the person's blood and on which the charge is based.

a. Roadside Screening

The authority for giving roadside screening tests is set out as follows:

ROADSIDE
SCREENING
s.254(2)

> **254.(2) Where a peace officer reasonably suspects that a person who is operating a motor vehicle or vessel or operating or assisting in the operation of an aircraft or of railway equipment or who has care or control of a motor vehicle, vessel or aircraft or of railway equipment, whether it is in motion or not, has alcohol in the person's body, the peace officer may, by demand made to that person, require the person to provide forthwith such a sample of breath as in the opinion of the peace officer is necessary to enable a proper analysis of the breath to be made by means of an approved screening device and, where necessary, to accompany the peace officer for the purpose of enabling such a sample of breath to be taken.**

An "approved screening device" is an instrument which can evaluate a person's blood alcohol level immediately. For example, the Alcohol Level Evaluation Roadside Tester (ALERT) is an electronic instrument that flashes red, yellow, or green when a driver breathes into it. If it flashes red, it indicates that the driver's blood alcohol level is over the 80-mg limit. If the device signals red, the driver will then be taken to the police station for the more precise breathalyzer test.

Notice that an officer can demand that a person take a screening test where the officer has a reasonable suspicion that the person has alcohol in his or her blood. This is a lower standard than that required for demanding a breathalyzer test which requires a "reasonable grounds" test.

b. Breathalyzer Tests

Section 254(3) provides:

BREATH-
ALYZER TEST
s.254(3)

> **254.(3) Where a peace officer believes on reasonable and probable grounds that a person is committing, or at any time within the preceding two hours has committed, as a result of the consumption of alcohol, an offence under section 253, the peace officer may, by demand made to that person forthwith or as soon as is practicable, require that person to provide then or as soon thereafter as is practicable**
>
> **(a) such samples of the person's breath as . . . are necessary to enable a proper analysis to be made in order to determine the concentration, if any, of alcohol in the person's blood, and to accompany the peace officer for the purpose of enabling such samples to be taken.**

c. Applying the Reasonable Suspicion and Reasonable Grounds Tests

At one time, the breathalyzer test under s.254(3) was the only test available for determining whether a person had committed an offence. Since the section required reasonable grounds before a demand could be made for a test, an officer had to have obvious evidence of impairment such as careless and erratic driving or physical signs of impairment before making a demand. Also the driver had to take the breathalyzer test at the police station.

The development of roadside screening devices has made controlling impaired driving less difficult. Under s.254(2) the police can demand that a person take a roadside screening test on reasonable suspicion that a person has alcohol in his or her body. A "reasonable suspicion" test is generally satisfied if the officer believes it is possible that the accused has alcohol in his body. On the other hand to have reasonable grounds the police officer must believe that the accused probably has committed the offence. The evidence from the roadside screening test gives the officer the grounds for demanding the breathalyzer test. Here is an example of how the two tests apply: A police officer observes Bill coming out of a tavern. Bill is walking in a perfectly normal manner, and appears to be in control of himself. Bill gets into his car and drives away. His driving is not erratic. Under s.254(3) the officer could not make a demand that Bill take a breathalyzer because he would not have reasonable grounds for believing Bill was driving while impaired. However, the officer could make a demand under s.254(2) for a roadside test, because it is reasonable to suspect that Bill, exiting from a tavern, has alcohol in his body while he is driving. In this example the officer could have made a demand for a breath sample as soon as Bill entered his car because, at that time, Bill would have had "care or control" of his car. If Bill fails the screening test, the officer will have reasonable grounds for demanding a breathalyzer test.

d. Random Stopping and the Charter

Most provinces today have legislation which allows for random stopping of vehicles or "spot checks". When a driver is stopped, the police will usually ask to see the driver's licence, car registration, and proof of insurance. If the officer reasonably suspects that the driver has consumed alcohol, the officer can ask the driver to take the roadside screening test. If the driver fails this test, the driver will be asked to accompany the police to take a breathalyzer test.

There have been several Charter challenges concerning the system for controlling drunk driving. One issue has been whether a person is detained when required to take either a roadside or breathalyzer test. If the person is detained, then under the Charter, he or she has a right to consult counsel and must be informed of that right. The Supreme Court of Canada has held that a person is detained if he or she is required to take either test. However, it is a justifiable limitation on the right to counsel to limit this right to situations where the more serious breathalyzer test is used.[26] In other words, there is no right to consult counsel before taking a roadside test. Similarly, random spot checks have been challenged as an arbitrary detention which infringes upon the Charter. Again the Supreme Court of Canada has said that random spot checks are a justifiable limitation on the right not to be arbitrarily detained. The objective of controlling the social evil of drunk driving is of sufficient importance to justify the infringement.[27]

F. REFUSAL TO TAKE A BREATHALYZER TEST

It is an offence under s.254(5) to refuse, without a reasonable excuse, to take a either a roadside screening test or a breathalyzer test, once the demand is made.

FAILURE TO COMPLY WITH DEMAND s.254(5)

1. Reasonable Excuse for Failure to Comply

In *R. v. Nadeau*,[28] the judge concluded that a "reasonable excuse" must entail some circumstance which renders compliance with the demand either extremely difficult, or likely to involve a substantial risk to the health of the person on whom the demand has been made. An example of a case where the court found that the accused had a lawful excuse because of "extreme difficulty" is *R. v. Cordeiro*.[29] The accused's dentures were so poorly fitted that, when he tried to give a breath sample, the dentures came loose, making it impossible for him to exhale enough for a proper reading.

In *R. v. Phinney*,[30] the Nova Scotia Court of Appeal held that there is not an all inclusive definition of reasonable excuse. In this case, the court held that the accused had an honest belief based on reasonable grounds that the machine was not functioning properly. This was a reasonable excuse for refusing the test.

In *R. v. Iron*,[31] the accused would have had to be driven 160 km, . . . with no place to stay or a way to get home, in order to take a breathalyzer test. The court held that he had a reasonable excuse for refusing.

2. Unacceptable Excuses

Examples of excuses which have not been judged reasonable are: Where

---

26. *R. v. Thomsen* (1988), 63 C.R. (3d) 1 (S.C.C.); *R. v. Therens* (1985), 45 C.R. (3d) 97 (S.C.C.).
27. *R. v. Hufsky* (1988), 63 C.R. (3d) 14 (S.C.C.).
28. (1974), 19 C.C.C. (2d) 199 (N.B.C.A.).
29. (Ont. Prov. Ct.), reported in *The Lawyers Weekly*, February 19, 1988.
30. (1979), 49 C.C.C. (2d) 81 (N.S.C.A.).
31. (1977), 35 C.C.C. (2d) 279 (Sask. Q.B.).

the accused had a sincere belief that the results would not be accurate because the accused had consumed alcohol after driving,[32] or was on medication,[33] where the accused was not being permitted to smoke,[34] where the accused would suffer a financial loss if he left his truck and its cargo which was likely to spoil.[35]

G. BLOOD TESTS

It is not always possible for a person to take the breathalyzer test. If there has been an accident, the driver may be injured or unconscious. In these situations the police can use s.254(3)(b) to demand a blood sample or s.256 to obtain a warrant for a blood sample where the person cannot consent. Section 254(3)(b) states:

WHERE BLOOD SAMPLE REQUIRED s.254(3)

254.(3) . . . the peace officer may . . . by demand made to that person . . . require that person to provide . . . [blood samples] . . .

(b) where the peace officer has reasonable and probable grounds to believe that, by reason of any physical condition of the person,

(i) the person may be incapable of providing a sample of his breath, or

(ii) it would be impracticable to obtain a sample of his breath.

WARRANT FOR OBTAINING BLOOD SAMPLE s.256

To use s.256 for obtaining a warrant for a blood sample, the officer must lay an information before a justice of the peace in person or by telephone to state there are reasonable grounds to believe that:

256. . . .

(a) a person has, within the preceding two hours, committed, as a result of the consumption of alcohol, an offence under section 253 and that person was involved in an accident resulting in the death of, or bodily harm to, any person, and

(b) a qualified medical practitioner is of the opinion that

(i) by reason of any physical or mental condition of the person that resulted from the consumption of alcohol, the accident or any other occurrence related to or resulting from the accident, the person is unable to consent to the taking of samples of his blood, and

(ii) the taking of samples of blood from the person would not endanger the life or health of the person.

---

32. *R v. Dunn* (1980), 8 M.V.R. 198 (B.C.C.A.).
33. *R. v. Frohwerk* (1979), 48 C.C.C. (2d) 214 (Man.C.A.).
34. *R. v. Leduc* (1987), 56 C.R. (3d) 270 (Que.C.A.).
35. *R. v. Gidney* (1987), 7 M.V.R. (2d) 90 (N.S.C.A.).

H. PENALTIES FOR DRINKING AND DRIVING OFFENCES

PENALTIES
FOR
IMPAIRED
AND OVER
80 mg
s.255 and s.259
Min:

FIRST
OFFENCE
Indictable or
summary
conviction
Fine $300,
3-month
driving
prohibition
2ND OFFENCE
Imprisonment
14 days,
6-month
driving
prohibition

SUBSEQUENT
OFFENCE
90-day
imprisonment,
one-year
driving
prohibition

Max. for first or
subsequent
offence:

Indictable: 5
years'
imprisonment,
3-year driving
prohibition;
summary
conviction: 6
months'
imprison-
ment, $2 000
fine, 3-year
driving
prohibition

IMPAIRED
CAUSING
BODILY
HARM
Indictable
Max: 10 years'
imprisonment

The penalties for drinking and driving offences are set out in s.255 which deals with fines and terms of imprisonment and s.259 which deals with court-ordered driving prohibitions. Offences under s.253 (impaired or over 80 mg/100 mL of blood) and s.254 (refusing to provide a breath or a blood sample) are hybrid offences. There is a minimum penalty for these offences regardless of whether the offence is treated as a summary conviction offence or as an indictable offence. These penalties are as follows:

1. for a first offence, a fine of not less than three hundred dollars, and a three-month driving prohibition;

2. for a second offence, to imprisonment for not less than fourteen days, and a six-month driving prohibition;

3. for each subsequent offence, to imprisonment for not less than ninety days and a one-year driving prohibition; . . .

The maximum penalties for first or subsequent offences are:

1. where the offence is prosecuted by indictment, to imprisonment for a term not exceeding five years and three years' driving prohibition;

2. where the offence is punishable on summary conviction, to a term of imprisonment not exceeding six months, a $2 000 fine, and three years' driving prohibition.

If the offence under s.253(a) (driving while impaired) causes bodily harm to any other person, the offence is indictable and punishable by a term of imprisonment of up to ten years and a ten-year driving prohibition.

If the offence of driving while impaired causes death, it is indictable and punishable by a term of imprisonment of up to fourteen years and a ten-year driving prohibition.

A person who has been found guilty of committing an offence under s.253 has one possibility for avoiding a conviction and the imposition of at least these minimum penalties. Section 255(5) of the Code allows for, under certain circumstances, the conditional discharge of a person who has committed the offence of impaired driving. A person who receives a discharge avoids having a conviction registered on his or her record and, thus, avoids some of the problems associated with having a criminal record. Under s.736 discharges are generally allowed for offences except for those that are punishable by a maximum of 14 years' imprisonment or those that have a minimum punishment. Section 255(5) creates an exception to s.736 to allow discharges for drinking and driving offences.

The reason that discharges are allowed for impaired driving cases under s.255(5) is the belief that many of these offenders are addicted to drugs or alcohol. Through treatment and hopefully the curing of their addiction is thought that future offences of impaired driving will be

and 10-year driving prohibition

IMPAIRED CAUSING DEATH
Indictable
Max: 14 years' imprisonment and 10-year driving prohibition

DISCHARGE FOR S.253 OFFENCE
s.255(5)

avoided. Section 255(5) is not in effect in every province. The federal government has left it up to the provinces to choose whether to allow this response for cases of impaired driving. At this time s.255(5) has been proclaimed in force in Nova Scotia, New Brunswick, Manitoba, Prince Edward Island, Alberta, Saskatchewan, the Yukon Territory, and the Northwest Territories.

The subsection states:

> (5) . . . a court may, instead of convicting a person of an offence committed under section 253, after hearing medical or other evidence, if it considers that the person is in need of curative treatment in relation to his consumption of alcohol or drugs and that it would not be contrary to the public interest, by order direct that the person be discharged under section 736 on the conditions prescribed in a probation order, including a condition respecting the person's attendance for curative treatment in relation to that consumption of drugs or alcohol.

I. DRIVING WHILE DISQUALIFIED

DRIVING WHILE DISQUALI-FIED
Hybrid
Max: indictable, 2 years' imprisonment, 3-year driving prohibition; summary conviction, 6 months' imprisonment, $2 000 fine, and 3-year driving prohibition

It is an offence under s.259(4) for a person to drive while disqualified. A person is disqualified from driving if a court has prohibited the person from driving or if the province has suspended the person's licence because of a conviction for an offence under s.253 or s.254.

Driving while disqualified is a hybrid offence. If it is treated as a summary conviction offence, the maximum penalty is a $2 000 fine, six months' imprisonment, and a three-year driving prohibition. If the offence is treated as indictable, the maximum penalty is two years' imprisonment and a three-year driving prohibition.

QUESTIONS FOR DISCUSSION AND REVIEW

1 Explain the differences between the federal and provincial powers to create driving offences.

2 What is the difference between driving that is criminally negligent and driving that is dangerous?

3 Annette is involved in an accident as a driver of a motor vehicle. What are Annette's legal responsibilities under the Criminal Code?

4 What is the difference between the offence of impaired driving and the offence of driving with 80 mg of alcohol in 100 mL of blood?

5 How have the courts defined "care and control" as used in s.253?

6 Explain the offence of driving while disqualified.

7 The accused was charged with having care and control of a motor vehicle while impaired. He was found by the police sleeping in his truck which was located on private property about eight to ten feet (two to three metres) from the road. His head was by the passenger's side door and his lower body which extended under the steering wheel was encased in a sleeping bag. The key was in the ignition and the stereo was playing loudly. The engine and lights were not on. His evidence was that a friend drove him to a party in the accused's truck. The accused was tired and went to sleep in the truck while waiting for his friend to drive him home. He testified that he had no intention of driving home. It was conceded that he was impaired at the time he was found by the police. The issue for the court was whether he had care and control. Should the accused be convicted? Discuss the arguments for and against.

See *R. v. Toews* (1985), 21 C.C.C. (3d) 24 (S.C.C.).

8 The accused was charged with dangerous driving. The evidence was that he had had very little sleep over a five-day period. He had worked an afternoon shift for three consecutive days and then spent two days helping his father move to a new residence. At the end of the fifth day he had one or two beers and then got in his car to drive to a restaurant for something to eat. On a busy four-lane highway he fell asleep at the wheel and collided with a car going the opposite way. He testified that he knew he was exhausted but felt that he was driving normally. Should he be convicted?

See *R. v. Mason* (1990), 60 C.C.C. (3d) (S.C.C.).

9 The accused was a passenger in his own car when the driver hit a pedestrian. The driver stopped about 100 feet (31 m) away from the accident, started to reverse, then got confused and drove about 600 feet (182 m) forward. The accused then took over driving, went another 100 feet (31 m) forward, turned around, and went back to the accident. The accused was charged with failure to remain. Should he be convicted?

See *R. v. Shea* (1982), 17 M.V.R. 40 (Nfld.C.A.).

TWELVE

Assaults and Related Offences Against the Person

Parts VIII and X of the Code

A. ASSAULT (PART VIII)

265.(1) A person commits an assault when

(a) without the consent of another person, he applies force intentionally to that other person, directly or indirectly;

(b) he attempts or threatens, by an act or gesture, to apply force to another person, if he has, or causes that other person to believe on reasonable grounds that he has, present ability to effect his purpose; or

ASSAULT
DEFINED
s.265

(c) while openly wearing or carrying a weapon or an imitation thereof, he accosts or impedes another person or begs.

(2) This section applies to all forms of assault, including sexual assault, sexual assault with a weapon, threats to a third party or causing bodily harm and aggravated sexual assault.

(3) For the purposes of this section, no consent is obtained where the complainant submits or does not resist by reason of

(a) the application of force to the complainant or to a person other than the complainant;

(b) threats or fear of the application of force to the complainant or to a person other than the complainant;

(c) fraud; or

(d) the exercise of authority.

Section 265 sets out the definition of assault. Notice that the section defines three different sets of circumstances in which an assault may occur. Under subs.(1)(a), force must be actually used, and lack of valid consent is an essential element. Where the use of force is only threatened or attempted, subs.(1)(b) requires that the person accused of assault must have either had the ability to carry out the assault or must have caused the victim to believe on reasonable grounds that the accused had the ability to carry out the assault. Subsection (1)(c) defines a specific situation in which it may be implied that the use of force is being threatened.

1. Assault: S.265(1)(a)

The British Columbia Court of Appeal has held that an assault is committed even though no degree of strength or power has been exerted. In *R. v. Burden*,[1] the victim was sitting on a bus when the accused sat next to her. The accused stared at the victim for a short time then put his hand on her thigh for between five to ten seconds. There were two other people on the bus at the time. In convicting the accused, the court quoted with approval the following passage from an eighteenth century English authority: "Battery [assault] seemth to be, when an injury whatsoever, be it ever so small, is actually done to a person of a man in an angry or revengeful, or rude, or insolent manner . . . . For the law can not draw the line between different degrees of violence and therefore totally prohibits the first and lowest stage of it, every man's person being sacred . . . ."

a. *Consent*

The main issue involving assault under s.265(1)(a) is whether the victim gave valid consent. This issue is important since lack of valid consent must be established before it can be said that an assault has occurred. Any touching of a person may be an assault if it is done without that person's consent. Thus, what in one situation might be a gesture of love and affection, in another situation might be a criminal assault. Of course, an accidental touching, for example, where André bumps into Bernadette on a crowded bus, would not be an assault, because even though there was no consent, André did not intend to touch Bernadette, and so the *mens rea* of the offence would be lacking.

Before a person can give his consent to an act, he or she must understand the nature of the act. The law draws a distinction between mere submission and positive consent. As one court stated: ". . . consent means an active will in the mind of the [victim] to permit the doing of the act complained of; and that knowledge of what is to be done, or of the nature of the act that is being done, is essential to a consent to the act."[2]

---

1. (1981), 64 C.C.C. (2d) 68 (B.C.C.A.).
2. *R. v. Lock* (1872) 12 Cox C.C. 244.

So, for example, doctors must inform patients of procedures they intend to perform to obtain valid consent. Some persons are incapable of giving consent, for example, insane persons or very young children. So, before a child receives medical treatment, unless emergency conditions exist, a doctor will obtain the consent of the child's parent or guardian.

Certain sports such as hockey involve physical contact. Courts have held that the players give implied consent to the use of force in these games. However, an assault may result where the amount of force used exceeds that to which consent has been given. In discussing the excessive use of force, one judge has said, ". . . there is a question of degree involved, and no athlete should be presumed to accept malicious, unprovoked or overly violent attack."[3] An example of a case where the use of force exceeded that to which consent was given is *R. v. Cey,*[4] where a fight broke out during a hockey game. One of the players involved in the fight walked over to a player who was just standing off to the side and hit him in an unprotected part of the head. The victim suffered an eye injury and had to stay in the hospital overnight for observation. The attacker was found guilty of assault.

Another type of case in which the question of consent arises is where two people agree to fight. Until recently, the law was not clear on whether the fact that the parties consented to fight could be a defence in cases where one person was injured; some courts had allowed the defence even if one person suffered bodily harm.[5] Other courts had followed the English common law, which says that a person cannot give valid consent to physical force used in anger or where it is likely to cause or does cause bodily harm. For example, in *R. v. Squire*[6] the court said "where two persons engage in a fight in anger by mutual consent, the blows struck by each constitute an assault on the other unless justifiable in self-defence."

The case which finally clarified the law was *R. v. Jobidon,*[7] in which the Supreme Court of Canada considered the issue. In this case, Haggart and Jobidon were drinking in a bar. Haggart walked over to Jobidon and punched him in the face because Haggart believed that a week earlier Jobidon had punched a friend of his. They started fighting. It appeared that Haggart was winning the fight but the owner of the bar broke up the fight and told Jobidon to leave. Jobidon waited outside the bar and when Haggart came out, they exchanged mutual invitations to fight. Jobidon rushed at Haggart and hit him in the head, knocking him unconscious and pushing him onto the hood of a car. He struck Haggart several more

---

3. *R. v. Maki* (1970), 1 C.C.C. (2d) 333 (Ont.Prov.Ct.).
4. (1989), 48 C.C.C. (3d) 480 (Sask.C.A.).
5. *R. v. Bergner* (1989), 36 C.C.C. (3d) 25 (Alta.C.A.).
6. (1975), 31 C.R.N.S. 314 (Ont.C.A.).
7. (1991), 66 C.C.C. (3d) 454 (S.C.C.).

times in the head. Haggart was taken to the hospital. He never regained consciousness and died the next day. Jobidon was charged with manslaughter (causing death by an unlawful act, assault). The trial judge found Jobidon not guilty because the two men had consented to fight. It did not matter that the fight was in anger, and that physical injury was intended. The judge also found that Jobidon did not intentionally exceed the consent which Haggart gave and that he struck the final blows in the reasonable but mistaken apprehension that Haggart was still capable of returning to the fight. The trial judge felt bound by the decision in *R. v. Dix*,[8] an earlier Ontario Court of Appeal decision which held that consent was a valid defence if the parties agree to a "fair fight" (for example, it wouldn't be a fair fight if the parties agreed to a fist fight and during the fight one party drew a knife). The decision of the trial judge was appealed. The appeal court reviewed the law on the issue of consent and held that the common law limitations on the defence of consent should apply to the Criminal Code offence of assault. The court concluded that *Dix*, the earlier case, was wrongly decided and should be overturned. The court stated:

> *The so-called consents to fight are often more apparent than real and are obtained in an atmosphere where reason, good sense and even sobriety are absent. In a case such as the one at hand it seems scarcely necessary to mention that often the results are very serious. To interpret the Criminal Code otherwise would continue to legitimize . . . uncivilized brawling.*

The court granted the appeal, set aside the acquittal, and entered a verdict of guilty in its place.

The Court of Appeal decision was then appealed to the Supreme Court of Canada, which dismissed the appeal. The court held that participants in consensual fist fights which cause "serious hurt or non-trivial bodily harm" are guilty of assault.

b. Consent Obtained by Threats or Fear of Using Force

The Ontario Court of Appeal[9] has held that the threat in this section refers to a threat of the use of force. In this case, the accused threatened to expose certain photographs of the victim. The Court stated that this is not the kind of threat contemplated by the subsection.

c. Consent Obtained Through Fraud

The British Columbia Court of Appeal[10] has held that the type of fraud contemplated by this subsection refers to the nature and quality of the act

---

8. (1972), 10 C.C.C. (2d) 324 (Ont.C.A.).
9. *R. v. Guerrero* (1988), 64 C.R. (3d) 65 (Ont.C.A.)
10. *R. v. Petrozzi* (1987), 35 C.C.C. (3d) 528 (B.C.C.A.).

and the identity of the accused. For example, a person, who poses as a medical doctor and, with a person's consent, physically examines the person, has obtained consent through fraud and can be charged with assault. In contrast, the court continued, it is not fraud, for example, for a person to falsely claim that he or she will pay for prostitution services the person is about to receive. The false statement does not refer to the act, the nature of the act, or the identity of the accused.

2. Assault: S.265(1)(b)

Actual physical contact is not required for an assault. Subsection (1)(b) defines an attempted or threatened use of force as an assault. An example of this type of assault is in *R. v. Judge.*[11] In this case a court of appeal upheld the conviction of an accused who, accompanied by other men, approached the victim, who was inside a locked car, and while using words and gestures which indicated he had a weapon, threatened to ''burn'' the victim. Similarly, pointing a gun at a person without a lawful excuse such as self-defence would be an assault.[12] Even where the accused does not intend to carry out the threat, if the victim reasonably believes that the accused has the ability to carry out the threat, the offence will have been committed. This point is illustrated by a New Brunswick case, *R. v. Horncastle,*[13] where an argument between a husband and wife led to the husband taking up a gun and threatening to shoot his wife. It was argued that the husband was not guilty of assault because the accused did not intend to actually shoot his wife. The Court of Appeal disagreed however and entered a verdict of guilty of assault. The court ruled that the making of the threat itself, coupled with the ability to carry it out, constituted the offence of assault.

Interestingly, the courts have held that words alone, no matter how threatening, do not constitute an assault. In the case of *R. v. Byrne,*[14] the accused was charged with robbery (i.e., assault with the intent to steal). The accused had walked up to the box office of a movie theatre and said to the cashier, ''I've got a gun, give me all your money or I'll shoot.'' Although he had a coat draped over his arm, no gun was visible. Then, while the cashier was gathering the money, the accused fled. The court held that the accused had not committed an assault since there were no acts or gestures accompanying his verbal threats and he could not, therefore, be found guilty of robbery as charged.

---

11. (1957), 118 C.C.C. 410 (Ont.C.A.).
12. *Kwaku Mensah v. R.* (1946), 2 C.R. 113.
13. (1972), 8 C.C.C. (2d) 253 (N.B.C.A.).
14. [1968] 3 C.C.C. 179 (B.C.C.A.).

3. The Permissible Use of Force

CORRECTION
OF CHILD BY
FORCE
s.43

Under certain circumstances, the law allows persons to apply physical force to other persons. For example, a peace officer or a person assisting a peace officer can use as much force as reasonably necessary to make an arrest.[15] Similarly, a person can use a reasonable amount of force to defend himself or herself, and his or her family, or property.[16]

Under s.43 of the Code, parents or a person standing in their place (e.g., a teacher)[17] can use a reasonable amount of force for the correction of a child. However, once the amount of force exceeds that which is reasonable and necessary under the circumstances, an assault has been committed. It is not always clear what is reasonable. In *R. v. LaFramboise*,[18] a father was convicted of assault for hitting his thirteen-year-old son on the buttocks and legs repeatedly with a piece of wood. The accused had slapped his son for being disruptive and the boy had slammed out of the house which the accused took as an act of defiance. The father then took the boy to the woodshed where he hit him with the wood. However, the accused's conviction was overturned on appeal.

The Supreme Court of Canada in *Ogg-Moss v. The Queen*[19] said that s.43 only allows force to be used for correction, that is, the education of the child, and is not a general authorization for the use of force. So where the child is mentally retarded and will not remember the "correction" within minutes of it being applied, this section cannot be used to justify the force.

B. THE OFFENCES OF ASSAULT

Once it is established that an assault as defined in one of the subsections of s.265 has taken place, the person who has committed the assault will be charged under one of the other Code sections which define the several different offences of assault. The reason that there is more than one offence of assault is because the nature and the seriousness of the assault will depend on other circumstances surrounding the actual use of, or attempted or threatened use of, force. For example, it is a more serious offence to commit an assault with a weapon than without one.

---

15. See Chapter Five, Pre-Trial Criminal Procedure.
16. See Chapter Four, Defences.
17. Although as a matter of policy, many school boards no longer allow teachers to use corporal punishment.
18. Reported in *The Lawyers Weekly*, January 25, 1991.
19. (1984), 14 C.C.C. (3d) 116 (S.C.C.).

1. Assault Under S.266

ASSAULT
s.266
Hybrid
Max: 5 years

266. Every one who commits an assault is guilty of
(a) an indictable offence . . .
or
(b) an offence punishable on summary conviction.

Assault under s.266 is the least serious type of assault. It applies when the assault consists only of threats or attempts, or when the victim has not suffered any bodily harm. This assault was formerly called "common assault" and is sometimes today referred to as level 1 assault.

2. Assault Under S.267

ASSAULT
WITH A
WEAPON OR
CAUSING
BODILY
HARM
s.267
Indictable
Max: 10 years

BODILY
HARM
DEFINED
s.267(2)

267.(1) Every one who, in committing an assault,
(a) carries, uses or threatens to use a weapon or an imitation thereof, or
(b) causes bodily harm to the complainant,
is guilty of an indictable offence . . .
(2) For the purposes of this section and sections 269 and 272, "bodily harm" means any hurt or injury to the complainant that interferes with the health or comfort of the complainant and that is more than merely transient or trifling in nature.

The meaning of bodily harm was discussed in *R. v. Dixon*,[20] a decision of the British Columbia Court of Appeal. The victim had been assaulted by the accused. Her injuries included small bruises on her face and shoulder and a laceration to the back of her head. She testified that she was "all better" within the month. The trial judge held that her injuries did not amount to bodily harm. The judge stated that there was no evidence that the injuries affected her health or comfort, and injuries which lasted no longer than a month were trifling and transient. The Court of Appeal disagreed and ordered that a conviction of assault causing bodily harm be entered against the accused. This court held that "transient and trifling in nature" refer to a very short period of time and injury of a very minor degree. While the decision did not define exactly a transient period of time, one judge stated that it is simply unsupportable to describe as transient an injury that lasts a month. Also, it is clear that, from the time of the injury until the time treatment was completed, the victim was deprived of a sense of comfort. The judge stated that, in this case, the trial judge's decision demonstrates an absence of any reasonable regard for the ordinary meaning of the words.

---

20. (1988), 41 C.C.C. (3d) 157 (B.C.C.A.).

The British Columbia Court of Appeal in *R. v. Brooks*[21] held that, for the offence of assault causing bodily harm, there is no requirement that the accused foresaw that bodily harm would result. In this case, the victim and his family were driving in their motorhome returning from a vacation at around midnight. The accused was driving his jeep on the same road behind the motorhome. For some reason the accused became enraged at the way the motorhome was being driven and forced it to the side of the road. The accused walked over to the motorhome reached in the window and pulled the victim from the vehicle. They were both immediately hit by a passing car and the victim was seriously injured. In this situation, it was irrelevant that the accused did not foresee the harm that resulted.

3. Assault Under S.268

**AGGRAVA-
TED ASSAULT
s.268
Indictable
Max: 14 years**

268.(1) Every one commits an aggravated assault who wounds, maims, disfigures or endangers the life of the complainant.

(2) Every one who commits an aggravated assault is guilty of an indictable offence and is liable to imprisonment for a term not exceeding fourteen years.

Courts have held that maiming means disabling a person so he or she is less able to fight or to defend himself or herself. Such injuries as broken limbs or loss of eyesight are results of maiming. Wounding involves breaking the skin, while to disfigure seems to mean harming a person so he or she is less physically attractive.[22]

4. Assault Under S.270

**ASSAULTING
A PEACE
OFFICER
s.270
Hybrid
Max: 5 years**

270.(1) Every one commits an offence who
(a) assaults a public officer or peace officer engaged in the execution of his duty or a person acting in aid of such an officer;
(b) assaults a person with intent to resist or prevent the lawful arrest or detention of himself or another person; or
(c) assaults a person
(i) who is engaged in the lawful execution of a process against lands or goods or in making a lawful distress or seizure, or

---

21. (1988), 41 C.C.C. (3d) 157 (B.C.C.A.).
22. See, for example, *R. v. Schutlz* (1962), 133 C.C.C. 174 (Alta.C.A.), on maiming; *R. v. Littletent* (1985), 17 C.C.C. (3d) 520 (Alta.C.A.), where a perforated eardrum was considered a wounding.

(ii) with intent to rescue anything taken under a lawful process, distress or seizure.
(2) Every one who commits an offence under subsection (1) is guilty of
(a) an indictable offence and is liable to imprisonment for a term not exceeding five years, or
(b) an offence punishable on summary conviction.

The common element of the offences listed under s.270 is the assault of a person who is engaged in an act of law enforcement such as a police officer making an arrest or a person seizing property under lawful process (e.g., a court order). A frequent question which arises under this section is whether the person assaulted was acting within the scope of authority at the time of the assault. If, for example, a police officer is assaulted while making an illegal arrest, the accused cannot be charged under s.270, although another type of assault may be charged. An interesting case which illustrates this point is *Carrier v. R.*[23] In this case, the police were investigating the theft of two wheels from a car. After searching the accused's trunk and finding nothing, the accused was told his car was being seized "to check it out." Apparently, the police wanted to take the car to the station to examine the wheels on the car. Upon being told that his car was being seized, the accused rolled up the car window, catching the police officer's arm between the glass and car frame, and drove off. The officer was able to free his arm but the accused then attempted to run him over. The court found that the police officer, by attempting to seize the car over the owner's objection and without arresting him, had exceeded the powers given to him. The accused, therefore, could not be convicted of assaulting an officer in the execution of duty. However, the court substituted a conviction of common assault (this is now assault under s.266) since the accused had used more force than necessary to resist the seizure of his car.

The extent of the police officer's authority is not always easy to determine. The Supreme Court of Canada considered this issue in *R. v. Stenning.*[24] The case involved police constables who, while investigating a disturbance outside a building and seeing a suspicious movement inside, entered the building through an open window. The police found two men in the building who refused to identify themselves. One of the men struck one of the constables in the face. It turned out that this man

---

23. (1972), 19 C.R.N.S. 308 (N.B.C.A.).
24. [1970] 3 C.C.C. 145 (S.C.C.). See also *R. v. Landry* (1986), 25 C.C.C. (3d) 1 (S.C.C.) in which the court upheld an assault conviction where police entered an apartment without a warrant to make an arrest. The accused resisted and was charged under what is now s.270. The court held that the police officer was in the execution of his duty when he had reasonable grounds for believing the person he was seeking was within the premises.

was the son of the owner of the building and was not involved in the outside disturbance. The court found that the accused was guilty of assaulting an officer in the execution of duty. The court stated:

> *Assuming that Wilkinson (the constable) did technically trespass on the premises, the fact remains that he was there to investigate an occurrence which had happened earlier in the evening, which involved the firing of a rifle. He was charged under s.47 of the* Police Act, R.S.O. 1960, c. 298, *with the duty of preserving the peace, preventing robberies and other crimes, and apprehending offenders. He was in the course of making an investigation, in carrying out that duty, when he was assaulted by the respondent.*

Both the *Stenning* case and the following case, *R. v. Tunbridge,*[25] which had the opposite result, demonstrate the difficulty in deciding when police are engaged in the execution of their duty. In *Tunbridge,* the police were called to investigate a domestic quarrel. The husband appeared to be intoxicated and the wife said she wished to take the children and leave the home. While the wife was dressing one child, the other child was taken by the father onto his lap. When the wife was ready to leave, the man refused to let the child go. The police then scuffled with the accused in an attempt to take the child from him. The man was charged with assault under s.246(2) (now s.270). The court directed that the accused be acquitted and stated:

> *In the absence of reasonable apprehension of injury to the child or of some breach of the peace I think the constables exceeded their duty when they purported to decide that the child should be taken from the father and then proceeded with their attempt physically to take it.*

C. THE OFFENCES OF SEXUAL ASSAULT

In 1983, the offences of rape and indecent assault were repealed and replaced by the new offences of sexual assault. Under these new offences, the victim can be either a man or a woman. The attacker can be of the same sex as the victim. Also a spouse can be charged with sexual assault. The old offence of rape was set out in Part V of the Code along with offences involving public morals and disorderly conduct. Sexual assault offences are with other offences against the person. This reorganization emphasizes that sexual assault involves physical violence to another person.

---

25. (1971), 3 C.C.C. (2d) 303 (B.C.C.A.).

1. Sexual Assault Under S.271

This is the least serious offence of sexual assault.

SEXUAL
ASSAULT
s.271
Hybrid
Max: 10 years

> **271.(1) Every one who commits a sexual assault is guilty of**
> **(a) an indictable offence and is liable to imprisonment for a**
> **term not exceeding ten years; or**
> **(b) an offence punishable on summary conviction.**

a. *The Meaning of "Sexual"*

The Code does not define the term "sexual", leaving this task to the courts. The Supreme Court of Canada considered this issue in *R. v. Chase*.[26] In this case, the accused, a neighbour, entered the home of the victim, a 15-year-old girl. Her brother was the only other person in the house. The accused seized the girl by the shoulders and grabbed her breasts. He was unable to touch her anywhere else because she fought back. The accused left the house when her brother called another neighbour. The trial court convicted the accused of sexual assault but the court of appeal overturned the conviction and substituted a conviction for assault on the grounds that "sexual" requires involvement of the genitalia. The Supreme Court of Canada disagreed and overturned the court of appeal's decision. The Supreme Court said that sexual assault does not depend solely on contact with any specific part of the human anatomy. The court stated: "Sexual assault is an assault committed in circumstances of a sexual nature such that the sexual integrity of the victim is violated." The court continued stating that the test for deciding whether the conduct has the required sexual nature is objective. The question is: "Viewed in the light of all the circumstances, is the sexual nature or carnal context of the assault visible to a reasonable observer?" Relevant factors are the nature of the conduct, the situation in which it occurred, the words and gestures accompanying the act, and all other surrounding circumstances including threats which may or may not be accompanied by the use of force.

In *R. v. Kindellan*,[27] the accused was a male stripper. As part of his act he would pull a female patron onto the stage, handcuff her, and pull her hands back and forth between his legs. He had performed this part of his act on more than 50 occasions. However, this time the woman complained and the accused was charged with sexual assault. The trial judge convicted him and his conviction was upheld on appeal. It was not relevant that the act was not done for sexual gratification but as part of his performance. The fact remained that the victim had suffered an affront to her sexual dignity.

---

26. (1987), 37 C.C.C. (3d) 97 (S.C.C.).
27. Reported in *The Lawyers Weekly*, September 16, 1988.

b. *Honest Mistake of Consent*

The defence of mistaken belief in consent may be raised by the accused in a sexual assault case and there have been several Supreme Court of Canada decisions considering this defence. In *Pappajohn v. The Queen*,[28] the Supreme Court held that an honest but mistaken belief that the victim consented is a defence. Furthermore, the belief does not need to be based on reasonable grounds although reasonableness is a factor in deciding whether the belief was honest. In this case, the victim was a real estate agent who was showing a house to the accused. Once they were in the house he attacked her, and he was charged with rape. (This case took place before the offence of rape was repealed.) He claimed that she consented. She claimed that she did not and there was evidence that she had attempted to fight back. Despite his claim of honest mistake, the accused was convicted because the court found that there was insufficient evidence to place the defence of honest mistake before the jury. The accused claimed that there was an undeniable consent. She claimed just the opposite. So, in other words, the accused was not really claiming that he misunderstood her but that she was lying. In this situation, the defence of honest mistake cannot be used.

After the decision in *Pappajohn*, the following was added to the Code:

PRESENCE OF REASONABLE GROUNDS FOR HONEST BELIEF s.265

265. . . .

(4) Where an accused alleges that he believed that the complainant consented to the conduct that is the subject-matter of the charge, a judge, if satisfied that there is sufficient evidence and that, if believed by the jury, the evidence would constitute a defence, shall instruct the jury, when reviewing all of the evidence relating to the determination of the honesty of the accused's belief, to consider the presence or absence of reasonable grounds for that belief.

This subsection appears to restate the law as developed by the courts. It indicates that the jury should consider the reasonableness of the belief when deciding if the belief was an honest mistake. However, it is clear that the jury is not required to find that the belief was reasonable for the defence to succeed.

Another case that illustrates the limits on this defence is *R. v. White*,[29] a decision of the British Columbia Court of Appeal. The accused was charged with break and enter and sexual assault causing bodily harm. He had broken into the house of his wife from whom he had been separated for two years. She testified that when she came home the accused

---

28. (1980), 52 C.C.C. (2d) 481 (S.C.C.).
29. (1986), 24 C.C.C. (3d) 1 (B.C.C.A.).

confronted her wearing surgical gloves and holding a pillow. She testified that he said he was going to rape and kill her. When she tried to scream, he first put the pillow, then a bandage he pulled from his pocket, over her face. He then hit her several times. After he hit her, they talked for about an hour and a half. Sometimes the accused was angry and at other times he said he loved her and did not want to hurt her. Finally they went to the bedroom where they had sexual intercourse. She testified that she agreed to have intercourse out of fear. As soon as he left the house she called the police. His evidence was that she had invited him to the house, that they had talked about various things, and that he had become angry at one point but had apologized. He said that she had suggested going to the bedroom. The court of appeal held that the defence of honest mistake was not available to him. On the evidence the jury had a choice of believing either his evidence that she had consented or the complainant's evidence that she didn't consent. The issue was consent and not mistaken belief.

The Supreme Court of Canada again considered this issue in *Laybourn, Bulmer and Illingworth v. The Queen*.[30] In this case the three accused were charged with the rape of a prostitute. Her evidence was that she went to a hotel room with one of the accused and had intercourse. The other two men then entered the room and forced her to return the money. She testified that she was frightened and wanted to leave but they told her that she would have to have intercourse with them for free. The accused testified that they thought she had consented to having sex with them. The Supreme Court held that the judge must only put before a jury defences which arise from the evidence. Where the accused raises the defence of honest mistake, the defence should only be put before the jury where "there is an air of reality" to the defence. The mere statement that the accused thought the complainant was consenting would not be enough.

Another limitation on the defence of mistaken belief is where the court finds "wilful blindness". This principle was discussed by the Supreme Court of Canada in *Sansregret v. The Queen*.[31] The accused was charged with rape on the grounds that the victim's consent had been extorted by threats or fear of bodily harm. The accused and the victim had been living together but she had broken off the relationship because of his violence toward her. A few days later, the accused broke into the victim's home at 4:30 a.m. armed with a file-like weapon. To calm the accused down she said that there was a chance of reconciliation and consented to having intercourse with him. After he left her home, she called the police and claimed to have been raped. The police investigated but no charges were laid. However, the accused's probation officer became involved and there was evidence that he had asked her not to press charges. Three

---

30. (1987), 33 C.C.C. (3d) 385 (S.C.C.).
31. (1985), 18 C.C.C. (3d) 223 (S.C.C.).

weeks later, the accused again broke into her house. She seized the phone to call the police but he ripped the phone out of the jack. He was armed with a butcher knife, and was furious and violent. The victim testified that she was in fear of her life and sanity. She again pretended that there was hope of reconciliation and consented to have intercourse with him. In the morning she drove the accused to the location he requested. She then went to her mother's home and called the police. At his trial, the accused was found guilty of breaking and entering and unlawful confinement but not guilty of rape. The trial judge found that, although there was no real consent, the accused "saw what he wanted to see, heard what he wanted to hear, believed what he wanted to believe." The judge then acquitted him of the rape charge because of his honest belief in her consent. The Supreme Court of Canada disagreed and held that the defence of mistake of fact is not available to the accused in this case because of his "wilful blindness". The court defined the term as follows: "wilful blindness arises where a person who has become aware of the need for some inquiry [in this case, whether the victim was giving true consent] declines to make the inquiry because he does not wish to know the truth. He would prefer to remain ignorant." In this case, because of the earlier episode and the rape complaint, proceeding "with intercourse in such circumstances constitutes . . . self-deception to the point of wilful blindness."

c. Where Consent Is No Defence

WHERE CONSENT NO DEFENCE s.150.1

EXCEPTIONS s.150.1(2)

Recall from Chapter Seven that there are certain sexual offences involving children where consent is no defence. With regard to sexual assault under s.271, s.272, or s.273, s.150.1 provides that consent is no defence where the complainant is under the age of 14. However, s.150.1(2) creates an exception to this rule. It provides that consent can be a defence to a charge under s.271 where the complainant is between the ages of 12 and 14 and the accused is:

a. 12 years of age or more but under the age of 16 years;

b. is less than two years older than the complainant; and

c. is neither in a position of trust or authority toward the complainant nor is a person with whom the complainant is in a relationship of dependency.

d. Where Mistake Made as to Age

Where the complainant's age is relevant to whether consent is valid, the accused may want to raise the defence of mistake of fact as to the complainant's age. Section 150.1 limits this defence. It provides:

> **150.1 . . .**
> **(4) It is not a defence to a charge under section . . .**

271, 272 or 273 that the accused believed that the complainant
was fourteen years of age or more at the time the offence is
alleged to have been committed unless the accused took all
reasonable steps to ascertain the age of the complainant.

In other words, the accused can raise the defence of reasonable mistake
of fact.

Both the general rule under s.150.1(1) where consent is not allowed as
a defence and the rule limiting the defence of mistake of fact as to age are
open to challenge under the Charter. Both may be violations of the
principle of fundamental justice (s.7) and a denial of equality under the
law (s.15).

2. Sexual Assault Under S.272

Sexual assault under s.272 is more serious than s.271 assault. It involves
either a weapon, actual or threatened bodily harm, or more than one
assailant:

SEXUAL
ASSAULT
WITH A
WEAPON,
THREATEN-
ING OR
CAUSING
BODILY
HARM
s.272
Indictable
Max: 14 years

> 272. Every one who, in committing a sexual assault,
> **(a) carries, uses or threatens to use a weapon or an imitation
> thereof,**
> **(b) threatens to cause bodily harm to a person other than
> the complainant,**
> **(c) causes bodily harm to the complainant, or**
> **(d) is a party to the offence with any other person, is guilty
> of an indictable offence. . . .**

3. Sexual Assault Under S.273

The most serious offence of sexual assault, aggravated sexual assault,
involves serious bodily harm to the complainant:

AGGRA-
VATED
SEXUAL
ASSAULT
s.273
Max: life
imprisonment

> 273.(1) Every one commits an aggravated sexual assault
> who, in committing a sexual assault, wounds, maims, dis-
> figures or endangers the life of the complainant.
> (2) Every one who commits an aggravated assault
> is guilty of an indictable offence . . . .

D. OTHER OFFENCES AGAINST THE PERSON

1. Intimidation

INTIMIDA-
TION
s.423
Summary
conviction

> 423.(1) Every one who, wrongfully and without lawful
> authority, for the purpose of compelling another person to
> abstain from doing anything that he has a lawful right to do,

or to do anything that he has a lawful right to abstain from doing,

(a) uses violence or threats of violence to that person or to his spouse or children, or injures his property,

(b) intimidates or attempts to intimidate that person or a relative of that person by threats that, in Canada or elsewhere, violence or other injury will be done to or punishment inflicted upon him or a relative of his, or that property of any of them will be damaged,

(c) persistently follows that person about from place to place,

(d) hides any tools, clothes or other property owned by or used by that person, or deprives him of them or hinders him in the use of them,

(e) with one or more other persons, follows that person, in a disorderly manner, on a highway,

(f) besets or watches the dwelling-house or place where that person resides, works, carries on business or happens to be, or

(g) blocks or obstructs a highway, is guilty of an offence punishable on summary conviction.

(2) A person who attends at or near or approaches a dwelling-house or place, for the purpose only of obtaining or communicating information, does not watch or beset within the meaning of this section.

The offence of intimidation is in Part X of the Code, Fraudulent Transactions Relating to Contracts and Trade. As the title and wording of the offence suggest, this offence has been used most often during trade disputes. Besetting and watching have been called the "legislative equivalent" to picketing.[32] Similarly, one purpose of s.423(2) is to clarify the conditions under which picketing is lawful.[33] However, s.423 does not apply only to trade and labour disputes but prohibits general types of conduct. So, for example, in *R. v. LeBlanc*,[34] a priest was convicted of an offence under s.423 where he made threats of violence against two Jehovah's Witnesses who were making house calls in his parish. After telling them to leave his parish, he said to them that the four men standing nearby might give them a "licking" and he would be glad to pay their fines. He and the four men then, in their cars, followed the couple's car for a few miles. The court held that the threats were made for the

---

32. *Allied Amusements Ltd. v. Reaney* (1937), 4 D.L.R. 162 (Man.C.A.).
33. *Canadian Dairies Ltd. v. Seggie* (1940), 74 C.C.C. 210 (Ont.Prov.Ct.).
34. [1964] 3 C.C.C. 40 (N.S.Cty.Ct.).

purpose of compelling the Jehovah's Witnesses to leave the area and to abstain from calling on people. Since the couple had a lawful right to propagate their religion in such a manner, the priest was guilty of the offence.

Before a person can be convicted of an offence under s.423 for doing one of the acts listed in (a) to (g), it must be proved by the prosecution that the purpose of the conduct was that set out in s.423(1). So, for example, in the case of *R. v. Brancombe*,[35] although it was proved that the accused had "besetted or watched" the dwelling place of the complainant, there was no evidence of what his purpose was. Since it was not shown that the accused's purpose was to compel the complainant to do something she had a lawful right to abstain from doing, or not to do something she had a lawful right to do, the Crown failed in making out its case against the accused, who was then found not guilty of the offence.

2. Kidnapping

KIDNAPPING
s.279(1)
Indictable
Max: life
imprisonment

279.(1) Every one who kidnaps a person with intent

(a) to cause him to be confined or imprisoned against his will,

(b) to cause him to be unlawfully sent or transported out of Canada against his will, or

(c) to hold him for ransom or to service against his will, is guilty of an indictable offence and is liable to imprisonment for life.

(2) Every one who, without lawful authority, confines, imprisons or forcibly seizes another person is guilty of an indictable offence and liable to imprisonment for a term not exceeding ten years.

UNLAWFUL
CONFINE-
MENT,
IMPRISON-
MENT, AND
FORCIBLE
SEIZURE
s.279(2)
Indictable
Max: 10 years

This section creates the offences of kidnapping, forcible seizure, confinement, and imprisonment. Kidnapping is the most serious offence and requires specific intent to carry out one of the purposes in subs.(1)(a) to (c).

The term "kidnapping" is not defined in the Code. It has, however, long been an offence at common law, being considered a form of aggravated false imprisonment. Many of the older English cases of kidnapping involved sending the victim out of the country.[36] However, an early Canadian case established that kidnapping does not necessarily mean

---

35. (1956), 25 C.R. 88 (Ont.C.A.).
36. For example, see: *Attorney General v. Edge* (1943), I.R. 115 and *R. v. Hale* (1974), 1 All E.R. 1107 where the historical sources of the offence are discussed.

that the stolen person must be taken out of the country.[37] This broader definition is reflected in the present wording of the section. Some help in defining the term is given by the English case of *R. v. Reid*.[38] In this case, a husband had been charged with kidnapping his wife. In finding that a man can be convicted of the offence even though the victim was his wife, the court accepted a definition of kidnapping that referred to the stealing, carrying away, or secreting of a person against that person's will. The offence, the court stated, is complete when the victim is seized and carried away.

The kidnapping must also be done "against the person's will." In the case of *R. v. Brown*,[39] the Ontario Court of Appeal considered the question: Is a person taken against his or her will if he or she willingly goes with someone else because of false statements made by that person? In this case, the accused picked up a ten-year-old girl by falsely telling her that her father had asked him to drive her to school. Instead, the accused drove the girl out of the city to an isolated spot. When he approached her, she attempted to get out of the car. The accused then choked her until she was unconscious. Believing her to be dead, he put her body in the car trunk and drove 25 miles (40 km) to a garbage dump where he threw the body and covered it with garbage. After the accused drove away, the girl escaped to a farm house. For the accused's defence, it was argued that since the child went with the accused willingly the accused could not be convicted of kidnapping.

The court, however, found the accused guilty of the offence since his actions of choking her, placing her in the trunk, and driving her to a garbage dump were, the court said, "clearly within the kidnapping section." However, the court also indicated that the kidnapping occurred as soon as the accused's false statements induced the victim to enter the car. In other words, a person does not act willingly when his or her actions are induced by false statements.

The offences under s.279 contain a reverse onus clause:

REVERSE ONUS s.279(3)

> **(3) In proceedings under this section, the fact that the person in relation to whom the offence is alleged to have been committed did not resist is not a defence unless the accused proves that the failure to resist was not caused by threats, duress, force or exhibition of force.**

The Ontario Court of Appeal in *R. v. Gough*[40] has held that this clause is an unconstitutional infringement of the Charter and is not valid. In this case, the accused had known the victim for about five years. At one point they were engaged to be married. The victim had broken off the engage-

---

37. *Cornwall v. The Queen*, (1872-3) 33 Upper Can.Q.B. 106.
38. *R. v. Reid* (1972), 2 All E.R. 1350 (C.A.).
39. (1972), 8 C.C.C. (2d) 13 (Ont.C.A.).
40. (1985), 43 C.R. (3d) 297 (Ont.C.A.).

ment, however, because of the accused's violence toward her. After breaking the engagement she went into hiding for three weeks. At the end of this time she left the house to run errands. She told her friend if she did not come back or was seen in the presence of the accused the police should be called. While on her errands, she did encounter the accused and went with him to a restaurant. In spite of her protests, he insisted on driving her home. They first went to a dental clinic where she paid a bill. He went into the clinic with her. They then went to a donut shop to continue their conversation. He again insisted on driving her home over her protests. Once they were in the car he said they were going for gas and then for a ride. When she said she did not want to go for a ride, she testified that an angry blank look came over his face. She thought he was going to hit her so she remained silent. They then drove for several days to the city where the victim's parents lived. They visited with her parents and spent the night. The next morning the police arrived. The accused was arrested and charged with kidnapping.

At the accused's trial, the judge instructed the jury that, to use the defence of consent, the accused was required to prove that the victim's failure to resist was not caused by threats, duress, force, or exhibition of force. The accused was found guilty and convicted.

The accused appealed the conviction to the Ontario Court of Appeal on the basis that s.279(3) violates the Charter. The court used the test set out by the Supreme Court of Canada in *R. v. Oakes*[41] and found that the clause does violate the Charter and is not a justifiable limitation because:

1. The clause requires the accused to prove the state of mind of the victim, that is, that the victim failed to resist because she consented and not because of threats. Proving the victim's state of mind is an unreasonably heavy burden to put on the accused.

2. The proved fact does not rationally tend to prove the presumed fact, that is, the proved fact that the victim did not resist does not tend to prove that the victim's failure to resist was caused by fear of threats.

The court allowed the appeal and ordered a new trial.

A decision of the Alberta Court of Queen's Bench,[42] also has found the subsection unconstitutional. It will be up to the Supreme Court of Canada to finally decide the constitutionality of s.279(3).

3. Unlawful Confinement

While kidnapping requires moving the victim from one place to another, unlawful confinement or imprisonment refers to physically restraining a person from moving from place to place. In *R. v. Gratton*,[43] the accused

---

41. (1986), 24 C.C.C. (3d) 321 (S.C.C.).
42. *R. v. Grift* (1986), 28 C.C.C. (3d) 120 (Alta.Q.B.).
43. (1985), 18 C.C.C. (3d) 462, leave to appeal to S.C.C. refused.

was charged with the unlawful confinement of a woman to whom he had been engaged. The victim's evidence was that she was home alone with her two children. At about 1:30 in the morning she heard a banging on her window; it was the accused. He then went to the back door and pounded on it. She agreed to let him in because she thought he would break the door down. She then asked the accused what he wanted. He rushed out to the porch and returned with a loaded shotgun. He then brought out her two children with the gun pointed at them and pulled the telephone from the wall. They then talked for a long time. At one point he became very angry and punched a hole through a wall. The police came to the door at about 5:45 in the morning. They found the victim hysterical, shaking, and trembling. She did not answer their questions but said, "I can't, he's going to kill me." They found the gun and shells which he had hidden when the police came to the door. The court held that there was ample evidence for a jury to find that the victim had been unlawfully confined. The confinement did not need to be for the whole period of time the accused was in the house but only for a "significant period of time." The use of the gun, pulling the telephone out of its connection, and displaying the gun in front of her children were all acts that must have had the effect of threatening her and overcoming her resistance.

4. Abduction

a. *Distinguished From Kidnapping*

Although there exist several different offences involving abduction, generally there are three differences between an abduction offence and kidnapping. First, the *mens rea* required for an abduction offence differs from that required for kidnapping. Second, the victim of the offence of abduction is always a young person (under 16 or 14, depending on the offence). Third, kidnapping requires a taking of the victim against the victim's will. Abduction is possible in some situations even though the victim consents.

b. *Abduction Under S.280*

ABDUCTION
OF PERSON
UNDER
SIXTEEN
s.280
Indictable
Max: 5 years

> 280.(1) Every one who, without lawful authority, takes or causes to be taken an unmarried person under the age of sixteen years out of the possession of and against the will of the parent or guardian of that person or of any other person who has the lawful care or charge of that person is guilty of an indictable offence and liable to a term of imprisonment not exceeding five years.
>
> (2) In this section and sections 281 to 283, "guardian" includes any person who has in law or in fact the custody or control of another person.

Before the changes to the Code in 1983, the offence which is now s.280 only applied to female victims who were taken (or abducted) for the purpose of marriage or illicit sexual intercourse. The present offence does not require any specific intent but only that the young unmarried person be taken against the will of the parent or guardian. Section 286 provides that the consent of the young person is no defence. It states:

> **286. In proceedings in respect of an offence under sections 280 to 283, it is not a defence to any charge that a young person consented to or suggested any conduct of the accused.**

So for example in *R. v. Langevin*,[44] the accused was found guilty of abducting two 14-year-old girls even though the court said that the girls had taken a very active if not leading part in the occurrence.

Section 285 does provide a defence however:

PROTECTION OF YOUNG PERSON DEFENCE s.285

> **285. No one shall be found guilty of an offence under sections 280 to 283 if the court is satisfied that the taking, enticing away, concealing, detaining, receiving or harbouring of any young person was necessary to protect the young person from danger of imminent harm.**

An element of the offence is that the person be taken out of the possession of his or her parents by the accused. So, if a person leaves home and later goes with the accused, the accused cannot be found guilty of abduction. Of course, if the accused aided the young person in leaving home by giving transportation or other encouragement, the fact that the person did not physically "take" the young person will not save the person. The case of *R. v. Blythe*[45] demonstrates the necessity of parental possession before the offence can be committed. In the *Blythe* case, a girl resided in the United States in the state of Washington. She received letters and money for tickets which persuaded her to leave her home and meet the accused in Victoria. The accused was charged with abduction but was found not guilty. The court held that when the girl arrived in Victoria, she had abandoned her father's possession by travelling to a foreign country. So, when the accused met her and took her to a boarding house where they spent the night, it could not be said that he had taken her out of her parent's possession. Although the letters and money from the accused encouraged her to leave, since they were received outside of Canada, the court had no jurisdiction over those events. In other words, the essential element of the offence, that is, being taken out of the

---

44. (1962), 133 C.C.C. 257 (Ont.C.A.).
45. (1895), 1 C.C.C. 263 (S.C.B.C.).

possession of her parents, had occurred in another country and, thus, the accused could not be found guilty of the offence in a Canadian court.

The case of *R. v. Cox*[46] considered the issue of whether a person is taken against the will of his or her parents when the parent allows the young person to be taken on the basis of the accused's fraudulent statements. In this case, the accused told the girl's mother that he needed a baby-sitter for his three children. The mother allowed her 15-year-old daughter to go with the accused in his car. When the accused did not turn at the street where he said his house was located, the girl became alarmed and escaped from the car. At his trial, it was found that the accused had used a false name and address and had lied about his employment situation. The Court of Appeal held that a consent obtained by fraud or trick is not consent and before a person can be said to do an act willingly, he or she must be consciously consenting to the act.

c. *Abduction Under S.281*

ABDUCTION OF PERSON UNDER 14 s.281 Indictable Max: 10 years

281. Every one who, not being the parent, guardian or person having the lawful care or charge of a person under the age of fourteen years unlawfully takes, entices away, conceals, detains, receives or harbours that person with intent to deprive a parent or guardian, or any other person who has the lawful care or charge of that person, of the possession of that person is guilty of an indictable offence and liable to imprisonment for a term not exceeding ten years.

Notice that this offence of abduction is committed even if the accused only "receives" or "harbours" the child. For example, if a 12-year-old child runs away from home and is allowed to stay in the home of a person, that person may be convicted of the offence if the necessary intent is proven. It will not matter that the person did not entice or encourage the child to leave home. Although the Ontario Court of Appeal[47] has held that, where a person detains a child, it is a necessary element of the offence that the detention be for the purpose of depriving a parent or guardian of possession.

The defence, to protect from harm (s.285 above), applies to this offence. Section 284 sets out another defence:

DEFENCE OF CONSENT s.284

284. No one shall be found guilty of an offence under sections 281 to 283 if he establishes that the taking, enticing away, concealing, detaining, receiving or harbouring of any young person was done with the consent of the parent, guardian or other person having the lawful possession, care or charge of that young person.

---

46. [1969] 4 C.C.C. 321 (Ont.C.A.).
47. *Bigelow v. R.* (1982), 69 C.C.C. (2d) 204 (Ont.C.A.).

Before s.282 and s.283, which deal with abductions by parents, were enacted, the cases reported under s.281 tended to involve separated parents who, in fighting over the custody of their children, engaged in child stealing. This section proved to be inadequate for dealing with the problem of parents abducting their own children. For example, where there was no custody order, it was not clear whether a parent could be guilty of an offence under this section. Thus, in *R. v. Kosowan*,[48] a court in Manitoba held that in the absence of a custody order restricting parental rights, each parent has an equal right to custody. Therefore, it is not an unlawful act for one parent to take children out of the custody of the other. This situation encouraged a parent who did not have custody, where no formal custody order existed, to take the children from the other parent, especially since the parent who had actual possession of the child had an advantage when seeking a custody order. In 1983, two new offences of abduction were added to the Code: one applies where a custody order exists (s.282); the other, where no custody order exists (s.283). Thus, under the present scheme, "stranger" abductions are charged under s.281. If a parent is the accused, the charge will be made under s.282 or s.283.

ABDUCTION
IN
CONTRAVEN-
TION OF
CUSTODY
ORDER
s.282
Hybrid
Max: 10 years

d. Abduction Under S.282

> **282.** Every one who, being the parent, guardian or person having the lawful care or charge of a person under the age of fourteen years, takes, entices away, conceals, detains, receives, or harbours that person, in contravention of the custody provisions of a custody order in relation to that person made by a court anywhere in Canada, with intent to deprive a parent or guardian, or any other person who has the lawful care or charge of that person, of the possession of that person is guilty of
> **(a)** an indictable offence and liable to imprisonment for a term not exceeding ten years; or
> **(b)** an offence punishable on summary conviction.

The elements of this offence are:

1. that the accused was a parent, guardian, or other person having lawful care or charge of a child under 14;

2. that the accused took the child;

3. that the taking was with the intent to deprive the parent, guardian, or person having lawful charge or care of possession of the child; and

4. that the taking was in contravention of the provisions of a custody order made by a court in Canada.

---

48. [1980] 6 W.W.R. 674 (Man.Cty.Ct.).

The defences under s.284 and s.285 are available to the accused. Another defence, where the accused was mistaken about the existence of a custody order, was allowed in *R. v. Ilczysyn*,[49] a decision of the Ontario Court of Appeal. The accused had lived with a man named West in a common-law relationship from August 1982 to March 1985. They had a child in September 1984. In March 1985, the accused was sent to a reformatory for an 18-month sentence. While she was in the reformatory, West applied for and obtained a custody order giving him exclusive custody of the child. The accused did not object. When the accused was paroled in August 1985, she resumed living with West. In January or February of 1986, she called her lawyer to find out if the custody order was still valid. Her understanding was that as long as she had resumed cohabiting with West, the order was no longer valid. She lived with West and the child until April when the couple had a "falling-out". In May she picked the child up from the babysitter and went to another city. About five weeks later she was apprehended and charged with abduction. The Court of Appeal held that she was mistaken about the validity of the custody order and that West had legal custody of the child. The rule that mistake of law is no defence does not apply as, in this case, to a mistake of civil law. Therefore, the court dismissed the Crown's appeal of her acquittal.

e. *Abduction Under S.283*

ABDUCTION
WHERE NO
CUSTODY
ORDER
s.283
Hybrid
Max: 10 years

> **283.(1) Every one who, being the parent, guardian or person having the lawful care or charge of a person under the age of fourteen years, takes, entices away, conceals, detains, receives or harbours that person, in relation to whom no custody order has been made by a court anywhere in Canada, with intent to deprive a parent or guardian, or any other person who has the lawful care or charge of that person, of the possession of that person, is guilty of**
>
> **(a) an indictable offence and liable to imprisonment for a term not exceeding ten years;**
>
> **(b) an offence punishable on summary conviction.**
>
> **(2) No proceedings may be commenced under subsection (1) without the consent of the Attorney General or counsel instructed by him for that purpose.**

As mentioned above, both parents, if married, and where no custody order exists, have equal right to custody of their children. Some provinces such as Alberta still recognize the concept of illegitimacy in their custody laws, so that if the child's parents are not married only the

---

49. (1988), 45 C.C.C. (3d) 91 (Ont.C.A.).

mother is the legal guardian of the child, although the father still has an obligation to support the child. Ontario is one of the provinces which no longer recognizes this concept in its laws and gives both parents equal right to custody.

An example of the application of s.283 abduction is the case of *R. v. Cook*,[50] a decision of the Nova Scotia Court of Appeal. The parents who were living in Ontario decided to separate. The mother left their five-year-old child with the father and moved to Nova Scotia. While the child was in Nova Scotia visiting with her mother, the mother filed an application for custody. On the date of the hearing the father arrived from Ontario and took the child, without the mother's consent, back to Toronto. He was charged with abduction under what is now s.284. The father's argument was that he was only doing what he was legally entitled to do. Their agreement when they separated was that he would have custody of the child. He felt that the custody application by the mother should have been made in Ontario, not Nova Scotia. He appealed his conviction of abduction. The Court of Appeal did not accept his argument. The court stated that: "Parliament clearly intended to prohibit the abduction of children by parents . . . . These provisions will force parents to seek the assistance of the courts before taking possession of a child without the consent of the other parent."

In this case, it was clear that the accused's intention was to deprive the mother of possession. The court confirmed his conviction.

Notice, that to bring a charge under this section, the consent of the Attorney General or counsel instructed by the Attorney General is necessary. This requirement indicates that the circumstances will be carefully considered before a charge will be laid.

PUBLIC INCITEMENT OF HATRED
s.319
Hybrid
Max: 2 years

5. Inciting Hatred

319.(1) Every one who, by communicating statements in any public place, incites hatred against any identifiable group where such incitement is likely to lead to a breach of the peace is guilty of

(a) an indictable offence and is liable to imprisonment for a term not exceeding two years; or

(b) an offence punishable on summary conviction

(2) Every one who, by communicating statements, other than in private conversation, wilfully promotes hatred against any identifiable group is guilty of

(a) an indictable offence and is liable to imprisonment for a term not exceeding two years; or

---

50. (1984), 40 C.R. (3d) 270 (N.S.C.A.).

(b) an offence punishable on summary conviction.

(3) No person shall be convicted of an offence under subsection (2)

(a) if he establishes that the statements communicated are true;

(b) if, in good faith, he expressed or attempted to establish by argument an opinion on a religious subject;

(c) if the statements were relevant to any subject of public interest, the discussion of which was for the public benefit, and if on reasonable grounds he believed them to be true; or

(d) if, in good faith, he intended to point out, for the purpose of removal, matters producing or tending to produce feelings of hatred towards an identifiable group in Canada.

These offences require the consent of the Attorney General before proceedings can start. "Communicating" [ss.(1)] includes by means of the telephone, broadcasting, or any other audible or visible means. An "identifiable group" [ss.(2)] is defined in s.318 as "any section of the public distinquished by colour, race, religion, or ethnic origin."

These offences have been rarely charged but two recent cases that were finally decided by the Supreme Court of Canada are of interest because they involve an application of the right to freedom of expression under the Charter. The cases were *R. v. Keegstra*[51] *and R. v. Andrews and Smith.*[52] Keegstra was a high school history teacher in Alberta who was charged with an offence under s.319(2). For years he had taught that the Holocaust (the killing of six million Jews during World War II) had never happened and that the story had been started by an international Jewish conspiracy. The charge resulted when a parent discovered what he was teaching and complained to the authorities. Andrews and Smith were from Toronto and were members of a Toronto-based political party which supported white supremacy. They were charged under s.319(2) for publishing a neo-Nazi magazine that claimed, among other things, that non-white and non-Aryan groups were inferior and responsible for violent crime in Canada.

In both cases, the accused argued that the offences for which they were charged violated their freedom of expression which is protected under the Charter. It was also argued that s.319(3)(a) creates a reverse onus clause that cannot be justified under s.1 of the Charter. The clause provides that an accused cannot be convicted if he or she can establish (i.e., prove on a balance of probabilities) that the statements were true. In other words, the Crown does not have to establish an element of the offence: that the statements are false.

The Alberta Court of Appeal in the *Keegstra* case held that s.319(2) was

---

51. (1990), 61 C.C.C. (3d) 1 (S.C.C.).
52. (1990), 61 C.C.C. (3d) 490 (S.C.C.).

unconstitutional and acquitted the accused. The Ontario Court of Appeal reached the opposite conclusion and held that in *Andrews* the offence does not violate the Charter.

The Supreme Court of Canada released concurrent judgments in the two cases. In a four-to-three split, the majority upheld the validity of the offence. The court agreed with the Alberta court that the offence violates the right to freedom of expression and that s.319(3)(a) creates a reverse onus clause. However, both the violation and creation of a reverse onus clause are justifiable limitations. After discussing the importance of freedom of expression in a democratic society, the court stated:

> *The suppression of hate propaganda undeniably muzzles the participation of a few individuals in the democratic process, and hence detracts somewhat from free expression values, but the degree of this limitation is not substantial . . . . [E]xpression can work to undermine our commitment to democracy where employed to propagate ideas anathematic to democratic values. Hate propaganda works in just such a way, arguing as it does for a society in which . . . individuals are denied respect and dignity because of racial or religious characteristics. This brand of expressive activity is wholly inimical to the democratic aspirations of the free expression guarantee.*

E. RECOGNIZANCES TO KEEP THE PEACE

**RECOGNI-
ZANCES TO
KEEP THE
PEACE
s.810**

810.(1) Any person who fears that another person will cause personal injury to him or his spouse or child or will damage his property may lay an information before a justice.

(2) A justice who receives an information under subsection (1) shall cause the parties to appear before him or before a summary conviction court having jurisdiction in the same territorial division.

(3) The justice or the summary conviction court before which the parties appear may, if satisfied by the evidence adduced that the informant has reasonable grounds for his fears,

(a) order that the defendant enter into a recognizance, with or without sureties, to keep the peace and be of good behaviour for any period that does not exceed twelve months, and comply with such other reasonable conditions prescribed in the recognizance as the court considers desirable for securing the good conduct of the defendant; or

(b) commit the defendant to prison for a term not exceeding twelve months if he fails or refuses to enter in the recognizance.

This section gives courts the authority to exercise what is sometimes called "preventative justice". By entering a recognizance the ***defendant*** agrees to keep the peace and to comply with any other conditions prescribed by the court. A "surety" is a person who is willing to be responsible for ensuring that the defendant keeps the peace. Sometimes a sum of money must be given to the court by the defendant or the surety as additional encouragement for the defendant to keep the peace. The money is forfeited if the defendant does not honour the recognizance. Although it is not necessary that an assault or any other offence be committed before a justice uses the powers given by this section, the powers can only be exercised upon "reasonable grounds" that a breach of the peace will occur in the future.[53]

In addition to the authority given to a justice under this section, there is a general authority derived from the common law to maintain order and preserve the peace by ordering persons who the justice thinks may breach the peace to enter a recognizance.[54] The difference between the common law authority and that given under s.747 was explained by a judge of the British Columbia Supreme Court in *R. v. White*[55] as follows:

> *Under s.717 [now s.810] of the Code a defendant cannot be bound over unless the magistrate is satisfied that the informant has reasonable grounds for his fears whereas the prerequisite to the exercise of the common law jurisdiction is that the magistrate (on facts established to his satisfaction) has probable grounds to suspect or be apprehensive that there may be a breach of the peace.*

In other words, under s.810, it is the informant who must have reasonable grounds for the fears of future injury, while under the common law, it is the justice who must have reasonable grounds for the fears. So, for example, a justice could require a person to enter a recognizance even though no other person had complained. This was, in fact, what the magistrate in the case of *R. v. White*[56] had attempted to do. He could not decide whether the informant or the defendant was telling the truth so ordered them both to enter recognizances. The British Columbia Supreme Court, however, found that the magistrate did not have reasonable grounds to exercise his common law authority since, unable to determine which person was telling the truth, he based his decision on speculation and conjecture as to what the actual facts of the case were.

---

53. For example, see *R. v. White* (1969), 5 C.R.N.S. 30 (B.C.S.C.).
54. For example, see *Mackenzie v. Martin* (1954), 180 C.C.C. 305 (S.C.C.), where it was established that the power exists in Ontario.
55. *Supra*, note 53.
56. *Supra*, note 53.

QUESTIONS FOR REVIEW AND DISCUSSION

1 Briefly describe the three sets of circumstances under which an assault may occur.

2 What positions have courts taken on the effect of the victim's consent when both parties have consented to a fight? What has the Supreme Court of Canada decided on the issue of consent?

3 Why does the law make an attempted or threatened use of force an offence?

4 Has the offence of assault been committed where the alleged assailant threatened a person with a weapon but did not actually intend to apply force to the victim? What further information, if any, do you need to answer this question?

5 Can threatening words alone constitute the offence of assault? Explain.

6 Discuss the circumstances under which the use of force may be lawful.

7 Why is there more than one offence of assault? What are they?

8 How does the Code define "bodily harm"?

9 Distinguish the following terms: "wounding", "maiming", and "disfiguring".

10 What are the elements of the offence of sexual assault?

11 What meaning has been given to the term "sexual" in the offences of sexual assault?

12 What does the law state about an honest mistake regarding consent?

13 What are some of the limits on using the defence of honest mistake in a sexual assault case?

14 What is the main difference between kidnapping and the offences of forcible seizure, confinement, and imprisonment?

15 Can a parent ever be found guilty of abducting his or her own child? Explain.

16 What was the Supreme Court of Canada decision in *Keegstra*?

17 What is a recognizance? a surety?

18 What is the main difference between the court's common law authority to order persons to enter recognizances and the authority given by the Code?

19 Is it necessary that an offence be committed before a judge can order a person to enter a recognizance?

20 Nareem and Fazil are two high school students. One afternoon they were playing basketball in the gym when Nareem ran into Fazil knocking him to the floor. Fazil got up angrily and punched Nareem in the mouth. At that point they began fighting violently until some

other students were able to separate them. Discuss. What charges if any could be laid against either student? What other information would you need?

21 The town of Marlboro closed off a downtown street one summer to create a mall. The area became a hangout for teenagers who sometimes became quite rowdy. One evening Constable Jones observed two young persons, a man and woman, kissing and wrestling in the middle of the sidewalk. Constable Jones told them to get up and stop acting like idiots. At that point another young woman, Molly Brown, yelled an obscenity at him. Jones then arrested Molly and attempted to take her to his police cruiser. By this time a crowd had developed and were making it difficult for Jones to escort Molly to his cruiser. While this was happening, Sandra stepped forward and slapped Jones in the face and was promptly arrested. Sandra was charged with assaulting a peace officer while engaged in the execution of his duty. Constable Jones gave evidence at her trial that he had not arrested Molly for yelling at him but said "his authority had been flaunted" and that he wanted to have her arrested "to prevent further trouble." Should the court find Sandra guilty of the charge? Explain. If not, what other offence could she be charged with?

See *R. v. Allen* (1971), 4 C.C.C. (2d) 194 (Ont.C.A.).

22 Sam Smith, age 19, had been dating Barbara Bright, age 15. Barbara's parents did not like Sam and thought he was a bad influence on their daughter. Last Wednesday they forbade Barbara to see him any longer. Friday night Barbara packed a suitcase and slipped out of the house. She went to Sam's apartment and told him that she had run away from home. He let her in and she spent Friday and Saturday nights at his apartment. Sunday night her parents found out where Sam lived. They went to Sam's place and forced her to go home with them. Can Sam be charged with abduction? What difference would it make if Sam had picked her up Friday night and driven her to his apartment? What if Sam had called her and encouraged her to leave home and live with him?

chapter

THIRTEEN

Offences Against Property Rights
Part IX of the Code

The offences covered in Part IX of the Code concern violations of a person's property rights. A property right includes a right of possession or ownership of a place or a "thing". Owning a car, or a home, or renting an apartment are examples of ways people obtain property rights. Common offences against property rights include theft and "breaking and entering." With the exception of the offences of robbery and extortion, these crimes do not involve personal violence.

A. THEFT

1. Elements of the Offence

Briefly, theft is the act of a person who dishonestly takes property belonging to another with the intention of depriving the owner of it either permanently or temporarily. Section 334 states that unless the law provides otherwise, where the value of the property stolen exceeds $1 000 or the thing stolen is a testamentary instrument (e.g., a will), theft is an indictable offence. (Theft that is indictable may be referred to as "theft over".) Thefts of property, where the thing stolen is not a testamentary instrument and is worth $1 000 or less, are hybrid offences.

Section 322(1) of the Code defines the offence of theft:

**THEFT
s.322
Indictable
if property a
testamentary
instrument or
value exceeds
$1 000
Max: 10 years
Otherwise
hybrid
Max: 2 years
[s.334]**

> **322.(1) Every one commits theft who fraudulently and without colour of right takes, or fraudulently and without colour of right converts to his use or to the use of another person, anything whether animate or inanimate, with intent,**
>
> **(a) to deprive, temporarily or absolutely, the owner of it, or**

277

a person who has a special property or interest in it, of the thing or of his property or interest in it;

(b) to pledge it or deposit it as security;

(c) to part with it under a condition with respect to its return that the person who parts with it may be unable to perform; or

(d) to deal with it in such a manner that it cannot be restored in the condition in which it was at the time it was taken or converted.

(2) A person commits theft when, with intent to steal anything, he moves it or causes it to move or to be moved, or begins to cause it to become movable.

a. "Converting" Property

A person converts property to his or her use when the person has legally obtained the property but fails to return it. So, for example, a person who borrows library books and does not return them, with the intent of depriving the owner (the library) of the books, has committed theft. An example of theft by conversion is given in the case of *R. v. Johnson*.[1] In this case, the accused opened a bank account and was accidently given the number of an account that had not yet been used. The person who had the account then made several deposits in it. When the accused discovered the increase in the account balance, he immediately withdrew the money. His conviction was upheld on appeal.

The taking or converting can be absolute or temporary. Therefore, an illegal borrowing is also theft.

The victim of the theft does not need to be the owner of the thing. A person who has a special property interest in a thing is, for example, a person who has rented it. One case has even held that a neighbour taking care of a dwelling-house in the owner's absence had a special property interest in the house.[2]

b. Taking or Converting "Anything"

In most situations, it is clear what "anything" means. A recent Supreme Court of Canada case, however, had to decide whether the offence of theft had taken place in an unusual situation. In *R. v. Stewart*,[3] the accused was hired by union organizers to obtain a list of names and addresses of about 600 employees of a hotel who the organizers were trying to unionize. Stewart approached a security guard and offered him money to obtain the information. The security guard went to the police

1. (1978), 42 C.C.C. (2d) 249 (Man.C.A.).
2. *R. v. Rodrique* (1987), 61 C.R. (3d) 381 (Que.C.A.).
3. (1988), 63 C.R. (3d) 305 (S.C.C.).

instead. The police taped a conversation between the guard and Stewart and eventually charged him with counselling theft. The case was eventually appealed to the Supreme Court of Canada on the issue of whether the term "anything" in s.322 includes confidential information. It was agreed by the Crown and defence that no written list or other tangible thing was involved. The confidential information was to be copied or memorized. In an unanimous decision the court held that confidential information is not property. The decision said: "to be the object of theft, 'anything' must be property in the sense that to be stolen it has to belong in some way to someone. For instance, no conviction for theft would arise out of a taking or converting of the air that we breathe, because air is not property."

The decision also pointed out that there was a policy reason for not expanding the meaning of property for the offence of theft. For example, if a person memorized confidential information knowing that it was stolen, that person could be charged with having possession of stolen property for every day that the person remembered it. As well, society's best interests are served by a free flow of information. The court went on to say that it may be that confidential information should be protected somehow under the Criminal Code. This, however, is a job for Parliament, who should enact appropriate legislation.

c. *Fraudulently and Without Colour of Right*

(i) Fraudulently

Some courts have held that fraudulent conduct requires a dishonest or immoral intent. In *Cooper v. R.*[4] the accused was charged with the theft of an aircraft. The accused went to the grounds of the flying school where he had begun taking flying lessons. Using a canoe he went out to the aircraft which was moored at a buoy. Without permission he got in and started the plane, intending to bring it alongside a dock. He missed the dock once and was making a second attempt when he was stopped. The evidence indicated that the accused intended only to show the plane to some friends. The court found the accused not guilty of the charge of theft. It held that he had not taken the aircraft fraudulently. Even though the accused had taken the plane within the meaning of s.322 (he deprived the owner of it temporarily), he did so only to show it to his friends and thus, he did not take it with a criminal, or dishonest, intent.

In *Handfield v. R.*[5] the accused was charged with the theft of an election poster. His defence was lack of criminal intent. He and two of his brothers spent the evening together. On their way home they passed the

4. (1946), 2 C.R. 408 (N.S.C.A.).
5. (1953), 17 C.R. 343 (Que.C.A.).

residence of someone on which was standing an election poster, inviting the electorate to vote Progressive Conservative. The accused removed the poster and placed it on the lawn of a person they knew to be a Liberal party supporter. One of the accused said that he took the poster to "play a trick" and that he never meant to steal it.

The court held that the accused did not take the election poster fraudulently. The judgment concluded: "What was done may, to some people, seem reprehensible and might possibly subject the accused to some punitive measures, but not in my opinion subject them to conviction as common thieves and to a criminal record for the future."

In *R. v. Kerr*,[6] the accused was celebrating a victory in a retriever dog championship competition. For some reason, the accused and two companions went to the International Airport where they were seen by a cleaner at the airport. All three were staggering and acting in a foolish manner. The accused was carrying one of the ashtrays belonging to the airport. The cleaner saw the ashtray being carried out by the accused. The ashtray was of a floor type and several feet in height. The behaviour of the men made the cleaner think that the ashtray was being carried away as a prank, and he thought it would be left outside the airport door. Later two police officers visited the accused's home and saw the ashtray resting on the lawn in front of the house. The accused said he did not mean to take the ashtray, and that he had intended to return it but the police arrived before he was able to do so. The court decided that the accused did not commit the offence of theft: "The circumstances in connection with the accused's stupid and foolish actions clearly showed the absence of any criminal intent."

However, court decisions have not been consistent, and the "prank" defence does not always succeed. In *Bogner v. The Queen*,[7] the accused had taken a rocking chair off the porch of a hotel. They were chased by the wife of the owner of the hotel. She saw a police car and informed the police of what had happened. The accused were later arrested by the police for theft. At their trial they testified that the taking of the chair was a joke and that they had meant to return it later. Their conviction was upheld on appeal. The court stated that the offence was complete when the chair was taken without any justification. The owner had been deprived of it. It was not necessary to prove a general dishonest state of mind.

(ii) Without colour of right

The term *colour of right* under s.322 generally refers to a situation where a person asserts a possessory right, that is, a claim of ownership or lawful possession, to the thing which is alleged to have been stolen. In other

---

6. [1965] 4 C.C.C. 37 (Man.C.A.).
7. (1975), 33 C.R.N.S. 349 (Que.C.A.).

words, if someone puts forth what he or she believes to be an honest claim of ownership, even though the person is mistaken, the person will have a colour of right to the "thing" and cannot be found guilty of the offence of theft.

In *R. v. Wudrick*,[8] the accused, who was a railway employee, believing certain watermelons in a car on the railroad tracks had been abandoned, took two. In fact, the melons had not been abandoned and the accused was charged with theft. The accused's defence was that he had a "colour of right," in other words a possessory claim to the watermelons. The court concluded the accused's belief, that the melons were waste and that there was nothing wrong in taking them, was an honest belief. The accused was, in such circumstances, acquitted of the charge.

In *R. v. Howson*,[9] the accused was charged with the theft of a car. The complainant parked his car on a private parking lot without the permission of the owner. The accused, at the request of the superintendent of the lot, towed the complainant's car to his premises where it remained until the complainant found it there. The complainant demanded the return of his car but the accused refused to release it until he was paid a towing and storage charge. The complainant eventually paid the amount demanded, under protest, recovered his car and laid an information charging the accused with stealing his car.

The accused, in actual fact, could not legally keep the complainant's car. The accused stated he took the car believing, honestly, that he had a possessory claim to it until such time as he was paid a towing and storage charge. In other words, the accused claimed he honestly believed he had a "colour of right" to the car. The court accepted this argument and he was acquitted on the charge of theft.

2. The Doctrine of Recent Possession

Courts have developed through case law the doctrine of recent possession. This doctrine states that where it is proved that the accused had possession of recently stolen property, and no explanation has been given for having possession, the **trier of fact** (jury or judge if no jury) may, but not must, draw an inference that the accused is guilty of theft or offences incidental to theft (e.g., break and enter or possession of stolen property). The inference may be drawn even if there is no other evidence of guilt. The Supreme Court of Canada recently affirmed this doctrine in the case of *R. v. Kowlyk*.[10] There had been three break and enters in the Winnipeg area over a short period of time. The police arrested the

---

8. (1959), 123 C.C.C. 109 (Sask.C.A.).
9. [1966] 3 C.C.C. 348 (Ont.C.A.).
10. (1988), 43 C.C.C. (3d) 1 (S.C.C.).

accused's brother and brought him to the house that he shared with the accused. When they arrived, the brother yelled to the accused, "The police are here." The accused ran upstairs and started to go out a window, but he stopped once he saw the police outside. When the house was searched, the police found items from the three break and enters in the accused's locked bedroom, in the same containers as described when they were stolen. The accused was charged with break and enter.

The Supreme Court of Canada upheld the accused's conviction, stating that, under the doctrine of recent possession, the accused may be found guilty even though there is no other evidence of guilt. This doctrine does not apply, however, if the accused offers an explanation which might reasonably be true, even if the trier of fact is not satisfied with its truth. In that case, the Crown would have to prove all of the elements of the offence beyond a reasonable doubt. So, for example, Allen is charged with possession of stolen property, a television set. The television does not look new and Allen tells the court he bought it from a friend who said she did not need it any more. If Allen's explanation might be reasonably true, the Crown will have to prove every element of the offence of possession of property obtained by crime beyond a reasonable doubt, including that Allen knew that the television was stolen.

B. SPECIFIC THEFT OFFENCES

The Criminal Code contains a number of specific theft offences. Some of these are described in the following paragraphs. If the section which sets out the specific offence does not contain a penalty, the general penalty set out in s.334 applies; see page 277.

1. Theft of Gas, Electricity, or Telecommunications

Section 326 provides:

THEFT OF TELECOM-MUNICATION SERVICE
s.326
Penalty
[s.334]

326.(1) Every one commits theft who fraudulently, maliciously, or without colour of right,

(a) abstracts, consumes or uses electricity or gas or causes it to be wasted or diverted; or

(b) uses any telecommunication facility or obtains any telecommunication service.

(2) In this section and in section 327, "telecommunication" means any transmission, emission or reception of signs, signals, writing, images, sounds or intelligence of any nature by wire, radio, visual, or other electromagnetic system.

Section 326(1)(a) deals with situations in which gas, electricity, or a telecommunication service is stolen. For example, a person who diverts electricity from a public utility commission so that it does not pass through the commission's meter can be charged with theft of electricity.

In *R. v. Brais*,[11] the accused was charged with theft for fraudulently obtaining long-distance telephone services. An operator of the telephone company took a call from the accused who said she wanted to make a credit card call to Toronto. The accused gave the Toronto number and the credit card number. The call lasted 64 minutes and the charge for it was $41.60. After 30 minutes the telephone company made certain checks and found that the card number was not genuine. For this reason, the telephone company could not charge the call to anyone. The court held that the accused placed the telephone call intentionally, without mistake, and with knowledge that she was obtaining the call by using a credit card number which did not exist. The accused was convicted.

POSSESSION OF DEVICE TO OBTAIN TELECOM-MUNICATION SERVICE s.327(1) Indictable Max: 2 years

Section 327(1) creates the offence of making, owning, or selling, any instrument or device which is designed to obtain a telecommunication service (telephone, telegram, etc.) without paying for the "service". For example, a de-scrambler for intercepting pay television signals and computer software for making long-distance telephone calls without charge are such devices.

THEFT BY PERSON REQUIRED TO ACCOUNT s.330(1) Penalty [s.334]

2. Theft by a Person Required to Account

Section 330(1) provides:

> **330.(1) Every one commits theft who, having received anything from any person on terms that require him to account for or pay it or the proceeds of it or a part of the proceeds to that person or another person, fraudulently fails to account for or pay it or the proceeds of it or the part of the proceeds of it accordingly.**

Section 330(1) covers situations in which an accused has received money, or a "thing", from one person and must turn it over to another person. In *R. v. Mckenzie*,[12] a taxi driver was convicted of theft under s.330, because he failed to turn over to the taxi's owner all of the fare money he owed to the owner, his employer. In *Washington State v.*

---

11. (1972), 7 C.C.C. (2d) 301 (B.C.C.A.).
12. (1971), 4 C.C.C. (2d) 296 (S.C.C.).

Johnston,[13] the Supreme Court of Canada held that the element of fraud cannot be inferred just because the accused did not return the goods within a reasonable time. In other words, the Crown must prove fraudulent intent.

THEFT BY
HUSBAND OR
WIFE
s.329(1)(2)
Penalty
[s.334]

3. Theft by Husband or Wife

Section 329 provides:

> **329.(1) Subject to subsection (2), no husband or wife, during cohabitation, commits theft of anything that is by law the property of the other.**
>
> **(2) A husband or wife commits theft who, intending to desert or on deserting the other or while living apart from the other, fraudulently takes or converts anything that is by law the property of the other in a manner that, if it were done by another person, would be theft.**

If a husband and wife are still living together, neither spouse can be convicted of theft if he or she takes property belonging to the other. However, if one of the spouses deserts, intends to desert, or is living apart, and takes property belonging to the other, he or she has committed theft.

The property taken must belong, in law, to the other spouse. For example, if a car is the object taken, the car, in most situations, would have to be registered in the name of the "wronged" spouse. Or, for example, if one spouse is given a gift by the other, and the spouse giving the gift has relinquished all control over it, the gift is "by law" the property of the other.

Section 329(3) states:

> **329.(3) Every one commits theft who, during cohabitation of a husband and wife, knowingly,**
>
> **(a) assists either of them in dealing with anything that is by law the property of the other in a manner that would be theft if they were not married; or**
>
> **(b) receives from either of them anything that is by law the property of the other and has been obtained from the other by dealing with it in a manner that would be theft if they were not married.**

---

13. (1988), 40 C.C.C. (3d) 546 (S.C.C.). This case concerned an extradition hearing. The accused was to be extradited to the state of Washington from which he fled after being convicted and imprisoned for theft. The court had to decide whether the offence of theft in Washington, which did not require fraudulent intent, was the same as in Canada before a fugitive could be extradited.

If a third party assists one of the spouses in taking property belonging, in law, to the other, he or she will be guilty of theft. Also, if the third party receives property from one of the spouses and the property was stolen by the spouse, the third party will also be committing theft. In such situations the third party must know the spouse is removing property which belongs to the other before the offence of theft can be made out. For example, if a wife removed from the matrimonial home her husband's stamp collection and gave the collection to her brother, who was aware of the husband's ownership of the collection, he also would be guilty of theft.

C. OFFENCES RESEMBLING THEFT

1. "Joy-Riding"

It is possible to "take" a motor vehicle or vessel without the consent of its owner, and *not* be committing the offence of theft. This offence is loosely referred to as "joy-riding". Section 335 provides:

TAKING
MOTOR
VEHICLE OR
VESSEL
WITHOUT
CONSENT
s.335
Summary
conviction

> **335. Every one who, without the consent of the owner, takes a motor vehicle . . . with intent to drive [or], use . . . or cause it to be driven, [or] used . . . is guilty of an offence punishable on summary conviction.**

Notice that joy-riding is a summary conviction offence. Since most cars are worth more than $1 000, a young person, for instance, who takes a car for a "joy-ride" intending to return it can be charged with this offence rather than the more serious offence of "theft over". The Supreme Court of Canada has held that joy-riding is not an included offence in theft. However, in certain situations, either offence could be charged. It is then up to the Crown to decide which offence to charge.[14]

In *R. v. Wilkins*,[15] the accused took a police officer's motorcycle, while the latter was standing on the sidewalk making out a ticket, intending for a joke to drive it a short distance. He was charged with theft of the motorcycle under s.283 (now s.322). The court held that the accused should have been charged under s.295 (now s.335) and that he was not guilty of theft. In its judgment, the court stated:

> *In the instant case, the facts could not possibly justify a conviction of theft. The accused did not intend to steal the vehicle, that is, to convert the property to his own use, but only to drive it as contemplated by s.295 [s.335]. His intention was merely to play a joke on the policeman — the*

---

14. *LaFrance v. The Queen* (1973), 13 C.C.C. (2d) 289 (S.C.C.).
15. (1964), 44 C.R. 375 (Ont.C.A.).

intention to perpetrate this joke, stupid though it was, is incompatible with the evil intent which is inherent in the crime of theft.

2. Fraudulent Concealment

Section 341 creates the offence of fraudulent concealment:

FRAUDULENT CONCEAL- MENT s.341 Indictable Max: 2 years

341. Every one who, for a fraudulent purpose, takes, obtains, removes or conceals anything is guilty of an indictable offence . . .

Section 341 is designed to cover situations in which the thing taken is hidden in the hope that the owner will not be able to find it. For instance, if a deceased had made two wills, and neglected to destroy the first, an accused who concealed the second, because it "cut out" an inheritance which the first granted, would be guilty of fraudulent concealment under s.341.

THEFT OF CREDIT CARD s.342(1) Hybrid Max: 10 years

3. Taking of a Credit Card

Section 342(1) deals with the theft or forgery of a credit card.

342.(1) Everyone who,
(a) steals a credit card,
(b) forges or falsifies a credit card,
(c) has in his possession, uses or deals in any other way with a credit card that he knows was obtained
    (i) by the commission in Canada of an offence, or
    (ii) by an act or omission anywhere that, if it had occurred in Canada, would have constituted an offence, or
(d) uses a credit card that he knows has been revoked or cancelled is guilty of
(e) an indictable offence . . . or
(f) an offence punishable on summary conviction.

4. The Unauthorized Use of Computer Facilities

The offence of unauthorized use of computer facilities is in s.342.1:

UNAUTHOR- IZED USE OF COMPUTER s.342.1 Hybrid Max: 10 years

342.1(1) Every one who, fraudulently and without colour of right,
(a) obtains, directly or indirectly, any computer service,
(b) by means of an electro-magnetic, acoustic, mechanical or other device, intercepts or causes to be intercepted, directly or indirectly, any function of a computer system, or
(c) uses or causes to be used, directly or indirectly, a

computer system with intent to commit an offence under paragraph (a) or (b) or an offence under section 430 in relation to data or a computer system

is guilty of an indictable offence . . . or is guilty of an offence punishable on summary conviction.

5. Taking From Mail

Section 356 creates a special offence for the theft of mail:

THEFT FROM
MAIL
s.356
Indictable
Max: 10 years

356.(1) Every one who
(a) steals
    (i) anything sent by post, after it is deposited at a post office and before it is delivered,
    (ii) a bag, sack or other container or covering in which mail is conveyed, whether or not it contains mail, or
    (iii) a key suited to a lock adopted for use by the Canada Post Corporation, or
(b) has in his possession anything in respect of which he knows that an offence has been committed under paragraph (a),
is guilty of an indictable offence . . . .

D. ROBBERY

1. Elements of the Offence

ROBBERY
c.343
Indictable
Max: life
imprisonment
[s.344]

Section 343 of the Code defines the offence of robbery:

343. Every one commits robbery who
(a) steals, and for the purpose of extorting whatever is stolen or to prevent or overcome resistance to the stealing, uses violence or threats of violence to a person or property;
(b) steals from any person and, at the time he steals or immediately before or immediately thereafter, wounds, beats, strikes or uses any personal violence to that person;
(c) assaults any person with intent to steal from him; or
(d) steals from any person while armed with an offensive weapon or imitation thereof.

Section 2 of the Criminal Code provides that "to steal" means "to commit theft." However, robbery, as opposed to theft, involves the threat or actual use of violence against a person or property. Generally, assault is a *lesser included offence* for robbery. However, not every robbery will include an assault. For example, robbery under s.343(d) does not involve assault.

The violence used to commit the robbery need not be severe, nor cause injury to the victim. Generally, any form of physical interference, from a push to a punch, will amount to "violence" for the purposes of s.343. However, it is necessary that some violence be used in the committing of a robbery to distinquish the offence from theft. For example, suddenly snatching a purse may be theft rather than robbery if there is no violence used and the victim offers no resistance.[16] However, if, in order to get the purse, the accused had to "lock" his hand around the wrist of the purse-holder, or even "shake" the purse in order to force the victim to let it go, the offence of robbery would be committed, because violence was used.[17]

Similarly, a threat of any form of violence will generally bring the accused's action within the offence of robbery.

2. Robbery Under S.343(a)

Section 343(a) sets out the basic definition of the offence of robbery, that is, theft accompanied by actual violence, or by threats of violence. To "extort" means to compel, or to force. The violence or threat of violence need not be directed at the person being robbed. If the accused struck an innocent bystander at the scene of the theft, he would be guilty of robbery. The Ontario Court of Appeal in *R. v. Sayers and McCoy*[18] held that robbery under this section does not require that the accused be armed: the threat of violence is enough. In *Sayers*, the accused entered a bank at about 12:30 in the afternoon. While one of the accused stood at the door and watched for police the other jumped on the counter and yelled at the cashiers: "This is a robbery [or hold-up] in progress . . . Give me the money . . . I'm not going to hurt anyone." He went up to two tellers and grabbed the cash from their drawers. When he came to the third cashier and tried to open the cash drawer, he found it was locked. He screamed at her: "Unlock the drawer, this is a robbery." The bank employees testified that they were concerned and afraid. Neither of the accused had weapons. After taking the money, the accused fled on foot and were apprehended by the police. The appeal court held that the words and gestures of the accused "could only have the effect of causing reasonable apprehension of physical harm unless the tellers complied with the demand." This conduct falls within the definition of robbery under s.343(a). The appeal court set aside their acquittal and entered convictions for robbery.

---

16. *R. v. Picard* (1976), 39 C.C.C. (2d) 57 (Que.Sess.Ct.).
17. *E.G.R. v. Trudel* (1984), 12 C.C.C. (3d) 342 (Que.C.A.).
18. (1983), 8 C.C.C. (3d) 572 (Ont.C.A.).

3. Robbery Under S.343(b)

Assault is a lesser included offence for robbery under this subsection.

The Ontario Court of Appeal in *R. v. Oakley*[19] has held that the words "uses any personal violence" are coloured by the preceding words, "wounds, beats [or] strikes" and, therefore, for robbery under this subsection, there must be more than a "technical assault", that is, something more than touching without consent. In this case, the accused was a passenger in his sister-in-law's car when he began hallucinating. He thought his sister-in-law was the devil and that she was taking him to the hospital to be killed. He put the car into park while it was moving, causing it to come to an abrupt stop. He then demanded the keys from her. When she refused, he took the keys from her and told her to get out of the car and then drove off. The court held that in this case no robbery had occurred under s.343(b) because the assault was only technical.

4. Robbery Under S.343(c)

Section 343(c) provides that, whether or not a theft takes place, if the victim was assaulted with the intent to steal, the offence of robbery is still mitted. If an accused knocked someone to the ground with the intent to grab his wallet, and was interrupted by a witness's screams, causing him to flee before he could get the wallet, he would still have committed the offence of robbery.

5. Robbery Under S.343(d)

Section 343(d) provides that robbery is committed if a person steals while he or she is armed with an offensive weapon or with an imitation of an offensive weapon. Section 2 of the Code defines what is meant by the word "offensive weapon":

> **"offensive weapon" or "weapon" means**
> **(a) anything used or intended for use in causing death or injury to persons whether designed for that purpose or not, or**
> **(b) anything used or intended for use for the purpose of threatening or intimidating any person.**

Almost any object can be an offensive weapon. The person must be armed with some "thing" however. In *R. v. Sloan*,[20] the accused was

19. (1986), 24 C.C.C. (3d) 351 (Ont.C.A.).
20. (1974), 19 C.C.C. (2d) 190 (B.C.C.A.).

charged with attempted robbery under s.343(d). The accused, whose head and upper body were partially covered with a bed sheet, had come to a hotel in the middle of the night and ordered the night-desk clerk to open the office where the money was kept. The clerk refused. He was prodded backwards in the chest by something protruding from under the sheet. He said to the accused, "Don't push me, I've got a couple of cracked ribs." The accused replied, "If you don't open that door, you'll be in worse shape." The clerk turned and, in so doing, hit the protruding object and discovered it was a finger, not a gun barrel. At that point, the accused fled.

The court held that the accused did not have an "offensive weapon or an imitation thereof." Part of the judgment states:

> *In this case, all that is shown is that the accused . . . simulated the conduct of a man armed with a weapon. He acted a part or played out a pantomime to give the impression that he had a weapon. While the conduct might have justified a conviction under para.(a) (theft with threat of violence) or (c) (theft with assault) . . . it does not meet the requirements of . . . (d). To arm oneself with a weapon means to equip oneself, to acquire, to become possessed of some instrument which is either a weapon or an imitation of a weapon. I am not of the opinion that in these circumstances a man can be armed with his own finger and I am satisfied that the word "imitation" as used in s.302(d) [now s.343(d)] refers to an imitation of the weapon and cannot be stretched to include a simulation of conduct or actions.*

6. Robbery of Mail

STOPPING
MAIL WITH
INTENT
s.345
Indictable
Max: life
imprisonment

Section 345 defines a special offence for robbing anything that is used to convey or transport mail. It states:

> **345. Every one who stops a mail conveyance with intent to rob or search it is guilty of an indictable offence . . . .**

E. EXTORTION

Section 346 defines the offence of extortion:

EXTORTION
s.346
Indictable
Max: life
imprisonment

> **346.(1) Every one commits extortion who, without reasonable justification or excuse and with intent to obtain anything, by threats, accusations, menaces or violence induces or attempts to induce any person, whether or not he is the person threatened, accused or menaced or to whom violence is shown, to do anything or cause anything to be done.**
>
> **(1.1) Every one who commits extortion is guilty of an indictable offence . . .**

(2) A threat to institute civil proceedings is not a threat for the purposes of this section.

Extortion is essentially equivalent to the word "blackmail". An extortion occurs when one person threatens another with some consequence, such that the person is forced to commit an act, or to omit doing something which he or she otherwise would have done, if not threatened.

In *R. v. Natarelli and Volpe*,[21] the accused were convicted of extortion for threatening the life of the victim if he did not deliver to them a large sum of money. In this case, the Supreme Court of Canada stated that there were three ingredients to the offence of extortion:

1. that the accused has used threats,
2. that he has done so with the intention of obtaining something by the use of threats, and
3. that either the use of the threats or the making of the demand for the thing sought to be obtained was without reasonable excuse or justification.

With respect to requirement 3, above, the court in *Volpe* said that once "it is proved that the accused made threats to cause death, or bodily harm, with intent to obtain the money sought, then they are guilty of extortion regardless of whether they honestly believed that they had a right to the money." In other words, a person cannot threaten another with death, or harm, in an attempt to force him to do something, even if he honestly believes he has reasonable justification for making the threat. An example of a threat which is justified is the threat of a creditor to turn over an account to a collection agency, in an attempt to get payment from a person who owes the creditor money. However, if the creditor threatened the person with violence if payment was not made on time, even though the creditor is owed the money, the creditor would have no reasonable justification for making such a threat.

1. Threat or Menace

It is an essential element of the offence that there be a threat, accusation, menace, or violence. In *R. v. Rousseau*,[22] the Supreme Court of Canada found that the offence had not occurred because none of these elements were present. In this case, the accused was a lawyer who had been representing two men who were charged with theft. The men were employees of a security company which was under contract to protect the

---

21. (1967), 1 C.R.N.S. 302 (S.C.C.).
22. (1985), 21 C.C.C. (3d) 1 (S.C.C.).

premises from which the goods were stolen. The accused approached the lawyer for the security company and offered to get the charges dropped in exchange for some money. The accused had already worked out a deal with the police to have some of the charges dropped. Although the accused was guilty of obstructing justice, he was not guilty of extortion.

The threat or menace need not amount to a threat to harm or murder the victim. A threat, for example, by someone to do damage to the victim's property is sufficient for the purposes of s.346. For example, a threat to break a person's windows, or let air out of the person's tires, could probably qualify as extorting threats.

2. "Anything"

The British Columbia Court of Appeal has held that the word "anything" in this offence has a wide and unrestricted meaning. Therefore, an act of sexual intercourse can be the anything "extorted".[23]

3. Threat to Sue

Section 346(2) provides that a threat to take someone to court in an attempt to force him to do something is *not* a threat for the purpose of committing the offence of extortion. Therefore, if Kevin threatened to sue Wilf in an attempt to get Wilf to pay for damages Wilf caused to Kevin's property, Kevin would not be committing the offence of extortion.

F. BREAK AND ENTER

Section 348 defines the offence of break and enter:

BREAKING
AND
ENTERING
WITH INTENT
s.348(1)
Indictable
Max: life
imprisonment

348.(1) Every one who
(a) breaks and enters a place with intent to commit an indictable offence therein,
(b) breaks and enters a place and commits an indictable offence therein, or
(c) breaks out of a place after
(i) committing an indictable offence therein, or
(ii) entering the place with intent to commit an indictable offence therein,
is guilty of an indictable offence . . . .

---

23. *R. v. Bird*, [1970] 3 C.C.C. 340 (B.C.C.A.).

1. The Presumptions and the Charter

Chapter Two discussed reverse onus clauses, statutory presumptions, and the Charter. It explained how many of these clauses are being struck down as violations of the presumption of innocence. Although there are many presumptions and reverse onus clauses in other parts of the Code, a concentration of them may be found in the offences of break and enter. These clauses are all open to challenge under the Charter. Existing case law will be mentioned in the discussion which follows. Some of these decisions are from provincial courts of appeal. Of course, in the end, it is up to the Supreme Court of Canada to finally decide whether any particular clause is invalid for infringing the Charter.

2. Break Defined

Break is defined in s.321:

BREAK DEFINED s.321

> **321. In this Part,**
> **"break" means**
> **(a) to break any part, internal or external, or**
> **(b) to open any thing that is used or intended to be used to close or to cover an internal or external opening.**

"Breaking" can involve "jimmying" a door or window, "picking" a lock, or breaking a window. However, "breaking" also includes a number of ways of entering a place that one would not normally associate with the word "breaking". Opening a door with a stolen or "found" key, lifting a latch, raising an already open window, or simply opening an unlocked door, are all examples of breaking for the purposes of the offence of breaking and entering.

In *R. v. Jewell*,[24] the accused was charged with "breaking and entering" under s. 348. An excerpt from the court's decision summarizes the facts:

> *The building which is the subject of the charge is a house which had been unoccupied for a considerable period of time. It was in a somewhat dilapidated condition and not habitable at the date of the alleged offence. The accused entered the house through a screen door and an inner door, both of which were open wide enough to permit the accused to enter without further opening the doors.*

The accused's evidence, which was the only evidence on this point, was as follows:

---

24. (1975), 22 C.C.C. (2d) 252 (Ont.C.A.).

Q. **And do you remember entering the house in question?**

A. Yes, I do.

Q. **Yes?**

A. I entered through, well, it's the westerly door, and I didn't have to force it open. It was open. When we walked up, the screen door was open, the door was open wide enough to walk through without having to push it any further.

Q. **You didn't even budge the door? Is that what you are saying?**

A. I didn't budge it at all.

The accused admitted that he entered the house for the purpose of stealing something from the house.

The court concluded that because the accused entered through an already open door it could not be said that he "broke into" the building. However, in *R. v. Bargiamis*,[25] it was held that further opening an already ajar door did constitute "breaking". In the *Bargiamis* case, the door was open about one-half inch (about two centimetres) and the accused pushed it open to allow himself space to enter.

In sum it would appear that if an accused is to be said to have "broken into" (or out of) a place he or she must have gained entrance (or exit) by having used some force to "assist" in the entry. If the accused is able to enter through an already open door or window, he or she will not have broken into the place.

3. Enter Defined

Enter is defined by s.350:

ENTER
DEFINED
s.350

> **350.(a) a person enters as soon as any part of his body or any part of an instrument that he uses is within any thing that is being entered; and**
>
> > **(b) a person shall be deemed to have broken and entered if**
> >
> > > **(i) he obtained entrance by a threat or artifice or by collusion with a person within, or**
> > >
> > > **(ii) he entered without lawful justification or excuse, the proof of which lies upon him, by a permanent or temporary opening.**

An entrance is made as soon as any part of the body of the accused, or any part of the instrument used by him or her, is within any part of the place being entered. For example, if an accused is caught by police with a

---

25. (1970), 10 C.R.N.S. 129 (Ont.C.A.).

hand inside a window which the accused opened, the accused has entered the place for the purpose of s.348.

In *R. v. Marshall*,[26] the accused was charged with "breaking and entering." A police officer on patrol noticed a window pane in the premises pushed in about one foot (30 cm). The window pane consisted of six glass panels, five of which were broken. One police officer searching in the vicinity of the broken window found the accused lying on his back on the ground concealed in a trench some five feet (one and one-half metres) from the building. His hand was cut and his left cowboy boot was off. He was arrested.

At the trial, the accused gave this testimony:

> *I was standing there and I went across the street to take a leak and I was standing in an empty yard there and I seen all these cars going by so I went a little further in over by the building there and I went like this, leaning against the building there and the window broke and then this here. So I was mad and I went like this, I just swung. I may have swung twice, I don't remember but I swung once and I hit the bottom and then I don't know. I think I had a piece of glass or something in my boot cause when I moved it hurt so I took my boot off and I was trying to empty it out and I heard the police coming so I laid down in the grass because I was scared. I thought I was going to be charged with wilful damage or something. I had no intention of entering the building whatsoever, I know the man that owns the building very well and there was nothing I wanted of his.*

It was acknowledged by all parties, including the accused, that there had been a "breaking". But it was further held that there had been an "entering" as well. Even though the accused had only put his hand through the window in the process of breaking it, that was enough to constitute an entering. It was, therefore, established that the accused had broken and entered the building. However, it was not proved that he had done so with the intent to commit an indictable offence and he was acquitted.

Section 350(b)(i) provides that if a person gains entry by threats or with the help of a person inside he will still have "broken and entered."

Section 350(b)(ii) states that a person is presumed to have broken and entered a building if the person entered through a "permanent or temporary opening." Open doors and open windows are not permanent or temporary openings. In *R. v. Sutherland*,[27] the accused entered through a garage "enclosed on three sides and open on one end for the entrance of a car." He entered for the purpose of stealing gasoline and was charged with "breaking and entering." The court held that the

26. (1970), 1 C.C.C. (2d) 505 (B.C.C.A.).
27. (1967), 50 C.R. 197 (B.C.C.A.).

"opening" in the garage was really not an opening but was, in fact, "an entrance." An opening in s.350 refers to a hole in a wall, or door, or an opening where a door or window has not yet been placed. Areas where people usually enter buildings are not "openings."

Section 350(b)(ii) also contains a reverse onus clause. The phrase, "the proof of which lies upon him," means that it is up to the accused to show that the entrance was made with *lawful justification*. This element has been challenged as a violation of the presumption of innocence. For example in *R. v. Singh*,[28] the Alberta Court of Appeal held that the effect of this section is that once it is proven that the accused entered he or she will be deemed to have broken in unless the accused proves on a balance of probabilities that he or she entered with a lawful justification or excuse. The court held that this section creates an unjustifiable reverse onus provision. An accused could be convicted of break and enter where a reasonable doubt exists that he or she entered without lawful justification or excuse. However, to save the section, the court held that the section could be applied without the phrase "the proof of which lies upon him." In other words, the Crown must prove beyond a reasonable doubt that the accused entered without lawful justification.

An example of lawful justification is the case of *R. v. Farbridge*.[29] In this case, the accused entered a department store during business hours with the intent to hide in the store until it was closed and then steal clothing. The Alberta Court of Appeal held that he had not broken and entered under s.350(b) because he entered with lawful justification, that is, with the lawful justification that any person has for entering a store during business hours.

4. Place Defined

Section 348(3) defines the term "place":

PLACE
DEFINED
s.348(3)

    348.(3) For the purposes of this section and section 351, "place" means
    (a) a dwelling-house;
    (b) a building or structure or any part thereof, other than a dwelling-house;
    (c) a railway vehicle, vessel, an aircraft or a trailer; or
    (d) a pen or enclosure in which fur-bearing animals are kept in captivity for breeding or commercial purposes.

5. Intent to Commit an Indictable Offence

Once it is established that the accused "broke" into or out of a "place," it

---

must still be shown that (1) he or she committed an indictable offence, or (2) he or she entered with the intent to commit an indictable offence.

The most common indictable offence that is the object of a break-in is theft. However, any other indictable offence can be the object of a break-in under a "breaking and entering" charge. For example, assault may be the indictable offence which is the object of the break-in.

In *Macleod v. R.*[30] the accused, after being ordered out of his host's home where he had been drinking, returned and broke into the home to retrieve a bottle of liquor which he had brought to the home earlier. The accused was acquitted on a charge of "breaking and entering" because he did not break and enter with an intent to commit an indictable offence. See also the *Marshall* case discussed above.

For the same reason, if someone breaks into a cottage only to seek shelter, that person will not have committed an offence under s. 348, because, in such a situation, there is no intent to commit an indictable offence.

6. Presumption of Intent

Section 348(2) provides:

**PRESUMP-
TION OF
INTENT TO
BREAK-IN OR
BREAK-OUT
s.348(2)**

348.(2) For the purposes of proceedings under this section, evidence that an accused

(a) broke and entered a place or attempted to break and enter a place is, in the absence of any evidence to the contrary, proof that he broke and entered the place or attempted to do so, as the case may be, with intent to commit an indictable offence therein; or

(b) broke out of a place is, in the absence of any evidence to the contrary, proof that he broke out after

> **(i) committing an indictable offence therein, or**
> **(ii) entering with intent to commit an indictable offence therein.**

This subsection creates a presumption of intent that requires evidence that the accused did not break into or out of the place for the purpose of committing an indictable offence. Although this evidence would usually come from the accused, it is possible that the evidence could also arise out of the Crown's case. If "evidence to the contrary" is presented, the Crown must prove every element of the offence beyond a reasonable doubt. The application of this presumption and the meaning of the phrase "evidence to the contrary" was considered by the Supreme Court of Canada in *R. v. Proudlock*.[31] In this case, the accused had been drinking

---

30. (1968), 2 C.R.N.S. 342 (P.E.I.S.C.).
31. (1978), 43 C.C.C. (2d) 321 (S.C.C.).

at a party in an apartment above a restaurant. He had been living in the apartment with the son of the owner of the restaurant. At some time in the evening he broke into the restaurant by breaking a window and climbing through. He encountered the janitor in the restaurant who asked him what he was doing. The accused replied that he had been given the key by the owner's son and was looking for some soup. He then left by the back door. Later he was questioned by the police. When asked why he had broken into the restaurant, he said that he did not know why but he had no intention to steal anything. At his trial, the judge said that he didn't believe the accused's testimony that he didn't intend to steal anything but that his testimony was evidence to the contrary and therefore the Crown had to prove the offence beyond a reasonable doubt. The case was appealed on the issue of whether evidence that is disbelieved is "evidence to the contrary." The Supreme Court disagreed with the trial judge. The court held that evidence which is disbelieved is not evidence to the contrary. To rebut the presumption, the evidence must be believable and raise a reasonable doubt. The Supreme Court ordered that a conviction be entered against the accused.

The decision in *Proudlock* was made before the Charter was enacted so the Supreme Court did not deal with the issue of whether the section violates the Charter. However, this section has been found to violate the Charter by the British Columbia Court of Appeal in *R. v. Slaven*.[32] The accused in this case was found in a locked parking area of an apartment building by the apartment manager. When confronted, the accused ran out of the area to where the police were waiting. He was charged with breaking out with intent. The appeal court said that the presumption of intent violates the presumption of innocence under the Charter because:

In order to avoid a conviction, the accused . . . has the burden cast upon him to rebut the presumption [of intent] by ensuring that there is evidence to the contrary before the court . . . . And the evidence to the contrary must be sufficient to raise a reasonable doubt that the accused committed an indictable offence . . . or that he entered in the first instance with the intent of committing an indictable offence.

However, the court finally held that the presumption is saved by s.1 of the Charter. The court relied on evidence that personal property crimes have reached epidemic proportions in this country and that the presumption only gave the Crown an "evidentiary assist". Therefore, the presumption of intent is a reasonable and justifiable limit under s.1 of the Charter.

---

32. 64 C.C.C. (3d) 29 (B.C.C.A.).

G. BEING UNLAWFULLY IN A DWELLING-HOUSE

Section 349 provides:

BEING UNLAWFULLY IN DWELLING-HOUSE
s.349
Indictable
Max: 10 years

349.(1) Every one who without lawful excuse, the proof of which lies upon him, enters or is in a dwelling-house with intent to commit an indictable offence therein is guilty of an indictable offence . . . .

(2) For the purpose of proceedings under this section, evidence that an accused, without lawful excuse, entered or was in a dwelling-house is, in the absence of any evidence to the contrary, proof that he entered or was in the dwelling-house with intent to commit an indictable offence therein.

The place entered must be a dwelling-house. This term is defined in s.2 as follows:

2. . . .
"dwelling-house" means the whole or any part of a building or structure that is kept or occupied as a permanent or temporary residence, and includes
(a) a building within the curtilage of a dwelling-house that is connected to it by a doorway or by a covered and enclosed passageway, and
(b) a unit that is designed to be mobile and to be used as a permanent or temporary residence and that is being used as such a residence . . .

Examples of dwelling-houses include apartments and motel or hotel rooms. Even a tent that people intend to sleep in has been considered a dwelling-house. The term "curtilage" refers to buildings close by a dwelling which are used for domestic or family activities, that is, a garage or shed.

For the purpose of s.349, "enters" has the same meaning as it does under s.348 and as it is defined under s.350.

To commit an offence under s.349, a person does not have to "break" in. In other words, if a person walked through an open door into a dwelling-house, although he or she could not be found guilty of the offence of "breaking and entering" (s.348), the person could be found guilty of unlawfully being in a dwelling-house. Also, the person does not need to enter for the purpose of committing an indictable offence. In other words, the person can form the intent once in the dwelling-house.

This offence has two elements that have been attacked as violations of the Charter right to be presumed innocent. First, subs.(1) sets out a reverse onus clause that the accused must prove that the entry was lawful. Second, subs.(2) sets out a presumption that evidence that the entry was unlawful is, in the absence of evidence to the contrary, evidence that the accused entered or was in the dwelling-house for the purpose of committing an indictable offence. Both of these elements were considered by the Ontario Court of Appeal in *R. v. Nagy*.[33] In this case, the accused entered the unlocked door of the house of M at about 3:00 in the afternoon. M was sleeping upstairs when he was awakened by someone downstairs saying hello. M asked the accused, who by this time was on the third stair leading upstairs, what he wanted. The accused said something about being stuck and needing a tow. There was some evidence that he turned his back to M and took off rubber gloves. The accused then called to a person in the car which was running in the driveway. Next, the accused's son entered the house and asked M if he owned a dog and said that there was an injured dog on the road. At that point, M's son walked in and the accused and his son left. M's son followed them and could find neither a stuck car nor an injured dog.

The trial judge convicted the accused of being unlawfully in the house. He rejected the accused's explanation because it was "incapable of belief" and held that there was no evidence to the contrary for explaining the accused's presence in the house.

The Court of Appeal held that the "without lawful excuse" requirement in subs.(1) is an element of the offence and that the accused must prove on a balance of probabilities that there was a lawful excuse for being in the dwelling-house. The court, however, did not consider the constitutionality of the subsection because in this case it was not necessary. The Crown had proved that the accused's entry was unlawful without using the reverse onus clause. With regard to subs.(2), the court found that the subsection infringed upon the presumption of innocence: first, because a person who enters a dwelling-house without a lawful excuse is not necessarily doing so with the intent to commit an indictable offence; and, second, the subsection may require a person to testify or give evidence to avoid a conviction where the Crown has not proved every element of the offence beyond a reasonable doubt. This requirement violates the accused person's right to remain silent, which is an underlying principle of the presumption of innocence. However, the court held that the violation could be justified under s.1 of the Charter since the objective of protecting people and property from the crimes of break and enter are sufficiently pressing to justify an infringement of the Charter.

---

33. (1988), 45 C.C.C. (3d) 350 (Ont.C.A.).

H. OFFENCES INVOLVING POSSESSION

The next two offences to be discussed, possession of instruments for break-in and possession of property obtained through the commission of an indictable offence, share the element of possession as the *actus reus* of the offence.

1. Possession

Possession is defined by s.4(3) of the Code:

POSSESSION DEFINED s.4(3)

> **4.(3)(a) a person has anything in possession when he has it in his personal possession or knowingly**
>
> **(i) has it in the actual possession or custody of another person, or**
>
> **(ii) has it in any place, whether or not that place belongs to or is occupied by him, for the use or benefit of himself or of another person; and**
>
> **(b) where one of two or more persons, with the knowledge and consent of the rest, has anything in his custody or possession, it shall be deemed to be in the custody and possession of each and all of them.**

Possession under both (a) and (b) of s.4(3) require (1) the knowledge of what the "thing" is and (2) a measure or right of control over the thing.

a. *Knowledge*

Even though a person has personal possession of the thing, for the law to consider the person to be in possession the accused must know what the thing is. This requirement of knowledge for possession was set out by the Supreme Court of Canada in the case of *Beaver v. The Queen*.[34] The accused was charged with possession of a narcotic and with trafficking in a narcotic. The evidence was that he sold a package of morphine to an undercover police officer. His defence was that he honestly believed that the package only contained powdered milk sugar. The Supreme Court of Canada allowed his defence to the charge of possession. The court stated:

> *To constitute possession within the meaning of the criminal law it is my judgment that where as here there is a manual handling of the thing it must be co-existent with knowledge of what that thing is, and both these elements must be co-existent with some act of control (outside of public duty).*

However, the defence failed for the charge of trafficking since the offence only requires that a person "hold out" anything to be a narcotic.

---

34. (1957), 118 C.C.C. 129 (S.C.C.).

b. Control

Control over the thing does not necessarily mean actual physical or manual control. Control refers to exercising authority over the thing. For example, a person can have control even if the person allows someone else to keep the thing.

2. Constructive Possession and Control

Possession under s.4(3)(b) is called constructive possession because the person does not have actual possession of the thing. Constructive possession requires knowledge, consent, and a measure of control. The case that decided that control is necessary for constructive possession is the Supreme Court of Canada decision in *R. v. Terrence*.[35] The accused was charged with being in possession of a stolen automobile in which he was a passenger. The evidence was that he was watching television one night when a friend, Hayes, arrived and asked if anyone wanted to go for a ride. The accused said "Sure" and went with Hayes. The car which was being driven by Hayes was eventually stopped by the police. The accused was charged with and convicted of possession. The accused appealed his conviction. The issue on appeal was, regardless of whether an accused knows a vehicle is stolen, is a measure of control necessary for the charge? The Supreme Court of Canada agreed with the Court of Appeal and held that a measure of control is necessary for constructive possession. His appeal was allowed and his conviction was overturned.

Consent can provide the element of control. In *R. v. Chambers*,[36] the accused was charged with possession of narcotics for the purpose of trafficking. She was living with her boyfriend who she knew was importing drugs. When their house was searched, drugs were found in her closet in the bedroom they shared. The Ontario Court of Appeal held that the required element of control was that she could choose to consent or not to consent to the drugs being stored in her closet.

POSSESSION OF BREAK-IN INSTRUMENT s.351(1) Indictable Max: 10 years

3. Possession of Break-In Instrument

Section 351 makes it an offence for a person to have possession of break-in instruments. The section states:

> **351.(1) Every one who, without lawful excuse, the proof of which lies on him, has in his possession any instrument suitable for the purpose of breaking into any place, motor vehicle, vault or safe under circumstances that give rise to a**

---

35. (1983), 4 C.C.C. (3d) 193 (S.C.C.).
36. (1985), 20 C.C.C. (3d) 440 (Ont.C.A.).

reasonable inference that the instrument has been used or is or was intended to be used for any such purpose is guilty of an indictable offence . . . .

In *Mongeau v. R.*,[37] the accused was arrested along with L. The accused was driving L's car when he was stopped by a police officer and asked for his driving licence and the car registration.

The arresting officer testified that he had no particular suspicion of either of the parties, and that he was merely making a routine "spot" check. He asked the accused to open the trunk of the car, which the latter proceeded to do. Observing a pack-sack, the officer asked what it contained. The accused said that he thought the pack-sack contained tools because he could see a wooden handle sticking out of the top of the bag.

As the two of them were examining the trunk, another police officer, who had remained in the police car, noticed L, who had stayed in his automobile, open the door and deposit another bag underneath the car. When this was examined, it was found to contain dynamite, caps, and fuse. Both men were then arrested and charged under s.351.

The accused argued that he did not have possession of the tools and dynamite, and only guessed that the bag in the trunk contained "ordinary tools". He further explained he was driving the car, which was L's, because L had an injured foot.

The court acquitted him for the following reasons:

1. While the accused was in control of the automobile in which the articles were found, his control was merely due to the fact that he was sitting in the driver's seat at the time the police stopped the automobile to check it. The checking of the car was merely routine and the police officer testified that he had no suspicion of either of the parties.

2. The mere fact that the accused was driving the car at the time on behalf of the owner, who was also present in the car, did not establish that he had control over, or even knowledge, of the tools or dynamite.

3. The explanation of the accused was a reasonable one under the particular circumstances of the case and he was entitled to the benefit of any doubt that might arise in respect of the offence.

a. Instruments Suitable for Breaking-In

In *R. v. Hayes*,[38] the accused was found in possession of certain documents. These documents consisted of elaborate plans or sketches of two villages in Ontario showing the exact location of two banks, and containing a minute and detailed description of the interior of one of them. The documents also contained recipes for making explosives, information

---

37. (1957), 25 C.R. 195 (Que.C.A.).
38. (1958), O.W.N. 449 (Ont.C.A.).

about bullet-proof vests, and descriptions of other instruments. The sole question for determination in the case was whether the documents, or plans, found in the possession of the accused, came within the category of "instruments for house-breaking, vault-breaking or safe-breaking." The court concluded a *"breaking" instrument* necessarily implies an object, article, or tool, which may be used to break something in the sense of the meaning of "break" as it is defined by s.321. Objects such as crowbars, jacks, screwdrivers, or even bent coat-hangers, are all capable of being described as "breaking" instruments. Having thus defined instrument, the court decided that the documents in the possession of the accused could not be classified as "house, vault or safe-breaking" instruments.

Another case which considered the issue of whether the articles found in the possession of the accused were break-in instruments is *R. v. Betzischek*.[39] In the trunk of a motor vehicle, owned by the accused, the police seized a briefcase in which was found bottles containing nitric and sulphuric acid, bicarbonate of soda, a measuring bottle and a cup, rubber gloves, and a plastic spatula. The evidence established the chemicals and implements were all necessary for making nitroglycerin, a powerful explosive used for safe-breaking. Glycerin, an essential ingredient for making the explosive, was not found in the possession of the accused. However, glycerin has several legitimate uses and is readily available at any drugstore.

The court concluded: "Having in mind that the only purpose that could be served by using all the objects found was to make nitroglycerin they are in my opinion substantial things having physical characteristics enabling them to be used to facilitate a breaking and constitute therefore an instrument for safe-breaking."

b. Reasonable Inference

Once it is shown that a person possessed instruments that could be used for "breaking into any place, motor vehicle, vault or safe," it must then be demonstrated that a reasonable inference can be drawn from the circumstances that the instruments were used or were intended to be used to break into a place, motor vehicle, safe, or vault.

In *R. v. Kozak and Moore*,[40] the accused were found with screwdrivers, a pair of pliers, a metal expandable tool, a wrench, two pallet knives, and two pairs of gloves. The question was whether these "otherwise innocent instruments" were to be used for an intended break-in. The accused were observed to be studying the rear door of an apartment building with the assistance of binoculars. Also found in the possession of the accused was a card, on which was written the licence plate number of the car

39. [1963] 3 C.C.C. 286 (Ont.C.A.).
40. (1975), 30 C.R.N.S. 7 (Ont.C.A.).

owned by the occupant of the apartment. The court held that such circumstances could be capable of giving rise to a reasonable inference that the instruments in possession of the accused were to be used to break into the apartment they were studying.

A case which reached the opposite conclusion is *R. v. Sullivan and Godbolt*,[41] where the accused was found in possession of possible safe-breaking instruments — a set of pole-climbers, a three-pound hammer, two pieces of soap, steel punches, pieces of wire, a pair of pliers and a quantity of rubber tape. The court believed his evidence that all of this material and the instruments could be, and were intended to be, used for a legitimate contracting business purpose.

The Supreme Court of Canada has considered whether the offence of possessing break-in instruments contains a reverse onus clause in the phrase "every one who without lawful excuse, the proof of which lies on him . . . ." In *R. v. Holmes*,[42] the accused was charged with possession of break-in instruments when he was found with a pair of vice grips and a pair of pliers. Before entering a plea to the charge, the accused applied to have the indictment quashed on the grounds that the section offends the Charter. The Supreme Court of Canada agreed with the decision of the Ontario Court of Appeal that held this offence does not contain a reverse onus provision. The Crown must prove all three elements of the offence beyond a reasonable doubt: (1) that the accused had possession (2) of break-in instruments (3) under circumstances which give rise to a reasonable inference that the instruments had been or were intended to be used for the purpose of a break-in. Once these three elements are proved, then the onus shifts to the accused to raise a defence, that is, to present evidence that raises a reasonable doubt. The phrase then is superfluous. The accused has the same defence that would be available even if those words were not contained in the offence. The Supreme Court dismissed the accused's appeal and sent the case back for trial.

4. Possession of Property Obtained by Crime

a. *Elements of the Offence*

Section 354 provides that it is an offence for a person, knowingly, to have in his or her possession any "thing" (either in whole or in part) which was obtained directly, or indirectly, by the commission of an indictable offence. Also, if a person has in his or her possession proceeds of a transaction involving a thing obtained by a crime, the person is guilty of an offence under s.354. This offence is often used for possession of stolen

---

41. (1946), 1 C.R. 164 (B.C.C.A.).
42. (1985), 41 C.C.C. (3d) 497 (S.C.C.).

POSSESSION
OF PROPERTY
OBTAINED BY
CRIME
s.354(b)
Indictable if
property is a
testamentary
instrument or
its value
exceeds $1 000
Otherwise
hybrid
Max: 2 years
[s.355]

property. Section 355 makes this offence indictable if the subject matter is a testamentary instrument or if it is worth more than $1 000. In other situations, the offence is hybrid.

Section 354(1) states:

> **354.(1) Every one commits an offence who has in his possession any property or thing or any proceeds of any property or thing knowing that all or part of the property or thing or of the proceeds was obtained . . . directly or indirectly from**
> **(a) the commission in Canada of an offence punishable by indictment, or**
> **(b) an act or omission anywhere that, if it had occurred in Canada, would have constituted an offence punishable by indictment.**

Paragraph (b) applies to the situation where the thing is obtained by a criminal act outside of Canada. As long as the act is one which would be an indictable offence if performed in Canada, possession of the thing is an offence.

The elements of an offence under s.354 are that the accused has a thing (1) in his or her possession (2) knowing it was obtained by the commission of an indictable offence in Canada or by an act committed outside of Canada which would have been an indictable crime within Canada.

b. *Possession*

The definition of possession in s.4(3) was discussed on page 301. Section 358 further provides that for the purposes of s.354 (also s.342, theft, and s.356(1)(b), theft from mail) the offence of "having in possession" is complete when a person has, alone, or together with another, possession or control over the "thing" or aids in concealing or disposing of it. So, for example, a person who helps someone sell stolen property is considered to have possession.

In *R. v. Kinna*,[43] one of the issues considered was whether the accused had possession of a stolen typewriter. According to the evidence, the accused and W were in the accused's room in downtown Vancouver. After some time, W went across to his own room and brought back a typewriter into the accused's room. W then said it would have to be sold as they needed money. He spoke of the typewriter in terms indicating it had been stolen. W went into a store to sell the typewriter while the accused remained outside. A police officer saw him there and questioned him. The accused told the officer a false story, and W was arrested in the store. The accused was not arrested until the next day.

---

43. (1951), 11 C.R. 292 (B.C.C.A.).

The court held that the accused did not have possession of the typewriter. Mere knowledge that a thing is stolen is insufficient, and a person (the accused) cannot be said to consent to possession by another (and thereby be in possession himself), unless he, the accused, has some control over the thing. The court concluded that the accused did not have a measure of control over the typewriter.

c. Knowledge

For a successful conviction of a charge under s.354, it must be proved that the accused knew the "goods" which are the subject of the charge were obtained by an indictable crime. If a person has his or her suspicions aroused but then deliberately or recklessly omits to make further inquiries, he or she will be deemed, as a matter of law, to have "guilty knowledge". That is, it will be assumed he or she was aware that the goods in question were obtained by an indictable offence.

An example of a case of "turning a blind eye" is *R. v. Marabella*.[44] The accused, a scrap or salvage dealer, was charged with having possession of stolen copper. The police seized, in a salvage yard, over a ton of new copper which was proved to have been stolen a few nights earlier from a manufacturing company. The accused had delivered the copper to the salvage-yard owner after having purchased it from B. The main issue in the case was whether the accused should have known the copper was stolen, considering the circumstances in which B sold it to him.

B was not connected with a business which sold copper. The copper was purchased at a private residence, and copper is not normally found at a private residence. It was not a purchase of a quantity of scrap material. The copper was bulky, heavy, and from its size, shape, and appearance, the accused must have known it was new and unused. The accused did not deal in new copper. There was also the matter of the price paid. The price paid by the accused, according to his statement, was 25 cents a pound. This was little more than one-half of the amount normally paid even for scrap copper. Even in view of all of the unusual and suspicious circumstances described above, the accused never questioned B as to the source of the copper.

The court concluded that in such circumstances, the accused was guilty of having possession of stolen property. He *deliberately* refrained from asking for further information to avoid obtaining knowledge which would have been dangerous to him, namely that the copper was stolen. If a person *consciously omits* to ask questions because he wishes to remain in ignorance, he is deemed to have "guilty knowledge."

---

44. (1957), 177 C.C.C. 78 (Ont.C.A.).

d. Possession of a Stolen Motor Vehicle

Section 354(2) deals with situations in which a motor vehicle is the thing in possession. If a person has in his or her possession a motor vehicle with a tampered identification number, the vehicle is presumed to have been stolen or obtained by another crime.

Section 354(2) states:

PRESUMP-
TIONS
REGARDING
POSSESSION
OF A STOLEN
MOTOR
VEHICLE
s.354(2)

354.(2) In proceedings in respect of an offence under subsection (1), evidence that a person has in his possession a motor vehicle the vehicle identification number of which has been wholly or partially removed or obliterated or a part of a motor vehicle being a part bearing a vehicle identification number that has been wholly or partially removed or obliterated is, in the absence of any evidence to the contrary, proof that the motor vehicle or part, as the case may be, was obtained, and that such person had the motor vehicle or part, as the case may be, in his possession knowing that it was obtained,

(a) by the commission in Canada of an offence punishable by indictment, or,

(b) by an act or omission anywhere that, if it had occurred in Canada, would have constituted an offence punishable by indictment.

(3) For the purposes of subsection (2), ''vehicle identification number'' means any number or other mark placed upon a motor vehicle for the purpose of distinguishing the motor vehicle from other similar motor vehicles.

Section 354(2) contains two presumptions: (1) that a vehicle that has had its identification number removed partially or wholly has been obtained through the commission of an indictable offence and (2) that the person who has possession of the vehicle had knowledge that the vehicle was obtained through the commission of an indictable offence. To rebut these presumptions, the accused must only raise a reasonable doubt. However, if they are not rebutted, the jury, or judge if there is no jury, must conclude that the presumed facts are true. Both of these presumptions have been challenged as violations of the Charter's presumption of innocence.

In *Re Boyle and the Queen*,[45] the Ontario Court of Appeal considered the constitutionality of these presumptions. The court held that the first presumption is constitutionally valid. The fact that a vehicle identification number has been obliterated is cogent evidence that at some time the

---

45. (1983), 5 C.C.C. (3d) 193 (Ont.C.A.).

vehicle was stolen or otherwise obtained through the commission of a crime.

The court found, however, that the second presumption is invalid. It is not reasonable that people other than car dealers would even be aware of the location of vehicle identification numbers. Further, the presumption is not limited to recently stolen vehicles. So that, upon proof, if a person has possession of a vehicle that has its identification number obliterated, that person may be found guilty of possession even though there is no evidence that the person knew the vehicle was stolen. For these reasons, the second presumption is not a justifiable limitation on the presumption of innocence, but is arbitrary and not reasonable. However, the offence can still operate without this presumption.

In other words, the Crown has the burden of proving guilty knowledge as it has for any other element of the offence.

QUESTIONS FOR REVIEW AND DISCUSSION

1 Is a property right the same as ownership? Explain.

2 If a person "takes" a transistor radio on Friday, without the owner's consent, and returns it undamaged on the following Monday, has he committed the offence of theft? Explain.

3 What is theft by "conversion"?

4 What does "colour of right" mean?

5 Is it possible to steal confidential information? Explain.

6 Explain the "doctrine of recent possession."

7 Explain the elements of the offence of joy-riding. What is an important reason for this offence?

8 What is the offence of fraudulent concealment? Make up an example.

9 How is the offence of theft related to the offence of robbery?

10 Jocelyn grabs at Noreen's purse. She holds tight. Without actually touching her, Jocelyn "wrenches" the purse out of Noreen's hands. Noreen stumbles but does not fall. Is Jocelyn guilty of robbery?

11 What are the elements of the offence of extortion ?

12 What constitutes a threat for the purposes of extortion?

13 Define for the purposes of "breaking and entering" the following words:
   a "breaking"
   b "entering"
   c "place"

14 How have courts dealt with the presumption of intent under s.348(2)?

15 What is the difference between the offence of "breaking and entering" and being unlawfully in a dwelling-house?

16 How does the criminal law define the term "possession"?

17 What are break-in instruments?

18 What are the elements of the offence of possessing property obtained by crime?

19 Does a person have to know for certain that an object is stolen before being convicted of possession of property obtained through the commission of an indictable offence? Explain.

20 Jean-Marc and Louise are husband and wife. Before the marriage, Jean-Marc collected valuable coins. After his marriage to Louise, Jean-Marc stopped collecting but he did keep all of the coins he had collected before the marriage. Louise took the coins one day, without letting her husband know, and sold them for $500. She spent the money on herself. Jean-Marc did not discover the coins were missing until a month later. His wife pretended she didn't know what had happened to them. Could Louise, the wife, be convicted of theft if it is found out it was she who took the coins?

21 A was convicted of possession of break-in instruments under s.351. He was arrested while carrying bolt cutters, vice grips, pliers, and broken bicycle locks as he was entering the unlocked parking lot of an apartment building. He appealed his conviction. Consider the elements of the offence under s.351. What do you think he based his appeal on?

FOURTEEN

False Pretences, Fraud, and Forgery

Parts IX and X of the Code

The offences discussed in this chapter might be most aptly described as "crimes of deceit." Like theft, these offences are against property rights and do not usually involve violence.

A. FALSE PRETENCES

1. False Pretences Defined

Section 361 defines the term "false pretence":

FALSE
PRETENCE
DEFINED
s.361

> **361.(1) A false pretence is a representation of a matter of fact either present or past, made by words or otherwise, that is known by the person who makes it to be false and that is made with a fraudulent intent to induce the person to whom it is made to act upon it.**
>
> **(2) Exaggerated commendation or depreciation of the quality of anything is not a false pretence unless it is carried to such an extent that it amounts to a fraudulent misrepresentation of fact.**

A false pretence is therefore (1) a representation, by words or other means (e.g., an act) (2) about facts, past or present, (3) that the accused knows to be untrue and (4) made with dishonest intent to make someone do something. For example, Albert falsely tells Bryce that he has $5 000 in his bank account so that Bryce will accept a cheque as payment for a motorcycle which Albert wants to buy. If Bryce accepts the cheque and gives the bike to Albert, Albert will have obtained the bike by false pretences.

The false statement must be about an existing or past fact. So, assume Albert had told Bryce that he would pay for the motorcycle in a week and Bryce gave him the motorcycle on the basis of that promise. If Albert did not pay Bryce at the end of the week, Albert would not be guilty of an offence based on a false pretence because Albert did not make a representation about a fact, past or present. His representation was about a future event. However, Albert could be charged with theft or fraud (see discussion of fraud below).

Section 361(2) provides that if a person exaggerates about the quality of an article, for example, by stating that his or her car is in good condition when, in fact, he or she knows it is in poor shape, this exaggeration will probably not amount to a false pretence. The exaggeration must be such that it comes close to being an outright lie.

2. The Offences of False Pretences

Section 362 sets out the offences which involve false pretences.

a. *False Pretences Under S.362(1)(a)*

FALSE
PRETENCE
s.362
Indictable if
property a tes-
tamentary
instrument or
value exceeds
$1 000
Max: 10 years
Otherwise
hybrid; 2 years

> **362.(1) Every one commits an offence who**
>
> **(a) by a false pretence, whether directly or through the medium of a contract obtained by a false pretence, obtains anything in respect of which the offence of theft may be committed or causes it to be delivered to another person;**
>
> **(2) Every one who commits an offence under paragraph (1)(a)**
>
> **(a) is guilty of an indictable offence . . . where the property obtained is a testamentary instrument or where the value of what is obtained exceeds one thousand dollars; or**
>
> **(b) is guilty**
>
> > **(i) of an indictable offence, . . . or**
> >
> > **(ii) an offence punishable on summary conviction, where the value of what is obtained does not exceed one thousand dollars.**

Section 362(l)(a) covers the general situation in which property is obtained by false pretences. Anything that is capable of being stolen is capable of being obtained by false pretences.

In general, courts have held that to establish an offence under s.362(l)(a), it is necessary to prove that the accused received more than mere possession of the property. Although court decisions have not been totally consistent, most decisions have held that the owner of the property must intend to transfer ownership or at least some property interest, as distinct from possession. Under the common law, the difference between taking possession and obtaining ownership was one of the distinctions between theft and false pretences. Theft involved taking possession but not ownership while false pretences involved getting ownership of the thing. For example, a person who steals a car has possession but not ownership while a person who through false representation talks someone into transferring ownership of the car has not committed theft. This point is illustrated in *R. v. Arsenault*.[1] The accused was charged on two counts of false pretences. The false pretence used in both cases was a "bad" cheque (he lied about the amount of money in his bank account). In the first instance, he purchased electric clippers which were sold and delivered to the accused on the faith of the cheque. In the second instance, a cheque was used as a down payment on a car. However, the vendor refused to deliver the car to the accused until his cheque had cleared, and his conditional sale agreement had been accepted and discounted by the finance company. The accused then persuaded the vendor to let him test the car, but instead of returning it, he drove it to Mexico.

The accused was convicted of false pretences in the case of the clippers. However, with respect to the car, he was found not guilty. The court held that the accused acquired only possession of the car because the vendor did not intend to transfer ownership of it and, as a consequence, he did not commit the offence of "false pretences" within the meaning of s.362(l)(a). The court concluded the proper charge against the accused should have been theft of a motor vehicle or fraud (discussed below).

Another example of a case that distinquishes between theft and false pretences is *R. v. Dawood*.[2] In this case the accused was charged with theft. She had gone into a department store and switched price tags on a jumper and blouse so that the item she wished to buy had a lower price tag. She paid for the item at the check-out counter and was then apprehended by the store detective who had observed her actions. Her conviction for theft was quashed by the Alberta Court of Appeal. The court reasoned that when she paid for the item she became the owner of the clothes.

b. False Pretences Under S.362(4)

Writing "bad" cheques is specifically dealt with under s.362(4) which states:

> **362.(4) Where, in proceedings under paragraph (1)(a), it is shown that anything was obtained by the accused by means of a cheque that, when presented for payment within a reasonable time, was dishonoured on the ground that no**

---

1. (1970), 11 C.R.N.S. 366 (B.C.C.A.).
2. (1975), 27 C.C.C. (2d) 300 (Alta.C.A.).

PRE-
SUMPTION
OF FALSE
PRETENCES
FOR WRITING
BAD
CHEQUES
s.362(4)

funds or insufficient funds were on deposit to the credit of the accused in the bank or other institution on which the cheque was drawn, it shall be presumed to have been obtained by a false pretence, unless the court is satisfied by evidence that when the accused issued the cheque he believed on reasonable grounds that it would be honoured if presented for payment within a reasonable time after it was issued.

This subsection creates a presumption that a person who writes a bad cheque did so under false pretences. Like other presumptions, it has been challenged under the Charter. The Alberta Court of Appeal has held that the subsection is of no force or effect because it violates the presumption of innocence.[3] Conversely, courts in Saskatchewan and Ontario have held that the section is valid.[4]

c. Obtaining Credit by Fraud or False Pretences

Section 362(1)(b), (c), and (d) reads as follows:

OBTAINING
CREDIT BY
FALSE
PRETENCES
OR FRAUD
s.362(3)
Indictable
Max: 10 years

362.(1) Everyone commits an offence who . . .

(b) obtains credit by a false pretence or by fraud;

(c) knowingly makes or causes to be made, directly or indirectly, a false statement in writing with intent that it should be relied on, with respect to the financial condition or means or ability to pay for himself or any person, firm or corporation that he is interested in or that he acts for, for the purpose of procuring, in any form whatever, whether for his benefit or the benefit of that person, firm or corporation,

    (i) the delivery of personal property,

    (ii) the payment of money,

    (iii) the making of a loan,

    (iv) the extension of credit,

    (v) the discount of an account receivable, or

    (vi) the making, accepting, discounting or endorsing of a bill of exchange, cheque, draft, or promissory note; or

(d) knowing that a false statement in writing has been made with respect to the financial condition or means or ability to pay of himself or another person, firm or corporation that he is interested in or that he acts for, procures upon

---

3. *R. v. Driscoll* (1987), 38 C.C.C. (3d) 28 (Alta.C.A.).
4. *R. v. Bunka* (1984), 12 C.C.C. (3d) 437 (Sask.Q.B.), *R. v. Johnson*, a decision of the Ont. Ct. of Justice reported in *The Lawyers Weekly*, July 12, 1991.

the faith of that statement, whether for his benefit or for the benefit of that person, firm or corporation, anything mentioned in subparagraphs (c)(i) to (vi).

Section 362(3) provides:

> **362.(3) Every one who commits an offence under (b), (c) or (d) is guilty of an indictable offence . . . .**

Paragraph (b) creates the general offence of obtaining credit by false pretences. Paragraphs (c) and (d) define specific false pretence situations involving the establishment of a "phony" credit rating.

Paragraph (b) would be applicable, for example, if a person deliberately gave false information about his or her assets to a bank officer when negotiating a loan. However, to obtain a conviction it would be necessary to establish that the loan officer relied on the false information when deciding to grant the loan. For example, in *R. v. Winning*,[5] the accused obtained a credit card by giving his correct name and address, but lying about his financial worth. The evidence showed that credit was not advanced to the accused on the basis of the false information but on the basis of an independent credit investigation. Therefore, the court held the offence was not made out and acquitted him.

The false pretence in paras.(c) and (d) must be made in writing with the object to procure one of the benefits listed within the subsection, that is, obtain delivery of personal property or money, or obtain a loan or an extension of credit, etc. For example, Naomi owns a company and drafts a letter which falsely describes the company's worth. Naomi presents this letter to several creditors and they, relying on the letter, loan Naomi money. In such circumstances, Naomi would be guilty of an offence under s.362(1)(c).

It was necessary to make the offence of obtaining credit by false pretences a separate offence because "credit" does not fall within the term "anything", that is, credit cannot be stolen. On the other hand obtaining credit by fraud is included in the general offence of fraud.

B. FRAUD

1. Definition

Fraud is defined by s.380 of the Code:

> **380.(1) Every one who, by deceit, falsehood or other fraudulent means, whether or not it is a false pretence within the**

---

5. (1973), 12 C.C.C. (2d) 449 (Ont.C.A.).

FRAUD
s.380
Indictable
if property a
testamentary
instrument or
exceeds $1 000
Max: 10 years
Otherwise
hybrid
Max: 2 years

meaning of this Act, defrauds the public or any person, whether ascertained or not, of any property, money or valuable security,

    (a) is guilty of an indictable offence . . . where the subject-matter of the offence is a testamentary instrument or where the value of the subject-matter of the offence exceeds one thousand dollars; or

    (b) is guilty

        (i) of an indictable offence . . . or

        (ii) of an offence punishable on summary conviction, where the value of the subject-matter does not exceed one thousand dollars.

To commit fraud the person must know the act is dishonest and must also intend to act dishonestly. This point is illustrated in the case of *R. v. Bobbie*,[6] where the accused who was an officer of a trust company made unauthorized loans to a customer. The customer failed to repay the loans and the trust company suffered a loss. The officer's defence was that he believed that the loans would be approved and that he had only made an error in judgment but he did not intend to act dishonestly. He was convicted at his trial of fraud and attempted fraud. On appeal, the Ontario Court of Appeal held that the trial judge misdirected the jury when stating that the issue was whether the act was objectively dishonest. The trial judge should have instructed the jury that to prove dishonesty there must be evidence not only that the act was objectively dishonest but also that the accused knew the act was dishonest and intended to act dishonestly. The appeal court ordered a new trial.

2. Other Fraudulent Means

The classic definition of fraud is found in an old English case, *Re London and Globe Finance*: "To defraud is to deprive by deceit: it is by deceit to induce a man to act to his injury. More tersely, it may be put that to deceive is by falsehood to induce a course of action."[7]

However, fraud under the Criminal Code has a broader meaning. The offence of fraud under the Code can be committed by "other fraudulent means" as well as by deceit and falsehood. The Supreme Court of Canada has held that "other fraudulent means" includes not only deceits and falsehoods but any other means that can be characterized as dishonest. In *R. v. Olan, Hudson and Harnett*,[8] the directors of a company sold blue-chip securities to raise funds so the company could purchase shares

---

6 (1988), 43 C.C.C. (3d) 187 (Ont.C.A.).

7. [1903] 1 Ch. 728.

8. (1978), 41 C.C.C. (2d) 145 (3d) (S.C.C.).

in a company whose major asset was an unsecured debt owed to another company controlled by two of the accused. In other words, the company sold its high quality securities to purchase shares in a company in poor financial shape. Since the directors are the "mind" of the corporation, it could not be said that they were deceived, although the act was dishonest in that it was not done for the benefit of the corporation but for the personal benefit of the accused. The court held deception of the corporation is not an essential element of the offence. The two essential elements are dishonesty and deprivation, that is, prejudice or risk of prejudice to the economic interests of the victim.

Another case that considered the phrase "other fraudulent means" is *R. v. Kirkwood.*[9] The accused was the owner of a video store and had been making illegal copies of video tapes to sell or rent. The trial judge dismissed the charges of fraud against the accused because there was no relationship between the accused and the "victim" of the crime, the holder of the copyright. The trial court said for the offence of fraud, the accused must cause the victim to act to his or her detriment. The Court of Appeal disagreed with this narrow interpretation: it stated that where fraud is based on deceit or a falsehood, it may be that a relationship between the victim and accused must exist. However, where the charge is based on "other fraudulent means" as in this case, it does not matter that the victim was unaware of the accused's actions. Deprivation is satisfied by injury to the economic interests of the victim. Intent to injure the economic interests of the victim can be inferred from the accused's willingness to deal in the copied tapes.

3. Fraud and False Pretences

The offence of fraud is a broader offence than false pretences. In other words, the offence of fraud includes false pretences but also other forms of deceit. The federal Law Reform Commission, in its working paper "Theft and Fraud", gives this example of how the offences overlap:

> *A merchant selling water as gin obtains money by false pretences; a contractor paid on the basis of a bogus promise to repair a roof obtains money by fraud. The former can be convicted under s.320(1)(a) [now s.362] or s.338(1) [now s.380], the latter only under s.338(1) [i.e., s.380].*[10]

The Commission has recommended repealing the offences of false pretences and having only one offence of fraud to avoid overlap.

---

9. (1983), 5 C.C.C. (3d) 393 (Ont.C.A.).
10. Law Reform Commission of Canada, Working Paper 19, *Criminal Law, Theft and Fraud* (Ottawa: 1977).

4. Examples of Fraud

In *R. v. Kribbs*,[11] the accused was charged with defrauding A of a sum of money. He obtained the money by taking advantage of his relationship with A, who was in a condition of senility and dependent upon him. The accused obtained the money by getting A to transfer his money into a joint bank account. He then withdrew large sums of A's money. The accused was convicted of fraud under s.338 (now s.380). In substance what the accused did was to, by deceit, defraud A of his money.

In *R. v. McLean and Janko*,[12] the accused, M, was charged with committing fraud contrary to what is now s.380. M, a used car dealer, made a practice of getting customers to sign offers to purchase at a price agreeable to the customer, and said he was willing to give delivery at the set price. Afterwards he would refuse to approve such offers and attempt to get the customer to pay more for the car, or enter into some other deal more advantageous to him. This latter process, known as "bumping" or "jacking", was entrusted to his sales manager. A, a customer, paid the agreed price of $320 for a car, was promised delivery and was then sent to J, who tried to get the customer to pay a further $100 for the car, or buy another with the money he had already paid. A refused and demanded that he receive the car that had been promised him or get his money back. When J failed to deliver the car or return the money A went to the police. The court held that because M made a false promise (that the customer would receive a particular car for his money), a promise which from the start he never intended to keep, he was guilty of committing fraud.

5. Examples of Specific Fraud Offences

This section describes crimes that concern illegal business practices that tend to cheat the public.

FRAUDULENT MANIPULATION OF THE PRICE OF STOCKS OR SHARES s.380(2) Indictable Max: 10 years

Section 380(2) is a specific type of fraud concerned with the manipulation of price of stocks or shares or anything else offered for sale to the public. It states:

> **380.(2) Every one who, by deceit, falsehood or other fraudulent means, whether or not it is a false pretence within the meaning of this Act, with intent to defraud, affects the public market price of stocks, shares, merchandise or anything that is offered for sale to the public, is guilty of an offence . . . .**

USING MAIL TO DEFRAUD s.381 Indictable Max: 2 years

Section 381 provides that a person who uses the mail to send letters or circulars concerning schemes designed to deceive or defraud the public is guilty of an indictable offence.

---

11. [1968] 1 C.C.C. 345 (Ont.C.A.).
12. [1963] 3 C.C.C. 118 (B.C.C.A.).

FRAUDULENT MANIPULA-TION OF STOCK EXCHANGE TRANS-ACTIONS
s.382
Indictable
Max: 5 years

Section 382 makes it an indictable offence for a person to manipulate the stock market by creating a misleading or false appearance of active public trading.

Sections 385 and 386 cover any fraudulent behaviour involved in the sale or mortgaging of property, that is, fraudulent activities on the part of a mortgagor, or vendor of property. Specifically, s.385 provides:

FRAUDULENT CONCEAL-MENT OF TITLE DOCUMENTS
s.385
Indictable
Max: 2 years

> **385.(1) Every one . . .**
> **(a) with intent to defraud and for the purpose of inducing the purchaser or mortgagee to accept the title offered or produced to him, conceals from him any settlement, deed, will or other instrument material to the title, or any encumbrance on the title,**
> **or**
> **(b) falsifies any pedigree upon which the title depends, is guilty of an indictable offence . . .**

Section 386 states:

FRAUDULENT REGIS-TRATION OF TITLE
s.386
Indictable
Max: 5 years

> **386. Every one who, as principal or agent, in a proceeding to register title to real property, or in a transaction relating to real property that is or is proposed to be registered, knowingly and with intent to deceive,**
> **(a) makes a material false statement or representation,**
> **(b) suppresses or conceals from a judge or registrar, or any person employed by or assisting the registrar, any material document, fact, matter or information, or**
> **(c) is privy to anything mentioned in paragraph (a) or (b), is guilty of an indictable offence . . . .**

FALSE PROSPECTUS, ETC.
s.400
Indictable
Max: 10 years

Section 400 makes it an indictable offence to, among other things, make a false statement about a company to induce persons to become shareholders, to deceive shareholders, or to induce anyone to put up security or advance money for a company.

C. PERSONATION

PERSON-ATION WITH INTENT
s.403
Indictable
Max: 14 years

If a person "passes himself or herself off" as another for a criminal purpose, the person has committed an offence under s.403:

> **403. Every one who fraudulently personates any person, living or dead,**
> **(a) with intent to gain advantage for himself or another person,**

(b) with intent to obtain any property or an interest in any property, or
(c) with intent to cause disadvantage to the person whom he personates or another person,
is guilty of an indictable offence . . . .

The intent to gain an advantage or cause a disadvantage required for this offence has a broad meaning. For example, in *Rozon v. The Queen*,[13] the accused, upon being asked to identify himself, handed to the police officers a medical insurance card belonging to another person. He did so in order to avoid being arrested on a warrant issued against him. In the circumstances the accused was convicted of "personation" because he deliberately, and in bad faith, showed the police the insurance card of another in order to gain the "advantage" of avoiding arrest on a warrant outstanding against him.

In a similar case, *R. v. Dozois*,[14] the accused, D, whose driver's licence was suspended, was convicted of "personation" when he used his passenger's licence, after being stopped by police for a traffic violation.

In *R. v. Hetsberger*,[15] the accused purchased a plane ticket in another person's name to help N be admitted to the United States. The court convicted the accused, noting that the advantage obtained need not be an economic one. Gaining illegal entry into the United States could be considered an advantage for this offence.

D. FORGERY

1. Elements of the Offence

Section 366(1) defines the offence of forgery:

FORGERY DEFINED s.366

366.(1) Every one commits forgery who makes a false document, knowing it to be false, with intent
(a) that it should in any way be used or acted upon as genuine, to the prejudice of any one whether within Canada or not; or
(b) that a person should be induced, by the belief that it is genuine, to do or to refrain from doing anything, whether within Canada or not.

Section 366(3) states:

366.(3) Forgery is complete as soon as a document is made with the knowledge and intent referred to in subsection (1),

13. (1975), 28 C.R.N.S. 232 (Que.C.A.).
14. (1974), R.L. 285 (Que.C.A.).
15. (1980), 51 C.C.C. (2d) 257 (Ont.C.A.).

notwithstanding that the person who makes it does not intend that any particular person should use or act on it as genuine or be induced, by the belief that it is genuine, to do or refrain from doing anything.

Section 367(1) provides:

PENALTY FOR FORGERY
s.367
Indictable
Max: 14 years

367.(1) Everyone who commits forgery is guilty of an indictable offence . . . .

Before an accused can be convicted of the offence of forgery, it must be proved that he or she (1) knowingly made a false document with (2) intent it be used (3) as if it were genuine in such a way that someone is prejudiced.

Section 366(2) and s.321 define false document.

2. False Document Under S.366(2)

FALSE DOCUMENT UNDER s.366(2)

366.(2) Making a false document includes
(a) altering a genuine document in any material part,
(b) making a material addition to a genuine document or adding to it a false date, attestation, seal or other thing that is material, or
(c) making a material alteration in a genuine document by erasure, obliteration, removal or in any other way.

To make a "material addition or alteration," or to change a "material part" of a document, is to change an important part of the document. For example, to change the date on a cheque is to alter a material part of the cheque. In *R. v. O'hearn*,[16] the accused got an 87-year-old man, L, to subscribe to *Maclean's* magazine for a year. L gave the accused a signed cheque with the marginal figures "315" inserted, but the amount otherwise blank. The accused gave L a receipt for $3.15, the cost of the subscription. The accused afterwards altered the cheque to read $31.50 and filled in the words for that amount in the appropriate space. The court held the alteration of the figures constituted an alteration of a material part of the cheque.

3. False Document Under S.321

The Supreme Court of Canada in *Gaysek v. The Queen*,[17] held that because of the use of the word "includes" in s.366 the term "false document" also

---

16. [1964] 3 C.C.C. 296 (B.C.C.A.).
17. (1971), 2 C.C.C. (2d) 545 (S.C.C.).

includes the definition in s.321. Section 321 defines a false document as follows:

> **321.** **"false document" means a document**
> **(a) the whole or a material part of which purports to be made by or on behalf of a person**
> > **(i) who did not make it or authorize it to be made, or**
> > **(ii) who did not in fact exist;**
> **(b) that is made by or on behalf of the person who purports to make it but is false in some material particular;**
> **(c) that is made in the name of an existing person, by him or under his authority, with a fraudulent intention that it should pass as being made by some person, real or fictitious, other than the person who makes it or under whose authority it is made.**

Under the common law a false document was described as "one that tells a lie about itself," but not about its contents. Thus, forgery consisted of the falsification of the document itself and not in merely making false statements. If a letter is supposed to have been signed by Paula but was in fact signed in Paula's name by Evelyn, without Paula's permission, and a third party is led to believe it is Paula's letter, the letter is a false document. It tells a lie about itself, the lie being that the letter is signed by Paula. If the same letter had actually been signed by Paula, even though the contents of the letter may have been completely untrue, the letter would not be a false document. It does not tell a lie about itself. The lie is in the information, not in the letter.

However, in the *Gaysek* case, the Supreme Court of Canada gave "false document" a broader meaning. The accused in this case prepared false inventory sheets for about 20 Becker Milk stores and certified that the information was correct. The accused was acquitted of forgery at his trial because the trial judge held that the false inventory sheets were not false documents as required by the Code for the offence of forgery. The information contained in the inventory sheets was false, not the document itself. The Supreme Court, after concluding that the definition of false document in s.321 applied, held that any document that is false in some "material particular" (that is, in some significant part) is a false document. In this case, a document that is false in reference to the very purpose for which the document was created is certainly one which is false in a "material particular". The inventory sheets in question contained false information as to the very matter which they purported to certify and so were false in a number of material particulars and therefore each was a false document. The Supreme Court ordered a new trial.

4. Corroboration

Section 367(2) states:

CORROB-
ORATION
REQUIRED
FOR FORGERY
CONVICTION
s.367(2)

> **367.(2) No person shall be convicted of an offence under this section on the evidence of only one witness unless the evidence of that witness is corroborated in a material particular by evidence that implicates the accused.**

"An offence under this section" refers to the offence of forgery. Section 367(2) means that additional, independent evidence is required to strengthen, or support, the testimony of a single witness before a conviction for forgery can be made out.

E. UTTERING

Section 368 states:

UTTERING
FORGED
DOCUMENT
s.368
Indictable
Max: 14 years

> **368.(1) Every one who, knowing that a document is forged,**
> **(a) uses, deals with, or acts on it, or**
> **(b) causes or attempts to cause any person to use, deal with, or act on it,**
> **as if the document were genuine, is guilty of an indictable offence . . .**
> **(2) For the purpose of proceedings under this section, the place where a document was forged is not material.**

Section 368 creates the offence of "uttering" a forged document. Generally, uttering means to pass, or to cause to have passed, as if it were genuine, a forged document. If a person takes to a bank a forged cheque *knowing* it to be forged whether or not the person was the one who forged the cheque, and attempts to cash it, the person is guilty of an offence under s.368. Similarly, if a person, knowing a cheque is forged, gives it to another, who has no knowledge of the forgery, with a request that the person cash it, the person who caused the other to pass the cheque is guilty of "uttering".

An example of committing the offence of uttering is in the case of *R. v. Paquette*.[18] The accused was a notary who was charged with uttering a forged document. He had notarized the signature of a person on a document that had not been signed in his presence (the law requires notaries to actually witness the signature before signing the document).

---

18. (1979), 45 C.C.C. (2d) 575 (S.C.C.).

In other words, the notary attests that the signature on the document was made in his or her presence. Therefore, the document was a forgery because of s.366(2)(b) (adding a false attestation). However, he was not charged with forgery but with uttering. The Supreme Court of Canada agreed with the dissenting judge at the Court of Appeal and held that the accused was guilty of uttering because he affixed the false document to a mortgage and had thus acted on it.

F. OFFENCES RESEMBLING OR RELATED TO FORGERY

There are a number of other offences resembling or related to the offence of forgery. Some of these offences are described in the following paragraphs.

1. Forgery Equipment

EXCHEQUER BILL PAPER, PUBLIC SEALS, ETC.
s.369
Indictable
Max: 14 years

Section 369 provides that it is unlawful (without the proper authorization) to make, or possess, exchequer bill paper, revenue paper, or paper that is used to make bank notes, or any paper that is intended to make bank notes, or any paper that is intended to resemble any of the above. Section 369 also states that it is unlawful to make, or possess, any machinery, or instrument that is intended to be used to commit forgery.

An offence under s.369 is indictable.

2. False Messages

Section 371 states:

TELEGRAM, ETC., IN FALSE NAME
s.371
Indictable
Max: 5 years

> **371. Every one who, with intent to defraud, causes or procures a telegram, cablegram or radio message to be sent or delivered as being sent by the authority of another person, knowing that it is not sent by his authority and with intent that the message should be acted on as being sent by his authority, is guilty of an indictable offence . . . .**

3. Forging a Trademark

There are a number of offences that deal with trademarks. Generally, a trademark is an identification of a company's product or property. Trademarks are the property of a company. Only that company may use the trademark, unless it grants permission allowing another company to make use of the trademark.

Section 406 states:

FORGING A TRADEMARK DEFINED s.406

406. For the purposes of this Part, every one forges a trade-mark who

(a) without the consent of the proprietor of the trade-mark, makes or reproduces in any manner that trade-mark or a mark so nearly resembling it as to be calculated to deceive; or

(b) falsifies, in any manner, a genuine trade-mark.

Section 407 then provides:

THE OFFENCE OF FORGING TRADEMARK s.407 Hybrid Max: 2 years [s.412]

407. Every one commits an offence who, with intent to deceive or defraud the public . . . forges a trade-mark.

Section 410 has wider application:

OTHER OFFENCES IN RELATION TO TRADE-MARKS s.410 Hybrid Max: 2 years [s.412]

410. Every one commits an offence, who with intent to deceive or defraud,

(a) defaces, conceals or removes a trade-mark or the name of another person from anything without the consent of that other person; or

(b) being a manufacturer, dealer, trader or bottler, fills any bottle or siphon that bears the trade-mark or name of another person, without the consent of that other person, with a beverage, milk, by-product of milk or other liquid commodity for the purpose of sale or traffic.

In *R. v. Irvine,*[19] the accused, a manufacturer, was convicted under s.410 when he filled bottles with his own product and then marked these bottles with another company's name.

G. COUNTERFEIT MONEY

1. Definition

Counterfeit money is defined by s.448:

COUNTER-FEIT MONEY DEFINED s.448

448. In this part,

"counterfeit money" includes

(a) a false coin or false paper money that resembles or is apparently intended to resemble or pass for a current coin or current paper money,

(b) a forged bank-note or forged blank bank-note, whether complete or incomplete,

---

19. (1905), 9 C.C.C. 407 (Ont.C.A.).

(c) a genuine coin or genuine paper money that is prepared or altered to resemble or pass for a current coin or current paper money of a higher denomination,

(d) a current coin from which the milling is removed by filing or cutting the edges and on which new milling is made to restore its appearance,

(e) a coin cased with gold, silver or nickel, as the case may be, that is intended to resemble or pass for a current gold, silver or nickel coin, and

(f) a coin or a piece of metal or mixed metals that is washed or coloured by any means with a wash or material capable of producing the appearance of gold, silver or nickel and that is intended to resemble or pass for a current gold, silver or nickel coin.

The word "current" as it is used in the counterfeiting sections usually means that the money counterfeited (copied) must be negotiable, or still "in circulation".

In *Robinson v. The Queen*,[20] the accused had in his possession a number of counterfeit United States "1941/42" dimes. The peculiarity in their dating gave them a numismatic value of between $100 and $800. The accused argued that the dimes were not intended to resemble, or pass as, "current" coins, within the definition of "counterfeit money". They were for the purpose of sale as a numismatic curiosity and not for circulation as legal tender.

A representative of the Treasury Department of the Secret Service in Washington D.C. gave the following evidence with respect to the dimes:

Q. **I have in this plastic bag one hundred and forty-six 1941/42 U.S. dimes. Are these currency in the United States?**

A. Most definitely.

Q. **Are they legal tender?**

A. They are.

Q. **And if they were genuine, would they be legal tender today?**

A. They would be, sir.

The court held that the coins' primary characteristic was that they were counterfeits of "current" coins and that they were intended to resemble such coins. The accused was, therefore, convicted of having counterfeit money in his possession.

---

20. (1973), 10 C.C.C. (2d) 606 (S.C.C.).

2. Offences Involving Counterfeit Money

There are several offences involving the use of counterfeit money. It is an offence to make, to have possession of, or to utter counterfeit money. (See s.449 to s.453). It is also an offence to make, repair, buy, sell or have possession of equipment for making counterfeit money (see s.458).

QUESTIONS FOR REVIEW AND DISCUSSION

1 Explain some of the differences and similarities among the offences of theft, false pretences, and fraud.

2 **a** How does the Code define "false document"?

  b How has the Supreme Court of Canada defined "false document"?

3 Define the elements of the offence of forgery.

4 What is "counterfeit money"?

5 Christian takes possession of a used car from Bill and promises to pay for it in one week. Christian does not have any intention of paying Bill for the car. What is he guilty of?

6 Brady buys a motorcycle from Marilyn. He gives Marilyn a postdated cheque in payment for the "bike". On the date for which the cheque is endorsed Marilyn discovers that Brady's bank account has insufficient funds to cover the amount of the cheque. Has Brady committed an offence? Explain your answer.

7 Ian is applying to join the Canadian Armed Forces. He never finished high school but provides the recruiting officer with a copy of a high school transcript on which he has put his name. Has Ian made a false document? What offence or offences could he be charged with? What if Ian had in fact graduated from high school? Ian lists all of the subjects he studied at high school but he lies about some of the marks which he received. Has Ian made a false document? Explain. What other information might you need? What offence or offences could he be charged with? Explain.

chapter

FIFTEEN

Mischief, Arson, and Cruelty to Animals

Part XI of the Code

Generally, the offences in this part concern interferences with or acts against private property that do not involve taking possession; for example, acts of vandalism can be a type of mischief. However, the offences may involve danger or harm to persons such as the offence of arson.

A. MISCHIEF

MISCHIEF DEFINED
s.430

MISCHIEF CAUSING DANGER TO LIFE
Indictable
Max: Life imprisonment
[s.430(2)]

MISCHIEF TO PROPERTY OVER $1 000, DATA, OR TESTA-MENTARY INSTRUMENT
Hybrid
Max: 10 years
[s.430(3)]

430.(1) Every one commits mischief who wilfully

(a) destroys or damages property;
(b) renders property dangerous, useless, inoperative or ineffective;
(c) obstructs, interrupts or interferes with the lawful use, enjoyment or operation of property; or
(d) obstructs, interrupts or interferes with any person in the lawful use, enjoyment or operation of property.
(1.1) Every one commits mischief who wilfully
(a) destroys or alters data;
(b) renders data meaningless, useless or ineffective;
(c) obstructs, interrupts or interferes with the lawful use of data; or
(d) obstructs, interrupts or interferes with any person in the lawful use of data or denies access to data to any person who is entitled to access thereto.

Mischief that causes actual danger to life is an indictable offence. Mischief in relation to property or to data is a hybrid offence.

MISCHIEF TO OTHER PROPERTY
Hybrid
Max: 2 years
[s.430(4)]

The term "property" refers to both real property and personal property. In brief, real property consists of immovable things (or real estate), that is, land and things attached to the land (e.g., a house or garage). Personal property consists of movable things such as automobiles and furniture. Data is defined in s.342.1 as:

> . . . **representations of information or of concepts that are being prepared or have been prepared in a form suitable for use in a computer system.**

There are many ways of committing the offence of mischief. For example, mischief in regard to personal property may occur by:

a. damaging a car by breaking the car's radio antenna,
b. rendering a car dangerous by tampering with the brake system of the car, and
c. obstructing the use of the car by blocking a public highway.

Mischief in regard to real property may occur by:

a. damaging a building by breaking its windows,
b. rendering the building dangerous by weakening a step in a stairway, or
c. obstructing the use of the building by barricading the entrance so that no one can get in.

An example of mischief in relation to data would be the alteration of a computer disk so that the data stored on it cannot be accessed by its owner.

The important issue in many mischief cases is whether the damaging, rendering dangerous, or obstructing was done wilfully. Wilfully usually means intentionally, or as one judge has put it: "Wilfully means not merely to commit an act voluntarily but to commit it purposely with an evil intention, or in other words it means to do so deliberately, intentionally, and corruptly and without any justifiable excuse."[1]

So, for example, if a student breaks a window in his school building, it must be shown that the student broke the window deliberately and with a criminal (i.e., evil) intent. The student would not be guilty of mischief if the window was broken accidentally or with a justifiable excuse (e.g., to escape from a fire).

Section 429(1) extends the meaning of "wilfully" when it is mentioned in Part XI of the Code to include recklessness:

WILFULLY EXTENDED TO RECKLESSNESS
s.429(1)

> **429.(1) Every one who causes the occurrence of an event by doing an act or by omitting to do an act that is his duty to**

---

1. *R. v. Duggan* (1906), 12 C.C.C. 147 (Man.C.A.).

> **do, knowing that the act or omission will probably cause the occurrence of the event and being reckless whether the event occurs or not, shall be deemed, for the purposes of this Part, wilfully to have caused the occurrence of the event.**

In other words, a person may not intend to damage property but if the person did some act and knew that the damage would probably occur and took an unjustifiable risk that the damage would not occur, then the person will be considered to have wilfully or intentionally caused the damage if it occurs.

The wilfulness of an interference with property was considered by the Supreme Court of Canada in *McKenna v. R.*[2] The accused drove his car onto a railway track, left it there, and walked away. A short time later, a train crashed into the car. When questioned by the police, the accused stated that he parked his car on the track, that he did not think that trains travelled on that track, that he had taken the keys and turned off the lights, and that he had walked four miles (six and one-half kilometres) for help. Later, after being told of the crash, he said the car was stuck rather than parked. At the time of being questioned by the police the accused could walk without assistance but staggered and appeared to be intoxicated. He was charged with wilfully obstructing the lawful use of property and he was convicted of the charge. The court concluded that the interference with the railway track was wilful, but it did not specify whether the accused had acted with criminal intent or had acted recklessly.

In *R. v. Wendel*,[3] the accused and other youths were charged with breaking and entering with the intent to commit mischief. Early in the evening, they had obtained some beer. They drank some of the beer while sitting under a bridge. They then went to an apartment building, and found a vacant apartment with a slightly open door. They went in and drank their beer. Later, the caretaker of the building came to the apartment and could not get in because the door had been locked from the inside. There was no question that they had broken and entered into the apartment. The only question was whether they intended to wilfully obstruct or interfere with the lawful use of the apartment. The court held that even under the extended meaning of wilfully in s.429(l), the accused were not guilty. He and the others entered the apartment for the purpose of drinking beer, not for the purpose of obstructing or interfering with the use of the property.

The extended meaning of wilfully (i.e., recklessness) was applied in *R. v. Gotto.*[4] The accused and a group of others ransacked a car. In order to

---

2. [1961] S.C.R. 660 (S.C.C.).
3. [1967] 2 C.C.C. 23 (B.C.C.A.).
4. [1974] 6 W.W.R. 454 (Sask.Dist.Ct.).

provide light so that he could see under the front seat, the accused set fire to a road map which he found in the car. He left the map near the car when he and the others left. The car caught fire and was destroyed. The accused argued that he was not guilty because he had not wilfully set fire to the car. However, the court disagreed and held that his conduct fell within the meaning of "wilfully" as defined under s.429(1). He knew that damage to the car would probably result if he did not take precautions to remove the risk of the fire destroying the car. He made no attempt to remove the risk and was reckless about whether or not the damage would occur.

A trivial interference with property will not be considered mischief. In *R. v. Chapman*,[5] the accused was charged with wilfully interfering with the lawful use of property. The accused, who was 18 years old, and two younger companions were walking along a street late at night when they saw a small car parked in the street. As a prank, they pushed the car 10 to 30 feet (3 to 9 m) down the street and left the scene. They did not try to start the car and it was not damaged in any way. The only inconvenience to the owner of the car was that he had to walk an extra 10 to 30 feet (3 to 9 m) the next morning to his car. The court found the accused not guilty. There was no significant interference with the use of the car or intention to interfere with the lawful use of the car.

Mischief charges may result during a labour dispute such as a strike. An example of such a case is *R. v. Mammolita*,[6] a decision of the Ontario Court of Appeal. In this case, there was a legal strike of employees at a factory in Thunder Bay. Several months after the employer had obtained an injunction limiting pickets to 10, 75 to 100 people formed a picket line and blocked the management and office personnel from entering the building. The police were called and were able to form a wedge, allowing only management to pass through. Police took photographs of the strikers and eventually 33 people were charged with mischief for wilfully obstructing or interfering with the lawful use and operation of the property of the company. The accused were acquitted at their trial on the grounds that their mere presence and passive acquiescence at the time did not make them liable for the offence. The Court of Appeal disagreed and ordered a new trial. The court stated:

> . . . [A] person may be guilty as a principal of committing mischief . . . if he forms part of a group which constitutes a human barricade or other obstruction. The fact that he stands shoulder to shoulder with other persons even though he neither says anything nor does anything further may be an act which constitutes an obstruction. However, criminal liability only results if the act is done wilfully. . . . It may not be very difficult to infer

---

5. [1969] 3 C.C.C. 358 (B.C.Cty.Ct.).
6. (1983), 9 C.C.C. (3d) 85 (Ont.C.A.).

that a person standing shoulder to shoulder with other persons in a group so as to block a roadway knows that his act will probably cause the obstruction and is reckless if he does not attempt to extricate himself from the group.

However, in general, the law allows the right to strike and picket. Section 480 provides

STRIKING
AND
PICKETING
NOT
MISCHIEF
s.430

430.(6) No person commits mischief within the meaning of this section by reason only that

(a) he stops work as a result of the failure of his employer and himself to agree on any matter relating to his employment; or

(b) he stops work as a result of the failure of his employer and a bargaining agent acting on his behalf to agree on any matter relating to his employment; or

(c) he stops work as a result of his taking part in a combination of workmen or employees for their own reasonable protection as workmen or employees.

(7) No person commits mischief within the meaning of this section by reason only that he attends at or near or approaches a dwelling-house or place for the purpose only of obtaining or communicating information.

B. ARSON

For the offence of arson to be committed, there must be a burning of property. In *R. v. Jorgenson,*[7] the meaning of "burning" was explained:

There must be actual combustion, although it is not necessary for the material to blaze openly, so long as it comes to a red heat. Charring, that is, the carbonization of the material by combustion, is evidence of burning, but blackening of the material not accompanied by any degree of consumption is not nor is mere scorching . . . . So long as there is burning in that sense, the extent and duration of the fire is immaterial, and the damage may be insignificant.

In *Jorgenson*, the accused was charged with setting fire to a building. The only evidence of burning on the building consisted of three blister marks on a small area of the paint on a metal door. The court held that the blistering did not amount to burning because there had been no consumption of material.

There are several offences involving "arson" or the criminal setting of fires or explosions.

---

7. (1955), 111 C.C.C. 30 (B.C.C.A.).

1. Arson Causing Danger to Human Life

The most serious arson offence is the following:

ARSON CAUSING DANGER TO HUMAN LIFE
s.433
Indictable
Max: 14 years

433. Every person who intentionally or recklessly causes damage by fire or explosion to property, whether or not that person owns the property, is guilty of an indictable offence . . . where

(a) the person knows that or is reckless with respect to whether the property is inhabited or occupied; or

(b) the fire or explosion causes bodily harm to another person.

2. Arson Causing Damage to Property

Where there is no danger to human life, a person who sets a fire can be charged under s.434:

ARSON CAUSING DAMAGE TO PROPERTY
s.434
Indictable
Max: 5 years

434. Every person who intentionally or recklessly causes damage by fire or explosion to property that is not wholly owned by that person is guilty of an indictable offence . . . .

Where there is a serious threat to the health, safety, or property of another person, a person who causes a fire or explosion can be charged under s.434.1:

ARSON TO OWN PROPERTY
s.434.1
Indictable
Max: 14 years

434.1 Every person who intentionally or recklessly causes damage by fire or explosion to property that is owned, in whole or in part, by that person is guilty of an indictable offence . . . where the fire or explosion seriously threatens the health, safety or property of another person.

3. The Fraudulent Burning of Property

The offence of fraudulently burning property is contained in s.435:

ARSON FOR FRAUDULENT PURPOSE
s.435
Indictable
Max: 10 years

435.(1) Every person who, with intent to defraud any other person, causes damage by fire or explosion to property, whether or not that person owns, in whole or in part, the property, is guilty of an indictable offence . . .

(2) Where a person is charged with an offence under subsection (1), the fact that the person was the holder of or was named as beneficiary under a policy of fire insurance relating to the property in respect of which the offence is alleged to have been committed is a fact from which intent to defraud may be inferred by the court.

This offence applies to the situation where, for example, a person burns down a building he or she owns to collect the fire insurance money.

4. Arson by Criminal Negligence

ARSON BY
NEGLIGENCE
s.436
Indictable
Max: 5 years

436. Every person who owns, in whole or in part, or controls property is guilty of an indictable offence . . . where, as a result of a marked departure from the standard of care that a reasonably prudent person would use to prevent or control the spread of fires or to prevent explosions, that person is a cause of fire or explosion in that property that causes bodily harm to another person or damage to property.

(2) Where a person is charged with an offence under subsection (1), the fact that the person has failed to comply with any law respecting the prevention or control of fires or explosions in the property is a fact from which a marked departure from the standard of care referred to in that subsection may be inferred by the court.

C. CRUELTY TO ANIMALS

1. General

CAUSING
UNNEC-
ESSARY
SUFFERING
s.446
Summary
conviction

446.(1) Every one commits an offence who

(a) wilfully causes or, being the owner, wilfully permits to be caused unnecessary pain, suffering or injury to an animal or bird;

(b) by wilful neglect causes damage or injury to animals or birds while they are being driven or conveyed;

(c) being the owner or the person having the custody or control of a domestic animal or bird or an animal or bird wild by nature that is in captivity, abandons it in distress or wilfully neglects or fails to provide suitable and adequate food, water, shelter and care for it;

(d) in any manner encourages, aids or assists at the fighting or baiting of animals or birds;

(e) wilfully, without reasonable excuse, administers a poisonous or injurious drug or substance to a domestic animal or bird or an animal or bird wild by nature that is kept in captivity or, being the owner of such an animal or bird, wilfully permits a poisonous or injurious drug or substance to be administered to it;

(f) promotes, arranges, conducts, assists in, receives money for, or takes part in a meeting, competition, exhibition, pasttime, practice, display or event at or in the course of which captive birds are liberated by hand, trap, contrivance or any other means for the purpose of being shot when they are liberated; or

(g) being the owner, occupier or person in charge of any premises, permits the premises or any part thereof to be used for a purpose mentioned in paragraph (f).

(2) Every one who commits an offence under subsection (1) is guilty of an offence punishable on summary conviction.

The meaning of "unnecessary suffering" in s.446(l)(a) was discussed in *R. v. Linder*.[8] The charge of causing unnecessary suffering to a horse was laid by an officer of the Society for the Prevention of Cruelty to Animals. The horse was a bucking horse and was being used in a bucking contest in a rodeo. The prosecution argued that unnecessary suffering was being caused by the use of a "bucking strap". The procedure was to place the horse in a chute with this strap loosely around the back of the horse's belly and in front of its rear legs. When the chute was opened to let the horse out, the strap was drawn tight which had the effect of making the horse buck more strenuously. The bucking, which lasted for about ten seconds, loosened the strap. The court held that no offence had been committed. The intent of the section was to make it an offence to cause unnecessarily substantial suffering to any animal. The court found that the strap did nothing more than excite or irritate the horse to more strenuous bucking. This did not cause any injury, not even an abrasion of the animal's skin.

A case which reached the opposite result was *R. v. Menard*,[9] in which the accused operated an animal shelter. Stray animals that were not claimed within a certain period were killed. The animals were placed in a small chamber which was then filled with carbon monoxide. The evidence was that the animals would die within two minutes but would be conscious for 30 seconds during which they would experience pain and suffering. There was also evidence that the suffering of the animals could be lessened by a simple modification of the system which was not expensive, and the accused had been informed of this possibility. The Court of Appeal held that the killing of stray dogs was justified but that the accused could have easily modified his system so that the animals would not suffer. Therefore, the court allowed the appeal and found the accused guilty.

Under s.446(3) a person who fails to exercise reasonable care or supervision of an animal, thereby causing it pain, will be considered to have "wilfully" caused the pain. However, this is only a presumption and may

8. (1950), 97 C.C.C. 174 (B.C.C.A.).
9. (1978), 43 C.C.C. (2d) 458 (Que.C.A.).

be rebutted if the accused can produce some evidence that he did not wilfully cause the pain, even though having failed to exercise reasonable care.

Another presumption is in s.446(4) which states that a person who was present at the fighting or baiting of animals or birds will be considered to have encouraged or assisted at such fighting or baiting in violation of s.446(l)(d). This can be rebutted by the accused showing some evidence that, even though he or she was present, he or she was not encouraging or assisting.

INJURING OR ENDANGER-ING CATTLE s.444 Indictable Max: 5 years

The purpose of s.446(1)(f) was considered in *Prefontaine v. R.*[10] The court held that the subsection was intended to prevent the use of live captive birds in trap shooting of any kind.

2. Harming Cattle

INJURING ANY ANIMAL OTHER THAN CATTLE s.445 Summary conviction

It is an offence to wilfully (a) kill, maim, wound, poison or injure animals, or (b) place poison in such a position that it may easily be consumed by animals. If any of these acts are done in regard to cattle, then it is an indictable offence under s.444. The term "cattle" is defined in s.2 and includes a horse, mule, ass, pig, sheep, or goat. If any of the above acts are done in regard to animals that are not cattle and are kept for a lawful purpose, then a summary conviction offence is committed under s.445.

D. LEGAL JUSTIFICATION AND COLOUR OF RIGHT

Section 429(2) provides a defence to any charge of mischief, arson, or cruelty to animals.

COLOUR OF RIGHT s.429(2)

429.(2) No person shall be convicted of an offence under sections 430 to 446 where he proves that he acted with legal justification or excuse and with colour of right.

A person acts with "legal justification or excuse" when that person's actions are permitted by law. This legal permission for acts which would otherwise be unlawful can be based on either the common law or statutory law. For example, there are provincial statutes which allow the killing of a dog that is found injuring or killing cattle.

"Colour of right" means an honest belief in a state of facts which, if it actually existed, would be a legal justification or excuse.[11] However, simply having an honest belief is not enough. There must be reasonable grounds for the belief.[12] The accused must prove beyond a reasonable

---

10. (1973), 26 C.R.N.S. 367 (Que.C.A.).
11. See the defences of mistake of fact and mistake of law in Chapter Four.
12. *R. v. Ninos and Walker*, [1964] 1 C.C.C. 326 (N.S.C.A.)

doubt that he or she had the honest belief, but it is not necessary to prove that the right actually existed.[13]

Following are three cases in which colour of right was a defence to a charge of wilfully damaging property:

In *R. v. Pimmett*,[14] the accused was charged with wilfully damaging a telephone pole which was located on his land. Many years earlier, a telephone line to a summer hotel was erected across the property of the accused. The telephone company had never acquired a right to use the land for this purpose. Without deciding whether or not the accused actually had the right to remove the pole, the court held that the accused was not guilty because he reasonably believed that he had the right to remove the pole which he considered a nuisance.

In *R. v. Adamson*,[15] the accused was charged with wilfully damaging another's land by crossing the land with a load of hay. The accused believed that she had a right to cross the land because the municipality had passed a resolution authorizing the accused to do so. The municipality had the authority to open temporary roads across private property but a resolution of the municipal council did not have the effect of opening the road. In short, the resolution was merely a preliminary step before the municipality's decision became law. The court held that the accused had colour of right for crossing the land because the municipality had the right to open temporary roads and the accused had an honest belief, based on reasonable grounds, that the resolution had that effect.

In *R. v. Johnson*,[16] the accused was charged with wilfully damaging the fence of Mott. In this case, there was some confusion as to whether or not the accused had a right of way over Mott's land. The court held that the accused had reasonable grounds for honestly believing that he did have a right of way. Therefore, he had colour of right for taking down part of a fence which was blocking his use of the right of way. In other words, the accused may not, in fact, have had a legal right or justification for damaging part of the fence. But, he had an honest belief, based on reasonable grounds, that he had such a right. Therefore, he was not guilty of the offence of wilfully damaging Mott's fence.

Notice that s.429(2) says that the accused must prove "that he acted with legal justification or excuse and with colour of right." Although it appears that both legal justification or excuse and colour of right must be proved in order for the accused to have a defence, the courts have interpreted "and" to mean "or". Thus, the accused may prove either legal justification or colour of right as a defence to a charge of mischief, arson, or cruelty to animals.

13. *R. v. Lilly* (1983), 5 C.C.C. (3d) 1 (S.C.C.).
14. (1931), 56 C.C.C. 363 (Ont.C.A.).
15. (1916), 56 C.C.C. 440 (Sask.C.A.).
16. (1904), 8 C.C.C. 123 (Ont.C.A.).

In general, a person who owns something may legally damage or destroy it. However, s.429(3) clarifies this right:

> **429.(3) Where it is an offence to destroy or to damage anything,**
>
> **(a) the fact that a person has a partial interest in what is destroyed or damaged does not prevent him from being guilty of the offence if he caused the destruction or damage; and**
>
> **(b) the fact that a person has a total interest in what is destroyed or damaged does not prevent him from being guilty of the offence if he caused the destruction or damage with intent to defraud.**

Under para.(a), it is no defence to a charge of mischief, for example, for an accused to say that he or she was partial owner of the thing which was damaged. If Lillian, Nicole, and Gerald jointly own a building, Lillian's partial ownership of the building does not give Lillian a right to tear down the building and replace it with a swimming pool. Lillian would have to get the permission of Nicole and Gerald. Under para.(b), even if Lillian had total ownership, Lillian would not have a defence to a charge of arson if she burned the building with the intent to defraud an insurance company.

QUESTIONS FOR REVIEW AND DISCUSSION

1 Make up several examples of conduct that would be covered by the offence of mischief.

2 What is the meaning of "property" in Part XI of the Criminal Code?

3 What is the meaning of "wilfully" in Part XI of the Criminal Code?

4 Which of the following would be sufficient evidence of burning in an arson case? (a) blackening of the material, (b) scorching of the material, (c) charring of the material, (d) flames on the material, (e) blistering of the material

5 List the offences of arson. Which is the most serious? Why do you think this offence is the most serious?

6 Explain the difference between legal justification and colour of right.

7 Roger is irritated with his neighbour because the neighbour drives a noisy motorcycle which keeps Roger awake at night. So, Roger solves the noise problem by setting fire to the motorcycle. Under what section should Roger be charged?

8 Alec operates a slaughterhouse. He slaughters hogs by shackling a hind leg, hoisting the hogs to a height of fifteen feet and then slitting their throats. He is charged with causing unnecessary pain and suffer-

ing to an animal, contrary to s.446(1)(a). Should he be convicted? What else, if anything, do you need to know?

See *R. v. Pacific Meat Co. Ltd.* (1958), 119 C.C.C. 237, 27 C.R. 128 (B.C.).

9 Kate's cattle frequently break through weak spots in a fence and graze on Gaby's property. Gaby is willing to share in the cost of building a new fence, but Kate refuses. In frustration, Gaby puts poison on the area of his property where the cattle graze and one cow dies as a result. Gaby honestly believed that he had the right to use the poison because Kate had refused to have the fence repaired. Is Kate guilty of an offence? Why?

Appendix A

Narcotic and Drug Offences

The Narcotic Control Act (NCA) and the Food and Drugs Act (FDA) together outline several offences aimed at controlling the illegal use of drugs. The two main drug offences under each are: "possession" and "trafficking".

A. THE NARCOTIC CONTROL ACT

A narcotic is defined as any substance, or anything that contains any substance, which is listed in the schedule to the Act. The list is very long and includes the opium poppy and any drug that can be manufactured from it, including opium itself, morphine, codeine, and heroin. Also included are cocaine, methadone, and marijuana.

The NCA specifies six offences with respect to narcotic drugs:

1. possession,
2. trafficking,
3. possession for the purpose of trafficking,
4. failure to disclose previous prescriptions,
5. importing and exporting, and
6. cultivation of opium poppy or marijuana.

1. Possession

Section 2 of the Narcotic Control Act provides that "possession" means possession as defined in s.4(3) of the Criminal Code. Court decisions on the meaning of possession were discussed in Chapter Thirteen.

Under s.3 of the NCA possession is a hybrid offence.

The following cases provide examples of various situations in which the accused were charged with possession of a narcotic.

In *R. v. Harvey*,[1] the accused was a passenger in a motor vehicle when it was stopped by the police. A search of the car uncovered marijuana and methedrine in a box hidden under a mat near the gear shift. The accused denied knowledge of the drug's presence. He stated that he was riding in

---

1. (1969), 7 C.R.N.S. 183 (N.B.C.A.).

the car because the driver needed someone with a licence. The court held that even if the accused was aware of the drugs' existence, he did not have them in his possession. There was no evidence that he and the driver were engaged in joint ownership of the drug. That is to say, the accused did not have a measure of control over the marijuana and methedrine.

In *R. v. Brady; R. v. Maloney; R. v. McLeod,*[2] the accused were charged with possession of hashish. The accused were present while two others produced hashish and made cigarettes containing the substance. The accused did not smoke or in any other way handle the hashish. The court held that the accused knew the other two persons present were handling a narcotic. However, they did not have any measure of control over it, and their mere presence while others were smoking hashish was not enough to constitute possession.

In *R. v. Caldwell,*[3] the accused, with a number of other persons, was found in a house during a drug raid. The accused had lived in the house for two weeks. Large quantities of drugs were found, some in a bathroom, some hidden under a mattress. No drugs were found in the accused's physical presence. The court concluded that the accused was in possession of the drugs. Although he did not have physical possession it could be inferred from the above facts that he did have knowledge, and control or a right of control, over the drugs.

2. Trafficking and Having Possession for the Purpose of Trafficking

Section 4 of the NCA makes it an indictable offence to traffic in or have possession for the purpose of trafficking.

Traffic is defined in s.2 of the act as follows:

> **2. . . .**
> **traffic means**
> **(a) to manufacture, sell, give, administer, transport, send deliver or distribute, or**
> **(b) to offer to do anything referred to in paragraph (a) otherwise than under the authority of this Act or the regulations.**

Trafficking in a narcotic drug includes giving a drug to a person. On the other hand, conveying, carrying, or moving a narcotic from one place to another for one's own use does not constitute trafficking.

The following cases considered the question of whether or not the accused trafficked in narcotics.

---

2. (1972), 19 C.R.N.S. 328 (Sask. District Ct.).
3. (1972), 7 C.C.C. (2d) 285; 19 C.R.N.S. 293 (Alta.C.A.).

For the offence of trafficking to be completed, the accused does not have to actually handle the drugs. He need only exercise control over them. In *R. v. MacFadden*[4] the accused phoned a delivery service and asked that a parcel be delivered to a garage operator. The parcel contained cannabis. The accused was aware of this fact but the garage operator was not. The accused was arrested before he could retrieve the parcel after it had been delivered to the garage. The accused argued that his actions did not amount to trafficking. The court disagreed and concluded that the accused "did traffic" the cannabis because he exercised control over it.

In *R. v. Chernecki*[5] the accused was asked by an undercover police officer if he could get hold of some heroin. The accused stated that he could. The two travelled by car to a cafe. The officer gave the accused $20 and the latter went into the cafe. The officer waited in the car. On his return the accused told the officer that they would have to go to a hotel room to pick up the heroin. On the way to the room the officer arrested the accused and charged him with trafficking. The accused was convicted; he undertook to procure the narcotic, and deliver it to the officer. In such circumstances a conviction for trafficking was made out.

In *R. v. Young*[6] the accused was living in Vancouver and his friend, G, lived in Sechelt. The accused and his wife planned to take up residence with G in his house in Sechelt. G, with money provided by himself and the accused, in equal portions, arranged to buy one kilo of marijuana in Vancouver for $225 and arranged with the accused to transport the drug to Sechelt. The accused was arrested and charged with trafficking in the process of delivering the marijuana. G, called as a defence witness, said that it was for, "our own personal use." G also admitted that the drug was "half mine."

The accused contended that he had purchased the marijuana on behalf of himself, and G, for their personal use, and that therefore it could not be said he was trafficking when he transported the drug to his friend's house. The court, however, stated that the fact the accused was transporting the marijuana not only for himself, but also for another, and the fact it might be used by others, sufficed to support a conviction of trafficking. The facts demonstrated there was something more extensive than mere conveying, or carrying or moving of the marijuana incidental to one's own use.

3. Failure to Disclose Previous Prescriptions

Section 3.1 makes it a hybrid offence for failing to disclose to a "practitioner" the particulars of previous narcotics or prescriptions for narcotics

---

4. (1972), 16 C.R.N.S. 251 (N.B.C.A.).
5. (1972), 16 C.R.N.S. 230 (B.C.C.A.).
6. (1971), 14 C.R.N.S. 372 (B.C.C.A.).

obtained up to 30 days prior to the seeking of a narcotic or a prescription for a narcotic. A practitioner is defined in s.2 of the Act as: ". . . a person who is registered and entitled under the laws of a province to practice in that province the profession of medicine, dentistry or veterinary medicine."

4. Importing and Exporting

Section 5 of the NCA makes importing into Canada or exporting from Canada an indictable offence.

Until 1987, there was a minimum penalty of seven years' imprisonment for anyone convicted of importing or exporting narcotics. This offence could be committed regardless of the amount of the drug brought into the country and even if it was brought in for personal use only. In 1987 the Supreme Court of Canada held that the minimum penalty was "cruel and unusual punishment " under the Charter and of no force or effect.[7]

5. Cultivation of Opium or Marijuana

Section 6 of the NCA makes it an indictable offence to cultivate opium poppy or marijuana.

6. Searches Under the Narcotic Control Act

The authority to search under the NCA is broader than the power under the Criminal Code.

a. *With a Warrant*

A search warrant is needed under the NCA is if the place to be searched is a dwelling-house.

Section 12 of the Act reads:

> **12. A justice who is satisfied by information . . . that there are reasonable grounds for believing that there is a narcotic, by means of or in respect of which an offence under this Act has been committed, in any dwelling-house may issue a warrant . . . authorizing a peace officer named therein at any time to enter the dwelling-house and search for narcotics.**

Section 11 of the Act allows the police to search any person who is found in the dwelling-house (or any other place) at the time of the search.

---

7. *R. v. Smith* (1987), 34 C.C.C. (3d) 97 (S.C.C.).

However, the Supreme Court of Canada held in *R. v. Debot*[8] that, before searching a person, the Charter requires that the officer have reasonable grounds to believe that the person searched is in possession of drugs.

The police officer may only be granted a warrant if he or she reasonably believes there are narcotics to be found in the house. A warrant to search for anything other than narcotics cannot be issued under the NCA. If the thing sought is something other than a narcotic or something that may be evidence of the possession of, or the trafficking of, a narcotic, the police would have to seek a warrant under s.487 of the Criminal Code.

Unlike a warrant under s.487, a warrant under the NCA can be used at any time of the day or night without the need for a special endorsement to that effect. Also, the actual powers of search are extremely wide. Section 14 provides:

> **14. For the purpose of exercising authority pursuant to any sections 10 to 13, a peace officer may, with such assistance as that officer deems necessary, break open any door, window, lock, fastener, floor, wall, ceiling, compartment, plumbing fixture, box, container or any other thing.**

A decision of the Ontario Court of Appeal[9] has held that this section allows police to make unannounced entries and to break open any door if necessary to gain entry. The decision said that the provisions of the NCA recognize that police need special powers when dealing with drug offences. In this case, the police had reliable information that a place was being used to sell cocaine and the door would be barred. Therefore, the police were justified in forcing entry without announcing themselves. However, the Charter still applies and when the police use force they must be able to justify its use. In *R. v. Genest*,[10] the Supreme Court of Canada also recognized that police may need to use force but it said: "The greater the departure from the common law and the Charter, the heavier the onus on the police to show why they thought it necessary to use force in the process of an arrest or a search." For example, the police may need to act quickly to preserve evidence or where there is a real threat of violence.

b. *Without a Warrant*

Section 10 of the NCA allows a police officer to, at any time:

> **10. . . . without a warrant enter and search any place other than a dwelling-house, . . . in which the peace officer**

---

8. (1989), 52 C.C.C. (3d) 193 (S.C.C.).
9. *R. v. Gimson* (1990), 54 C.C.C. (3d) 232 (Ont.C.A.).
10. (1989), 45 C.C.C. (3d) 385 (S.C.C.).

believes on reasonable grounds there is a narcotic by means or in respect of which an offence under this Act has been committed.

The Ontario Court of Appeal in *R. v. Rao*[11] has held that a warrantless search of a place is only justified if it is not practical to obtain a warrant. In other words, this section is inoperable because of the Charter if it is practicable to get a warrant. So, for example, vehicles, vessels, and aircraft can be searched without a warrant because they may move away. However, there must be reasonable grounds for believing that drugs are present; mere suspicion is not enough. Chapter Five discussed reasonable grounds for conducting a search.

The Supreme Court of Canada has held that where a warrantless search takes place and where there is an allegation of a Charter violation, the onus shifts to the Crown to show on a balance of probabilities that the search was reasonable.[12]

Chapter Five discussed the reasoning used by the courts in deciding whether evidence obtained from a search that violates the Charter should be admissible.

B. FOOD AND DRUGS ACT

The FDA classifies drugs as controlled or restricted. In general controlled drugs are those which can only be obtained by prescription from a physician. Restricted drugs can only be possessed by persons with special permission, for example, for research.

"Possession", as it is used in the FDA, has the same meaning as it does in s.4(3) of the Criminal Code (see Chapter Thirteen).

Trafficking for the purposes of the FDA is defined by s.38 and s.46 as follows:

"traffic" means to manufacture, sell, export from or import into Canada, transport or deliver, otherwise than under the authority of this Part or the regulations.

The meaning of trafficking under the FDA is narrower than under the NCA in that trafficking does not include giving a drug to a person as it does under the NCA.

---

11. (1984), 12 C.C.C. (3d) 97 (Ont.C.A.).
12. *Collins v. The Queen* (1987), 33 C.C.C. (3d) 1 (S.C.C.).

1. Restricted Drugs

Restricted drugs include LSD, MDA, harmaline, mescaline, and peyote. A complete list of restricted drugs is in schedule H of the Act. It is illegal to have possession of, or to traffic in, any restricted drug without a special licence. Under s.47 and s.48 the offences of having possession of and trafficking in a restricted drug are hybrid offences.

2. Controlled Drugs

Controlled drugs include amphetamines, barbiturates, benzphetamines, and methamphetamines. Controlled drugs are listed in schedule G of the Act. Only trafficking, possession for the purpose of trafficking in controlled drugs, and failure to disclose a previous prescription are offences. In other words, the mere possession of a controlled drug is not an offence. However, possession of large quantities of a controlled drug, without good reason, will raise a strong suspicion that the drug is in possession for the purpose of trafficking.

Section 39 makes trafficking in a controlled drug a hybrid offence. Section 38.1 makes failure to disclose a previous prescription a hybrid offence.

3. Searches Under the FDA

The authority to search under the FDA is the same as the authority under the NCA.

Appendix B

Young Offenders Act

A. INTRODUCTION

Since the turn of the century Canada has had special legislation to deal with young people who break the law. The principle underlying this legislation has been that young people should be treated differently from adult offenders in the criminal justice system. In practice this means that a separate court system and detention facilities exist for young people.

In 1982, Canada enacted a new law to deal with young people, the Young Offenders Act (YOA), although certain provisions of it did not come into effect until 1985. This legislation replaced the Juvenile Delinquents Act (JDA) and made major changes in the handling of young offenders.

The philosophy of the JDA was that young children who broke the law should be treated as "misguided", needing care and protection. It looked at juvenile delinquency as a social welfare problem. So, for example, young people were not charged with specific offences but with "delinquency" which included not only criminal offences but also provincial law violations such as truancy as well as a catch-all offence of "sexual immorality and similar forms of vice." Thus, the JDA handled a wide range of youths, from those who committed true criminal offences to youths with problems more related to child protection. Because the JDA was seen as helping and not punishing youth, rights and liberties were not emphasized. For example, court hearings often took place without legal representation for the youth.

In contrast to the social welfare approach of the JDA the YOA sets up a more legalistic system which acknowledges that the legislation is criminal law. Section 3 of the YOA is a declaration of philosophy which outlines the underlying principles of the Act. It is to be used as a guide for judges in applying and interpreting other provisions of the Act. It expresses the spirit in which the act should be understood. It states:

> **3.(1) It is hereby recognized and declared that**
> **(a) while young persons should not in all instances be held accountable in the same manner or suffer the same consequences for their behaviour as adults, young persons who commit offences should nonetheless bear responsibility for their contraventions;**

347

(b) society must, although it has the responsibility to take reasonable measures to prevent criminal conduct by young persons, be afforded the necessary protection from illegal behaviour;

(c) young persons who commit offences require supervision, discipline and control, but, because of their state of dependency and level of development and maturity, they also have special needs and require guidance and assistance;

(d) where it is not inconsistent with the protection of society, taking no measures or taking measures other than judicial proceedings under this Act should be considered for dealing with young persons who have committed offences;

(e) young persons have rights and freedoms in their own right, including those stated in the Canadian Charter of Rights and Freedoms or in the Canadian Bill of Rights, and in particular a right to be heard in the course of, and to participate in, the processes that lead to decisions that affect them, and young persons should have special guarantees of their rights and freedoms;

(f) in the application of this Act, the rights and freedoms of young persons include a right to the least possible interference with freedom that is consistent with the protection of society, having regard to the needs of young persons and the interests of their families;

(g) young persons have the right, in every instance where they have rights or freedoms that may be affected by this Act, to be informed as to what those rights and freedoms are; and

(h) parents have a responsibility for the care and supervision of their children, and, for that reason, young persons should be removed from parental supervision either partly or entirely only when measures that provide for continuing parental supervision are inappropriate

. . .

This declaration sets out to balance two principles. First, that society has an interest in being protected from the criminal conduct of young persons. Therefore, young people are to be held accountable for their crimes through criminal legislation. Since young people are held accountable for their criminal conduct, it is only fair that they be given the same rights and protections as other people in our society who are charged with committing crimes. The second principle is that young people who break the law should not be treated exactly like adults who break the law. There is a recognition that young people require special treatment: they not only need "discipline and control" but also "guidance and assistance."

So, for example, in recognizing that young people have special needs, the declaration states that young people should only be removed from the supervision of their parents if necessary and that it may be best to avoid court altogether.

B. MAIN FEATURES OF THE YOA

1. Court

Trials of young offenders are held in youth courts, which are organized by the provinces.

2. Age

The JDA applied to children who were at least seven. The upper limit was set by provincial law and ranged from 15 to 17 depending on the province. The YOA sets a standard age: 12 to and including 17 across the country. For the purposes of the Act, the young person's age is determined at the time the offence was alleged to have been committed. If the young person becomes an adult during the trial, the case continues in youth court as if the person were still a young person.

Children under 12 who break the criminal law are handled under provincial legislation, usually child welfare laws.

3. Offences

The YOA only applies to young people who are charged with criminal offences. Young people who break provincial laws are handled under provincial legislation.

4. Pre-Trial Procedures and Rights

Young people have the same rights as adults when detained or arrested, for example, the right to remain silent, the right to know the reasons for the detention, and the right to counsel. In addition, they have a right to be informed of their rights.

a. *Right to Counsel*

The right to counsel is treated very specifically and seriously by the Act at all stages from the first detention through to any court hearing. A step-by-step process for encouraging young people to be represented is set out in s.11. It states that the youth has a right to personally retain and instruct counsel, which means that the lawyer must take instructions from the youth and not, for example, the young person's parents. The police must not only inform the youth of the right to counsel but give the youth the opportunity to consult counsel. Section 56 of the Act states that no oral or written statement made by the youth to the police can be used unless

56.(2) . . .

(a) the statement was voluntary;

(b) the person to whom the statement was given has, before the statement was made, clearly explained to the young person, in language appropriate to his age and understanding, that

> (i) the young person is under no obligation to give a statement,
>
> (ii) any statement given by him may be used as evidence in proceedings against him,
>
> (iii) the young person has a right to consult another person in accordance with paragraph (c), and
>
> (iv) any statement made by the young person is required to be made in the presence of the person consulted, unless the young person desires otherwise;

(c) the young person has, before the statement was made, been given a reasonable opportunity to consult with counsel or a parent, or in the absence of a parent, an adult relative, or in the absence of a parent and an adult relative, any other appropriate adult chosen by the young person; and

(d) where the young person consults any person pursuant to paragraph (c), the young person has been given a reasonable opportunity to make the statement in the presence of that person.

The exception to the above is given in s.56(3) which provides that these requirements do not apply where a young person gives a "spontaneous statement" to a peace officer before the officer can comply with the requirements.

If the young person waives the rights under s.56, the waiver must be in writing.

If the youth is not represented by a lawyer at any court hearing (e.g., a hearing on pre-trial release) under s.11, the judge must advise the youth of the right and give the youth the opportunity to consult a lawyer. If the youth cannot afford a lawyer, the court must refer the youth to the province's legal aid plan or if that is not available, the judge can direct the Attorney General of the province to appoint a lawyer for the youth.

The youth may also choose to be represented by any other adult who the court considers suitable. If the judge finds that the interests of the youth are in conflict with the interests of the youth's parents, or that it is not in the best interests of the youth to be represented by the same counsel as the parents, the judge can direct that the youth be represented by counsel independent of his or her parents.

b. *Pre-Trial Release*

Young people have the same rights as adults to be released while awaiting trial. Under s.7 they are to be held separate and apart from adults unless this is not possible because of the youth's safety or of the safety of others or because there is no youth facility within reasonable distance.

To avoid detention, s.7.1 allows the court to place the young person under the supervision of a responsible person.

5. Notice to Parents

Parents have a right to be given notice as soon as possible that their child has been detained pending court appearance under s.9. The notice, either oral or written, must give the place of detention and the reason for the arrest. The parent must receive written notice where the young person is issued a summons or appearance notice, released on a promise to appear, or has entered a recognizance. Where the whereabouts of the parents are unknown or it appears that no parent is available, notice can be given to an adult relative who is known to the young person and seems likely to assist the young person or, if no such adult relative is available, to any adult known to the young person and who seems likely to assist the young person.

If the parent does not voluntarily attend the court hearing, the court can order the parent to appear.

6. The Trial

Under s.12 when the youth first appears in court the judge must:

> **(a) cause the information to be read to the youth,**
> **(b) where the youth is not represented by counsel advise the youth of the right to be represented,**
> **(c) if the youth appears without counsel, be satisfied that the youth understands the charge, explain to the youth that the youth may plead guilty or not guilty, and enter a plea of not guilty if the judge feels that the youth does not understand the charge counsel, ...**

The trial of a young offender is like the trial of an adult except that jury trials are not allowed. The Crown has the burden of proving the case beyond a reasonable doubt, and the youth can raise whatever defences apply. Witnesses are examined and cross-examined. The youth will be found guilty or not guilty. The trials are generally open to the public. However, s.39 allows the judge to exclude the public if the judge is of the opinion that:

39.(1). . .

(a) . . . any evidence or information presented to the court . . . would be seriously injurious or seriously prejudicial to

(i) the young person who is being dealt with in the proceeding

(ii) a child or young person who is a witness in the proceedings

(iii) a child or young person who is aggrieved by or the victim of the offence charged in the proceedings, or

(b) that it would be in the interests of public morals, the maintenance of order or the proper administration of justice to exclude any or all members of the public from the court room.

However, under s.38 the name of the youth cannot be reported in the media unless a special court order is obtained. A police officer can apply to the court for permission to publish the name of the youth or information which would help identify the youth where the officer can show that the youth is a danger to others and publication of the name of the youth will help in apprehending the youth. The order ceases to have effect two days after it is made.

7. Transfers to Adult Court Under S.16

If a youth is 14 at the time of the alleged offence and has been charged with an indictable offence other than the ones listed in s.553 (these are the less serious indictable offences) the young person, the young person's counsel, the Attorney General, or the agent of the Attorney General can apply for the case to be transferred to an "ordinary" (adult) court. The court must give the youth, the youth's parents and the Attorney General the opportunity to be heard on the issue.

Until the Act was amended in 1991, in making its decision whether to transfer the case, the court was directed to consider both the interests of society and the needs of the young person; the Act did not specify whether the interests of society or the needs of the youth should be paramount.[1] Subsequently, many legal critics felt that the Act should be changed to put the interests of society first. Parliament agreed with this position, and in 1991 the Act was amended to alter the test used for transferring cases to ordinary court. Section 16.(1.1) states:

---

1. In fact, the Ontario Court of Appeal held that neither criterion — neither the interests of society nor the needs and interests of the youth — was to be given greater importance in deciding whether a transfer should be made. See *R. v. M.A.Z.* (1987), 35 C.C.C. (3d) 144 (Ont.C.A.); leave to appeal to S.C.C. refused May 23, 1987.

(1.1) In making the determination . . . the youth court shall consider the interest of society, which includes the objectives of affording protection to the public and rehabilitation of the young person, and determine whether those objectives can be reconciled by the youth remaining under the jurisdiction of the youth court, and if the court is of the opinion that those objectives cannot be so reconciled, protection of the public shall be paramount and the court shall order that the young person be proceeded against in ordinary court in accordance with the law ordinarily applicable to an adult charged with an offence.

The factors that the court considers in making its decision are the same as before the amendments. Under s.16(2), the court is directed to consider:

(a) the seriousness of the alleged offence and the circumstances under which it was committed

(b) the age, maturity, character, and background of the young person and any record or summary of previous findings of delinquency under the Juvenile Delinquents Act . . .

(c) the adequacy of the Act and the adequacy of the Criminal Code or other Act of Parliament that would apply if a transfer order were made to meet the circumstances of the case

(d) the availability of treatment or correctional facilities

(e) any representations made to the court by or on behalf of the young person or by the attorney general or his agent

(f) any other factors the court considers relevant.

Prior to the amendments, the great disparity between penalties in the youth and adult systems were criticized by legal analysts and the media, particularly in cases of young persons convicted of murder. Under the adult system a person convicted of first degree murder must receive a sentence of life imprisonment and must usually serve 25 years before being eligible for parole. A conviction for second degree murder carries a penalty of life imprisonment and at least ten years before eligibility for parole. A young person convicted of first or second degree murder in youth court would face a maximum penalty of three years in custody. The 1991 amendments dealt with this disparity in two ways. First, if a case is transferred to adult court, the Criminal Code was amended so that a young person convicted of first or second degree murder will still be given a sentence of life imprisonment but may be eligible for parole in 5 to 10 years. Second, the YOA was amended so that a young person convicted of first or second degree murder must receive a disposition of three years in custody and two years of supervision in the community. It is also possible, at the end of the young person's custody period, where the Attorney General can show that there are reasonable grounds to believe that the young person is likely to commit an offence causing the death of or serious harm to another person prior to the expiration of the disposition, for the Attorney General to apply to court to have the youth serve the remainder of the disposition in custody.

8. Dispositions Under S.20

The Act uses the term "disposition" rather than "sentence" for a young person found guilty of an offence. In general, dispositions are limited to a two- or three-year period except where the youth is convicted of murder (see above discussion of the penalty for a murder conviction in youth court). The possible dispositions are set out in s.20. They include:

1. an absolute discharge — this means that although the young person has been found guilty, a conviction is not entered against the young person; therefore, the young person can truthfully state that he or she has never been convicted of a crime, for example, on a job application
2. a fine not exceeding $1 000
3. an order for the young person to make financial compensation to the victim
4. restitution of property to the victim
5. a community service order
6. probation for a period not exceeding two years
7. custody order
   a. not exceeding two years
   b. or three years where the penalty for an adult would be life imprisonment

A custody order must specify whether it is for open or closed custody. Open custody would be something like a group home or foster home. Closed custody involves security measures such as locked doors and windows.

8. an order for detention in a treatment facility if the young person, the parents, and the hospital consent

9. Reviews of Dispositions Under S.28 to S.31

Unlike the process of sentencing an adult, the youth court may stay involved in the case after a disposition is made. For example, if a custody order for more than one year is made, the case must be brought back by the provincial director of the Act for review at the end of one year. Any custody order may be reviewed on the request of the youth, the youth's parents, or Attorney-General or his or her agent, after six months. The grounds for review are set out in s.28(4):

(a) . . . that the young person has made sufficient progress to justify a change in the disposition;

(b) . . . that the circumstances that led to the committal to custody have changed materially;

(c) . . . that new services or programs are available that were not available at the time of the disposition; or

(d) on such other grounds as the youth court considers appropriate.

Section 28(17) states that after reviewing the disposition the court may:

(a) confirm the disposition;

(b) where the young person is in secure custody, order the young person to be placed in open custody; or

(c) release the young person from custody and place the youth on probation . . .

The court may also review dispositions that do not involve custody on the application of the youth, parent, Attorney General, his or her agent, or provincial director. The grounds for review in s.32(2) are:

(a) . . . that the circumstances that led to the disposition have changed materially;

(b) . . . that the young person . . . is unable to comply with or is experiencing serious difficulty in complying with the terms of the disposition;

(c) . . . that the terms of the disposition are adversely affecting the opportunities available to a young person to obtain services, education or employment; or

(d) on such other grounds as the youth court considers appropriate.

Under s.32(7), after reviewing the disposition the court may:

(a) confirm the disposition;

(b) terminate the disposition and discharge the young person from any further obligation of the disposition; or

(c) vary the disposition or make such new disposition . . . other than a committal to custody, for such period of time, not exceeding the remainder of the period of the earlier disposition, as the court deems appropriate in the circumstances of the case.

Subsection (8) provides that the disposition cannot, without the consent of the young person, be made more onerous on review. Subsection

(9) provides that the court may extend the time for complying with the disposition up to 12 months after the disposition would have expired where the court finds that the youth needs more time to comply.

10. Alternative Measures Under S.4

The Act allows provinces to set up alternative measure programs. These are also called diversion programs. The purpose of the programs is to allow the youth to avoid appearing in court. They are based on the idea that it is sometimes harmful for a young person to go through the formal criminal justice system. For example, by going through a trial, the youth may see himself or herself as a criminal and behave accordingly. Diversion programs allow a response to the behaviour that attempts to avoid the youth being "labelled" or "stigmatized" a young offender. These programs might, for example, involve the youth making restitution to the victim or in doing a community service. The youth must agree to participate in the program. There must be enough evidence against the youth that the offence could have been prosecuted and the youth must accept responsibility for the offence.

Until recently it was not clear whether provinces had to set up alternative measure programs. In a 1988 decision the Ontario Court of Appeal[2] held that it was a violation of the equality rights under the Charter for some but not all provinces to have these programs. On appeal the Supreme Court of Canada[3] held otherwise and stated that the Act does not make these programs mandatory.

11. Termination of Disposition and the Use of Records

The philosophy of the Act is that young people should not be unnecessarily burdened with a "record" as a young offender. On the other hand, the Act also recognizes the importance of maintaining records for investigating crime and for having a person's record if that person is again before the courts. The Act tries to balance these two interests.

There are two sections dealing with young persons and their records after the disposition is completed.

a. Termination of Disposition

Section 36 provides that, for many purposes, once the young person has completed the disposition or been given an absolute discharge he or she will be deemed not to have been found guilty or convicted of an offence.

---

2. *R. v. S. (S.)* (1988), 63 C.R. (3d) 64 (Ont.C.A.).
3. *R. v. S. (S.)* (1990), 57 C.C.C. (3d) 115 (S.C.C.).

For example, once a young person completes the terms of probation he or she is deemed not to have been convicted of any offence. On job application forms, for example, the young person can state that he or she has not been convicted of an offence. This allowance is only the general rule, however. The exceptions are stated in s.36(1):

> . . .
>
> **(c) the young person may plead autrefois convict in respect of any subsequent charge relating to the offence [in other words, the young person cannot be charged with the offence again]**
> **(d) a youth court may consider the finding of guilt in considering an application for a transfer to ordinary (adult) court . . .**
> **(e) any court or justice may consider the finding of guilt in considering an application for judicial interim release or in considering what dispositions to make or sentence to impose for any offence, and**
> **(f) the National Parole Board or any provincial parole board may consider the finding of guilt in considering an application for parole or pardon.**

Except for para.(c), which is to protect the young person, the above circumstances apply to situations where the young person has become involved in actual or alleged criminal activity. Therefore, if the young person has no further dealings with the criminal justice system, the convictions will be treated as if they do not exist.

b. The Use of Records

Section 40 to s.43 set out the various organizations which can keep records of offences. Records may be kept by the police force responsible for investigating the offence and in a central repository kept by the RCMP. Also certain government agencies and organizations may keep records. As well the court which deals with the case can keep records.

Section 44.1 deals with disclosure of these records. In general, disclosure of records is only allowed in certain circumstances, for example, if the youth is again before the courts for a disposition or adult sentencing.

Section 45 sets out the rules for non-disclosure and the destruction of records. In brief the section provides that after certain crime-free qualifying times records kept under s.40 to s.43 may not be available for inspection. For example, records cannot be inspected after five years from the time a young offender was found guilty of a summary conviction offence or two years from the time a young person consented to participate in an alternative measures program.

Records kept in the central repository must be destroyed after the qualifying period. However, other records ". . . may, in the discretion of the person or body keeping the record, be destroyed at any time before or after the circumstances set out . . . are realized. . ." [s.45(3)].

After the qualifying time set out in s.45, the young person is deemed "not to have committed any offence to which a record kept pursuant to sections 40-43 relates . . . ."

Glossary

ACCESSORY AFTER THE FACT A person who receives, assists, or offers comfort to a party to an offence for the purpose of enabling that person to escape.

ACQUITTED An accused who is found not guilty of the offence will be acquitted of the charge by the court.

ACTUS REUS Latin for guilty action, meaning the physical element of a crime.

ADVERTENTLY NEGLIGENT Said of a person actually aware of the risk of his or her conduct. See *inadvertently negligent*.

AIDING OR ABETTING Helping or encouraging a person to commit an offence.

APPELLANT The person (or party) appealing the decision of a court.

ARREST Detaining a person who has been charged with an offence for the purpose of bringing the accused before the court.

ARREST WARRANT An order issued by a judge or justice of the peace commanding the police to bring the named person before the court.

ATTORNEY GENERAL The provincial or federal member of the cabinet responsible for the administration of justice.

BALANCE OF PROBABILITIES The burden of proof in civil cases. The burden is met if it can be said that it is more likely than not that the defendant has committed the wrong. See *defendant*.

BEYOND A REASONABLE DOUBT The burden of proof on the prosecution in a criminal trial. The accused's guilt must be proved beyond a reasonable doubt. See *reasonable doubt*.

BREACH OF THE PEACE A situation that involves a threat of violence such as when a group of people are loitering and threatening to become violent.

CANADIAN CHARTER OF RIGHTS AND FREEDOMS That part of the Constitution which sets out individual rights and freedoms.

CASE LAW The body of law which consists of the decisions of judges. See *common law*.

CIVIL NEGLIGENCE A wrong under civil (private) law where a person has failed to meet the standards of a reasonable person.

CIVIL WRONGS Private wrongs that give the victim a right to sue for compensation in a civil court.

CLAIM OF RIGHT An honest belief in the right to possess property. Where a person is in possession of property under a claim of right, the person is protected from criminal liability for defending the possession. See *colour of right*.

COLOUR OF RIGHT A defence to a charge of theft where the accused honestly but mistakenly believed that he or she had a possessory right to the property. See *claim of right*.

COMMON LAW The body of laws developed by judges following the rule of precedent when making decisions in cases. See *case law*.

COUNSEL The lawyer acting in legal proceedings — e.g., Crown counsel, defence counsel.

CRIMINAL CODE A federal law which is the main source of criminal law in Canada. It sets out offences, penalties, and rules of procedure.

CRIMINAL NEGLIGENCE An offence under the Criminal Code. Any conduct or breach of a legal duty which shows a wanton or reckless disregard for the lives or safety of others.

CRIMINAL PROCEDURE The rules which must be followed when enforcing the criminal law, for example, the rules for making a valid arrest or the steps to be followed in a trial.

CROWN ATTORNEY The lawyer who represents the government in prosecuting criminal cases.

CULPABLE HOMICIDE Causing death that is a criminal offence: murder, manslaughter, or infanticide.

DAY Defined in the Criminal Code, s.2, as ". . . the period between six o'clock in the forenoon and nine o'clock in the afternoon of the same day."

DEFENCE A justification or excuse for committing what would otherwise be an offence.

DEFENDANT In a criminal case, the person charged with a crime. In a civil case, the person being sued.

DETENTION A person is detained when he or she submits or acquiesces to the deprivation of liberty when the person believes there is no choice to do otherwise.

DISSENTING OPINION In an appeal that has been heard by more than one judge, the minority opinion.

DUAL PROCEDURE OFFENCE An offence which can be tried by summary conviction procedure or indictment. The decision on how to try an offence is made by the Crown Attorney. See *hybrid offence*.

DUTY COUNSEL A lawyer "on duty"

who is paid by legal aid to assist persons who have been arrested or detained.

DWELLING-HOUSE Defined in s.2 of the Criminal Code as ". . . the whole or any part of a building or structure that is kept or occupied as a permanent or temporary residence. . . ."

FUNDAMENTAL JUSTICE (PRINCIPLES OF) A right under the Charter not to be deprived of life, liberty, or security of the person except in accordance with the principles of fundamental justice. Sections 8 to 14 of the Charter are specific applications of the principles of fundamental justice, for example, the right to be secure against arbitrary search and seizure.

GENERAL INTENT OFFENCES Offences which require an intent to achieve the immediate result. See *specific intent offences*.

HOLDING IN THE CASE The court's decision in a case. The majority opinion in a case where more than one judge hears a case and more than one opinion is given.

HYBRID OFFENCE An offence which can be tried by summary conviction procedure or indictment. The decision on how to try the offence is made by the Crown Attorney. See *dual procedure offence*.

INADVERTENTLY NEGLIGENT Said of a person not aware of the risk being taken although a reasonable person would have been aware of the risk. See *advertently negligent*.

INDICTABLE OFFENCE The most serious crimes which are tried by indictment.

JUSTIFIABLE LIMITATION A term used in s.1 of the Charter which refers to a law which violates a Charter right but is upheld because it is a justifiable limitation in a free and democratic society.

LAWFUL JUSTIFICATION Where a person's conduct which would otherwise be criminal is allowed by law.

LESSER INCLUDED OFFENCE Also, lesser offence or included offence. Refers to an offence which has some but not all of the elements of the major offence.

MENS REA The mental element of a crime. Latin for "guilty mind".

MISTAKE OF FACT An error as to some circumstance, which results in the committing of a crime.

MISTAKE OF LAW An error as to the legal status of a circumstance or fact.

NIGHT Defined in the Criminal Code, s.2 as ". . . the period between nine o'clock in the afternoon and six o'clock in the forenoon of the following day."

NON-CULPABLE HOMICIDE Causing death that is not a criminal offence, that is, justifiable or excusable.

NOTWITHSTANDING/OVERRIDE CLAUSE Refers to section 133 of the Charter, which allows the federal or a provincial government to enact a law that violates the Charter if certain criteria are met.

OBJECTIVE FORESIGHT A description of a mental state where a reasonable person would have foreseen the consequences of the conduct.

OBJECTIVE *MENS REA* A description of a mental state which refers to the standard of a reasonable person in the position of the accused.

OFFICIALLY INDUCED ERROR A defence to a charge of committing a regulatory offence that the accused broke the law because he or she was misled by an official in charge of enforcing the law.

PAROLE The serving of part of a term of imprisonment in the community under supervision.

PAROLE BOARD The administrative board which decides whether a person should be released on parole. See *parole*.

PARTIES (TO A CRIME) The people who can be charged with a particular crime.

PERSONAL PROPERTY Tangible property that is not real property. See *real property*.

PRECEDENT (RULE OF) A precedent is a rule to be followed in similar cases. The rule of precedent states that when making a decision a judge must follow the decisions of (i.e., apply the same rule of laws as) higher court judges in cases with the same or similar fact situations. A judge must also attempt to follow decisions of same-level courts.

PRESUMPTION OF INNOCENCE The right to be presumed innocent until proven guilty in a fair and public hearing by an impartial tribunal. This right is guaranteed by the Charter. It means that the burden of proving the charge is on the prosecution.

PRINCIPAL OFFENDER The party to an offence who actually commits the *actus reus* and has the *mens rea* for the offence.

PROSECUTOR The person, usually a Crown Attorney, who presents the case against the defendant.

REAL PROPERTY Land and everything attached to it, for example, houses and trees. See *personal property*.

REASONABLE DOUBT Real doubt which an honest juror has after considering all the circumstances of the case which results in the juror being unable to say, "I am morally certain of the accused's guilt". See *beyond a reasonable doubt*.

REASONABLE GROUNDS In general, reasonable grounds are grounds which would lead an ordinary, prudent, and cautious person to have a strong and honest belief about the situation at issue.

REBUTTABLE PRESUMPTION A fact that is presumed to exist until rebutted by the accused. See *statutory presumption*.

RECKLESSNESS A type of mental element that may be required for a crime. Where a person does not intend a certain consequence but knows that the consequence is possible and chooses to run the risk that the consequence will not occur.

RECOGNIZANCE An agreement or promise made by an accused to pay a certain amount of money to the court if the accused fails to appear at a future court date.

RESPONDENT The person (or party) responding to an appeal of a court decision.

REVERSE ONUS CLAUSE An element of an offence which shifts part of the burden of proof to the accused in a criminal trial. Reverse onus clauses are subject to attack under the Charter for offending the presumption of innocence.

RIGHT TO REMAIN SILENT A principle of fundamental justice. A right of an accused person guaranteed by the Charter which flows from the presumption of innocence to say nothing before the trial. The right is also consistent with the burden of proof being on the prosecution to prove the case against the accused.

SEARCH WARRANT An order issued by a justice of the peace commanding the police to search a particular place for named items.

SPECIFIC INTENT OFFENCES Offences which require an additional intent beyond the intent to achieve the immediate result. An intent to further an illegal goal. See *general intent offences*.

STARE DECISIS Latin for "to stand by". Refers to the rule that judges must follow the decisions used in earlier cases when the facts are the same or similar. See *precedent (rule of)*.

STATUTE LAW Law made by our elected representatives.

STATUTORY PRESUMPTION An element of an offence where a fact is presumed to exist until the accused disproves it. Statutory presumptions are subject to attack under the Charter as violations of the presumption of innocence. See *rebuttable presumption*.

STRICT LIABILITY OFFENCES Offences for which the Crown only has to prove the *actus reus*. The accused will be convicted unless he or she can establish that he or she acted with due diligence.

SUBJECTIVE FORESIGHT/AWARENESS A description of a mental state where the accused actually foresaw the consequences of his or her conduct.

SUBJECTIVE INTENT A type of *mens rea* where the accused actually intended the consequences of his or her conduct.

SUMMARY CONVICTION OFFENCE The least serious criminal offences which are tried by summary conviction procedure.

SURETY A person who signs a recognizance with an accused and thereby agrees to be responsible for ensuring that the accused appears for his or her court date.

TRIER OF FACT In a trial with a judge and jury, the jury is the trier of fact, that is, it must decide what happened in the case.

Where there is no jury, the judge is trier of fact. See *trier of law*.

TRIER OF LAW In a trial, the judge is the trier of law, that is, he or she must decide what law applies to the case. See *trier of fact*.

UNCONSTITUTIONAL The term used to describe a law which violates the Charter and is not a justifiable limitation of a right.

WILFUL BLINDNESS A type of *mens rea* where the accused is aware of the need to make an inquiry but chooses not to, that is, chooses to remain ignorant.

Index

STUDENT REPLY CARD

In order to improve future editions, we are seeking your comments on *Criminal Law and the Canadian Criminal Code*, Second Edition, by Barnhorst/Barnhorst/Clarke.

   After you have used the book, please answer the following questions and return this form via Business Reply Mail. *Thanks in advance for your feedback!*

1. Name of your college or university: _____

2. Major program of study: _____

3. Your instructor for this course: _____

4. Were any chapters or sections of this text *not* assigned as course reading?_____
   If so, please specify those chapters or sections:

5. How would you rate the overall accessibility of the content? Please feel free
   to comment on reading level, writing style, terminology, layout and design
   features, and such learning aids as chapter objectives, summaries, and appendices.

6. What did you like *best* about this book?

7. What did you like *least*?

If you would like to say more, we'd love to hear from you. Please write to us at the
address shown on the reverse of this card.